P9-DMF-647

Invitation to Critical Thinking

1
FIRST
CANADION
EDITION

JOEL RUDINOW

SANTA ROSA JUNIOR COLLEGE

VINCENT E. BARRY

BAKERSFIELD COLLEGE

MARK LETTERI

WINDSOR, ONTARIO

THOMSON
NELSON

Australia   Canada   Mexico   Singapore   Spain   United Kingdom   United States

THOMSON

NELSON

Invitation to Critical Thinking, First Canadian Edition

by Joel Rudinow, Vincent E. Barry, and Mark Letteri

Associate Vice President, Editorial Director:
Evelyn Veitch

Editor-in-Chief, Higher Education:
Anne Williams

Acquisitions Editor:
Bram Sepers

Marketing Manager:
Sandra Green

Developmental Editor:
Natalie Barrington

Photo Researcher:
Kristiina Bowering

Permissions Coordinator:
Kristiina Bowering

Content Production Manager:
Lara Caplan

Production Service:
International Typesetting and Composition

Copy Editor:
Kathy van Denderen

Proofreader:
Debra Gates

Indexer:
Brenda Miller

Production Coordinator:
Ferial Suleman

Design Director:
Ken Phipps

Interior Design Modifications:
Fernanda Pisani

Cover Design:
Johanna Liburd

Cover Image:
Nguyen Thai/ShutterStock

Compositor:
International Typesetting and Composition

Printer:
Thomson West

COPYRIGHT © 2008 by Nelson, a division of Thomson Canada Limited.

Adapted from *Invitation to Critical Thinking,* Fifth Edition, by Joel Rudinow and Vincent E. Barry, Published by Thomson Wadsworth. Copyright © 2004 by Thomson Wadsworth.

Printed and bound in the United States of America
1 2 3 4 09 08 07 06

For more information contact Nelson, 1120 Birchmount Road, Toronto, Ontario, M1K 5G4. Or you can visit our Internet site at http://www.nelson.com

ALL RIGHTS RESERVED. No part of this work covered by the copyright herein may be reproduced, transcribed, or used in any form or by any means—graphic, electronic, or mechanical, including photocopying, recording, taping, Web distribution, or information storage and retrieval systems— without the written permission of the publisher.

For permission to use material from this text or product, submit a request online at www.thomsonrights.com

Every effort has been made to trace ownership of all copyrighted material and to secure permission from copyright holders. In the event of any question arising as to the use of any material, we will be pleased to make the necessary corrections in future printings.

Library and Archives Canada Cataloguing in Publication

Rudinow, Joel
Invitation to critical thinking/Joel Rudinow, Vincent E. Barry, Mark Letteri.—1st Canadian ed.

First ed., published 1984, written by Vincent E. Barry.
Includes bibliographical references and index.
ISBN-13: 978-0-17-625147-5
ISBN-10: 0-17-625147-2

1. Critical thinking. 2. Logic. I. Barry, Vincent E. II. Letteri, Mark Robert, 1961– III. Title.
BC177.R75 2007   160
C2006-904601-8

PREFACE

Much has changed in the world since this book was first published, and so the book itself has had to change in order to remain in touch with the world inhabited by its students. Many of the examples we used in earlier editions have disappeared from common awareness down the memory hole into the dustbin of history, yet the need in this generation for basic critical thinking skills remains as deep and urgent as ever. For example, as this edition goes into production, our country reels from the arrest of a number of alleged "homegrown" terrorists. What should we think of this event? What is the evidence? What should we make of it? Which sources and authorities should we trust? What might have prompted such a development? What legal and political implications follow? Must we adjust our conceptualization of our culture in light of these considerations, and, if so, how? How should we look to the future? So, though we have had to overhaul the book's contents and examples considerably over time, the instructional agenda of improving thinking skills remains the same. We continue to focus on the recognition, analysis, evaluation, and composition of arguments as discursive tools of rational persuasion. In this edition, we have reworked the text with the aim of making it as useful as it can be for contemporary Canadian students by including a number of Canadian examples that students today can appreciate. Previous editions of this text have proven themselves in the classroom for more than twenty years—without exaggeration, a long time in the world of critical thinking books—but we have revised the text with the aim of even greater clarity and coherence.

New to the 1st Canadian edition are:

- Examples and illustrations that are Canadian or general in nature
- A revised and more effective argument casting system (Chapter 4)
- An improved coverage of language (Chapters 2 and 11)
- Many localized improvements prompted by the helpful comments of the referees of this edition, such as more thorough treatments of theories of truth, fallacies, concession claims, and categorical and truth functional logic.

Meanwhile, the technology of education has been revolutionized in the Information Age. The lecture/discussion approach typical of classroom management a generation ago now seems increasingly quaint and primitive by comparison with the 24-hour global virtual classroom imagined in so many of the educational planning documents we see today. The pace of change is all but overwhelming. One thing change has forced us to do, as authors of a textbook, is to think rather deeply about how we teach critical thinking and about *how* we *might* teach critical thinking. This has in turn brought into sharp focus two perennial challenges. The first challenge shows up in the observation—confirmed in our classroom experience over and over for years—that the critical thinking course seems generally to work best for those students who already think critically. Such students tend to develop and flourish in the course and seem to get a great deal out of it.

Conversely, the students who are most desperately in need of instruction in critical thinking tend to find the text and the course so profoundly baffling and disorienting that they easily give up on it before they show or see any progress—yet these are the students one most wants to reach. A second, and related, challenge concerns integrating two essential areas of instructional emphasis that nevertheless seem inevitably at odds with each other. On the one hand, we must break down the complexity of critical thinking into manageable chunks and provide the kind of exercises that move the student in an orderly way through the material, building skill from the ground up toward greater and more advanced mastery. This is especially important for the student who finds the material most challenging and unfamiliar. On the other hand, we must ground and motivate study by demonstrating the relevance of the material in "real-world" applications, where, unfortunately, one never finds it broken down according to the instructional agenda of the course, however well that agenda has been laid out.

We have taken several bold and, we hope, effective steps to adapt *Invitation to Critical Thinking* to these challenges in these times. On the real-world applications front, we have introduced an integrated series of Term Project assignments, distributed chapter by chapter throughout the text. Each Term Project assignment, indicated by this icon ⚖ applies the skill set covered in a particular chapter to a sustained project in which the student applies what he or she is learning to the study of a real-world problem or issue. With the support of InfoTrac College Edition, the series of Term Project exercises guides the student through the steps of selecting, defining, analyzing, and researching an issue; identifying, analyzing, and evaluating arguments; and, finally, designing and composing an argument in essay form.

Students can also access a companion website at http://www.criticalthinking1ce .nelson.com for additional study resources for each chapter: Chapter quizzes, summaries, and additional exercises are some of the highlighted features.

An instructor's manual—offering teaching suggestions, solutions, additional resources, and quizzes—and PowerPoint presentations for each chapter are also available on the instructor's side of the companion website.

I am especially honoured to serve as co-author of *Invitation to Critical Thinking,* First Canadian Edition, because it was one of the first (and best) texts that I used to teach reasoning at the start of my classroom career nearly twenty years ago. I must thank Joel Rudinow and Vincent E. Barry for their initial work on the previous U.S. editions. I offer my sincerest gratitude to Natalie Barrington of Thomson Nelson, who helped me so much as the developmental editor of this project. I also thank Cara Yarzab of Thomson Nelson, who served as acquisitions editor at the start of this undertaking. The production team of Lara Caplan, content production manager, Kristiina Bowering, permissions researcher, and Kathy van Denderen, copy editor, did a wonderful job readying this book for publication. I am indebted greatly to the referees whose many suggestions helped me to make the transition, sometimes challenging but always intriguing, from the 5th American edition to this 1st Canadian edition: Paul Bali, Ryerson University; Victoria Digby, Fanshawe College; Jason Galea, Humber College; William Sweet, St. Francis Xavier University. I offer my deepest appreciation to Dr. Brian MacPherson, to whose advice I turned on a number of occasions as I adapted the American text. My conversations with Jan Sobocan over the years informed the understanding of critical thinking that I embodied in this project, so I credit her influence as well. I also thank Ken Turner for his assistance in Canadianizing some of the examples from the 5th American edition. My many reasoning students over the years affected the shape of this book, so I am obliged to them, too. Finally, I am beholden to my family for their constant support throughout my many years of academic endeavours. My parents are a continuing source of encouragement. I dedicate my work here to JoAnne, my partner, and Marie, our daughter—the twin lights of my life.

MARK LETTERI

CONTENTS

UNIT TWO: ARGUMENT   71

Chapter 3: Argument Identification   73

Chapter 4: Argument Analysis I: Representing Argument Structure   94

Chapter 5: Argument Analysis II: Paraphrasing Arguments   125

UNIT THREE: DEDUCTIVE REASONING   143

Chapter 6: Evaluating Deductive Arguments I: Categorical Logic   145

Chapter 7: Evaluating Deductive Arguments II: Truth Functional Logic   186

UNIT FOUR: INDUCTIVE REASONING   213

Chapter 8: Evaluating Inductive Arguments I: Generalization and Analogy   215

Chapter 9: Evaluating Inductive Arguments II: Hypothetical Reasoning and Burden of Proof   241

UNIT FIVE: EVALUATING WHOLE ARGUMENTS   263

Chapter 10: Evaluating Premises: Self-Evidence, Consistency, Indirect Proof   265

Chapter 11: Informal Fallacies I: Language, Relevance, Authority   282

Critical Thinking

THE IMPORTANCE OF CRITICAL THINKING

At the moment Canada's Parliament lies battered by tremendous partisanship. The minority Liberal government is aligned with the New Democratic Party in an attempt to keep at bay the opposition Conservatives who, in conjunction with the Bloc Quebecois, nearly toppled the minority Liberal government on a vote of nonconfidence. The margin of victory was only one vote, a vote that did not even belong to a Member of Parliament: The Speaker of the House had to cast the deciding vote to break the 152-152 tie. This absolutely razor-thin result transpired only after a number of frantic efforts on both sides to gain advantage. Fellow politicians and media subjected independent MPs—those who do not

CP PHOTO/Jonathan Hayward

CLOSE CALL: Yes 153 No 152

Prime Minister Paul Martin addresses his caucus after winning a confidence vote on the budget by a single vote on May 20, 2005.

officially represent any political party, and whose votes are therefore "wild cards"—to intense questioning and pressure. Perhaps most surprisingly, Belinda Stronach, a Conservative MP with a high profile who had in the recent past run for the leadership of the Conservative Party, suddenly switched parties and accepted a cabinet position with the Liberals only days before the non-confidence vote. The Queen's simultaneous visit almost faded into the background as these vivid developments transpired.

These events elicited a welter of questions and concerns that are probably still prominent as you read this book. Is Canada's federal system of government "broken"? Is minority government a sensible way to run the country because it forces competing parties to compromise for the greater good, or is it too prone to division and disintegration? Are coalitions between parties an appropriate way to ensure that Parliament works, or do they defeat the ideal of a balancing plurality of political voices? Should we impose term limits on prime ministers, or would such limits infringe improperly on the rights of the electorate? Should elections be held at set intervals, as in the United States? Should we demand of the federal government greater transparency, accountability, and reporting, or would such a demand degenerate into biased attacks and more bloated bureaucracy? Should we take to task a ruling party that may be linked to the known or alleged sins and crimes of its preceding incarnation, or should we judge each regime independently? Is political regionalism—the reality of political differences along geo-cultural lines, such as Quebec or the West—a chronically destructive problem in Canadian political life, or can we find some way of transcending such divergences? How can we regenerate democratic life in Canada and strengthen it for future times of change? On whose ideas and words should we rely in attempting this revitalization? Persons and parties on all sides offer advice constantly, but these recommendations are often, by turns, vague, debatable, and inconsistent.

The issues here affect us collectively and as individuals. Delving seriously into—let alone resolving—such complicated and momentous matters requires an enormous amount of critical thinking: the willingness and ability to work through problems in a coherent, reasonable, and fair-minded way. Many Canadians, though, seem to feel helpless or resigned in the face of these subjects, perhaps even to the point of giving up on the electoral process. For example, federal voting levels are now chronically low. Talk shows, Internet forums, and newspaper editorial pages are filled with expressions of exasperation over a perceived dysfunctionality in Canadian government. As critical thinkers, we must acknowledge the existence of these and other items of national interest in a spirit of engagement and constructiveness.

Critical thinking can be extraordinarily challenging, though you should not fear such situations, or assume that all matters of critical thinking are difficult. Some questions are relatively easy to address, and while others may prove obstinate, we would do well always to remember this: The alternative to critical thinking, whatever its demands, is uncritical thinking, or not thinking at all. Uncritical thinking will not lead us far toward a solution. We can invoke the spirit of the famous remark attributed to Sir Winston Churchill: "Democracy is the worst form of government, except for all the rest." As critical thinkers, we have an obligation to identify the assumptions on which we base our beliefs and actions, seek all the information, evidence, and reasons that are relevant to the matter at hand, ponder these grounds methodically and without prejudice, and create the best formed, most reasonable judgment under the circumstances.

A profusion of interfering urges, pressures, inducements, and distractions make it hard, even for reasonable people, to reliably differentiate between reasonable and unreasonable beliefs and courses of action. In other words, many

DILBERT: ©Scott Adams/Dist. by United Feature Syndicate, Inc.

obstacles to critical thinking exist. (We will come back to this topic later in this chapter.) The reality of these obstacles also shows, though, why critical thinking is so important for us each as individuals. Critical thinking is empowering and can improve a person's chances of success in a career, as a consumer, and throughout the wide variety of social roles each of us may be destined to play. Critical thinking is empowering because it is essential to something even more fundamental and basic: *personal autonomy. Autonomy* comes from the Greek words *auto* for "self," and *nomos* for "regulation." An autonomous person is self-regulating or self-directing. Autonomy is empowering because it makes a person less dependent upon—and so also less vulnerable to—the dictates, directions, and influence of others. A person who can make up her own mind does not *need* others to tell her what to think or do, and so is less likely to be dominated by others.

Since, however, personal power can easily become perverted, we should be wary of the similar-*sounding* idea that critical thinking might enable us to gain power *over* others. We have seen some actual cases where people have tried to use some of the things they have learned in critical thinking to humiliate, control, or otherwise take advantage of people. We would say simply that to apply critical thinking toward such goals is to distort, misunderstand, and misuse it. Critical thinking should be thought of as liberating, not as a "power trip."

EXERCISE 1.1	Topic for Class Discussion

How might Canadians become more effective and autonomous in deciding how to improve their democratic system?

_____

_____

_____

_____

_____

_____

WHAT IS CRITICAL THINKING?

You are about to embark upon a course of study in critical thinking, and you have a right to know the meaning of the central term. *We conceive critical thinking as a set of conceptual tools with associated intellectual skills and strategies useful for making reasonable decisions about what to do or believe.* This fancy-sounding formulation can be condensed thus: critical thinking is using reason to make up your mind. The words *reason* and *reasonable* appear again. Maybe now would be a good time for us to define them.

The word *reasonable* derives from the word *reason*. *Reason* comes from the Latin word *ratio* for "calculation" or "computation," a highly disciplined use of intelligence for problem solving. *We conceive reason as the capacity to use disciplined intelligence to solve problems.* On this basis we can fairly easily explain the meaning of other words in the same family. For example, we can understand "reasoning" as using disciplined intelligence to solve a problem or determine a course of action. We can understand a "reasonable decision" as one arrived at through the use of reason. We can understand a "reasonable person" as one who (at least ordinarily) uses reason to decide what to do or believe. We can understand an "unreasonable person" as one who fails or refuses to use reason in deciding what to do or believe.

IS CRITICAL THINKING NEGATIVE? A lot of people seem to think that the word *critical* involves negativity almost by definition; criticism is fault-finding, a critic is a fault-finder, and so anything with the word *critical* in its name must be similarly concerned with finding faults and weaknesses and other negative things. This myth comes primarily, we think, out of a misunderstanding of the word *critical*. The word *critical* and its cognates, *criticism, critic, critique,* and so on, all derive from the Greek word *kritikos* for "discernment" or "the ability to judge," which in turn derives from the Greek word *krinein* for "decision making." This is the way we prefer to understand critical thinking: It is concerned with decision making—period. So, yes, critical thinking involves finding faults and entertaining negative considerations, but not *only* in finding faults and other negatives. It is equally concerned with recognizing strengths and other positives. Critical thinking is interested in the "pros" as well as the "cons."

EXERCISE 1.2 | **Topic for Class Discussion**

Assume that you are a basically reasonable person. Do you hold some beliefs that others might consider unreasonable? Why would they consider these beliefs unreasonable?

Reason is a pretty special and important capacity. Some have held that it is a distinctively human capacity. An old tradition defines humans as the "rational animals," the *only* species with the capacity to reason. Other animals have intelligence. According to this particular tradition, however, *only human beings cultivate and develop their intelligence through discipline so as to solve problems.* Others disagree with this view and think that evidence exists of reason and reasoning in the behaviour of at least some *non*human animals, too.

EXERCISE 1.3 | **Topic for Class Discussion**

What do you think about this? Do you think reason is a distinctively human capability? Why or why not?

Whether reason is a distinctively human characteristic or not, whether it is *confined to* the human species or not, it has certainly proven to be an important species survival trait in human beings. Without reason human beings would be severely handicapped in the struggle for survival. We can easily see how we come to recognize reason as an *essentially human* trait, one that pertains to human beings *as* human beings. This does not mean that all members of the species are equally reasonable, or equally reasonable at all times. What it does mean is that we *presume* that all members of the human species have reason—in other words, that they all have the capacity to cultivate and develop their intelligence through discipline so as to solve problems. We do not restrict this presumption to exclude any category of human beings. This presumption is not gender specific. It is not restricted by age, race, or ethnicity. It applies to all human beings as human beings.

EXERCISE 1.4 | **Topic for Class Discussion**

What do you think about this? Do you think reason is an "essentially human" trait? Why or why not?

DISCIPLINE In our definition of *reason,* the word *discipline* is central. So let us take a moment to reflect on the meaning of *discipline.* We should point out two things about this crucial concept right at the start. First, any discipline will have rules, or at least regularities of some kind. To master any discipline you need to learn the rules and regularities. Second, therefore, discipline takes practice. Music is a good example of a discipline. To become a musician you need to learn some rules and regularities by practising. The same is true of critical thinking. Some people worry that entering into a discipline with all its rules and regularities means submitting to some sort of enforced conformity to some rigid orthodoxy— in other words, that all critical thinkers must think in exactly the same way. This belief is worrisome because thinking is one way we become, manifest, and express ourselves as individuals. If we think for a minute, though, about the comparison to music as a discipline, we can dismiss this worry. All the great musicians throughout history have been highly distinctive individuals. The same is true of writing as a discipline. Practice leads to greater mastery, which opens up many avenues for individual self-expression. The same holds true for critical thinking.

IS THERE ROOM FOR CREATIVITY? When we said that critical thinking involves discipline, we meant that it involves mastering rules and regularities and requires practice. Sometimes people jump from this definition to the conclusion that critical thinking does not involve or encourage creativity. This conclusion stems in part from the (mistaken) idea that creativity is essentially a matter of *breaking* the rules. On the contrary, *following* the rules often vitally involves creativity. Sometimes an original, creative insight is required to know just how to interpret and apply the rules in a given situation. We often describe such situations as calling for "judgment" or "discretion." We hope and anticipate that you will recognize examples of this sort of situation from time to time as you work your way through this book.

EXERCISE 1.5 | Freewrite

Freewriting, like brainstorming, is a technique for liberating creative mental energy. When you freewrite, you don't worry about parallel sentence structure, split infinitives, sentence fragments, or any of the other editorial problems your instructors will nag you about when you're working on an essay. When you freewrite you don't worry about anything—even spelling—that might interfere with simply getting your ideas flowing and on paper.

OK. So here's the exercise: Now that you've learned how we define critical thinking, what do you think you can gain from studying it? Take out a fresh sheet of paper and freewrite for 15 minutes on the topic of what you hope and expect to get out of a course in critical thinking. Don't plan what you're going to write. Just start writing. And don't stop to reconsider, refine, edit, or correct what you've written. Just keep writing. If you can't think of a good way to begin, just complete this sentence: "What I hope and expect to get out of a course in critical thinking is . . ."

When you have written for 15 minutes, finish your thought and save what you've written. We'll be coming back to this. Ready? Go!

OBSTACLES TO CRITICAL THINKING

Naturally, what people actually gain from the study of critical thinking varies widely, depending on many variable factors. What we *hope* our students will take away from the course in the end boils down to this: Critical thinking is a natural development of your already existing reasoning capacity with many

DILBERT: © Scott Adams/Dist. by United Feature Syndicate Inc.

www.dilbert.com scottadams@aol.com

3-24-05 © 2005 Scott Adams, Inc./Dist. by UFS, Inc.

useful applications in your daily life. We *hope* that everyone who studies the concepts, skills, and strategies covered in this book will come to understand them as natural refinements of common sense. We expect that anyone who arrives at this understanding will find many occasions to apply critical thinking in his or her daily life.

Now this may sound nice, but it does give rise to a bit of a puzzle: We are saying that critical thinking is natural for us as human beings. When we pay attention to the way people actually think and behave, however, we get the impression that a lot of pretty "normal" people do not think critically all that much. Perhaps they think critically only about certain things on certain occasions, but not at all about other things (sometimes the things that matter most). This makes us wonder: Why is something as important and natural as critical thinking not more common? Why do so many people seem unable to tell the difference between thinking critically and thinking in completely *uncritical* ways? Why do so many people find critical thinking so *un*natural—not only difficult, but also difficult to *understand*—when they first begin to study it? As stated earlier in this chapter, we think the answer is that many *obstacles* to critical thinking exist—urges, pressures, inducements, and distractions that make it hard, even for reasonable people, to think critically. In addition we are taught to believe things and understand things in ways that confuse and mislead and otherwise interfere with the natural refinement of common sense. So, as it unfortunately turns out, many of us need to *unlearn* a fair amount before we begin to appreciate how "natural" critical thinking can be for us. Many people find that they need to radically reorient themselves and their thinking processes and to change some deeply engrained thinking habits as they learn what it is like to think critically.

People often seem ready to make up their minds to one degree or another on the basis of . . . what? In reality, people too frequently make up their minds on the basis of little or no particular information, from sources whose *identity* is vague and indeterminate, and whose credibility and reliability are simply assumed. Common sense tells us that in a general discussion, where conflicting ideas are advanced in competition against each other, the question must arise of whether one's ideas have enough of a basis to stand up and hold their own. So we find that we really *must* look more deeply into the sources of our information and the assumptions underlying our beliefs in order to think critically about what is at issue. Now, if people have not learned how to do this sort of thing, it can seem like "thinking in reverse," probably because, at least for a while, it seems to take us *further away* from making up our minds. The search for truth seems long and hard, which can be discouraging and can raise obstacles to critical thinking. Let us begin with a common myth: the notion that truth, at least in any strong sense, does not exist.

RELATIVISM/SUBJECTIVISM

Sometimes people get so discouraged they seem to give up on searching for the truth altogether. They even say things such as, "There's really no such thing as the 'truth,' at least not 'Truth' with a capital *T*."

What do you think about this? First, what do you think the statement "There's really no such thing as the 'truth,' at least not 'Truth' with a capital *T*" *means*? Second, do you think the statement is true, or untrue? Third, does it make sense to ask whether the statement is true?

No doubt this statement *might* mean quite a few things. They all probably boil down to some version or variation of this notion: *The so-called "truth" is always relative to some particular point of view in a strong sense—what is "true-for-me" may not be "true-for-you."* Therefore, "firm" or "objective" truth is either impossible or unknowable. More formally, x may be true (for me or us) and not true (for you) at the same time in the same respect, thus contravening Aristotle's principle of noncontradiction (a proposition cannot be both true and not true at the same time in the same respect). For example, you may claim that "the earth is flat" *really is* "true-*for-you*" even though it *really is* "false-*for-me*." Although this example is farfetched (you almost certainly do not believe that the earth is flat), consider a more prosaic example: The proposition "Second-hand cigarette smoke frequently causes cancer in bystanders" really is true (for you) *and* false (for me). In other words, the proposition is purportedly both true and false. (Another example: You might see statements that involve value—for example, moral statements—as "iffy" or controversial and thus under the sway of relativism. Nonetheless, we would still maintain that a proposition or an idea cannot be both true and false at the same time in the same respect. The fact that statements of value are sometimes troublesome to investigate or assess does not mean that we may ditch the principle of noncontradiction for the sake of convenience. We just need to try harder in such cases.) This position is often called "Relativism" (whether social or individual) or "Subjectivism" (when limited to individuals). Relativism/subjectivism is a big obstacle to critical thinking. We consider it a "myth," and propose to refute it with the following argument: You cannot say or believe that "Relativism" or "Subjectivism" is true without contradicting yourself. (Try it.) Therefore, saying or believing that "Relativism" or "Subjectivism" is true is unreasonable.

What do you think about this? Do you find this argument convincing? Explain why, or why not.

We should not be surprised if the question were to arise in this discussion of what exactly we mean by "truth." This turns out to be a surprisingly deep philosophical question because a number of competing "philosophical theories of truth" exist. If you are interested in learning about and considering these theories in detail, we recommend taking a course in metaphysics and/or epistemology.[1] Common theories of truth include the correspondence theory, the coherence theory, and the pragmatic theory. The correspondence theory holds that a proposition—such as, "Unless obstructed, objects fall to the ground"—is true when the proposition matches up with some feature of our world; in this case, the observable properties of physical things. Of course, not all features of our world are confirmable in this way. For instance, we could forward the proposition, "Fairness demands that we treat similar cases in a similar way," but the feature of reality with which our proposition must match up is more of a (supposed) moral intuition than a "fact" that we can simply read off the environment, as when we readily perceive objects falling down around us. In any case, the correspondence theory requires us to show how well our statements and beliefs *match up* with "what is the case" in "the world."

The coherence theory holds, roughly, that our beliefs must *hang together,* and that an allegedly true proposition must be consistent with other propositions that are (known to be) true. A simple example of consistency: If you believe in gravity as an explanatory principle (a general truth), you must also believe that this book will fall down if you let go of it (a specific truth). Another example of ideas hanging together: If you want to know whether you should cut your lawn short or leave it high, then learning that grass height and sound root systems are positively linked helps you get clear about the answer.

Finally, the pragmatic theory holds that truth is a function of practical states of affairs. A statement or belief is true if the practical results of believing it are reliably established. For instance, if you are set up on a blind date and conclude, on the basis of many clear incidents throughout the evening, that you and your date are basically incompatible, then it is true, as a matter of interpersonal fact, that you and the other person are incompatible. Indeed, we cannot conceive the truth of this idea as lying anywhere but in its concretely lived reality. In the simplest terms, a pragmatist asks the question, "Does this idea *work*?" In the case of our example, dismissing this pragmatically confirmed truth and merely hoping for the best on another date would be wrong-headed—the second date would not work!

For our purposes here in overcoming the obstacle to critical thinking posed by "Relativism/Subjectivism," we will assume a correspondence-type "common sense understanding" of the nature of "truth." We will assume that truth is a relationship between a belief or a statement on the one hand, and reality or the world on the other. A belief or statement is true if (and only if) it corresponds to something real. For example, if you believe or say that a hole is growing in the earth's ozone layer, your belief or statement is true if (and only if) there *really is* a growing hole in the earth's ozone layer. Now, on the basis of this conception of truth, what can we say about the search for truth? We can say that the search for truth can be long and hard. Scientists have been forced to work long and hard to understand the earth's ozone layer. To the extent that disagreement persists among scientists who have studied the earth's ozone layer, we should recognize that the search for truth may still be ongoing. In many instances, though, the search for truth is neither long nor hard at all. For example, finding out how much you weigh is not all that difficult, is it? In addition, note that our "matching up" common sense understanding of the nature of truth should also involve elements of the coherence and pragmatic approaches: Our beliefs should "hang together" and "work," too.

"LIMITED" RELATIVISM/SUBJECTIVISM

Often people will cling to some limited version of "Relativism/Subjectivism," even after granting that "Relativism/Subjectivism" cannot *generally* be true. A popular version of "Limited Relativism/Subjectivism" is based on a distinction between "matters of fact" and "matters of opinion, which goes something like this: "Factual matters" are matters that pertain to the "facts." The "facts," in turn, are those things that are provable or knowable beyond doubt or question. Everything else is a "matter of opinion." Furthermore, when it comes to matters of opinion, the "truth" does not exist, at least not "Truth" with a capital *T*.

EXERCISE 1.8 | **Topic for Class Discussion**

What do you think about this? Does the view of "Limited Relativism/Subjectivism" seem any more reasonable than "General Relativism/Subjectivism"? Explain why, or why not.

One way in which this sort of limited version of "Relativism/Subjectivism" may be stronger and more defensible than the general across-the-board version is that it is not so easily refuted by instantly deriving a self-contradiction from it. Nonetheless, it is a major obstacle to critical thinking. One big problem with this distinction is that almost everything, even science, turns out to be a "matter of opinion," simply because it is so hard to prove or know *anything* "beyond doubt or question." The problem arises when we give up the search for truth just because we recognize room for doubt and disagreement. Critical thinking does not give up the search for truth so easily. To overcome the obstacles to critical thinking posed by "Relativism/Subjectivism," whether limited or general, we must cultivate an attitude of *patience and tenacity in pursuit of the truth*. We will come back to this shortly.

EGOCENTRISM

Another big obstacle to critical thinking —a kind of opposite to "Relativism/ Subjectivism"—arises out of the tendency of people to cherish and defend those beliefs most closely associated with their identity. Even in science one can find examples of egocentrism standing in the way of critical thinking. Galileo's astronomical treatise, *Dialogue on the Two Chief Systems of the World* (1632), was a thoughtful and devastating attack on the traditional geocentric view of the universe proposed by the ancient Greek Ptolemy (second century A.D.) and accepted by most scholars and scientists of Galileo's time. Galileo's treatise was therefore an attack not only on the views that these authorities held, but also on the authoritative status that they were privileged to enjoy, and on their self-images. Their reaction was to censor Galileo. Pope Urban, who was persuaded that Simplicio, the butt of the whole dialogue, was intended to represent himself, ordered Galileo to appear before the Inquisition. Although never formally imprisoned, Galileo was threatened with torture and ordered to renounce what he had written. In 1633 he was banished to his country estate. His *Dialogue*, together with the works of Kepler and Copernicus, were placed on the Index of Forbidden Books, from which they were not withdrawn until 1835.

The tendency to cherish and defend those beliefs most closely associated with one's identity is not *un*natural. We are each naturally inclined to favour and defend ourselves and so also anything with which we identify ourselves. We are naturally "egocentric," in our thinking as well as in our interests and concerns. This natural and understandable tendency, if left unchecked, can, as in the case of Galileo and his contemporaries, close one's mind to the possibility that one is mistaken, which would surely stand in the way of thinking critically. In order to understand how to keep this natural inclination in healthy check, let us begin with a series of "thought experiments".[2]

EXERCISE 1.9 | Thought Experiment

Try saying, "Some of my beliefs are not true." Do you notice a problem with this statement? If so, explain. Do you nevertheless find it a reasonable thing to say about yourself? If so, explain.

Some people notice a problem when they say "Some of my beliefs are not true," because they recognize that part of believing something is believing that it *is* true. Some people find this problem manifesting itself at the level of their own particular beliefs: "If I were to do an inventory of my beliefs, wouldn't they *all* strike me as true?"

EXERCISE 1.10 | Thought Experiment

What do you think about this problem? Try the thought experiment in Exercise 1.9 using some of your own beliefs. Identify 5–10 beliefs that you have. Do they all strike you as true? Or does it occur to you to wonder whether any of them might not be true? What more general conclusion, if any, can you draw from these results?

What *is* a belief, anyway? Think of a belief as a kind of "investment of trust or confidence." A belief, like any other investment, can be difficult to abandon, even when evidence shows that it was a bad investment. Realizing and writing off a loss can be so painful that many a person will hang on to a bad investment in the hope that it will eventually turn around to be a good one. "Is this evidence really conclusive? Maybe there's something wrong with this evidence." Questioning the evidence against one of your beliefs is one thing, but when this reluctance to admit that you have made a bad investment in a belief rises to the level of *denying* or *refusing to heed* the evidence, then what we have is not critical thinking but wishful thinking.

EXERCISE 1.11 | **Thought Experiment**

What do you think you would do if you became aware of evidence indicating that one (or more) of your beliefs is not true?

Some people say, "If I found out that something was not true, I would just stop believing it." It would be nice if things were this simple, but we frequently do engage in wishful thinking, and we are capable even of profound self-deception. "How can this be?" you might wonder. "How can a person know that something is not true and continue to believe it? How can a person be both the successful deceiver and the victim of the deception at the same time?" These are good questions. The phenomenon of self-deception is deeply puzzling. It is a fact of human life, though, and we are sure that if you think for a minute or so you can come up with an example or two from your own experience of the sort of thing we have in mind. You probably know people who have on occasion talked themselves into believing things that they knew were not true; for example, that they were ready for a midterm exam when in fact they knew at some level that they were not really prepared. If we were *perfectly* rational creatures, we would no doubt recognize the inconsistency involved in self-deception, and so self-deception probably would never occur—but there is no doubt that it does occur.

Leon Festinger's theory of cognitive dissonance is germane. It holds that cognitive discrepancies (for instance, between what we believe at the moment and new but contrary information) cause us discomfort and that we are inclined to lessen such divergences, often by irrational means (say, by figuring that the new but contrary information must be faulty). We are rational creatures, but not perfectly so. We are also (in some ways and at some times) irrational creatures, and our wishes and desires often overwhelm our good sense. Therefore, we often persist in believing what we want to believe, or what we wish were true, in spite of what we know or have every good reason to believe.

EXERCISE 1.12 | **Thought Experiment**

A moment ago we imagined someone saying, "If I were to do an inventory of my beliefs, wouldn't they all strike me as true?" Try now to describe what it would actually be like to complete an inventory of your beliefs. How long would it take? How would you start? What kind of procedure would you use? How would you keep track?

After you've struggled with this task for a while, go ahead and write down an inventory of your beliefs on paper. Give yourself five minutes and see what you come up with.

Most people are immediately struck by the realization that they have many more beliefs to itemize than they ever would have imagined had they not been prompted to consider enumerating them. If you tried to organize an inventory of your beliefs by sorting them into categories, a similar realization occurs: Beliefs are of so many different *kinds*!

EXERCISE 1.13 | **Thought Experiment**

Do you have any beliefs about how many beliefs you have? For example, do you believe that you have more beliefs than you can count? If so, into what category would such a belief fall? When did you realize that you had beliefs of this sort? For example, were you aware that you had beliefs of this sort before you tried this thought experiment?

By this point, most people are struck by what might be described as a "Major Inventory Control Problem." This problem arises out of two conditions. First, uncertainty about the current inventory of beliefs holds sway. How many of these beliefs that I have just noticed have been here with me all along? How many more beliefs do I hold that I have yet to notice? Second, we must consider the dynamic condition of our belief systems. In other words, our belief systems are not static. They constantly undergo change and revision as we deal with incoming information. Consider how this process normally works. We live in what has come to be known as the "information age," a label that derives from the awesome volume of information bombarding us on a daily basis. Just think of the amount of material contained in the average metropolitan daily newspaper. Now multiply that by seven days a week, and then again by the number of metropolitan population centres that you can tally in a few short minutes. Now add to this weekly, monthly, quarterly, and annual publications, and books, radio, and television—the literally hundreds of separate stations, channels, and cable services, many of which broadcast round the clock. Now add the Internet! These should be enough to make the point that we cannot inspect most of the information that presses upon us, let alone truly absorb it.

Consequently, each of us has to be highly selective about where we direct our attention in this overwhelming flow of information. Actually, this is nothing new or peculiar to our age. In fact, it is part of the human condition—our ability to attend to information is always smaller than the amount of information at hand. If you are like most people, you continue to be selective even within the narrow range of information of which you become aware. You will actively incorporate some information into your belief system, while you will reject other information. What do you suppose are the main factors that govern this process? What do you suppose determines these selections? Among the most important and influential of these factors are the existing contents of our belief systems. What we already believe determines in large part the way we deal with incoming information. Our belief systems are "self-editing."

EXERCISE 1.14 **Topic for Class Discussion**

So, what do you suppose common sense would suggest at this stage about our selection of information?

Each of us has a large and constantly evolving belief system comprising a huge number of beliefs—so many that trying to count them seems crazy. Most of these beliefs we routinely just *assume*. In other words, we take them for granted. We regard them as true without questioning them, or determining the adequacy of whatever evidence may exist to support them, or wondering whence they came and whether those sources are reliable. So, if you are like most people, a large part of your belief system is probably "subterranean" and functions in a largely unexamined way, as a set of assumptions of which you are probably not even fully aware and that influences its own ongoing evolution. Based on the sheer *size* of a person's belief system, common sense surely suggests the strong probability that some of those beliefs are not true, especially as long as they remain unexamined.

EXERCISE 1.15 | **Thought Experiment**

Suppose that you were actually able to complete a thorough inventory of each and every one of your beliefs. Suppose further that you were able to weed out each and every false or dubious item from that inventory, and now here you are at the end, considering the very last item in the inventory: Belief #457,986,312 "Some of my beliefs are not true." What do you think you should do with this belief? Would you weed it out or not? Explain.

To overcome the obstacles to critical thinking posed by the pitfalls of egocentrism, we must cultivate an attitude of *intellectual humility*. In other words, we ought to recognize our fallibility or liability to error, while at the same time maintaining a patient and tenacious commitment to the pursuit of truth. As we shall see, however, even such a healthy attitude as intellectual humility can give rise to another kind of obstacle to critical thinking.

© The New Yorker Collection 1987 Al Ross from cartoonbank.com. All Rights Reserved.

"Logic—the last refuge of a scoundrel."

INTIMIDATION BY AUTHORITY

An authority is an expert source of information outside ourselves. The source can be a single individual (a parent, a teacher, a celebrity, a clergy member, the prime minister), a group of individuals (doctors, educators, a peer group, a national consensus), or even an institution (a religion, a government agency, an educational establishment). Whatever its form, authority can exert considerable influence on our belief systems. It is easy to see why this is so. Consider the difficulty in becoming an expert about *anything*. Nobody can ever hope to become an expert about *everything*. If we want to know something, we can almost always find someone who knows more about the subject than we do. So a person with a healthy attitude of intellectual humility is likely to find it helpful to consult authorities for their expert opinions.

EXERCISE 1.16 | **Thought Experiment**

Now go back and reconsider your belief inventory regarding sources. How many of the things that you believe can you trace back to your own direct experience? Take as an example some area of interest or concern that is of intimate personal importance to you (such as your physical health). How many of the things that you believe about your physical health have you derived from sources other than your own direct experience? In such cases can you identify the precise source of the belief? Explain.

If you are like the rest of us, chances are that you have gotten a lot of the things you believe from other sources. Beliefs about world history, the direction of the economy, the events of the day, the existence of God and an afterlife, the state of your health—what are the sources of all of these beliefs? Chances are that you got many of them by relying on the word of others, sources you are in effect trusting as authorities. Again, all this is perfectly normal and natural. Common sense should warn us, though, that trusting someone other than ourselves when we make up our minds involves risk. How do we know that the authority we trust is in fact reliable?

Beyond this inherent risk (a risk that can at least be managed) a deeper danger lurks. We can rely on authority so much that we stop thinking for ourselves. Such blind acceptance of and obedience to authority is of course incompatible with intellectual autonomy and critical thinking. Just how likely is it that an intelligent person would be susceptible to such a debilitating abuse of trust? How vulnerable are we really to the dictates of authority? How subtle might its negative influence be?

Consider a series of experiments conducted by psychologist Stanley Milgram in the 1960s.[3] Milgram's famous experiment consisted of asking subjects to administer strong electrical shocks to people the subjects could not see. The subjects were told that they could control the shock's intensity by means of a shock generator with 30 clearly marked voltages, ranging from 15 to 450 volts and labelled from "Slight Shock (15)" to "XXX—Danger! Severe Shock (450)." We should point out that the entire experiment was a setup: No one actually administered or received shocks. The subjects were led to believe that the "victims" were being shocked as part of an experiment to determine the effects of punishment on memory. The "victims," who were in fact confederates of the experimenters, were strapped in their seats with electrodes attached to their wrists "to avoid blistering and burning." The "victims" were told to make no noise until a "300-volt shock" was administered, at which point they were to make noise loud enough for the subjects to hear (for example, pounding on the walls as if in pain). The subjects were reassured that the shocks, though extremely painful, would cause no permanent tissue injury. When asked, a number of psychologists predicted that no more than 10 percent of the subjects would follow the instruction to administer a 450-volt shock. In fact, well over half did (26 out of 40). Even after hearing the "victims" pounding, 87.5 percent of the subjects (35 out of 40) followed instructions to increase the voltage. It seems clear that many intelligent people, when instructed by an authority, will act against their better judgment. To overcome the obstacles to critical thinking posed by the intimidating influence of authority, what we need is simply to maintain our *intellectual independence.*

CONFORMISM

Further experiments seem to show that not only are people's actions susceptible to external influence, but their judgment itself is susceptible as well. For example, look at the line segments in the accompanying figure. Which of the three lines below matches the one on the right?

A _____

B _____   _____

C _____

Do you trust your own perceptual judgment here? Line segment B obviously matches the line segment on the right. Do you think you could ever be persuaded to doubt your own perceptions and choose A or C? Maybe not, but experiments indicate that many people *can be* persuaded to alter their perceptual judgments, even when their judgments are obviously correct. These experiments involved several hundred individuals who were asked to match lines just as you did. In each group, however, one and only one subject was naive, that is, unaware of the nature of the experiment. The other individuals were instructed to make incorrect judgments in some cases and to exert peer pressure on the naive subject to change his or her correct judgment. The results: When subjects were not exposed to peer pressure, they inevitably judged correctly. Peer pressure, however, produces a measurable and significant tendency toward conformity, the tendency increasing as the majority increased toward unanimity.[4] What is most interesting about these results is what they show about the power of "peer pressure." Psychologically we are all, at some level, aware of our liability to error, even in our perceptual judgments. The fact that peer pressure is powerful enough to erode people's confidence in their own perceptual experience and judgment is nevertheless remarkable. Consider how much *more* intimidating peer pressure must be when applied to anything more remote from you than your very own perceptual experience and judgment!

What accounts for such intimidating power? Like many other creatures, human beings are social animals. Our chances of survival and of flourishing are greatly enhanced by association with others. We survive and do much better generally in groups than as individuals. Therefore, we are naturally fearful of isolation. At the same time, cooperation among individual members and group loyalty are both essential to the successful organization of any group, to the coordination of any group project, and to the maintenance of the group as a stable entity. So there is a natural tendency in any group toward conformity and orthodoxy. A hierarchy of authority arises within any group through which orthodoxy is established and conformity to it is reinforced. All this is perfectly natural and makes sense when it comes to survival value for the individual, for the group, and for the species. If, however, this natural and functional tendency exceeds healthy limits, the fear of isolation can overcome our basic common sense, increasing rather than minimizing our liability to error. To overcome the obstacles to critical thinking posed by the intimidating influence of authority, peer pressure, and orthodoxy, we need to cultivate and maintain *intellectual courage.*

ETHNOCENTRISM

Another major obstacle to critical thinking—a close relative of egocentrism—also arises out of our natural tendency as social animals to gather together in groups and to identify ourselves with and by way of our social groupings. To see how this happens, try the following little thought experiment.

EXERCISE 1.17 | **Thought Experiment**

Cultural Categories: How many distinct cultural groups can you identify in five minutes simply by describing yourself? "I am a(n) _____." (You could even start with your name [which identifies your family].)

However narrowly or broadly these groupings are defined—from kinship groupings (families) to something as broad as gender—cultural categories play an important role in the formation of our individual identities because we identify ourselves to a large extent by way of them. Ethnic consciousness, like self-awareness, and ethnic pride, like self-esteem, are important ingredients in a healthy personality and in society. Unfortunately, they each have corresponding perversions that, when they arise, stand as obstacles to critical thinking (and cause other serious problems as well).

The natural human tendency to be egocentric can also affect our attitudes regarding groups with which we identify. There is a tendency to believe in the superiority of our family, our circle of friends, our age group, our religion, our nation, our race, our ethnicity, our gender, our sexual orientation, and our culture. Thus, egocentricity, the view that mine is better (my ideas, my experience, my values, my agenda) becomes ethnocentricity, the view that ours is better (our ideas, our values, our ways).

In recent years cultural identity has gained recognition as a matter of political importance. Multiculturalism is high on the agenda of most educational institutions now sensitive to the importance of cultural diversity in the community and the curriculum. Instructors now strive to reflect multiple cultural perspectives in their courses (and authors in their textbooks). In critical thinking, cultural diversity and an awareness of alternative cultural perspectives are especially useful because of the limitations inherent in *any* given cultural perspective. An appreciation of cultural diversity contributes to open-mindedness, an essential ingredient of critical thinking. To overcome the obstacles to critical thinking posed by ethnocentrism, we must cultivate an attitude of *respectful intellectual tolerance* and maintain and strengthen our *intellectual humility*.

UNEXAMINED ASSUMPTIONS

At the time of this writing, Robert Pickton, a pig farmer from British Columbia, stands charged with 27 counts of murder. If convicted, he will be Canada's worst serial murderer. Many of Pickton's alleged victims were female prostitutes from Vancouver's notorious Downtown Eastside, a drug-infested slum. He incongruously hosted registered charitable social events on his property, which many prostitutes allegedly attended. The bulk of the evidence against Pickton comprises traces of DNA of many of the missing women that investigators found on his farm.

EXERCISE 1.18 | **Thought Experiment**

Do you find it difficult to "suspend judgment" on this shocking case? If someone asks you, "Do you think Pickton did it?" and you say sincerely, "I don't know," you are suspending your judgment. If you think Pickton is probably guilty, what assumption about the meaning of the DNA findings underlies your judgment?

Most people come to a point where it is no longer possible to suspend judgment. The urgency of the need we feel to initiate *some* plan of action makes the suspense unbearable. Though we may not *know* what has happened to any degree of certainty, we nevertheless feel we must do *something*. Therefore, we begin to make "assumptions." "Assumption" was one of the first words we needed to define clearly in order to avoid misunderstanding. So here is what we mean by assumption: *An assumption is a claim that is taken to be true without argument.* In this definition we use two terms, *claim* and *argument*, which also need to be explained. A claim is a statement that "claims for itself (whether rightly or wrongly) the value of being true." If someone says, "Hi. How are you?" this would not be a claim—the person is not using this language to make a statement that claims to be true. If someone asks you "What time is it?" this also would not be a claim. If, however, someone says, "Pickton must be guilty," the person is making a claim. Argument is a concept that we will define and develop in detail in Chapters 3, 4, and 5 of this book. For the time being just think of an argument as support for a claim. Therefore, an assumption is a statement that claims to be true and is taken to be true without support.

EXERCISE 1.19 | Find the Argument

Argument is a concept that we will define and develop in detail in Chapters 3, 4, and 5 of this book, but it is a concept we have already put to use. Where did we do this?

Perhaps you have heard the cliché, *Beware of assumptions; to "assume" makes an "ass" out of "u" and "me."* This is part of a widespread myth according to which *all* assumptions are suspect or dangerous, and so we should try to avoid making *any assumptions at all.*

EXERCISE 1.20 | Thought Experiment

Pick any topic or subject you like, and try thinking about it without making any assumptions.

The main problem with this widespread myth is that it is *practically impossible* to follow as a recommendation for how to conduct one's reasoning. The more seriously you take it, the more paralyzed you become. All reasoning must start somewhere. We cannot make utterly assumptionless statements. Every statement rests unavoidably on some further idea. Proving statements to someone else's satisfaction may require defending the deeper ideas on which your statements rest, but the chain of proof must end somewhere. For example, if you were to argue in favour of strengthening basic education in poverty-stricken countries on compassionate grounds, dialogical pressure might prompt you to add the clarification, "Of course, the United Nations Universal Declaration of Human Rights states clearly that everyone has a right to education." The idea that everyone has a right to education is or comes close to being an irreducible point of departure. You might try to go further and appeal to inherent human worth and dignity, but you probably would not be able to push your justification beyond such a point.

Of course risk is involved in making *any* assumption; namely, the risk that what you are assuming is not true. No doubt we are making some assumptions when we make this claim, but it seems clear that in practice it is *impossible* to reason about *anything* without making at least *some* assumption(s). Consequently, *some* risk is inherent and inevitable in reasoning as such. In other words, we cannot eliminate this risk entirely. This risk increases—in other words, assumptions are more "dangerous"—to the extent that assumptions remain *hidden*. As long as assumptions are hidden they are not open to discussion, to challenge, to debate, and to deliberate consideration (as any serious claim to the truth should be). So the obvious way to keep the risk down would be to *be aware of the assumptions we are making.* Thus, we would replace the cliché "Beware of Assumptions" with the maxim "Be Aware of Assumptions" and posit this as a critical thinking "Rule of Thumb."

CRITICAL THINKING TIP 1.1

~~Beware of Assumptions~~ BE AWARE of Assumptions.

An important corollary to this rule of thumb emerges: *Do not forget the assumptions you are making (do not forget that they ARE assumptions).* This is essential to avoiding one of those pitfalls that lead otherwise reasonable people into unreasonable beliefs and ill-advised courses of action. Assumptions in their essential nature—*by definition*—are "taken to be true without support." As we explained above, the risk of error increases as soon as we forget about the need to discuss, challenge, debate, and deliberately consider whether what we are assuming is really true. Do not forget the point we made earlier about the difficulty this poses for many people. Seriously examining assumptions, on the basis of which you thought you were going to make up your mind, can easily seem like thinking in reverse.

INFERENTIAL ASSUMPTIONS

Where should we look for assumptions? Common sense suggests that we should be especially vigilant in two particular directions. Where people are making "inferences," or are "drawing conclusions"—by which we mean reasoning from one claim to another—we should look for assumptions in between the claims in the inference.

EXERCISE 1.21 | **Identifying Hidden Assumptions ("Between the Lines")**

Suppose a fellow student says to you, "As a society we really shouldn't be relying on computers as much as we do." When you challenge her claim, she says, "Well, don't forget, computers are designed and built by human beings." What is she assuming?

Notice how the reasoning here goes from her *answer* back to the claim you challenged. How, though, does the reasoning get from the claim "computers are designed and built by human beings," to the claim you originally challenged "that we really shouldn't be relying on computers as much as we do"? An assumption exists here that serves as a missing link in the chain of reasoning. Can you figure out what this assumption is? Assumptions that play this sort of linking role are often called inferential assumptions, a concept we will return to in Chapters 3 and 4.

PRESUPPOSITIONS

Another important place to look for assumptions is "underneath" the claims being made. Sometimes in order to make any sense of what *is* stated or expressed explicitly, we are required to assume additional claims that are not stated explicitly.

EXERCISE 1.22 | **Identifying Hidden Assumptions ("Beneath the Surface")**

Go back and look at the first cartoon in this chapter. What assumptions do you have to make to understand the definition of Critical Thinking here?

As a response to the father's statements in the cartoon, the rhetorical question (indirect assertion)—"Wouldn't that teach them to believe anything they're told without applying any Critical Thinking?"—assumes that Critical Thinking involves inquiry and reflection, not merely accepting opinions from authorities. Assumptions of this kind—the kind that we must make in order for what *is* explicitly said to make sense—are often called "*pre*suppositions." We will develop this concept also in Chapters 3 and 4.

EXERCISE 1.23 | **Topic for Class Discussion**

On June 24, 1997, the United States Air Force issued its official explanation of the Roswell Incident. The Roswell Incident is probably the most famous incident of an alleged Earth landing of extraterrestrials, long thought by many UFO believers to involve a government cover-up because the sightings occurred and the debris was collected on and around a government military reservation (Roswell Air Force Base in New Mexico), and because the government maintained an official silence about the incident for 50 years. The official explanation was that an experimental high-altitude weather balloon and several humanoid crash test dummies had fallen to Earth from very high altitudes. Conspiracy theorists were not convinced and much debate ensued. Here is an opinion overheard on the radio. (How many assumptions can you identify?) "There's no government cover-up, and there were no aliens. Look, if you were an alien and you were scoping out the Earthly terrain, the last place you'd go would be to one of the most highly fortified and tightly secured military installations in the United States."

From this discussion of obstacles to critical thinking, a sort of "portrait of the critical thinker" begins to emerge. A critical thinker is a person who combines an array of "intellectual virtues" and displays these virtues in his or her intellectual life. A critical thinker is patient, tenacious, humble, courageous, tolerant, and respectful of diversity of opinion in pursuit of the truth. The critical thinker sticks with the search for truth. The critical thinker is not in a hurry to be done with the search for truth, although it may be long and arduous. The critical thinker is humble in recognizing his or her own limitations and liability to error. The critical thinker is also not easily intimidated by authority, popular opinion, or peer pressure. The critical thinker recognizes the value of diverse perspectives and viewpoints and is respectful of the views of others with whom he or she may disagree.

With this portrait of the critical thinker in mind, let us now return to a question we raised earlier in this chapter: How is it that reasonable people come to hold unreasonable beliefs? Chances are that this occurs because people have given up the search for truth, or lost their patience and jumped to a hasty conclusion in the search for truth, or become intimidated (lost their courage and independence), or become arrogant (lost their humility) in pursuit of the truth.

EXERCISE 1.24 | **Critical Thinking Self-Assessment**

Part 1, A critical thinking *"Role Model":* Based on your understanding of critical thinking as defined and explained so far in this chapter, identify the person(s) you think best exemplifies a critical thinker. Explain why you chose this person(s).

Part 2, A critical thinking *"Self-Assessment":* Assess your own habits of mind in light of the "intellectual virtues" found in the above portrait of the critical thinker.

In the search for truth I am,
Extremely patient, relatively patient, about average, somewhat impatient, very impatient.
Very tenacious, relatively tenacious, about average, will give up, will give up easily.
Etc.

LOOKING AHEAD: ISSUES AND DISPUTES

You may have heard the expression "Reasonable people may differ . . ." We call a topic of reflection or investigation about which reasonable people may differ an *issue.* Should there be a law against abortion? Should animals be used in medical experimentation? Does intelligent extraterrestrial life exist? What is the average temperature of the water in Lake Erie? Does a global environmental crisis truly exist? What drives people to commit acts of terrorism? Should the federal government overhaul its regional equalization payments? These are all questions to which a number of significant and conflicting alternative responses are both genuinely open and defensible. These are all good examples of our concept of an issue.

Sometimes it seems as though reasonable people may differ about anything, everything, even nothing at all. If only we could dispense with disputes over nothing at all. So before we begin to discuss issues, let us explain more deeply what we mean by *genuinely* disputable, by pointing out and setting aside another kind of thing that frequently *passes* for an issue.

MERE VERBAL DISPUTES

Philosopher William James tells the story about how on a camping trip everyone got into a dispute over the following puzzle:

> The corpus of the dispute was a squirrel—a live squirrel supposed to be clinging to one side of a tree-trunk; while over against the tree's opposite side a human being was imagined to stand. This human witness tries to get sight of the squirrel by moving rapidly round the tree, but no matter how fast he goes, the squirrel moves just as fast in the opposite direction, and always keeps the tree between himself and the man, so that never a glimpse of him is caught. The resultant problem now is this: *Does the man go round the squirrel or not?* He goes round the tree, sure enough, and the squirrel is on the tree; but does he go round the squirrel?[5]

James's idea was that although you can easily imagine people going round and round in an endless dispute over such a puzzle, you can just as easily dissolve the puzzle by drawing a simple terminological distinction: It all depends on what you mean by "going round" the squirrel.

> If you mean passing from the north of him to the east, then to the south, then to the west, then to the north again, obviously the man does go round him, for he occupies these successive positions. But if on the contrary you mean being first in front of him, then on the right of him, then behind him, then on the left, and finally in front again, it is quite as obvious that the man fails to go round him, for by the compensating movements the squirrel makes, he keeps his belly turned towards the man all the time, and his back turned away.[6]

Since it hardly matters which meaning of "going round" the squirrel applies, this could be called a "merely verbal" dispute. To put it another way, no *real* issue exists here; the dispute arises out of a simple "ambiguity" (for an explanation of this concept, see the section "Some Issues in the Use of Language" in Chapter 2) in the way the puzzle is worded. A similar example is the old dispute, "If a tree falls in the forest and nobody is there to hear it, is there a sound?" Clarifying the meaning of "sound" dissolves the dispute. If you are talking about sound *waves*, then presumably sounds occur whether or not anyone is there to hear the tree fall. If, however, you mean sound *sensations*—the experience of sound—then the falling tree makes no sound, for no one is there to experience the sound sensations.

On one hand, perhaps it would be nice if all issues were as trivial as these. Perhaps it would be nice if all disputes arose out of simple ambiguities and could be dismissed as mere "matters of semantics." On the other hand, perhaps it would be boring if all disputes were idle, and we had no real, serious, and urgent issues about which to argue. Reasonable people may differ here, possibly leading to another kind of idle dispute. In any case, most genuinely important disputes are concerned with genuine issues of one sort or another. The rest of this book will be devoted to developing and refining strategies and procedures for resolving serious disputes about real and important issues, which comprise a variety as wide as all of human interest and concern.

ISSUE ANALYSIS

CRITICAL THINKING TIP 1.2

"If we want to understand something very complex, we must approach it very simply, and therein lies our difficulty—because we always approach our problems with assertions, with assumptions or conclusions, and so we are never free to approach them with the humility they demand."

—Krishnamurti

Because they inherently involve conflict, all issues present a certain amount of psychological discomfort. They all seem to "cry out" for resolution, but a critical thinker must discipline herself to be patient in pursuit of the truth. Thus, another aspect of thinking critically that often gives the impression of "thinking in reverse" concerns issues and their analysis. Before we begin to "make up our minds" about how to resolve a given issue, it is useful to do some analysis of the issue itself.

Inherent complexity is one of the immediate challenges that most issues present. Take as an example the first of the issues we mentioned earlier: The question of whether there should be a law against abortion. Even though it is worded as a simple yes-or-no question, it is hardly a simple issue. The minute you look at the issue closely and begin to confront it seriously, you will see that what you have in front of you is not just one issue but a whole bunch of them, resembling a can of worms. This happens because there are *so many different things* under the umbrella heading of "abortion" about which reasonable people can disagree.

For example, reasonable people will disagree over whether abortion belongs in the same moral category as murder, or homicide, or elective surgery, or birth control. Reasonable people will disagree over whether a woman's reproductive processes are private, and so also over whether the government may legitimately interfere with her choices. Reasonable people will disagree over whether the fetus is a person or only a potential person. Reasonable people will disagree over whether potential persons have rights. Reasonable people will disagree over whether the right to life overrides other rights that may come into conflict with it, and over whether the right to life includes the right to use another person's body as a life-support system. Even among those who agree that the law *should* restrict abortion, reasonable people will disagree, for example, over whether the restriction should be total or partial, rigid or flexible, and if partial and flexible, over what the exceptions should be, and so on. So much complexity! It seems as though there might be too many dimensions of complexity to count.

The challenge this situation poses for human intelligence is confusion: another one of those things that make it difficult—even for reasonable people, and even when they are not distracted by external pressures or internal longings and fears—to discriminate between reasonable and unreasonable beliefs. Most interesting issues are deep and complex enough to present this sort of challenge. So the first step of issue analysis is to take apart the issue to see what subsidiary issues are contained within it.

EXERCISE 1.25 | **Issue Analysis I**

Set a timer for three minutes. Then brainstorm for subsidiary issues. See how many distinct issues you can see arising out of any one of the following issues:

- Should animals be used in medical experimentation?
- Does intelligent extraterrestrial life exist?
- What is the average temperature of the water in Lake Erie?
- Is there a global environmental crisis?
- What drives people to commit acts of terrorism?
- Should the federal government overhaul its regional equalization payments?

The next step is to find an approach to the issue that will help us to bring its complexity under intellectual control rather than allowing its complexity to confuse and overwhelm us. One approach that immediately occurs to many people is to narrow the focus of the inquiry. For example, rather than try to resolve the whole nest of issues arising out of the abortion debate, we might confine ourselves to the issue over whether the fetus is a person or only a potential person. This approach is a reasonable one and is often useful. Nonetheless, it never completely disposes of the problem. Suppose we do narrow our focus down to the issue over the status of the fetus. Is the fetus a person or just a potential person? Here again, the minute you look closely at this issue and begin to confront it seriously, what you will see is not just one issue but a whole bunch of them—a pile of concerns. What are the biological changes that take place during fetal development? How do the criteria for personhood relate to the biology of fetal development? Is personhood simply a biological matter, or is it an essentially political matter? Is it perhaps a spiritual matter? What precisely do we mean by the word *person*? What are the criteria for being a "person"?

LOGICAL PRIORITY

With any such complex inquiry, what we really need to do is to develop an *orderly agenda of inquiry*. An agenda is a list of things to do. The function of an agenda is to monitor progress, especially when we must keep track of a lot of things. An agenda of inquiry would contain a list of issues to resolve. Its function is to help you know whether you are making progress toward resolving the main issue (the issue with which you started) in which the others are embedded, rather than going round and round in circles or wandering aimlessly and getting lost in it all.

To develop an agenda, we must prioritize, which simply means putting things into some kind of serial order. In any agenda something has to come first, something has to come next, and so on. An agenda of inquiry may admit of several reasonable orders to follow and probably should always be open to revision. Nevertheless, some ways of ordering an agenda of inquiry are more logical than others. Suppose we start out trying to resolve the issue of what to do about the national issues mentioned at the start of this chapter. Very shortly we should notice that any resolution to this issue that we might consider presupposes some resolution to the subsidiary issue of the *causes* of the problems. This indicates that the issue as to the causes of the problems is "logically prior" to the issue as to the remedies. Similarly, any resolution to the issue of whether the fetus is a person will presuppose some resolution to the issue of what the criteria for personhood are. In other words, the issue of the criteria for personhood is logically prior to the issue of whether the fetus is a person. Whenever we notice this sort of relationship, it makes sense to address issues in the order of their logical priority.

EXERCISE 1.26 | **Issue Analysis II**

Now take the list of subsidiary issues you brainstormed in Exercise 1.25 and prioritize it.

ISSUE CLASSIFICATION

The next step of issue analysis comes from recognizing that different types of issues exist and that strategies and procedures appropriate for issues of one type may not be very appropriate for issues of other types. For example, the procedures for determining the average temperature of the water in Lake Erie will not be much use in resolving the question of whether animals should be used in medical experimentation. We propose to sort issues into three categories: factual Issues, evaluative Issues, and interpretive Issues.

In this connection we will use the terms *factual, evaluative,* and *interpretive* in a way that departs slightly but significantly from what we believe is current popular usage. Our impression is that people generally draw a sharp distinction between "factual" matters on the one hand and "evaluative and interpretive" matters on the other, but also that people generally do not draw any sharp and clear distinction at all between evaluative and interpretive matters. Popular usage seems to go something like this: Factual matters are matters that pertain to the facts. The facts are everything that is proven or known beyond doubt or question. Everything else (values, interpretations, whatever) is a matter of opinion and as such can never be proven or established as true.[7]

If you agree with any of this, we are going to try to talk you out of it. First, this way of talking and thinking fails to recognize the need for strategies and procedures to resolve issues about what the facts actually are. Second, it does not open up any useful strategic or procedural options for resolving evaluative or interpretive issues. We are therefore going to stipulate meanings with somewhat greater precision and utility than popular conventional usage has for the words *factual, evaluative,* and *interpretive.* We will use *factual* to refer to "matters that can be investigated by the methods either of *empirical science* or of *documentary research.*" We will use *evaluative* to refer to "matters that concern the *merits* of things." Finally, we will use *interpretive* to refer to "matters that concern the *meanings* of things."

These categories are neither mutually exclusive nor exhaustive. This means that a given issue may have aspects that belong to more than one of these categories or fall outside all of them. Bear in mind that the purpose of this categorical scheme has little to do with labelling issues or sorting them correctly. We are more concerned about clarifying the agenda of inquiry. Recognizing a given issue as belonging to a particular type is potentially valuable in determining what strategies and procedures will most likely lead to a resolution of the issue. To approach an issue as a factual issue is to raise questions of evidence. What sort of evidence is relevant and decisive? What evidence that bears on the issue is already available? What additional evidence is required? What sorts of experiments or research are needed in order to obtain that additional evidence? To approach an issue as an evaluative issue is to raise questions of standards. To approach an issue as an interpretive issue is to raise the question of interpretive hypotheses.

FACTUAL ISSUES

In modern Olympic history which nation has won the most medals in weight lifting? What city is the world's coldest national capital? What is the average temperature of the water in Lake Erie? All of these are factual questions. They illustrate what we mean by saying that factual matters can be investigated by doing empirical science or documentary research. If a dispute were to arise about any of these questions—say, for example, during a game of Jeopardy or Trivial Pursuit—well-established procedures are already available for settling it. We might look up the information in a reliable source (documentary research), or if the information is not already recorded, we could easily imagine the sort of scientific investigation by which the information could be gathered.

Having said that, you should also note right away that things are not always so simple with factual issues. Suppose that for some reason we needed to figure out how many feral cats live in the city of Kelowna, British Columbia. In this case the question is not theoretically difficult to answer. It is a simple factual matter of counting the cats. In practice, though, how in the world can anyone count all the feral (wild) cats in the city of Kelowna?! They run away. They hide. They breed like, uh, feral cats. So we would need to estimate the number in some way. In fact, things might not be simple, even with the simple (or simple-sounding) examples we mentioned above. Suppose we were asked to determine the average temperature of the water in the Pacific Ocean. You can begin to appreciate the difficulty of determining matters of fact.

Doing good science involves both evaluation and interpretation, as does doing good documentary research. The question of whether or not there is a global environmental crisis is a good example. Suppose we approach it initially as a factual question. What sort of evidence would be relevant? Suppose hard empirical evidence existed as to significant changes in weather patterns on a global scale. This would certainly be relevant evidence. Notice that evaluation (of the evidence) is already involved. "Hard" evidence *has merit;* "significant" changes *merit attention.* Supposing for the moment that we do have hard evidence of significant global weather anomalies; we would still need some understanding of their causes in order to answer our original question. This would involve interpreting the evidence we already have as well as additional evidence we may seek concerning, for example, extraordinary fluctuations in the average temperature in the Pacific Ocean, and so on. We will discuss all of this further in Chapters 8 and 9.

EVALUATIVE ISSUES

Now let us reconsider the first two issues we mentioned earlier. Should there be a law against abortion? Should animals be used in medical experimentation? One thing should be clear right away: Neither of these issues can be resolved *simply* as a matter of fact. We could not possibly hope to settle a dispute over the right and proper legal status of abortion by doing documentary research alone, nor could we hope to settle a dispute over the use of animals in experimental medicine on the basis of empirical science alone. This is not to say that documentation and empirical evidence are irrelevant to these issues. Just as evaluation and interpretation are important parts of any good factual inquiry, good science and documentary research often play a crucial role in evaluation and interpretation. Nonetheless, no amount of empirical evidence and documentation could possibly be *by itself decisive* in either of these issues. Thus, it makes sense to approach them initially not as factual issues, and the word *should* in the questions is a clue that they are each fundamentally evaluative issues, which raises the question of standards. What standards of evaluation concern us? In each of these issues we can see that moral or ethical standards are central, so they will need to be clarified in the course of the inquiry. Interpretive and factual questions will take their place in the agenda of inquiry as they arise in the process of clarifying and applying these moral or ethical standards. We will discuss this further in Chapter 10.

INTERPRETIVE ISSUES

Suppose that in her first speech before the United Nations General Assembly the newly appointed Canadian ambassador makes five explicit references, to fair trade, Arctic sovereignty, Canadian values, the treatment of detainees in the war on terrorism, and the importance of the U.N. and multilateral cooperation. Is Canada sending a message to United States? If so, what is the message? We could also take an example from our earlier list of issues: Should the federal government overhaul its regional equalization payments?

These questions indicate issues concerning what things mean, or how they should be understood. Such issues frequently arise in our attempts to understand things whose meanings may be flexible, complicated, multilayered, obscure, or even deliberately veiled. Issues of this sort are probably the most procedurally complex and difficult issues that we are likely to encounter in everyday discourse. They are also absolutely fundamental to the process of communication, since they concern the discernment of meaning. Indeed, many, perhaps most, of the exercises you will do throughout this book involve interpretation. Deciding whether or not a particular passage is an argument involves interpretation. Deciding whether or not a passage is intended to serve a persuasive, an expressive, or informative function involves interpretation. No single simple procedure exists for resolving interpretive issues or for settling interpretive disputes. Instead, many kinds of information are relevant to interpretation, some of which have already been mentioned and some of which we will discuss further in Chapters 2, 9, and 10.

For example, the conventions governing the use of a term or an expression are relevant to its interpretation. Similarly, so-called diplomatic conventions exist that are relevant to the interpretation of communications between one government—for example, through its U.N. ambassador—and another. In addition to conventions, information about the context surrounding a passage is relevant to its interpretation. Knowing that a particular speech was delivered before the U.N. General Assembly rather than, for example, by confidential communiqué to the American ambassador, is an important piece of information that can guide us closer to an accurate understanding of what was meant. Contextual information in the case of oral communication, as well as in film and video, includes facial expression, vocal inflection, bodily posture, timing, and so on.

Gathering and sifting evidence of such a wide variety, especially in living contexts where time is of the essence, is evidently a process of considerable complexity and subtlety. A good deal of disagreement exists among theorists about the proper procedures for doing interpretive work and how they should be applied in different sorts of interpretive controversy. Nevertheless, interpretation is something you are probably pretty good at by now. You no doubt already recognize that some interpretive issues can be resolved relatively firmly and easily, whereas others are more difficult and may be quite resistant to resolution. In disputed cases, perhaps the most useful procedural strategy is the use of hypothetical reasoning, which involves formulating and testing interpretive hypotheses. An hypothesis is a particular sort of conscious assumption. It is an idea we *assume* to be true for the purpose of exploring or testing it. This procedure also has important applications regarding factual issues. We will be discussing it in greater detail in Chapter 9.

EXERCISE 1.27 | **Issue Analysis III**

Number each of the following sets of questions or issues in ascending order of logical priority, first to last. Then classify each question or issue as to type. Explain your rankings and classifications.

- ☐ Should "hate speech" on the Internet be against the law?
- ☐ What is "hate speech"?
- ☐ Should the service provider or the government be responsible for the enforcement of regulations prohibiting "hate speech" over the Internet?
- ☐ What kinds of penalties should be imposed on people who post "hate speech" on the Internet?

- ☐ Is time travel possible?
- ☐ Is time travel technically feasible?
- ☐ Is the technical feasibility of time travel worth investigating?
- ☐ What is meant by "time travel"?

- ☐ What are the defining criteria for being a person?
- ☐ Should abortion be prohibited under criminal law as a form of homicide?
- ☐ Is abortion a form of homicide?
- ☐ Is the human fetus a person?

- ☐ Should same-sex couples be allowed to join in legally sanctioned marriages?
- ☐ Will the recognition of same-sex marriages undermine the purposes of legally sanctioned marriage?
- ☐ What purpose(s) is (are) served by the institution of legally sanctioned marriage?
- ☐ Could civilization survive the collapse of an institution as important as legally sanctioned marriage, as a result of the recognition of same-sex marriages?

COMPOSING AN ISSUE STATEMENT

An Issue Statement is a composition whose purpose is to communicate clearly an interest in a topic, a topic about which we anticipate disagreement among reasonable people. An Issue Statement can be composed very briefly—for example, as a single short sentence—or at greater length—for example, as the opening chapter of a book. The ability to compose issue statements is essential both to communicating successfully our own opinions and to understanding the viewpoints of others (as we will explain in Chapter 5). Either way, composing an Issue Statement can and should involve careful and appropriate use of the techniques of issue analysis discussed above in this chapter. Eventually, when you compose a complete argumentative essay, a well-crafted issue statement will be an important part of your essay's introduction. We will work on this in greater detail in Chapter 13.

EXERCISE 1.28 | Term Project: Issue Statement I

Compose a 250-word Issue Statement (one page standard, double-spaced) incorporating your results from Exercises 1.25 and 1.26. In your Issue Statement, try not to take sides.

EXERCISE 1.29 | Issue Statement II

Compose a 250-word Issue Statement (one page standard, double-spaced) presenting an issue of your choice. In your Issue Statement, try not to take sides.

ADDITIONAL EXERCISES

As you work through the exercises throughout this book, keep in mind what we said earlier about relativism and the search for truth. Some questions do not admit of a "correct" answer, and yet even in such cases, most likely some answers will be better than others. What matters most of all is how you reason your way to your answer, and whether your reasoning holds up under scrutiny. When you discuss these exercises, you should not be afraid to challenge answers that your instructor may offer, but you should also try to understand and appreciate the reasoning your instructor may offer in support of his or her preferred answers.

EXERCISE 1.30 Let us use the term *world-view* to refer to the living system of assumptions and other beliefs according to which a person views the world or deals with incoming information. One of the most valuable things about the diversity of cultures you will find on most contemporary college campuses is what you can learn from cultures other than your own about the limitations of your own world-view. Here is a little exercise in self-awareness and appreciation of cultural diversity: Try to identify three items in your own world-view that are not shared by, or conflict with, the world-view of a typical member of some identifiable culture other than your own. You may find it useful, perhaps even necessary, to approach one or more of your fellow students whose cultural heritage(s) differs from your own to learn a bit from them about the distinctive characteristics of their culture(s).

EXERCISE 1.31 Another valuable thing about cultural diversity is what you can learn about common or shared humanity. Here is a follow-up exercise in cultural awareness: Try to identify three items in your own world-view that are, or would be, shared by a typical member of some identifiable culture other than your own.

EXERCISE 1.32 From your own experience, give an example of "self-deception" in which you or someone you know well persisted in maintaining a belief in the face of powerful contradictory evidence. As best you can, explain how this was possible for you or a person you know well.

▨ **EXERCISE 1.33** Identify 10 beliefs that you hold on the basis of some external authority. As best you can, identify the authoritative source of the belief in each case. Then evaluate the authority. Is the authority generally reliable? Is the authority an appropriate one for the belief in question?

▨ **EXERCISE 1.34** Do you have access to the Internet? If so, this exercise won't need much in the way of explanation. (If you don't have access to the Internet, ask your instructor where you can get access to the Internet on your campus.) Search the Internet for "critical thinking," and log on the chart below what you find.

Internet Address	Site Name	Brief Description

▨ **EXERCISE 1.35** *"Freewrite Rewrite":* Now, with this introductory chapter under your belt, review what you wrote earlier in Exercise 1.5, your freewrite on what you hope and expect to get out of a course in critical thinking. Have your hopes and expectations changed in any way as a result of your reading and experiences in the course so far? Now, with the benefit of these experiences, edit your earlier thoughts into a short essay of one or two pages on the topic of what you hope and expect to get out of a course in critical thinking.

GLOSSARY

assumption   an unsupported claim
assumption, hidden   an unstated or implied assumption
assumption, inferential   hidden assumption that functions as added support linking a stated premise with a conclusion
authority   an expert or source of information outside ourselves
claim   a statement that is either true or false
Critical Thinking   a set of conceptual tools with associated intellectual skills and strategies useful for making reasonable decisions about what to do or believe

egocentrism   favouritism for oneself and the beliefs, values, traditions, and groups with which one identifies

ethnocentrism   favouritism for the beliefs, values, and traditions of one's ethnic group

issue   a topic of reflection or investigation about which reasonable people may disagree

issue, evaluative   an issue concerning the merits of things

issue, factual   an issue to be resolved by either the methods of empirical science or documentary research

issue, interpretive   an issue concerning the meanings of things

logical priority   a kind of order among issues where one issue presupposes a resolution of a second issue, the second is logically prior to the first

presupposition   assumption required in order to make sense of what is explicitly stated

reason   1. the human capability to use disciplined intelligence to solve problems
2. a claim used as a premise
3. a claim used as an explanation

relativism   the position that point of view, whether social or individual, determines truth to a high degree

subjectivism   the view that truth is relative or varies from individual to individual

truth   the agreement of an idea with reality; the matching up of a statement or belief with what really is the case in the world

world-view   the living system of assumptions and other beliefs through which a person receives and interprets new information

Go to http://www.criticalthinking1ce.nelson.com for additional study resources for this chapter.

ENDNOTES

[1] Metaphysics is the branch of philosophy concerned with the nature of reality; epistemology is the branch of philosophy concerned with belief and knowledge.

[2] This series of thought experiments is derived from Jonathan Bennett's unpublished lectures on Descartes, given at the University of British Columbia, 1970–1972.

[3] Stanley Milgram, *Obedience to Authority: An Experimental View* (New York: Harper & Row, 1974).

[4] See S. E. Asch, "Effects of Group Pressure Upon the Modification and Distortion of Judgment," in M. H. Guetskow (ed.), *Groups, Leadership and Men* (Pittsburgh: Carnegie Press, 1951); S. E. Asch, "Opinions and Social Pressure," *Scientific American* (September 1955): 31–35; S. E. Asch, "Studies of Individual and Conformity: A Minority of One Against a Unanimous Majority," *Psychological Monographs* 70 (1956): 9.

[5] William James, *Pragmatism*, Lecture II (Cambridge, MA: Harvard University Press, 1975).

[6] Ibid.

[7] This is a version of relativism.

CHAPTER 2

Language

"Some people have a way with words.
Some no have way." STEVE MARTIN

Sometimes people wonder why we have included a chapter on language in a book about thinking. Try to imagine what thinking would be like without language. Can you? In fact, the harder you try, the more you notice language creeping into the effort. The more you notice yourself trying to "put the ideas into words," so to speak, the more it seems clear that thinking, as we know it, cannot be separated from language. Language is a fundamental medium of our thinking—a basic environment and material within which our thoughts take form and gain expression. Other ways exist, too, perhaps, in which our thinking takes shape and comes out. Language (narrowly conceived, as words) is not the *only* thing to which you pay attention in finding out what and how people think. Posture, gesture, vocal inflection, timing, context, and other clues are all meaningful dimensions of human communication, and they frequently guide our interpretations of people's words. None is more important, though, than language itself. Language is most central and basic.

DOONESBURY © 2003 G. B. Trudeau. Reprinted with permission of UNIVERSAL PRESS SYNDICATE. All rights reserved.

Indeed, to say that posture, gesture, vocal inflection, timing, context, and so on are meaningful dimensions of human communication is almost as good as saying that they are linguistic dimensions of human communication—either part of language (more broadly conceived) or at least language-like. In any case, when you boil it all down, the most important and best way of finding out what and how people think is by attending to what they *say*.

WHAT IS LANGUAGE?

This is one of those questions you hope your children do not ask you when they are little and persistent in their curiosity, but here is a powerful way to approach a question like this: Focus on *function*.[1] For example, if we were trying to figure out or explain the nature of a telephone, a good place to begin would be to ask what a telephone is *for* and why it has the peculiar features it has—or what its peculiar features contribute to that purpose or goal. For example, a telephone has a handset with a distinctive shape. Why does it have that shape? The shape functions so that you can easily hold the thing in one hand while you talk into one end of it and listen at the other. This is a pretty useful combination of features to have in a device designed to enable people to have a conversation outside each other's physical presence. Thus, the essential function, as well as the functional essence, of a telephone is a technological means of remote conversation.

We should try to think about language in the same way. Linguistic communication involves a sender presenting an intended message to a recipient. Linguistic communication is successful when the receiver grasps the intended message of the sender but is unsuccessful when the receiver cannot understand or misunderstands the intended message. Language is a means of expressing thought and reasoning, so as critical thinkers we need to pay attention to the purposes and uses of language. We must be able to follow the *dialectic* of the encounter: the context and flow of inquiry or reasoning. We must also be able to follow the *rhetorical* unfolding of the encounter: the use of language to persuade (whether reasonably or unreasonably).

EXERCISE 2.1 | **Uses of Language**

Use your imagination. How many distinct uses of language can you list in five minutes?

Use or Function	Example

We imagine that you noticed language has a large and wide variety of actual and potential uses. Let us all marvel for just a moment at the flexibility, utility, and power of language as a set of tools. Language can be used to describe the world or some part of it, pose problems, suggest solutions, issue orders, make agreements, tell stories, tell jokes, sing songs, exchange greetings, buy things, sell things, make friends, insult enemies, and so on. Can we say that language serves any specific *single essential* function amid all this variety? First remember these points from Chapter 1: Human beings are social animals. Our chances of survival and of flourishing are greatly enhanced by association with others of our kind. We do much better in groups than as individuals. This places a high premium on *cooperation* and *coordination with others*. Thus, the essential function, as well as the functional essence, of language would seem to be *communication*. What exactly is communication? Communication is what we do to achieve "common understanding"—essential to cooperation and coordination—among two or more sentient beings.

All nonsymbolic reasoning takes place in natural language, whether in spoken or written mode. On the one hand, this sentence is an example of natural language in written mode—in this case, English (as distinct from French or Urdu or any of the other hundreds of natural languages in the world). On the other hand, "P ⊃ Q; P; ∴.Q" is an example of reasoning expressed in formal symbols or terms. As critical thinkers, we must attend carefully and become attuned to matters of word meaning and usage, the context and flow of inquiry or reasoning, and the use of language to persuade. Medieval schools emphasized as foundational the subjects of the *trivium* (in alphabetical order): grammar, logic, and rhetoric.

In a general sense, you should be analytical in your approach to language. You should not stray by arguing inappropriately with the substance of the point at hand. When critiquing the language of a piece of reasoning, you should avoid "arguing the issue itself." Note also that problems with language are a kind of deficit in reasoning, so you ought to address them as such.

FUNCTIONS OF LANGUAGE

Let us now consider the wide variety of actual and possible uses of language from the point of view of critical thinking. Given our understanding of critical thinking as a discipline for making reasonable decisions about what to do or believe, we would be sensible to single out several general uses or functions of language for special attention.

THE INFORMATIVE FUNCTION OF LANGUAGE

Let us begin with a concept we introduced in Chapter 1: *A "claim" is a statement that claims for itself (whether rightly or wrongly) the value of being true.* Writing in 370 B.C.E., Hippocrates, the father of Western medicine, wrote,

> Speaking generally, all parts of the body which have a function, if used in moderation and exercised in labours to which each is accustomed, become healthy and age slowly. But if unused and left idle, they become liable to disease, defective in growth, and age quickly.

Hippocrates was reporting the results of empirical observation and making general claims about how physical exercise and health are related, claims he clearly thought to be true and wanted others to accept as true. *When we use language in this way for making claims, language is performing its "informative" function.* Here are a few more typical examples:

> Ottawa, Ontario, is the capital of Canada.
> Laetrile is (or is not) an effective treatment for cancer.
> Canadian federal elections are held at least every five years but may also be held prior to the five-year mark at the government's discretion.
> Business administration is currently the most popular postsecondary major.
> One out of 10 Canadians has herpes.
> The New Democrats have twice formed the national government of Canada.

Notice that the last statement is false. "Informative," as we are using it here, includes *misinformation.* Not just true statements, but false statements, statements whose truth is not yet determined, or statements whose truth may be in doubt, such as "Extraterrestrial life exists" and "The next prime minister will be a Green Party member," all count as examples of the informative function of language.

THE EXPRESSIVE FUNCTION OF LANGUAGE

In addition to its utility for making claims and conveying information, language has an important and powerful potential to express and arouse emotion. A bumper sticker we used to see quite a lot reads:

Mean people suck!

Quite possibly, the authors of this statement, as well as some of those who drive around with this sticker on their cars, are making a claim they think is true. The main thing that this bumper sticker accomplishes, though, is to express an "attitude"—to vent and to arouse emotional energy. *Whenever we use language to vent or arouse feelings, it performs its expressive function.* Poetry furnishes some of the best examples of the expressive function of language:

So fair, so sweet, withal so sensitive,
Would that the Little Flowers were to live,
Conscious of half the pleasures which they give . . .
—William Wordsworth

Here again, though the poet *may* be making a claim he thinks is true and worth communicating about the aesthetic value of flowers, the poetry functions even more powerfully as an expression of emotion and to evoke an emotional mood in the reader. The importance of the expressive function of language for critical thinking has to do with the role of emotion in decision making. Emotional energy can be powerful, easily capable of overwhelming common sense. This is not to say that emotion should play *no role at all* in decision making. Emotional energy can and sometimes does reinforce and enhance a process of rational deliberation. In some cases, emotion is an expected part of a whole response, as when we offer a strong moral condemnation and naturally feel anger or disgust at the same time. Again, though, given our understanding of critical thinking as a discipline for making reasonable decisions about what to do or believe, we would do well to *be aware* of the expressive function and use of language insofar as it may interfere with rational decision making.

CRITICAL THINKING TIP 2.1

~~Beware of Emotion~~ BE AWARE of Emotional Language.

THE DIRECTIVE FUNCTION OF LANGUAGE

Let us focus once again on the functional essence of language and the survival value of coordination and cooperation for us as human beings. Any interest in coordination or cooperation quickly translates into an interest in other people's behaviour and ways of influencing it. How do we get other people to cooperate with us? How do we get them to do what we want? We say things such as,

> "Please pass the butter."
>
> "Caution: Keep hands and feet away while machine is in use."

Language serves a directive function when we use it in an attempt to influence the behaviour of another person. If someone is fortunate (?) enough to be in a position of power or authority, then perhaps this person can issue commands and give orders, but ordinarily when we are with our peers our directive uses of language take the form of requests and suggestions. When we make requests and offer suggestions, we generally are counting on at least a willingness to cooperate in the other party. What do we do, however, when we can neither command nor presuppose a willingness to cooperate? Generally speaking, what we need to do under these circumstances is *be persuasive.* We try to influence the beliefs and motivations behind the behaviour we want. Now of course, language is flexible and powerful enough to lend itself well to this purpose. Critical thinking is especially interested in this particular kind of directive use of language—what we will call *persuasive* language. This is where the directive function of language comes to incorporate the informative and expressive functions of language, because in order to influence people's beliefs and motivations, we must often convince people to accept certain claims as true, and arousing emotional energy often proves useful. For example, remember the quotation from Hippocrates we used above to illustrate the informative function of language:

> Speaking generally, all parts of the body which have a function, if used in moderation and exercised in labours to which each is accustomed, become healthy and age slowly. But if unused and left idle, they come liable to disease, defective in growth, and age quickly.

We encountered this quotation on the wall of our health club in the gymnasium; it was posted near the mirrored wall that faces you when you are on the exercise machinery. Next to the quotation is a life-sized photo-poster showing a young woman athlete in peak physical condition about to serve a volleyball. She looks GREAT! In this context the quotation is clearly being used persuasively as a motivator.

EXERCISE 2.2 | **Functions of Language**

For each of the following examples, determine the primary language function. (You may occasionally find more than one primary language function.) Be prepared to explain the reasoning behind your answer.

	Informative	"The suspect left the scene driving a green convertible with out-of-province plates."	Explain your answer:
	Expressive		
	Directive		
	Persuasive		

	Informative	"Follow Highway 12 west to Madras Road, take Madras to Szechuan Drive, then turn left and drive two kilometres till you see the golf course."	Explain your answer:
	Expressive		
	Directive		
	Persuasive		

	Informative	"We must all hang together or assuredly we shall all hang separately." —Ben Franklin (to other signers of the American Declaration of Independence)	Explain your answer:
	Expressive		
	Directive		
	Persuasive		

	Informative	Teenage moviegoer after seeing *Spiderman:* "Awesome!"	Explain your answer:
	Expressive		
	Directive		
	Persuasive		

	Informative	"Combine 2 cups water and 1 tablespoon butter and bring to a boil. Stir in rice and spice mix, reduce heat and simmer for 10 minutes."	Explain your answer:
	Expressive		
	Directive		
	Persuasive		

	Informative	"How 'bout that Mike Weir, ya know what I'm sayin'?!"	Explain your answer:
	Expressive		
	Directive		
	Persuasive		

	Informative	Noticing that it was five minutes past bedtime, Dad said, "Okay, pal, let's close the book now and go to bed."	Explain your answer:
	Expressive		
	Directive		
	Persuasive		

MEANING IN LANGUAGE

How do words come to mean what they mean? (This is another one of those questions you hope your children do not ask you when they are little and persistent in their curiosity.) Let us start by briefly examining a primitive theory: that words are labels for things. For example, the word *cat* functions as a label. It "stands for" and "points to" the animal. We use the word *cat* not only to identify an individual animal, distinguishing it from other things, but also for the purpose of categorization (grouping things together—in this case to refer to feline creatures). If you reflect for a moment, you can readily see how useful labels are. Just imagine how difficult it would be to talk about people in general if we did not have labels such as *humanity* or *people.* Imagine how hard it would be to talk about the functions of language if we did not have the word *function*—or some other word with the same function.

Labels also help us to point things out, or to refer specifically to some part of a complex situation, as in "Please pass the *butter.*" Labels help us orient ourselves in new and unfamiliar surroundings, as in "Where's the *restroom*?" Labels are like "verbal handles" enabling us mentally to come to grips with our world and our experience. The Arabic language offers more than five thousand words that pinpoint differences in age, sex, and bodily structure among camels. Consider how much more can be said—and thought—about camels in Arabic than in English. From this we can appreciate how tempting it may be to generalize from labels to the whole of language.

Next, how do labels come to mean what they mean? How does the word *cat* come to stand for the animal and the category? Speakers of English use *cat,* while speakers of French use *chat,* speakers of Spanish use *gato,* and speakers of German use *Katze.* These words are similar enough to make one wonder whether some "natural" connection exists between the label and its object. Some labels, such as *hiccup* and *splash,* do seem to have some sort of identifiable natural connection to the things for which they stand. A label that *sounds like* its object is called an onomatopoeia. Not all labels, though, have this sort of obvious and straightforward connection with their functions. In fact, most labels do not. Take, for example, the word *onomatopoeia*—or, for that matter, look at any of the

Used by permission of Johnny Hart and Creators Syndicate, Inc.

words in this sentence. Some of them—*for, at, any, the, in*—do not even seem to function as labels at all.

For a more comprehensive and deeply explanatory theory of meaning, we might do well to return to the notion of language's essential function, or functional essence, as a set of tools for achieving common understanding, and look at things such as this: Words are noises to which human beings have assigned "meanings." Speakers of English use *cat* to refer to feline creatures, while speakers of French use *chat,* speakers of Spanish use *gato,* and speakers of German use *Katze.* Such assignments of meaning to noises are not "required" or "natural." Any other sound *could* have been made to stand for what *cat* stands for in English, and likewise in the other language communities. These assignments of meaning are merely conventional; that is to say, they are based on human conventions or customs. Some words, such as *the, and, so,* and *on,* among other words, have meanings in accordance with their conventional uses; they play a role in putting words together into meaningful sentences. We can say much the same of syntax as of word meaning. Syntax refers to the structural regularities in the ways words are put together to communicate thoughts and ideas. In English we put adjectives before nouns, as in *white house.* In Spanish the adjective typically follows the noun: *casa blanca.* The difference is a matter of convention or custom.

So, what is a "convention"? *A convention is simply a behavioural regularity that we maintain and follow to solve problems of coordination.* Suppose that you and your friend are cut off in the middle of a cell phone conversation. Here you have what we might call a coordination problem. What each of you should do depends on what the other person does. If you both dial each other's cell phone number, you both get a busy signal. If you both hang up and wait, well, you wait. You get back in contact if, and only if, one of you dials while the other waits. What should you do? Suppose that in the past when this sort of thing has happened, you have always been the one to dial and that has worked, and you know it has worked, and your friend knows it has worked, and you know that your friend knows it has worked, and you know that your friend knows that you know this, and so on. Therefore, if you now dial the phone while your friend waits, and you do this because both of you are thinking that this will solve the coordination problem, because both of you know that it has worked in the past, you are following a "convention."[2] We could also call a convention a practice upon which we agree. The basic problems of communication, understanding one another and making oneself understood, are coordination problems. Language can usefully be understood as a vast system of conventions we learn to follow in order to solve such problems.

A number of interesting and important consequences follow from this way of viewing language. First of all, linguistic conventions are, in one sense, arbitrary. This means that they could have been other than they are. Indeed, linguistic conventions evolve, sometimes quite rapidly and dramatically. Though linguistic conventions could have been other than they are and may well change over time, they nevertheless do regulate meaningful discourse. Linguistic conventions are thus a lot like the rules in a game.

Think of the rules governing organized sports such as football or basketball and you will see what we mean. Canadian football is played on a 100-metre (approximately) or 110-yard field with 12 players on each side. In addition, the rules of a game can be changed by common consent. These rules are arbitrary; they could be other than what they are. For example, one rule in American football states that the dimension of the playing field between the end zones is 100 yards; another prescribes 11 players per team. The rules, whatever they are, do regulate the game. If you play Canadian football, you must observe its rules. If you choose to play American football, then you must play by its rules.

Similarly, in playing the language game, we must generally abide by the conventions of the particular language in which we are attempting to communicate. We can rightly expect others to do the same. Conventions in language are somewhat more flexible and informal than rules are in games. For one thing, you do not get thrown out of the game for committing five unconventional speech acts. Furthermore, sometimes violating a linguistic convention can be a highly creative and effective way of communicating something special and unique. Nevertheless, meaningful departures from the conventions of our language presuppose those conventions as generally binding. If this were not the case, departing from our language's conventions would lead to hopeless confusion.

In *Through the Looking Glass,* Alice and Humpty Dumpty have the following conversation:

> " . . . there are 364 days when you might get un-birthday presents."
>
> "Certainly," said Alice.
>
> "And only *one* for birthday presents, you know. There's glory for you!"
>
> "I don't know what you mean by 'glory'," Alice said.
>
> Humpty Dumpty smiled contemptuously. "Of course you don't—till I tell you. I meant, 'there's a nice knock-down argument for you!'"
>
> "But 'glory' doesn't mean 'a nice knock-down argument'," Alice objected.
>
> "When I use a word," Humpty Dumpty said, in a rather scornful tone, "it means just what I choose it to mean—neither more nor less."[3]

Just imagine the confusion that would reign if, like Humpty Dumpty, each of us used words to mean exactly what we wanted them to mean, "neither more nor less". To avoid such chaos and inconvenience, we generally presuppose a conventional interpretation of what someone says. If a writer or speaker does not indicate a departure from conventional usage, we normally assume that the person is following conventional usage. Of course, this works both ways, which is why generally speaking it is best to *follow conventional usage* when we try to communicate. When we do use a word in an unconventional way, we need to give our audience extra guidance to our meaning. If we do not, we are likely to lose them. Communication obviously breaks down when you and your audience are not coordinated regarding what you mean.

| EXERCISE 2.3 | "Communication Breakdown" |

Topic for Class Discussion: Here is an actual example of communication breakdown. Read the following news-paper story and then see if you can identify the factors that account for the breakdown in communication.

Neighbors Chop Down Redwood: Claim to Have Had Permission

An East Napa Street front yard is now barren, following a misunderstanding between neighbors.

When Rene Alonzo returned to Sonoma in early December, he drove straight past his East Napa Street home. Realizing his mistake, he backed up, parked and slowly got out of his car. Seeing his lawn, he gasped and fell back against the vehicle. The house was the same as always, but his prized old-growth trees were gone.

Alonzo had been away for six weeks. Caring for his wife who is in the hospital. He hoped to bring her back to the Sonoma house that she has owned for 35 years since before their marriage. But after seeing the property, Alonzo wanted to spare her the shock.

Three trees had been removed, along with hedges on the side of the house. Alonzo couldn't believe what he was seeing. "These trees are 150 years old," he said.

Alonzo said that a caretaker at the house had contacted him while he was away and said that the new neighbors had asked permission to remove a single overhanging branch from one of the trees. Alonzo agreed but said that he had no idea they were going to take out the entire trees. "We don't even know the neighbors. We've never even met them," Alonzo said.

Mona Couchman has lived at 351 East Napa Street with her husband and 3-year-old daughter since September. She said that her family decided to have the trees removed on the Monday after [American] Thanksgiving because they were top heavy and could possibly fall and hurt people. "Our neighbors are very upset about it, but it seems that this is an issue of dangerous trees," Couchman said.

Couchman said that she wanted to contact Alonzo, but the caretaker would not give her his number. She said that the caretaker understood that they were going to remove the trees and was surprised when Alonzo was shocked. "We're very reasonable people. We wouldn't do it if we knew how irate he would be," Couchman said. According to Couchman there was no mention of only removing one branch. "We never, ever said that," she said.

Alonzo claims that his property is worth half a million dollars less now that the trees are gone. "It would have been better if they knocked down part of the house. At least you could rebuild it," he said.

The incident was reported to the Sonoma Police Department, but Capt. Robert Wedell said that it is no longer being investigated as a crime because "there was no intent to do harm. It's now up to the parties to resolve it," Wedell said.[4]

DIMENSIONS OF MEANING: PRECISION AND CLARITY

In the story you just read, we see a pair of next-door neighbours who have never spoken to each other face-to-face, and probably never will. Their only communications so far have been through intermediaries, first the caretaker, and now lawyers. No doubt there are several important lessons to be drawn from this unfortunate tale. You can see, for instance, what people mean when they say, "Get it in writing." You can also see the importance of two dimensions of communication in particular, precision and clarity.

SOME ISSUES IN THE USE OF LANGUAGE   Let us now distinguish and define several important concepts concerning precision and clarity in communication that will prove increasingly useful as we proceed. Each of these can be a source of confusion in communication. We always hope to grasp the sender's intended message, but problems with the use of language can arise and compromise our effort at understanding.

To say that a term or expression is "ambiguous" is to say that it has more than one conventional meaning. In other words, it can be conventionally understood in more than one way. For example, the word *bank* can mean:

1. any piled up mass, such as snow or clouds
2. the slope of land adjoining a body of water
3. the cushion of a billiard or pool table
4. to strike a billiard shot off the cushion
5. to tilt an aircraft in flight
6. a business establishment authorized to receive and safeguard money, lend money at interest, etc.

On one hand, ambiguity gives language the flexibility to handle multiple meanings at once. Without ambiguity, many jokes, plays on words, puns, and much of the richness of poetry and literature in general could not exist. On the other hand, *ambiguity is a problem with the use of language when we are faced with a small set of possible meanings—two or three definite prospects—from which we are unable to extract the relevant meaning.* For example, consider this statement, "I'll give you a ring tomorrow."[5] Let us assume for the sake of the example that *ring* might mean phone call or that it might mean a piece of jewellery for a finger. With no additional information available, we cannot determine which meaning the writer or speaker intends (though, given our assumption, we know that the answer must be one or the other).

"Equivocation" is similar to ambiguity; it involves playing with multiple senses of a word between or across usages. *Equivocation is a problem with the use of language when we are faced with a set of at least two possible meanings—each of which is definite—such that we are able to verify that the sender uses a logically, dialectically, or rhetorically inappropriate or questionable meaning.* For example, consider, "Odd[1] things arouse human suspicion. But seventeen is an odd[2] number. Therefore, seventeen arouses human suspicion."[6] Odd[1] obviously means peculiar or unusual, while odd[2] obviously means a type of number. The conclusion of this reasoning depends on the word *odd* meaning the same thing in both instances, yet we can see clearly that it does not. The reasoner problematically shifts the meaning of the central term from the first usage to the second one.

Our discourse is filled with terms of evaluation: good, bad, better, worse, valuable, valueless, and so on. We must use such language to get along in the world.

Thus, evaluative language is *not* inherently inappropriate. *Evaluative language is problematic when (only when) either of two situations occurs:*

(1) *The evaluative language is demonstrably inappropriate in the context*

(2) *The evaluative language needs defence but the speaker/writer provides either no defence or inadequate defence (but better defence could be provided in principle).*

However you proceed, do not make the mistake of saying, "Evaluative language exists in this passage," as though you are offering a criticism. Simply pointing out the fact that someone uses evaluative language does not demonstrate the existence of a problem. Note also that words or expressions are not problematic merely because they are sophisticated.

Criticism 1 is fatal, so a critic bears a high burden of proof in making this type of criticism. Thus, you should level this charge *only* if you are absolutely certain of its aptness. For example, what if a critic of tough antismoking legislation were to refer argumentatively to opponents as "cigarette Nazis" for treating smokers "differently"? The expression "cigarette Nazis" is problematic evaluative language that muddies the dialectical waters. Comparing those concerned with public health to the brutal and murderous Nazi regime is unhelpful and perhaps even offensive to some. Stricter smoking regulations certainly involve distinguishing smokers and nonsmokers, but this is not inherently illegitimate. Instead, the writer must show why this distinction is inappropriate, which is not done in the statement here.

Criticism 2 may be strong, medium, or weak in gravity. For example, what if, in the context of reasoning, a critic were to call the members of the National Organization for the Reform of Marijuana Laws (NORML) Canada "misfits"? Assuming a lack of plausible supporting reasons, the critic uses problematic evaluative language in referring to the members in this way. Such negative evaluative language requires evidence and defence, but the writer provides none—unless the mere stance of the group is supposed to serve this purpose, which is not just dialectically unhelpful but decidedly uncharitable. Such language tends to "poison the well" against NORML Canada (and perhaps against liberalization advocates generally). Well poisoning may diminish or obviate rational thought, so critical thinkers are obliged to identify and eschew it.

Philosopher Trudy Govier says that euphemism may be a problem with language depending on the context. Euphemism is problematic if it treats lightly a hard reality that ought to be addressed as such. While the more common problem is language that is overly charged ("insane scheme" versus "questionable policy"), problematic euphemisms seem to fit into the category of problematic evaluative language, too, since undercharged language may be just as unhelpful or diversionary ("ethnic reconfiguration" versus "genocide"). Hence, problematic euphemisms comprise a subtype of problematic evaluative language.

Vagueness in language is another concern. *Saying that a term is "vague" means that it is not entirely clear when it does and does not apply.* In technical terms, *a vague term or expression is one that has an indefinite "extension"* (see the section on denotation and connotation below). For example, the word *bald* clearly applies to the comedian Colin Mochrie. It clearly does not apply to the actor Paul Gross. An indefinite area exists, however, between the extremes of "clearly bald" and "clearly not bald." Vagueness itself admits of degrees according to the size of the "grey area." Thus, *bald* is less vague than *happy*, and *vague* is itself pretty vague (which is a pretty vague thing to say). Consider the following exchange between a parent and a teenager. Parent: "Where did you go tonight?" Teenager: "Nowhere." Parent: "What did you do?" Teenager: "Nothing." Parent: "Whom did you see?" Teenager: "Nobody." The vagueness here, of course, is entirely intentional. The teenager utters words, but the parent cannot decipher the meanings of the terms (the parent clearly cannot take the terms in a strictly literal sense if the teenager really did leave the house to socialize).

On one hand, vagueness gives language the flexibility it needs to adapt to unforeseen and unforeseeable situations by leaving questions of definition and judgment open to deliberation in context. On the other hand, *vagueness is a problem with language when we are faced with a large set of possible meanings— more than three or four prospects—from which we are unable to extract the relevant meaning.* For example, imagine someone saying, "Our culture is permeated with violence of all sorts—assaults, threats, intimidation, unkind words, misunderstanding." If violence ranges from assaults to unkind words—assuming we can identify truly unkind words and distinguish them from sincere criticism—to a mild misunderstanding, what does the word *violence* mean? We have no clear sense of what violence means, or how all these things can be instances of violence, a term that people normally apply to forceful physical acts, not to mere disagreements.

The problem with vagueness is also a definitional problem, of course, as this attempt to define violence is hopelessly broad. Note that whether a word is vague depends upon the dialectical context. The mere fact that you do not know the meaning of a particular word does not make the word vague; for example, the word *quiddity*, when used in the context of medieval thought, is not vague, even if you as an individual happen not to know what it means. (Look it up now!) If possible, use a dictionary, conduct some contextual research, or consult with others before concluding that a word is objectionably vague. Note also that words or expressions are not vague merely because they are sophisticated.

| EXERCISE 2.4 | **Some Issues in the Use of Language** |

In each of the following examples highlight any terms or expressions that evidence ambiguity, equivocation, evaluation, or vagueness. Take special care to indicate any problematic uses of these features. Explain your answers.

	Explain your answers:
Rappers continue to get a bad rap in the press.	
How do reasonable people come to hold unreasonable beliefs?	
Headline: "Drunk Gets Nine Months in Violin Case"	
"Choose dates with a shiny skin."[7]	
The streets are perfectly safe here in Hazardville. It's the muggers you have to watch out for.	
Random urinalysis for drugs in safety-sensitive job categories does not constitute an unreasonable violation of privacy.	
A man walks up to the Zen Buddhist hot dog vendor and says, "Make me one with everything."	
Nuclear energy is just as natural as any other fuel, and cleaner than many already in use.	
All we need do is recognize the word "plastic" in plastic surgery to grasp its unnaturalness.	
When it comes to plastic surgery, we seem to forget that true beauty and self-respect come from within, not from a mercenary's scalpel.	
Let me reassure the public that your government is doing everything within its power to make sure that the travelling public is as secure against the threat of terrorism as it can possibly be.	
Canadian law does not prohibit people from burning flags as such acts are instances of political speech.	

DENOTATION AND CONNOTATION   Let us now look more closely at word meaning and develop an important distinction between two of its dimensions, denotation and connotation, starting once again with labels. Consider the word *bridge*. What does the word *bridge* mean? In one sense, as a label, the word means the object to which it refers or points. The word *bridge* points to a group of objects: bridges. This pointing-to relationship between a label and the things for which it is a label is called *denotation*. The set of things denoted by a term is called the term's *extension*. For example, the extension of the word *bridge* includes the Peace Bridge in Niagara Falls, Ontario; the extension of the word *building* includes the Calgary Tower. So we could also say that at least part of what the word *bridge* means is the whole set of things it denotes (in other words its extension), including the Peace Bridge; and part of what the word *building* means is its extension, including the Calgary Tower. The word *building* has a large and relatively diverse extension that includes the Calgary Tower, the Sydney Opera House in Australia, the Eiffel Tower in France, the lighthouse at Cap de Gaspé in Quebec, and the outhouse behind the barn. All these structures are buildings, but not everything is a building. This book is not a building. Not all structures are buildings, nor is everything built a building; the Peace Bridge is a structure, but not a building. Why is this so and how do we know? In many cases this is so and we know it to be so because we have *criteria* that determine the extension of the term. Bridges and buildings are bridges, or buildings, because they satisfy criteria that make them bridges or buildings rather than, say, tunnels or microchips. These criteria, which define the extension of the term, we call the term's *intension.* So we could also say that part of what the word *bridge* means is its intension, this set of criteria that define its extension. If the intension of a term is part of its meaning, we do not want to confuse it with what the term denotes. So we will say that it is part of the term's *connotation.*

In addition to the extension and the intension of a word—we will say these comprise the word's *literal* meaning—most words also come with a penumbra of additional meanings that arise out of their conventionally implied associations. For example, *prima donna* literally means "the principal female singer in an opera company," but the term has come to carry by conventional association the added meaning of "a vain, temperamental person." Consequently, using the term *prima donna,* especially outside the specialized context of opera, is an effective way of putting down someone. These additional meanings comprise the word's *connotations.* Similarly, the word *tabloid* literally means "a newspaper formatted at about half the size of a standard-size newspaper page and with no horizontal fold." But because many newspapers in tabloid format have tended toward journalistic sensationalism, the word *tabloid* conventionally carries an additional negative or pejorative connotation of disreputable journalism.

Of course, such connotations need not be derogatory. Many are complimentary. "Diplomat" sounds so much more respectable to many an ear than "politician." "Moderate" sounds so much more thoughtful than "wishy-washy." Here we can see the importance of language's expressive function to what we might call the "artistry" of persuasion. One can, through the careful selection of terms (choosing a word such as "artistry," for example) colour a statement emotionally.

EXERCISE 2.5 | Labels/Denotation/Connotation

Agenda for Class Discussion: One of the most astute observers of language these days is linguist Geoffrey Nunberg. He is a regular contributor to the National Public Radio program *Fresh Air,* whose hostess, Terry Gross, describes him as having "the best ear in America for listening to how the English language is changing, the best mind for interpreting those changes, and the most amusing way of explaining it all." Read the following selection, in which Nunberg comments on labels, changing conventions, denotations, and connotations. Here is an agenda of questions for class discussion (or an essay assignment).

1. What are the labels Nunberg is commenting on? (Note: There are more than two.)
2. Carefully describe the connotations of each of these labels.
3. What are Nunberg's explanation and assessment of these connotative developments?
4. Do you agree or disagree with what he says?

100% Solution

I got a mail-order catalog the other day from a company that specializes in home and health-care products—at least they used to call them products, but now that word's been entirely eliminated from their catalog in favor of the word 'solutions.' You can find seat cushions in the section on stress relief solutions, bathrobes in spa care solutions, and support bras in intimate apparel solutions.

The solutions game began in the early 1980s when companies like IBM started using the word to describe the packages of hardware, software and services they were selling to corporate customers. In a sense, it's just a new way of pitching your offerings as answers to customers' needs and anxieties, in the time honored tradition of ring around the collar and the heartbreak of psoriasis, except that the word 'solutions' makes its point in a proactive way. In the old days, when people said, 'I've got a solution for you,' you assumed that somebody had mentioned a problem somewhere along the line. Now the two have come unhitched.

Solutions aren't solutions for anything anymore. When you do a search on 'solutions' at the Web site of Compaq or Apple Computer you find that it's anywhere from two to three times as frequent as the word 'problems.' Business people don't like to hear talk about problems; it seems to betray a negative mind-set. If there are difficulties you absolutely have to mention, you try to find another name for them, as in, 'We had a number of challenges this quarter,' or, 'There are several known issues installing the beta release of the printer driver.'

By now there are hundreds of firms that have incorporated that word 'solutions' into their company names, and by no means all of them are high-tech. There's the beachwear-maker Sun Solutions, which is not to be confused with Solar Solutions, which sells propane ranges and composting toilets. And then there's Bright Horizons Family Solutions, an outfit that manages corporate daycare centers, whose portfolio presumably includes story hour solutions and snack solutions, not to mention nap solutions for clients with crankiness issues.

It's hard to think of a company that couldn't say it was in the solutions business now. Smuckers, your toast coating solutions provider. And in fact, one reason why so many companies are sticking the word into their names is that they don't have to let on as to what they're actually selling, particularly if they're still in the embarrassing position of making things. Things have low margins and high capital costs; they're expensive to ship; they lead to liability lawsuits. They get you in trouble with the EPA. If you make them domestically, you have to deal with unions. If you make them overseas, people get on your back for running sweatshops.

It's no wonder the manufacturing sector is a diminishing part of the American economy. In 1950, material goods made up more than half the GDP. Now they account for less than a quarter of it. And companies that aren't in the position to stop making things altogether can at least relabel them as solutions. It suggests that their products are just an ancillary sideline of their real business, like the terry cloth slippers they throw in when you go for a massage. That's the beauty of solutions, nobody has to tip their hands.

It's a perfect complement for those empty corporate names that marketing consultants paste together out of strings of chopped up syllables. Take the Ohio outfit called Amnova Solutions. What line of work would you say they're in? Client-server applications, health-care benefits administration, fabric transfers and decorative wall coverings? As it happens it's the last of those, but the others are just as plausible. These aren't like those old-fashioned corporate names that were designed to conjure up an image of a particular product made by a real company. You feel sorry for the members of a softball team who have to take the field with Amnova Solutions written on their uniforms.

Names like these are attempts to create pure brands; free signifiers that float in the ether, ready to light on anything that somebody's willing to pay for. That's what the new economy comes down to in the end: Just one big intersection with people at every corner holding signs that say, 'Will solve for cash.'[8]

EXERCISE 2.6 | Labels/Denotation/Connotation

For each of the following labels, give an example from its extension and two substitute labels, one with positive connotations and one with negative connotations.

Label	Example	Positive	Negative
Environmental Activist	David Suzuki	Defenders of the earth	Tree huggers
Spectator Sports			
Occupations			
Corporations			
Animals			

DEFINITIONS

A definition is an explanation *of the meaning of a term.* The word *definition* and its close relatives *define, definite, definitive,* and so on all derive from the Latin *definire,* which means "setting boundaries or limits." The most basic use we have for definitions is teaching people language. One simple sort of definition often used for the purpose of teaching language consists in pointing out *examples* of the term being defined. For example, if someone did not know what *reptile* meant, you could help the person by pointing out snakes, lizards, turtles, crocodiles, and so on. This kind of definition is called *ostensive definition*—from the Latin word for *show,* as in "*show* me what it means." Another basic strategy of definition, also useful for the purpose of teaching new or unfamiliar vocabulary, is the use of "synonyms." From the Greek for "same name," *synonyms* are words or expressions that have the same meaning. For example, suppose we came across the word *poltroon* (rhymes with "doubloon") in a line of verse about pirates. If we did not know that *poltroon* is a synonym for *coward,* we might easily wind up thinking that the line was about a parrot or a drunken sailor. Knowing the origin of a word can tell you a lot about what it means, and many

PEANUTS: © United Feature Syndicate, Inc.

® 1969 United Feature Syndicate, Inc. PEANUTS reprinted by permission of UFS, Inc.

words have fascinating histories—or *etymologies.* For example, the word *etymology* comes through Middle English and Old French from the Medieval Latin *ethimologia,* which is derived from the Latin *etymologia*, which comes from the Greek *etumologia*, which is based on the Greek word *etumon*, which means "true sense of the word." Help in understanding a new or unfamiliar term (such as *burqa* or *gigabyte*) is something even fluent speakers of any language need regularly, because language is dynamic and evolving constantly. This is why we have dictionaries—and why they need to be updated periodically.

WHAT DICTIONARIES DO NOT DO

In a good dictionary, in addition to the spelling and the pronunciation key, we are likely to find examples, synonyms, etymologies, and other information helpful in understanding the conventional meanings of words. However, a dictionary generally will not tell you the meaning of a word that someone is using in an unconventional way—although knowing what the word conventionally means is often helpful and maybe even essential for figuring out the unconventional meaning.

Suppose a writer or speaker wants to communicate an idea for which no conventionally understood term is exactly right. This could happen when some new invention or category arises (e.g., *gigabyte*). This can also happen with well-established vocabulary: We may need to depart from conventional usage and use words in unconventional ways to get across our meanings. We typically do this to achieve *greater precision* than we generally need for conventional purposes of communication. In specialized or technical disciplines, geometry, for example, words such as *point, line,* and *plane* have quite specific meanings much more precise than their conventional ones. In legal and other policy contexts, making distinctions and classifications more precisely than conventional vocabulary will express is often necessary. For example, "In this contract, for purposes of determining benefit eligibility a 'full-time employee' shall be defined as an 'employee working 25 hours or more per week.'" For these purposes we often stipulate definitions. The word *stipulate,* which comes from the Latin word for "bargaining," means "to specify as in an agreement." In effect, when we stipulate a definition we lay down the terms of an agreement about how a word should be used and understood in the context of some discourse, where conventional usage and understanding are inadequate or unsuitable in some way.

EXERCISE 2.7 | **Definition Scavenger Hunt**

- Make up one example of definition by synonymy.
- Find an example of definition by synonymy in a dictionary.
- Find one example of stipulated definition in this book.

In the next exercise we will look at something else that dictionaries don't generally do, or at least don't generally do well or reliably.

EXERCISE 2.8 | **Essential Definitions I**

Read the following list of words and put a check mark beside the ones you are confident that you know and understand.

- art
- beauty
- communication
- drugs
- entertainment
- freedom
- information
- jazz

- love
- music
- news
- obscenity
- pornography
- religion
- sign
- terrorism

We are willing to bet that you know and understand every word on this list. We are willing to bet that if you came across any of these words in a sentence, you would not need to consult a dictionary. We are sure that you are able to use any of these words quite comfortably and correctly in your own conversation and writing because you are already quite familiar with the conventional meanings of all of these words. Are we right?

■ EXERCISE 2.9 | **Essential Definitions II**

Now, go through the list of words in Exercise 2.8 and see how many of them you think you'd be able to teach to another person ostensively. Remember, this means being able to point out examples in order to indicate what the word means.

Is the list pretty manageable—or are you experiencing a little problem here and there with one or two of the more "abstract" words?

■ EXERCISE 2.10 | **Essential Definitions III**

OK. So now here's a real challenge: Take any of the words on the list and explain its intension. Remember what intension means: The intension of a word is the set of criteria that define the word's extension, which is the set of examples to which it conventionally applies.

Criteria, the plural form of *criterion,* derives from *krinein,* the same Greek root as "critical," which you remember from Chapter 1 concerns "decision making." *Criteria are rules or standards for decision making.* So, the criteria that define a word's extension would be the rules or standards according to which we decide whether the word applies or not. We expect that you will find this surprisingly hard. Take the word *music* for example. Remember, this is a word you know well. It is in your working vocabulary. You do not need a dictionary to help you understand the question, "Do you want to listen to some music?" You can easily identify examples of music. Now try to state the criteria according to which you decide whether something is music or not. This is not as easy as you might think.

What you are trying to state here is a kind of definition that we are going to refer to as an "essential definition." People have often described what we are challenging you to do here as stating the *essence*—or *essential nature*—of (in this case) music. Another way to describe what you are trying to do is this: Think of the extension of the word *music* as though it were a bounded territory—the things to which the word *music* conventionally applies, all the things in its extension, are "inside the boundaries of the territory"; things to which the word *music* does *not* apply are "outside the boundaries." So, what you are trying to do is produce a verbal map of the territory, or describe its boundaries in words. (Remember, the word *definition* comes from the Latin for "setting boundaries or limits.")

Now you might wonder why essential definitions are desirable. What special purpose or purposes do they serve? Assuming that people are familiar with the word we are defining, no need exists to teach it as a new vocabulary item. In that case, why would we need *any* sort of definition? Sometimes how we classify things is a matter of great importance. Suppose the government has just passed a new law that regulates the sale and distribution of "obscene" and "pornographic" materials to minors. Now suppose the local purveyor of recorded entertainment (CDs, tapes, videos) is brought up on charges of violating the law in connection with the sale of a Christina Aguilera music video to a 16-year-old. The case turns partly on whether or not the Christina Aguilera video is "obscene" and/or "pornographic," which turns on the criteria for "obscenity" and "pornography." Now these criteria would presumably be stipulated in the law. Suppose, however, that you are a government official and have to draft the law. You have the challenge of creating the wording of the criteria according to which others will decide whether something is "obscene" or "pornographic." So, we are back to the challenge of formulating the essential definitions. Why not just look these words up in a dictionary?

EXERCISE 2.11 | **Essential Definitions IV**

OK. Go ahead and try it. Go through the list of words in Exercise 2.8 again and see how many satisfactory essential definitions you can find in a good dictionary. Try the word *terrorism*.

Occasionally you may find a satisfactory essential definition in a dictionary. Nonetheless, you would be better off to approach this as a "figure it out" kind of a challenge rather than a "look it up" kind of a challenge. To see why this is so, we'll take the word *terrorism* as our example. Here is the definition of *terrorism* supplied by the *Canadian Oxford Dictionary:* "The systematic employment of violence and intimidation to coerce a government or community, esp. into acceding to specific political demands."[9] According to this definition, many acts of war, indeed any deliberate use of violence or intimidation, down to the actions of a nation that attempts to liberate civilians at risk of mass slaughter by another regime, would qualify as terrorism. Do we really want to define *terrorism* so broadly? Instead, do we want a definition that makes finer distinctions possible? Conventional usage of the term *terrorism* is, we think, slightly more selective—something similar to this: "Terrorism is when 'the bad guys' (the enemy) use terror, violence, and intimidation to achieve an end." Of course, this is a "double standard" and therefore is clearly useless for any serious discussion of international political conflict. Sometimes, as in connection with international politics, we are not in a position of authority to just stipulate a meaning that departs from general conventional usage. Such definitions truly need to be "negotiated."

In the obscenity and pornography example, we need a ruling as to whether or not the Christina Aguilera video is "obscene". An essential definition of *obscenity* should tell us what to look for in the video to see if it satisfies or fails to satisfy the criteria for "obscenity." In the case of the definition of *terrorism,* what we need is a set of criteria that will help us distinguish acts of terrorism from other kinds of behaviour that may or may not involve the use or threat of violence. We are now going to present some concepts and strategies for figuring out this sort of definition when just looking it up in a dictionary is not a satisfactory option.

NECESSARY AND SUFFICIENT CONDITIONS First, let us stipulate the definitions of two important ingredients of essential definitions: "necessary conditions" and "sufficient conditions." To fulfill its function, an essential definition must allow you to do two things: Rule things in and rule things out. Necessary and sufficient conditions are the parts of an essential definition that enable you to rule things in and rule things out.

A necessary condition is a characteristic or set of characteristics required *for membership in the word's extension.* To illustrate we will use a word that is quite a bit easier to define essentially than any of the words on the list in Exercise 2.8. Let us define the word *square* as used in plane geometry. The essential definition of *square* can be stated in two words: equilateral rectangle. A square is defined essentially as an equilateral rectangle. In this definition, both "equilateral" and "rectangle" indicate necessary conditions. In other words, it is required that something be both equilateral and rectangular in order to be included in the extension of the word *square*. If you find out that something is not equilateral or is not rectangular, you do not need to know anything more about it. You already know enough to rule it out.

A sufficient condition is a characteristic or set of characteristics that is by itself adequate *for membership in the word's extension.* Again, in the essential definition of *square* as an equilateral rectangle, the set of characteristics, equilateral and rectangle, together constitute a sufficient condition. In other words, if you find out that something is both equilateral and rectangular, you do not need to know anything more about it. You do not have to know its size, age, colour, value, or molecular structure. You already know enough to rule it in.

A "DIALOGICAL" APPROACH TO ESSENTIAL DEFINITIONS As we said, providing an essential definition of a word, such as *square*, is relatively simple and straightforward. *Obscenity* is harder to define. *Music* is *much* harder to define. In fact, words such as *music, art, information, jazz,* and *love,* and others, such as *justice, liberty, equality, racism, terrorism,* and so on are so hard to define in this way that many people give up the attempt. People who persist in the attempt to formulate essential definitions of these types of words are often called philosophers, and their attempted essential definitions are often called "philosophies" or "theories" and take a whole book to present and explain, as in "Kant's philosophy of art" or John Rawls's *A Theory of Justice.* This involves thinking in a careful and disciplined way about examples and the precise wording of the definition. We call the following approach "dialogical" because it goes back and forth in dialogue form. To illustrate it we will continue with the simple example we used above to explain necessary and sufficient conditions.

STEP 1 Formulate a definition. Just go for it. Write it down (so that it stays put and does not start changing and evolving before you get to Step 2). When we gave the essential definition of *square*, we were able to do it in two words, and we got to it in one step, without any of this back-and-forth business. Squareness is a pretty simple essence to capture in words, but that is pretty rare. We cannot expect to get to the essence in one step using two words terribly often. In most of the interesting cases, we are more likely going to need to try something and then tinker with it, refine it, and adjust it. This dialogical approach is designed to help the tinkering process stay on a productive track. So for purposes of illustration let us imagine that we had initially defined the word *square* as an "equilateral shape."

CRITICAL THINKING TIP 2.2:   Three Things to Avoid in Step 1

Circularity: A definition is circular if it defines a word in terms of itself. The problem with circularity is that it defeats the purposes of definitions. Once when we were learning French we ran across a conjugated form of the verb *fructifier*. Having no idea what this meant, we referred to the French/English dictionary in the back of the book, where we learned that *fructifier* is French for "to fructify." What we really needed to know was what "to fructify" means ("to fructify" is "to bear fruit"). We had already figured out the rest. The purposes of the definition will be defeated by circularity, whether what you are trying to do is teach the conventional meaning of a new or unfamiliar word, stipulate an unconventional meaning, or give an essential definition.

Obscurity: A similar problem results from obscurity. If the terminology in which the definition is formulated is even less familiar than the word being defined, or more difficult to grasp and understand, then the definition will be harder to understand than the word whose meaning it is supposed to explain. Now we cannot always avoid obscurity, especially in formulating an essential definition, because people are not all familiar with the same words. What is obscure to one reader may be quite familiar to another. Even more important, sometimes the ideas you will need to capture in words are themselves out of the ordinary, and only relatively obscure words will do the trick. You should try to keep the words as simple and familiar as the ideas with which you are working will permit.

Negativity: A definition should explain what a word means, not what it does not mean. Of course, some words defy affirmative definition. *Orphan* means a child whose parents are not living; *bald* means the state of not having hair on one's head. Unless negativity is an essential element in the meaning of the word, try to formulate the definition in the affirmative.

STEP 2   Critique Step 1 by example. Using what you know about shapes, you can see that something is not entirely right about the definition of *square* as an "equilateral shape." You can demonstrate this by means of an example:

The example does two important things. First, it exposes a flaw in the definition as formulated in Step 1, because the example fits all the criteria specified in the definition, but it is not a legitimate member of the extension of the word *square*. In other words, the example *refutes* the definition. *An example used for this purpose, or which accomplishes this purpose, we will call a "counterexample."* Two kinds of counterexamples exist: counterexamples that show the definition is "too broad" or "overly inclusive" or "lets in too much" (this is how the triangle example above works); and counterexamples that show the definition is "too narrow" or "overly restrictive" or "leaves out too much." An example that *is* a legitimate member of the extension of a word but does not satisfy all of the criteria specified in a proposed definition would show that the definition is too narrow. The second thing the counterexample does is point the way in Step 3.

STEP 3   Revise the original definition. What was wrong with the definition of *square* as an "equilateral shape"? Our first definition was too broad, as demonstrated by our counterexample in Step 2, so we know we need to make the definition more restrictive. This means adding another necessary condition. How shall we formulate it? The counterexample in Step 2 gives us good guidance here: not enough sides. So this is what we want to add to our definition in Step 3. So let us revise our definition to say that *square* means "equilateral quadrilateral." (*Quadrilateral*, of course, means "four-sided figure.")

STEP 4   Repeat Step 2 (critique Step 3 by example). Once again, using what you know about shapes you can see that something is still not entirely right about the definition of *square* as an "equilateral quadrilateral." You can demonstrate this by example:

STEP 5   Repeat Step 3 (revise the revised definition). What was wrong with the definition of *square* as an "equilateral quadrilateral"? Once again our definition was too broad, as demonstrated by our counterexample in Step 4, so we know we need to make the definition even more restrictive. That means adding another necessary condition. How shall we formulate it? The counterexample in Step 4 again gives us good guidance: The angles are not 90-degree angles. So that's what we want to add to our definition at this point. And so we arrive at this: *square* means "equilateral rectangle." (*Rectangle* of course means" "four-sided figure with 90-degree angles.")

STEP 6   Keep going as needed. At this point the process is complete for the essential definition of the word *square* because it is not possible to refute our current definition by example. Anything that fits all the criteria specified in our current definition will turn out to be a legitimate member of the extension of the word, and vice versa: Any member of the extension will turn out to satisfy all the criteria in our definition. The word and our definition are *co-extensive,* which means they have the same extension. This is how we know we are done.

EXERCISE 2.12 | **Essential Definitions V**

Critique the following formulations as though they were intended to function as essential definitions. Explain your criticisms. Use examples where appropriate.

Too Broad	A "dinosaur" is an extinct animal.	Explain your answer:
Too Narrow		
Circular		
Unclear or Figurative		

Too Broad	"Sexual assault" is forcing a person to have sexual contact without the person's consent.	Explain your answer:
Too Narrow		
Circular		
Unclear or Figurative		

Too Broad	"Faith" is the substance of things hoped for, the evidence of things not seen. 　　　　—Hebrews 11:1	Explain your answer:
Too Narrow		
Circular		
Unclear or Figurative		

Too Broad	"Economics" is the science that treats of the phenomena arising out of the economic activities of men in society. 　　　—J. M. Keynes	Explain your answer:
Too Narrow		
Circular		
Unclear or Figurative		

Too Broad	A "circle" is a closed plane curve.	Explain your answer:
Too Narrow		
Circular		
Unclear or Figurative		

Too Broad	"Circular": of or pertaining to a circle; the property of circularity.	Explain your answer:
Too Narrow		
Circular		
Unclear or Figurative		

Too Broad	"Pornography" is any pictorial display of human sexuality or nudity.	Explain your answer:
Too Narrow		
Circular		
Unclear or Figurative		

Too Broad	A "definition" is an explanation of the meaning of a term.	Explain your answer:
Too Narrow		
Circular		
Unclear or Figurative		

	Too Broad	"Alimony": that's when two people make a mistake and one of them continues to pay for it.	Explain your answer:
	Too Narrow		
	Circular		
	Unclear or Figurative		

GENUS AND DIFFERENTIA A related strategic approach involves a two-step procedure and the concept of categories:

STEP 1 Locate the extension of the term you are defining within some larger category (called the "genus"). So, for example, squares are part of the larger category of plane geometric figures.

STEP 2 Now specify the feature or set of features (called the "differentia") that distinguishes the extension you are defining from the rest of the larger category. In this case you want to specify the feature or set of features that distinguishes squares from the rest of the plane geometric figures.

Term	Larger Category	Distinguishing Characteristics
square	plane geometric figure	with four equal sides and 90-degree angles

Similarly:

Term	Larger Category	Distinguishing Characteristics
spoon	utensil	consisting of a small, shallow bowl with a handle, used in eating or stirring
watch	machine	portable or wearable for telling time
ethics	branch of philosophy	concerned with morality

Notice that the definition of *square* we formulated using the dialectical approach is worded differently than the one we formulated using genus and differentia. Nonetheless, the two definitions, "equilateral rectangle" and "plane geometric figure with four equal sides and 90-degree angles," are synonymous. They express the same criteria. The necessary and sufficient conditions for being in the extension of *square* are the same in either case. These two strategic approaches can also be effectively combined. If you are stuck, you can use the genus and differentia approach to formulate an initial definition, and you can use the dialectical approach to critique and refine a definition by genus and differentia.

Let us reflect for a moment on the importance of the material we have just covered. Think about why words are important. Think about all the things you do with words. Think about what obstacles you would face if you suddenly found yourself in a community or a part of the world where no one spoke your language. Think about what your life would be like if you were suddenly deprived of the ability to speak or write or make yourself understood with words. Think about the importance of mutual understanding—to you personally, to the maintenance of any sort of interpersonal relationship, to world affairs. Think about how misunderstanding arises. Keep these thoughts in mind as you study further in this book.

ADDITIONAL EXERCISES

EXERCISE 2.13   Spend a few (5–10) minutes observing what happens in some open public area, such as a busy intersection, a campus quadrangle, or a shopping mall. Write a paragraph that contains a strictly factual descriptive account of what you observed. Next, write a paragraph that, besides being informative, is also entertaining. Next, write a paragraph that uses the information in a persuasive way.

Factual

Informative and Entertaining

Persuasive

▧ **EXERCISE 2.14** Explain both the conventional meaning and the current emotional connotations of the following terms:

- socialist
- conservative
- liberal
- welfare queen
- Barbie
- welfare state
- big business
- family entertainment
- adult entertainment
- urban
- foreign debt relief

- fundamentalist
- extremist
- universal health care
- drug-free zone
- gay
- higher learning
- ivory tower
- free trade
- free market
- free world
- inner city

▧ **EXERCISE 2.15** In traffic, have you ever noticed how anyone driving slower than you are is an "idiot," while anyone driving faster than you are is a "maniac"? The same thing can be called by different names, depending on whether one is for it or against it. For example, if you're in favour of a proposal to outlaw retail discounts on certain merchandise, you might call it the "fair trade practices act"; if you're against it you might call it a "price-fixing law." Take a current issue or piece of legislation and give it a favourable and an unfavourable name by which it could be designated.

▧ **EXERCISE 2.16** Imagine that you have created a successful national consulting firm specializing in political slogans. Your clients cover the spectrum of issues and interest groups. This month the following groups have scheduled rallies in major cities to further their cause. Your job is to come up with a set of five catchy slogans for each group that successfully communicates the group's message. You're also scheduled to address a national radio audience at the end of the month on the topic of "Successful Strategies for Political Communication." You plan to use the work to explain the secrets of your success to your current roster of clients.

- MADD (Mothers Against Drunk Driving)—demanding tougher penalties for drunk driving
- PETA (People for the Ethical Treatment of Animals)—opposing KFC Canada's involvement with the treatment of animals
- Montreal ACT-UP—demonstration in support of accelerating the pace of AIDS research
- NORML Canada—supporting the legalization of cannabis
- DARE (Drug Abuse Resistance Education)—keeping cannabis classified as an illegal substance

- Greenpeace—supporting a moratorium on logging in old-growth forests
- Sensible Harvesting Coalition—supporting the rights of private interests to harvest timber resources on private lands
- Safeguard Our Families Canada—opposing a permit for an all-ages rap concert
- Canadian Liberty Defence Group—counterdemonstration against censorship
- Big Dig Properties Ltd.—With the approval of the municipality, a real estate developer wants to dig up and move an ancient cemetery to make way for condos
- The Prince Edward Society for the Preservation of History and the Maritimes Genealogical Association launch a lawsuit and begin a public awareness campaign to prevent the cemetery relocation

EXERCISE 2.17   In each of the following examples highlight any terms or expressions that are used in an ambiguous way, and highlight any terms or expressions that are vague. Explain your answers.

	Explain your answers:
Asked why he robbed banks, notorious bank robber Willy Sutton replied, "That's where the money is."	
He was thrown from the car as it left the road. Later he was found in the ditch by some stray cows.	
As the great magician David Copperfield drove south along Main Street, he suddenly turned into a side street.	
American baseball pitcher Tug McGraw, asked if he preferred Astroturf to grass, said, "I don't know. I never smoked Astroturf."	
"Sexual harassment" means "any conduct, comment, gesture or contact of a sexual nature "(a) that is likely to cause offence or humiliation to any employee; or "(b) that might, on reasonable grounds, be perceived by that employee as placing a condition of a sexual nature on employment or on any opportunity for training or promotion."[10]	

■ **EXERCISE 2.18** How many definitions can you find in the first two chapters of this book? List them in the chart below.

Page #	Term defined	Definition

■ **EXERCISE 2.19** In the following examples highlight any terms or expressions that are either undefined and should be defined, or are defined in some incorrect or inadequate way and should be redefined. Explain your answers.

	Explain your answers:
I don't know why some people get so mad about major corporations that "use" the public. Such practices are part of the meaning of free enterprise, which everyone knows is the foundation of our economic and thus sociopolitical institutions. Free enterprise means that all of us should do what we think is best for ourselves. That's all business is doing—looking out for itself. If consumers are deceived or damaged, then that's their fault. Let them take a page from the book of free enterprise and look out for themselves. Instead of condemning business for being ambitious, aggressive, shrewd, and resourceful, we should praise it for acting in accordance with the ideals of free enterprise.	

Murder is whatever prevents a life from coming into existence. By this account, abortion is murder. All societies have proscriptions against murder, and rightly so. There is no more heinous act than to take the innocent life of another. A society that does not stand up to murderers cannot call itself truly civilized. It's obvious, then, that if Canada is worthy of the term "civilized," it must prohibit abortion and deal harshly with those who have committed or commit abortions, since these people are murderers.	Explain your answers:

EXERCISE 2.20   At the end of Chapter 1 (Exercise 1.28) we asked you to compose a one-page Issue Statement. Now review and revise that composition. Identify any key terms or concepts in your first draft relevant to understanding the issue. Make sure that these terms are clearly defined. Check to see that you are using terms in ways that are consistent with conventional usage, or that where you depart from conventional usage, your intended meaning is clear. Check your draft for emotionally loaded descriptions or labels. Where a detectable bias exists, try to reformulate the wording to eliminate it. Remember the distinction between the informative and the persuasive uses of language. An Issue Statement should not be a persuasive composition.

GLOSSARY

ambiguity, problematic   we are faced with a small set of possible meanings—two or three definite prospects—from which we are unable to extract the relevant meaning (cf. problematic vagueness)

ambiguous   a term or expression with more than one conventional meaning (cf. equivocal)

analysis   the process of breaking down things into their constituent elements

connotation   the intension plus the emotional impact of a term

convention   a behavioural regularity followed to prevent or solve interpersonal coordination problems

counterexample   example used to refute a general claim, as for example in a definition

definition   an explanation of the meaning of a term or expression

definition, essential   definition that gives a term's intension

definition, ostensive   definition by example

definition, stipulative   definition that specifies an unconventional meaning of a term for use in a specific context of discourse

denotation   the relationship between a word and the objects to which it "points"

dialectic   the context and flow of inquiry or reasoning

differentia   characteristics that distinguish the extension of a term from the genus

equivocal   a term or expression with more than one meaning that is used at least twice (cf. ambiguity)

equivocation, problematic   we are faced with a set of at least two possible meanings—each of which is definite—such that we are able to verify that the sender uses a logically, dialectically, or rhetorically inappropriate or questionable meaning

etymology   the history of a word

evaluative   a term that expresses a favourable or unfavourable judgment

evaluative language, problematic   we are faced with evaluative language that (1) is demonstrably inappropriate in the context or (2) suffers from (i) a lack of needed defence or (ii) inadequate defence (but better defence could be provided in principle)

explanation   language used to facilitate understanding

extension   the set of objects denoted by a term

genus   larger category within which the extension of a term is located

intension   the criteria that define the extension of a term

necessary condition   a necessary condition is a characteristic or set of characteristics required for membership in the word's extension

rhetoric   the use of language to persuade (whether reasonably or unreasonably)

sufficient condition   a characteristic or set of characteristics that is by itself adequate qualification for membership in the word's extension

synonymy   sameness of meaning

vague   a term or expression with an indefinite extension

vagueness, problematic   we are faced with a *large* set of possible meanings—more than three or four prospects—from which we are unable to extract the relevant meaning (cf. problematic ambiguity)

verbal dispute   a dispute arising out of overlooked verbal ambiguity

Go to http://www.criticalthinking1ce.nelson.com for additional study resources for this chapter.

ENDNOTES

[1] The Greek philosopher Aristotle was an early developer of this approach. For a more recent treatment of this concept as a general strategy, see David N. Perkins, *Knowledge as Design* (Hillsdale, N.J.: Erlbaum, 1986).

[2] This account of linguistic convention is derived from Jonathan Bennett, *Linguistic Behavior* (London: Cambridge University Press, 1976) and David Lewis, *Convention* (Cambridge, MA: Harvard University Press, 1969).

[3] Lewis Carroll, *Through the Looking Glass*, in *The Complete Works of Lewis Carroll* (New York: Random House, 1936), 214.

[4] William Wetmore, "Neighbors Chop Down Redwood, Claim to Have Had Permission," *Sonoma Index-Tribune*, Tuesday, December 25, 2001, 1. Reprinted with permission of the *Sonoma Index-Tribune*.

[5] *A Dictionary of Philosophical Terms and Names,* http://www.philosophypages.com/dy/a4.htm#amb.

[6] *A Dictionary of Philosophical Terms and Names,* http://www.philosophypages.com/dy/e5.htm#eqvn, with superscript numerals added.

[7] http://www.accidentalhedonist.com, "Date Tips" 6/21/05.

[8] "100% Solution," from *Fresh Air,* July 18, 2001, NPR. For more, see, Geoffrey Nunberg, *The Way We Talk Now* (New York: Houghton Mifflin, 2001). Reprinted by permission of Geoffrey Nunberg.

[9] *Canadian Oxford Dictionary* (Don Mills, Ontario: Oxford University Press, 2004), 1607.

[10] Canada Labour Code, Part Iii, Division Xv.1, 247.1

UNIT TWO
Argument

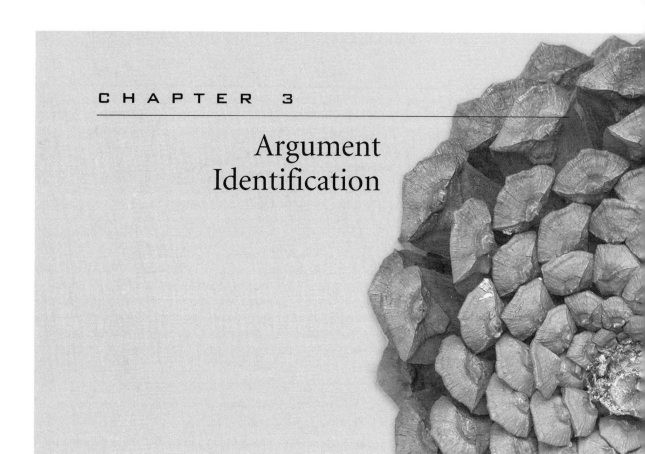

CHAPTER 3

Argument Identification

$\mathbf{L}$et us now suppose that you and some other reasonable person find yourselves divided over an issue—say, for example, whether the public health care system in Canada should change to a mixed system with both public and private elements. One of you holds the opinion that the system should remain public only, while the other thinks that a two-tiered approach is fairer and more sensible. What do reasonable people do when they recognize they are divided over an issue? They argue. In this chapter we will introduce and develop the concept of an "argument" as both a product of critical thinking and an object to which critical thinking is applied.

The word *argument* bears more than one sense. For clarity let us centre on one of its conventional meanings and set aside the other as outside our focus of primary concern. In this book we are primarily concerned with the sense of the word *argument* in which an individual person *makes* or *offers* an argument, not the sense in which two people *have* an argument. In the sense of the word with

© The New Yorker Collection 2004 Bruce Eric Kaplan from cartoonbank.com. All Rights Reserved.

"What about here? This looks like a good spot for an argument."

which we are primarily concerned, an argument can be defined as *a composition whose primary purpose is to persuade a person by appealing to the person's reasoning capability.* To reinforce this distinction, consider the following portion of the Monty Python's Flying Circus "Argument Clinic" sketch. A customer, played by Michael Palin, enters the reception area requesting an argument and is sent down the hall to room 12A, where he finds an attendant, played by John Cleese.

Monty Python's "Argument Clinic"

Customer: Is this the right room for an argument?

Attendant: I told you once.

C: No you haven't.

A: Yes I have.

C: When?

A: Just now.

C: No you didn't.

A: I did.

C: Didn't!

A: Did!

C: Didn't!

A: I'm telling you I did.

C: You did not!

A: Oh, I'm sorry. Just one moment. Is this the five-minute argument or the full half hour?

C: Oh, just the five minutes.

A: Ah, thank you. Anyway, I did.

C: You most certainly did not.

A: Look, let's get this thing clear. I quite definitely told you.

C: No, you did not.

A: Yes I did.

C: No you didn't.

A: Yes I did!

C: No you didn't!

A: Yes I *did!*

C: No you *didn't!*

A: Yes I *DID!*

C: No you *DIDN'T!*

A: *DID!*

C: Oh now look. This isn't an argument.

A: Yes it is.

C: No it isn't. It's just contradiction.

A: No it isn't.

C: It IS!

A: It is NOT!

C: Look. You just contradicted me.

A: I did not.

C: Oh, you did.

A: No, No, No.

C: You did just then!

A: Nonsense.

C: Oh, this is futile . . .

A: No it isn't.

C: I came here for a good argument.

A: No, you didn't. No, you came here for an *argument*.

C: Well, an argument isn't just contradiction.

A: Can be.

C: No it can't. An argument is a connected series of statements intended to establish a proposition.

A: No it isn't.

C: Yes it is. It's not just contradiction.

A: Look if I'm going to argue with you I must take up a contrary position.

C: Yes, but that's not just saying "No it isn't."

A: Yes it is.

C: No it *ISN'T!*[1]

The humour here depends on both senses of the term *argument*. What the attendant is offering is a perverse trivialization of the kind of argument that two people "have." In this sense *argument* is synonymous with *dispute*—a kind of verbal conflict, which Cleese's character has reduced in this scene to mere mechanical contradiction of whatever Palin's character says. Again, this is not the sense of the word *argument* with which we are primarily concerned in this book.

Palin's character is interested in something more substantial, and he gives a definition:

> An argument is a connected series of statements intended to establish a proposition.

This is an alternative to the functional definition given previously. It also gives the intention of the word *argument* in the sense with which we are primarily concerned, but it does so by reference to structural features rather than function. In other words, *an argument is a composition consisting of a set of claims one of which, called the "thesis" or "conclusion," is understood or intended to be supported by the other(s), called the "premise(s)."* The two definitions, functional and structural, are closely linked (because the structure suits the function) and can be combined as follows. *An argument is a composition—whose primary purpose is to persuade a person by appealing to the person's reasoning capability—consisting of a set of claims, one of which, called the "thesis" or "conclusion," is understood or intended to be supported by the other(s), called the "premise(s)."* To persuade someone by appealing to the person's reasoning capability, typically one presents a composition consisting of a series of claims, some of which support others. In what follows we will be using both parts of this definition. The functional part of the definition will serve as a basis for argument identification. The structural part of the definition will serve as a basis for argument analysis.

DEFINITION

An argument is a composition—whose primary purpose is to persuade a person by appealing to the person's reasoning capability—consisting of a set of claims, one of which, called the "thesis" or "conclusion," is understood or intended to be supported by the other(s), called the "premise(s)."

Our study of argument can be divided into four main skill areas: argument identification, argument analysis, argument evaluation, and argument design and construction. Argument identification involves recognizing arguments and distinguishing them from other sorts of material. Argument analysis involves taking arguments apart and understanding how they are put together and designed to work. Argument evaluation involves appraising the arguments' strengths and weaknesses. Argument design and construction involve generating original arguments of our own.

Here is a simple example of an argument: "Canadians wait too long for access to many public health care services. Some degree of medical privatization would help this problem. Therefore, Canada should take immediate steps to introduce two-tiered health care." "Canada should take immediate steps to introduce two-tiered health care" is the claim the others are intended to support and establish. For the purposes of our study of critical thinking, the relationships of support are the ones that matter here. We want to focus our attention on the "argumentative structure" of the composition—rather than, for example, its grammatical structure. If we wanted, we could combine all three claims in the above argument into a single sentence. "Since Canadians wait too long for access to many public health care services and some degree of medical privatization would help this problem, Canada should take immediate steps to introduce two-tiered health care." So, here is a point to bear in mind as you proceed: Although the grammatical structure of a passage is *sometimes* a good guide to its "argumentative structure," we want to uncover the "argumentative structure" (*regardless of its grammatical structure*).

ARGUMENT IDENTIFICATION

Arguments are compositions in language, which as you know is an immensely flexible medium of expression. Open any magazine or daily newspaper and you will find a wide variety of material composed in language, including some arguments. Listen to any conversation and you will hear many things occurring, quite possibly including argumentation. It is not so difficult to identify cases of verbal conflict, especially when you are involved. Identifying arguments, though, in the sense relevant to our purposes, can be much more difficult, especially when arguments are embedded in larger, more complex contexts. This is in part because recognizing arguments involves recognizing the speaker's or the writer's intentions and because speakers and writers can have complex intentions and do not always make their intentions perfectly clear in what they write and say.

Distinguishing arguments from explanations, or from jokes, entertainment, greetings, narratives, or instructions, is a matter of discerning the author's intentions to persuade by appeal to reason. Sometimes it is clear that what the author is trying to do is to persuade by appeal to reason. In that case what the author has put forward is clearly an argument. Take note: Faulty or questionable appeals to reason still count as arguments. Other times, however, we can clearly see that the author is trying to do something other than persuade by appeal to reason. In that case what the author has put forward is clearly not an argument. Sometimes an author may even be trying to do two or more things at once: persuade by appeal to reason and to amuse the reader. Other times we are just not clear about what the author is trying to do.

We often make claims without arguing for them: "Hockey is a popular sport in Canada. Baseball is a popular sport in the United States. North American–style football is generally played in winter. Soccer is played throughout the world." These claims are nonargumentative. None of them is intended to support or establish any of the others; so, taken as a group, they do not constitute an argument.

We also make claims when we try to explain things: "The class on the history of music has been cancelled for lack of enrollment"; "The horse was frightened by a snake in the grass"; "Last night's rain made the streets wet." These are explanatory claims. They help explain something: the cancellation of the class, the spooking of the horse, the wet pavement. They are, in other words, presumably intended to help someone understand something better.

The basic difference between such nonargumentative passages and arguments is one of intent or purpose. If people are interested in establishing the truth of a claim and offer evidence intended to accomplish such, then they are making an argument. If, however, they regard the truth of a claim as nonproblematic, or as already having been established and are trying to help us understand *why* it is the case (rather than *establish that it is* the case), then they are explaining. Thus, when we say, "The streets are wet because it rained last night," ordinarily we would not be trying to establish that the streets are wet. Presumably that fact is already apparent to any observer, and so we would more likely be offering an explanation of how the streets got that way. If, however, we say, "You should take your umbrella today because the forecast calls for rain," ordinarily we would not understand the statement that you should take your umbrella as an established truth, because advice like this ordinarily is not offered to people we think are already convinced. Thus, in this case we are more likely setting forth an argument. Notice that the word "because" occurs in both the explanation and in the argument—but that it fulfils different purposes in the two cases. In the case of the explanation, "because" serves to indicate an idea that elaborates upon an accepted fact; while in the case of the argument, "because" serves to indicate a reason given to prove a claim that is debatable or not yet embraced. Both instances of "because" involve answering questions (*Why* are the streets wet? *Why* should you take your umbrella?), but the dialectical intentions behind the usages differ.

EXERCISE 3.1 | **Argument Identification**

Which of the following passages express or contain arguments? You can use either the functional or the structural parts of the definition of "argument," or both, to make your determination. Explain your answer.

Argument	"A principle I established for myself early in the game: I wanted to get paid for my work, but I didn't want to work for pay." —poet Leonard Cohen	Explain your answer:	
Explanation			
Other			

	Argument	"I object to lotteries because they're biased in favour of lucky people."	Explain your answer:
	Explanation		
	Other		

	Argument	"The most serious issue facing journalism education today is the blurring of the distinctions between advertising, public relations, and journalism itself."	Explain your answer:
	Explanation		
	Other		

	Argument	"Even the most productive writers are expert dawdlers, doers of unnecessary errands, seekers of interruptions—trials to their wives and husbands, associates, and themselves. They sharpen well-pointed pencils and go out to buy more blank paper, rearrange their office, wander through libraries and bookstores, change words, walk, drive, make unnecessary calls, nap, day dream, and try not 'consciously' to think about what they are going to write so they can think subconsciously about it." —Donald M. Murray, *Write before Writing*	Explain your answer:
	Explanation		
	Other		

	Argument	"Gentlemen of the jury, surely you will not send to his death a decent, hard-working young man, because for one tragic moment he lost his self-control? Is he not sufficiently punished by the life-long remorse that is to be his lot? I confidently await your verdict, the only verdict possible: that of homicide with extenuating circumstances." —Albert Camus, *The Stranger*	Explain your answer:
	Explanation		
	Other		

	Argument	"It seems that mercy cannot be attributed to God. For mercy is a kind of sorrow, as Damascene says. But there is no sorrow in God; and therefore there is no mercy in him." —Thomas Aquinas	Explain your answer:
	Explanation		
	Other		

	Argument	"I knew a guy once who was so influenced by statistics, numbers ruled his entire life! One time he found out that over 80 percent of all automobile accidents happen within five miles of the driver's home. So he moved!"	Explain your answer:
	Explanation		
	Other		

		"Willy Loman never made a lot of money. His name was never in the paper. He's not the finest character that ever lived. But he's a human being, and a terrible thing is happening to him. So attention must be paid. He's not to be allowed to fall into his grave like an old dog. Attention, attention must be paid to such a person." —Arthur Miller, *Death of a Salesman*	Explain your answer:
	Argument		
	Explanation		
	Other		

ARGUMENT ANALYSIS

As we indicated earlier, argument analysis involves taking apart arguments into their structural elements so as to better understand how they are designed and intended to work. Argument analysis is a natural extension of argument identification, because argument identification already involves recognizing a set of claims as composed for a certain intended purpose.

PREMISES AND CONCLUSIONS

If an argument is a set of claims, some of which are understood or intended to support the other(s), then we may proceed to define two important basic concepts for both argument identification and argument analysis: the concepts of premise (sometimes written as *premiss* in logical discourse) and conclusion. *The **premises** of arguments are the claims offered in support of the **conclusion**. The **conclusion** is the claim that the **premises** are offered to support.*

Thus far we have considered two simple arguments:

(1) Canadians wait too long for access to many public health care services. Some degree of medical privatization would help this problem.

Canada should take immediate steps to introduce two-tiered health care.

(2) The weather forecast calls for rain.

You should take your umbrella today.

The solid line indicates the transition from supporting material to what the material supports, or from premise(s) to conclusion. Statements above the line are the premises; statements below the line are conclusions. We will call this line the *inference line.* The word *inference* refers to the step we take in our minds from the premise(s) to the conclusion. As soon as you recognize something as an argument, you are in position to take a positive first step in argument analysis: Identify the conclusion. Let's make this a "rule of thumb" for argument analysis.

CRITICAL THINKING TIP 3.1

First Find the Conclusion.

SIGNAL WORDS

As we mentioned earlier, identifying arguments can be difficult, especially when they are embedded in larger contexts, because recognizing arguments involves recognizing the author's intentions. Similarly, identifying the premises and conclusion of an argument can be difficult, especially when we find them embedded in longer passages. If you read and listen carefully, however, you can pick up clues to the presence of arguments and to the identity of premises and conclusions in written or spoken discourse. One of the most important clues is the *signal word,* or *signal expression.* Speakers and writers can and often do signal their intentions by using a word or an expression to indicate the presence of a premise or conclusion or relationship of support. Here are some of the words and phrases that conventionally indicate conclusions:

TABLE 3.1   Conclusion Signals

- so
- therefore
- thus
- consequently
- it follows that
- as a result
- hence
- in conclusion
- shows that

On first reading a passage, circling the signal words when you come across them is often useful, especially if the passage you are reading is long and complex. Doing so alerts you to the crucial relationships of support within the passage, and thus gives you "landmarks" to its argumentative structure.

> Canadians wait too long for access to many public health care services. Some degree of medical privatization would help this problem. (Therefore,) Canada should take immediate steps to introduce two-tiered health care.

Noticing the word *therefore* in the last sentence helps us locate the argument's conclusion: "Canada should take immediate steps to introduce two-tiered health care." It also helps us recognize that the first two claims are offered as reasons or premises in support of that conclusion.

Just as *therefore* is conventionally used to signal a conclusion, several conventional ways to signal a premise or premises exist. Here are some of the words and phrases that conventionally indicate premises:

TABLE 3.2   Premise Signals

- since
- because
- for
- follows from
- after all
- due to
- inasmuch as
- insofar as

Again, in reading a passage, circling such expressions so as to locate and keep track of premises can be quite useful.

> (Since) Canadians wait too long for access to many public health care services and some degree of medical privatization would help this problem, Canada should take immediate steps to introduce two-tiered health care.

In this passage the word *since* introduces the premises that support the arguer's position in favour of two-tiered health care.

Now having said this, we need to add two words of caution: first, a reminder about the contextual nature of language. Many of the words that are conventionally used to signal arguments also have other conventional applications. So you cannot simply rely on the presence of the signal words listed above as an absolutely foolproof indication of the presence of an argument. For example, if we compare:

> "You should take your umbrella (because) the forecast calls for rain."

with

> "The streets are wet <u>because</u> it rained last night."

we see that the first sentence is an argument in which the word *because* introduces a premise, but the second sentence is an explanation. In the second sentence, the word *because* introduces a claim whose intended function is not to *prove* or *establish* but rather to *explain* the wetness of the streets. In some cases, then, the intended function of the word *because* is clear, but in other cases terms of this sort (such as *since* and *for*) can be ambiguous. Sometimes these terms function to indicate the presence of an argument, and sometimes not. Like most interpretive work, identifying arguments—and even recognizing an expression as an argument signal—is in large measure dependent on context.

A second caution is that many of the arguments you will encounter contain no signals. Sometimes you are just supposed to "get" that an argument is what is being presented.

"Look, if we have to wait too long for health care and privatization would help, why *shouldn't* we introduce a two-tiered system?"

This passage, in one sentence, still makes three claims. The passage is evidently an argument, because one of the claims made in it is evidently supported by the others. How can we tell this? Start by taking the sentence as a whole and asking yourself, what is its *point?*

EXERCISE 3.2 | **Find the Conclusion**

Highlight the point of the passage:

"Look, if we have to wait too long for health care and privatization would help, why shouldn't we introduce a two-tiered system?"

We expect that you will have zeroed in on the question at the end, "why shouldn't we introduce a two-tiered system?" Even though the point is expressed in the grammatical form of a question, a claim emerges here: "We *might as well* introduce a two-tiered system." Now ask the natural next question, "*Why* should we accept this claim?" As soon as you ask this "Why" question, you can see that the rest of the sentence is responding to your question with two additional claims: "We have to wait too long for medical care" and "privatization would help." In effect, the author has anticipated a challenge—naturally arising in the mind of any reasoning being, that a controversial claim should be given some rational support—and has tried to meet this challenge. These two additional supporting claims are therefore the argument's premises. Notice once again that it is the argumentative structure, not the grammatical structure, that matters for our purposes in critical thinking. Notice also that in any passage of argumentative material, argument analysis boils down simply to figuring out what supports what.

EXERCISE 3.3 | **Argument Signals**

Circle the signals, and then highlight the conclusions in the following passages:

- Our whole class has to stay after school for an hour. So I'm going to need a ride home, because the bus leaves right after school.

- Human beings and many higher animals have very similar neurophysiological structures. Humans and animals exhibit many of the same behavioural responses to stimuli. It is reasonable to suppose that animals feel pain and pleasure as we humans do.

- "And he went from there, and entered their synagogue. And behold, there was a man with a withered hand. And they asked him, 'Is it lawful to heal on the Sabbath?' so that they might accuse him. He said to them, 'What man of you, if he has one sheep, and it falls into a pit on the Sabbath, will not lay hold of it and lift it out? Of how much more value is a man than a sheep? So it is lawful to do good on the Sabbath'." (Matthew 12:9–12)

- Two out of three people interviewed preferred Tub-o-Suds to another soap. Therefore, Tub-o-Suds is the best soap available.

- In the next century more and more people will turn to solar energy to heat their homes because the price of gas and oil will become prohibitive for most consumers and the price of installing solar panels will decline.

- People who smoke cigarettes should be forced to pay a health insurance surcharge since they know smoking is bad for their health, and they have no right to expect others to pay for their addictions.

- It's no wonder that government aid to the poor fails. Poor people can't manage their money.

- Even though spanking has immediate punitive and (for the parent) anger-releasing effects, parents should not spank their children, because spanking gives children the message that inflicting pain on others is an appropriate means of changing their behaviour. Furthermore, spanking trains children to submit to the arbitrary rules of authority figures who have the power to harm them. We ought not to give our children those messages. Instead, we should train them either to make appropriate behavioural choices or to expect to deal with the related natural and logical consequences of their behaviour.

- Public schools generally avoid investigation of debatable issues and instead stress rote recall of isolated facts, which teaches students unquestioningly to absorb given information on demand so that they can regurgitate it in its entirety during testing situations. Although students are generally not allowed to question it, much of what is presented as accurate information is indeed controversial. But citizens need to develop decision-making skills regarding debatable issues in order truly to participate in a democracy. It follows then that public schools ought to change their educational priorities in order to better prepare students to become informed, responsible members of our democracy.

- Ever since the injury to Mats Sundin, the rest of the Toronto Maple Leafs forwards have been under pressure to produce. But since their won/lost record is the best in the NHL, we must conclude that the loss of Sundin, while damaging to their overall offence, has not been devastating.

- Late Night Radio Talk Show Host: "I've heard more heart attacks happen on Monday than on any other day of the week, probably because Mondays mark a return to those stressful work situations for so many of you. So let's all call in sick this Monday, ok, folks, because we don't want any of you to check out on us."

- Since capital punishment is a form of homicide, it requires a strong justification. Simple vengeance is not an adequate justification for homicide. Therefore, since there is no conclusive evidence that capital punishment deters violent crime, capital punishment is not justified.

DEEPER ANALYSIS

Recognizing that people generally require reasons to persuade them to accept a controversial claim, we set forth an argument. In the argument additional claims are made in support of the claim we are trying to persuade people to accept. These additional claims, however, may be challenged as well. Recognizing this, authors frequently anticipate the need to supply further support for the premises of their arguments—in other words, to build in arguments for the premises of their arguments. For this reason arguments often call for in-depth analysis, as layer upon layer of support may require.

> Canadians wait too long for access to many public health care services, (because) such services tend to be overly bureaucratized. Some degree of medical privatization would help the problem, (because) privatization gives vendors a heightened motivation to increase efficiency. (Therefore,) Canada should take immediate steps to introduce two-tiered health care.

Circling the signal words in the above passage helps us to recognize several important features of this argument's structure. It enables us to notice first that the premise "Canadians wait too long for access to many public health care services" has embedded in it an additional claim, "such services tend to be overly bureaucratized." Once we see this we can also recognize that this embedded claim is intended to support the one in which it is embedded. Similarly, we notice that the premise "some degree of medical privatization would help the problem" is now followed by a further supporting claim: "privatization gives vendors a heightened motivation to increase efficiency."

From this relatively brief example, you can already see that a great deal of complexity can be packed into a few words. So you can also easily imagine the challenge involved in taking apart a large and complex argument and keeping track of all of the relationships of support between its many claims. In Chapter 4 we will give you a few tools for coping with this kind of challenge. We will also revisit this example. In the meantime, here is one more example to prepare you for the next exercise. Consider the following passage:

> Canada must do much more to address Aboriginal land claims, (since) many major Aboriginal land claims still have not been resolved satisfactorily. (For example,) many claims in British Columbia are still in early or intermediate stages.

The conclusion of the passage is, "Canada must do much more to address Aboriginal land claims." The arguer supports this conclusion by offering the premise, "Many major Aboriginal land claims still have not been resolved satisfactorily." (The premise indicator word here is *since*.) The arguer also offers support for this premise: "Many claims in British Columbia are still in early or intermediate stages." (The premise support indicator term here is *for example*.) The premise support is just one instance that the arguer could have adduced (we can imagine a raft of other facts and considerations that the arguer could have marshalled), but the point is that the argumentative structure here is complex: We see a conclusion (or overall conclusion, if you prefer) supported directly by one premise, which is itself supported by another contributing premise.

■ EXERCISE 3.4 | **Argument Analysis/Layers of Support**

Circle the signals, and then highlight the conclusions in the following passages. Next, highlight the premises. Use a second colour to highlight premises that support the conclusion *directly,* and a third colour to highlight premises that support other premises.

- The mother-in-law can't be the murderer. The victim, a vigorous 90-kilogram athlete, was strangled by the murderer's bare hands. The murderer must have very well developed upper-body strength. The mother-in-law is a frail 80-year-old woman.

- Part of believing something is believing that it's true. So if I were to do an inventory of my beliefs, they'd all seem true to me. Or, to put it another way, if I knew something was false, I wouldn't believe it. So it doesn't really make sense for me to say that some of my own beliefs are false.

- I've been mistaken in the past. I've learned on numerous occasions, and pretty much throughout my life, that things that I believed to be true were really false. Why should it be any different now? So if I were to do an inventory of my beliefs, I probably wouldn't notice the false ones, but I'd still bet there are some in there somewhere.

- "Nor is there anything smart about smoking. A woman who smokes is far more likely than her nonsmoking counterpart to suffer from a host of disabling conditions, any of which can interfere with her ability to perform at home or on the job. . . . Women who smoke have more spontaneous abortions, stillbirths, and premature babies than do nonsmokers, and their children's later health may be affected."[2]

- "Since the mid '50's, for example, scientists have observed the same characteristics in what they thought were different cancer cells and concluded that these traits must be common to all cancers. All cancer cells had certain nutritional needs, all could grow in soft agar cultures, all could seed new solid tumors when transplanted into experimental animals, and all contained drastically abnormal chromosomes—the 'mark cancer'."[3]

HIDDEN DEPTHS

In Chapter 1 we explained how important it is to be aware of the assumptions that may be involved in the reasoning under analysis, and that one of the important places to look for hidden assumptions is "underneath" the claims being made in the argument. We defined *presuppositions* as the kind of assumption that must be made in order for what is explicitly said to make sense. In the example below, from one of the exercises at the end of Chapter 1, an argument is made against the claim that extraterrestrial aliens crash-landed at the U.S. Air Force Base at Roswell, New Mexico.

> If you were an alien trying to scope out earthly terrain, the last place you'd go would be to one of the most highly fortified and tightly secured military installations in the United States.

Notice that this argument presupposes alien reasoning as essentially similar to our own human reasoning, in particular that aliens would be able to recognize a military installation as such if they saw one, and that they would recognize such a place as dangerous and to be avoided.

Just as people sometimes put forward arguments without signals, leaving it up to the listener or reader to recognize the argument as such, they also frequently put forward arguments that aren't completely stated. Sometimes what is hidden is the part of the argument we want to find first. Sometimes it is the argument's point, or conclusion, that we are just supposed to "get." Suppose that you are standing in line at the polling place on election day, waiting to have your

---

EXERCISE 3.5 | **Argument Analysis/Hidden Presuppositions**

What presuppositions can you identify in the argument used in Exercise 3.2?

"Look, if we have to wait too long for health care and privatization would help, why shouldn't we introduce a two-tiered system?"

Presuppositions:

_____

_____

_____

---

registration verified and to receive your official ballot, and you overhear the official say to the person in front of you:

> I'm sorry, sir, but only those citizens whose names appear on my roster are eligible to vote, and your name does not appear.

Clearly something further is implied here. The implied conclusion, which is evidently intended to follow from the two claims explicitly made, is that the person in front of you is not eligible to vote. This example, then, does express an argument. Recognizing it as such depends upon recognizing that the two explicitly stated claims "point to" the unstated conclusion.

EXERCISE 3.6 | **Argument Analysis/Unstated Conclusions**

Each of the following arguments has an unstated conclusion. Formulate the conclusion.

1. I'm sorry, but you may stay in the country only if you have a current visa, and your visa has expired.
   Therefore,

---

2. God has all the virtues, and benevolence is certainly a virtue.
   Therefore,

---

3. Either the battery in the remote control is dead or the set's unplugged, but the set is plugged in.
   Therefore,

---

4. All mammals suckle their young, and all primates are mammals, and orangutans are primates.

   Therefore,

5. Software is written by human beings, and human beings make mistakes.

   Therefore,

6. Legislation that can't be enforced is useless, and there's no way to enforce censorship over the Internet.

   Therefore,

In Chapter 1 we explained that another one of the important places to look for hidden assumptions is "between" the claims being made in the argument. We defined *inferential assumptions* as the kind of assumptions that play the role of "missing links in a chain of reasoning." Suppose once more that you are standing in line at the polling place on election day and you overhear the official say to the person in front of you:

> I'm sorry, sir, but only those citizens whose names appear on my roster are eligible to vote.

Here again the context makes it clear that the official is offering support for the claim that the person in front of you is not eligible to vote. In addition to the unstated conclusion, though, an unstated premise emerges:

> Your name does not appear on my roster.

Implied conclusions and premises are important parts of the logical structure of the arguments in which they occur, and they need to be taken into account in our analyses and evaluations of such arguments. How do we tell that there is an unstated claim ("that the person's name does not appear on the roster of eligible voters") in the last example? So now let us look between the premise and conclusion:

> Only those citizens whose names appear on my roster are eligible to vote.
> _____
> Therefore you are not eligible to vote.

EXERCISE 3.7 | Argument Analysis/Hidden Inferential Assumptions

Each of the following arguments has an unstated premise. Formulate the missing premise.

1. "Canadians wait too long for access to many public health care services, because such services tend to be overly bureaucratized."

2. All propaganda is dangerous. Therefore, network news is dangerous

Because

3. The Toronto Maple Leafs will play in the Stanley Cup Final because the Eastern Conference champion always plays in the Stanley Cup Final,

And

4. Everything with any commercial potential eventually gets absorbed into the corporate world, so the Internet will eventually get absorbed into the corporate world

Because

5. Hip-hop is a fad, so it will surely fade,

Because

The missing premise "Your name does not appear on my roster" is clearly implied, because it would seem to be the only way to get from the explicitly stated premise to the conclusion.

Formulating the premise is the most challenging kind of argument analysis, for the obvious reason that some of the things for which we are trying to account are hidden. In Chapter 5 we will give you a few additional tools for coping with this kind of challenge.

We will close this introduction to argument analysis with a few more exercises and examples to practise on.

ADDITIONAL EXERCISES

The following additional exercises should help you determine your readiness to move on to Chapters 4 and 5.

EXERCISE 3.8 In each of the following examples, check all issue categories that apply. Most important, explain each classification you make.

		The game has been delayed	Explain your answer:
	Argument	because of rain.	
	Explanation		
	Other		

		"While taking my noon walk today, I had more morbid thoughts. What is it about death that bothers me so much? Probably the hours. Melnick says the soul is immortal and lives on after the body drops away, but if my soul exists without my body I am convinced all my clothes will be loose fitting."	Explain your answer:
	Argument		
	Explanation		
	Other		
		—Woody Allen	

		I've heard more heart attacks happen on Monday than on any other day of the week, probably because Mondays mark a return to stressful work situations for so many.	Explain your answer:
	Argument		
	Explanation		
	Other		

		Because the two complaints so fundamentally contradict one another, evidence that can be brought forward on behalf of the first tends to call into question the accuracy of the second; and conversely, evidence that can be summoned up on behalf of the second works to undermine the first.	Explain your answer:
	Argument		
	Explanation		
	Other		
		—Elaine Scarry, *On Beauty and Being Just*	

		"One woman told me that brown spots, a bugaboo to older women, were twice as numerous on the left side of her face and arm due to daily use of her car. The right, or interior, side of her face and right arm showed far fewer brown spots. Since these unattractive marks seem to be promoted by exposure to the sun, either cover up or use a good sunscreen."[4]	Explain your answer:
	Argument		
	Explanation		
	Both		
	Other		

	Argument	"In bureaucratic logic, bad judgment is any decision that can lead to embarrassing questions, even if the decision was itself right. Therefore no man with an eye on a career can afford to be right when he can manage to be safe."[5]	Explain your answer:
	Explanation		
	Both		
	Other		

■ **EXERCISE 3.9**   Using the punctuation and signals as clues to the missing elements, fill in the blanks of the following "argument skeletons" with the letter **P** (for premise), **PS** (for premise support), or **C** (for conclusion).

- _____ and _____. So, _____.
- _____, because _____, since _____.
- Inasmuch as _____, _____, for _____.
- _____. Therefore, since _____, _____.
- _____. Therefore, _____, since _____.
- _____. This follows from _____, and _____.

■ **EXERCISE 3.10**   Construct an argument based on each of the argument skeletons in Exercise 3.9.

■ **EXERCISE 3.11**   Assume that each of the following passages is an argument. Fit the claims in each passage into the argument skeleton provided.

- Postsecondary education affects one's earning potential. Research shows that postsecondary graduates make more money over a lifetime than non-postsecondary graduates do.

  _____ for, _____.

- This new diet won't help me lose weight. No diet I've ever tried has worked.

  _____. So, _____.

- Bill must be a poor student. Bill spends most of his time watching sports on television. _____ since _____.

- Students come to school to learn. Students should have no say in curriculum decisions. Because _____, _____.

■ **EXERCISE 3.12**   For each of the following passages, either highlight or state the conclusion.

- "Yond Cassius has a lean and hungry look .... Such men are dangerous."[6]
- "Only demonstrative proof should be able to make you abandon the theory of Creation; but such a proof does not exist in nature."[7]

- "When we regard a man as morally responsible for an act, we regard him as a legitimate object of moral praise or blame in respect of it. But it seems plain that a man cannot be a legitimate object of moral praise or blame for an act unless in willing the act he is in some important sense a 'free' agent."[8]

EXERCISE 3.13 Arrange the following eight sentences to produce a logically coherent argument.

- First among them is that learning another language provides one with entry into a different world-view from one's own.

- If we are serious about making diversity a central narrative in the schooling of the young, it is necessary for our students to learn to speak at least one language other than English fluently.

- The reasons for serious second-language learning are various.

- But if our schools pay little attention to other languages, most of our population will remain monolingual.

- One might also add that in preparing our young for the 21st-century economy, bilingualism (at least) would seem to be a necessity.

- Educational visionaries insist that competence in using computers is essential in a global economy, apparently believing that speaking another language is not.[9]

EXERCISE 3.14 At the end of Chapter 1 (Exercise 1.28) you were instructed to draft a one-page Issue Statement, which you revised at the end of Chapter 2 (Exercise 2.20). Now you should try a little research. Research essentially means finding out something we do not already know. In researching an issue we need to gain access to reliable information relevant to our topic, and most important, since our topic is the subject of debate and disagreement among reasonable people, we need to gain access to arguments of a reasonably high standard representing the diversity of opinion on our topic. Go to InfoTrac College Edition and research the issue articulated in your Issue Statement. (An access card is packaged with each new book). Your goal is to identify at least three extended arguments representing at least two distinct positions on your issue. We recommend looking ahead to the section in Chapter 13 on "Research and the Media."

GLOSSARY

analysis   the process of breaking down complex things into their constituent elements
argument   (defined functionally): a composition whose primary function is to persuade a person by appealing to the person's reasoning capability; (defined structurally): a composition consisting of a set of claims one of which, called the "thesis" or "conclusion," is supported by the other(s), called the "premise(s)"

conclusion   the claim in an argument supported by the premise(s)

premise(s)   the claim(s) in an argument that support the conclusion

signal word   word indicating the presence of an argument or argument part

thesis   conclusion, especially in an extended argument

unstated claim   any claim in an argument that is not explicitly stated

Go to http://www.criticalthinking1ce.nelson.com for additional study resources for this chapter.

ENDNOTES

[1] "The Argument Clinic," *Monty Python's Flying Circus—Just the Words* Volume 2 by Monty Python, Methnen Publishing Ltd. Reprinted by permission.

[2] Jane E. Brody and Richard Engquist, "Women and Smoking," Public Affairs Pamphlet 475 (New York: Public Affairs Committee, 1972), 2.

[3] Michael Gold, "The Cells That Would Not Die," in "This World," *San Francisco Chronicle,* May 17, 1981, 9.

[4] Virginia Castleton, "Bring Out Your Beauty," *Prevention,* September 1981,108.

[5] John Ciardi, "Bureaucracy and Frank Ellis," in *Manner of Speaking* (New Brunswick, N.J.: Rutgers University Press, 1972), 250.

[6] William Shakespeare, *Julius Caesar.*

[7] Moses Maimonides, *The Guide for the Perplexed.*

[8] C. Arthur Campbell, "Is 'Freewill' a Pseudo-Problem?" *Mind,* 60, no. 240 (1951), 447.

[9] Neil Postman, *The End of Education* (New York: Vintage/Random House, 1996), 149–50. Used with some adaptation.

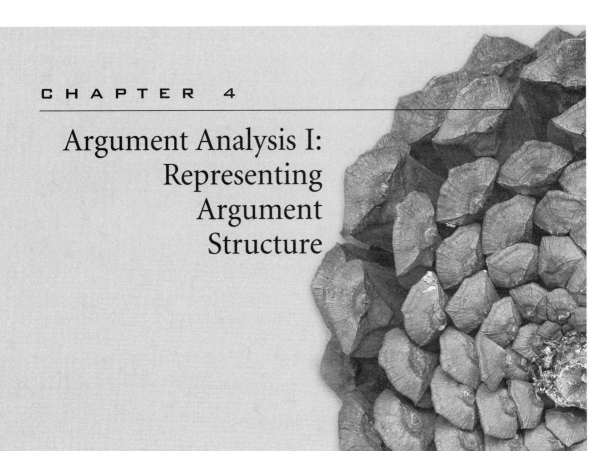

CHAPTER 4

Argument Analysis I: Representing Argument Structure

THE GOAL OF ARGUMENT ANALYSIS

The basic purpose of analysis—the intellectual process of taking apart complex things into their more basic elements—is to help us understand complex matters. In Chapter 1 we applied analysis to issues. In this chapter we will apply analysis to arguments. Argument analysis is important in critical thinking as a crucial first step toward argument evaluation. In this connection, we should bear in mind what we said in Chapter 1 about being patient in pursuit of the truth. When we are involved in an issue, especially in the heat of discussion, as soon as we recognize an argument emerging we may feel ready to endorse or reject it, often simply on the basis of whether or not we agree with its point. Before we pass judgment as to the

© The New Yorker Collection 1985 Gahan Wilson from cartoonbank.com. All Rights Reserved.

"But I see you're having difficulty following my argument.

merits of an argument, however, we need to make sure that we have understood the argument accurately, fairly, and in detail. This is the goal of argument analysis, and the main reason it comes *before* argument evaluation is that it makes no sense to pass judgment on something we do not adequately understand.

In Chapter 3 we defined an argument as (a) *a composition, whose primary purpose is to persuade a person by appealing to the person's reasoning capability,* and (b) *a composition comprising a set of claims one of which, called the "thesis" or "conclusion," is understood or intended to be supported by the other(s), called the "premise(s)."* Just as the functional part of the definition (a) is a good basis for argument identification, the structural part of the definition (b) will now serve as a basis for argument analysis. Breaking down an argument into its constituent elements is a matter of taking it apart structurally. The crucial structural relationships in arguments, as you can see clearly in the structural definition, are relationships of support. So argument analysis really boils down to figuring out what supports what. With short and simple arguments, this can be a relatively easy thing to do, especially if the argument is fully expressed, with signal words clearly indicating the identity of the conclusion and which claim(s) support it. Many of the arguments you will encounter in real life, though, are more challenging and difficult to process. An argument may be long and complex. It may be less than fully expressed. Parts of the argument may be veiled or implied, or perhaps just not worded clearly. Material that is extraneous to the argument may surround or be mixed in with the claims that make up the argument. In this chapter we offer you strategies and suggestions for analyzing arguments that present these challenges.

A good place to begin is with the goal of argument analysis: a fair and an accurate understanding of the argument in detail. How do we know if we have achieved this goal? How do we tell whether our understanding of someone else's argument is fair and accurate? One obvious way to proceed is to compare our understanding of the argument to the author's understanding of it. If we could talk directly with the author of the argument, we might say something similar to this:

> If I understand your argument correctly, your point is . . .
>
> or
>
> Are you saying . . . ?

and then restate the argument to the author in our own words. The author could then tell us whether we got it right or whether our understanding is mistaken in any way.

Obviously we cannot *always do* this. We cannot expect to be able to check the accuracy of our grasp of *every* argument directly with its author. Nevertheless, this is a pretty good way to understand the goal of argument analysis. *Can we take apart the argument and reassemble it in our own words without changing what it means or how it is designed to work as a tool of rational persuasion? In a word, can we "paraphrase" the argument?* This is a good test, indeed probably the best test, of the adequacy of our grasp of another person's argument. In the end it is the paraphrase that matters. The paraphrase is the measure of the degree to which we have succeeded in achieving the goal of argument analysis. We will return to paraphrasing in Chapter 5.

ELEMENTARY PROCEDURES

People who have a great deal of practice and experience with arguments and argumentation can often go straight to paraphrasing, and they can do this accurately and intuitively—that is, without resort to any other procedures. When we are just beginning the study of arguments, though, and our intuitions are not grounded in extensive experience and practice, additional techniques and procedures may be not only useful but also essential in establishing a firm footing in argument analysis.

CIRCLING AND HIGHLIGHTING

Let us begin with three simple procedures introduced in Chapter 3. When we recognize that an argument exists, a useful first step is to scan the passage for signal words and circle any that we find, as, for example, in the following passage:

Canadians wait too long for access to many public health care services, (because) such services tend to be overly bureaucratized. Some degree of medical privatization would help the problem, (because) privatization gives vendors a heightened motivation to increase efficiency. (Therefore,) Canada should take immediate steps to introduce two-tiered health care.

The second step is to identify the argument's conclusion and highlight it, as follows:

EXERCISE 4.1 | **Highlighting**

You do the highlighting. We will show you WHERE.

Canadians wait too long for access to many public health care services, (because) such services tend to be overly bureaucratized. Some degree of medical privatization would help the problem, (because) privatization gives vendors a heightened motivation to increase efficiency. (Therefore,) CANADA SHOULD TAKE IMMEDIATE STEPS TO INTRODUCE TWO-TIERED HEALTH CARE.

The third step is to challenge the argument's conclusion, in effect asking *why* we should accept it as true. We will then find that wherever the passage responds directly to this question, premises exist, which we could highlight in a new colour to distinguish these premises clearly from the argument's conclusion, as follows:

EXERCISE 4.2 | **Highlighting**

You do the highlighting. We will show you **where.**

Canadians wait too long for access to many public health care services, (because) such services tend to be overly bureaucratized. **Some degree of medical privatization would help the problem,** (because) privatization gives vendors a heightened motivation to increase efficiency. (Therefore,) CANADA SHOULD TAKE IMMEDIATE STEPS TO INTRODUCE TWO-TIERED HEALTH CARE.

We may discover deeper layers of support by repeating the third step. We now challenge the argument's premises highlighted above, asking why we should accept *them* as true. We will then find that wherever the passage responds directly to *this* question, further premises exist, which we could highlight in a new colour to distinguish them clearly from the claims that they support, as follows:

EXERCISE 4.3 | **Highlighting**

You do the highlighting. We'll show you *where.*

Canadians wait too long for access to many public health care services, (because) *such services tend to be overly bureaucratized.* **Some degree of medical privatization would help the problem,** (because) *privatization gives vendors a heightened motivation to increase efficiency.* (Therefore,) CANADA SHOULD TAKE IMMEDIATE STEPS TO INTRODUCE TWO-TIERED HEALTH CARE.

Circle the signal words, highlight the premises, and indicate the conclusions in the following examples:

(a) Since it is only a matter of time before Canada's submarine fleet becomes obsolete, and since the funds that would be used to develop this technology are sorely needed to reform health care, now is not the time to invest in a new submarine fleet.

(b) The history of technology shows that all technology eventually becomes surpassed and outmoded. Therefore, it is only a matter of time before Canada's submarine fleet becomes obsolete, and since the funds that would be used to develop this technology are sorely needed to reform health care, now is not the time to invest in a new submarine fleet.

(c) A new submarine fleet is necessary for national defence in this age of possible terrorist infiltration by sea. After all, any defence system that relies just on surface detection raises the risk of terrorist infiltration by sea, and this is not a realistic option in today's world. A new submarine fleet is the only option yet proposed that does not rely on plain sight detection.

MAPPING

Many people find it helpful to visualize argument structure. One of the simplest ways of visualizing argument structure is through spatial relationships. This approach to conceptualizing arguments is similar to the graphic techniques that some students use to make notes. In the next section, we will introduce a fully detailed formal scheme for mapping arguments. By using only two dimensions (easiest to handle on a sheet of paper), and using the above example, we can arrange the claims in the argument to reflect the hierarchy and structure of the relationships of support as so:

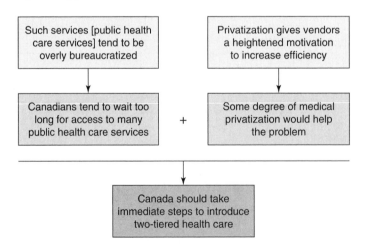

The conclusion appears at the bottom of the diagram, supported by two main premises (the ones closest to the conclusion), each of which is supported in turn by a further contributing premise. Note that the main premises "Canadians tend to wait too long for access to many public health care services" and "Some degree of medical privatization would help the problem" are linked by an addition (+) symbol: They are logically dependent premises that simply *must* be taken together if the intended conclusion is to make sense. Just one or the other would not get us to the conclusion as stated. Not all premises are dependent or linked. Some are independent: They support other propositions individually, not collectively. For example, the premises that support or contribute to the two main premises are not linked with any other propositions. Whether a premise can stand on its own in support of another proposition or whether it must be taken in conjunction with other elements depends on the case in question.

A system like this could be easily expanded to represent deeper and more elaborate argument analysis. In this same example in Chapter 3, we noted that additional claims were presupposed and implied within the argument. The claim that public health care services tend to be overly bureaucratized presupposes that they usually involve many organizational channels and restrictions. In addition, the claim that privatization gives vendors a heightened motivation to increase efficiency depends upon the idea that people tend to act more effectively when their own money is immediately at stake. These hidden elements might be represented in the following diagram:

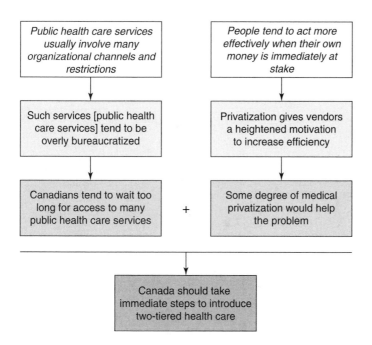

The use of *italics* sets apart these new elements as implied or hidden in the original passage. Getting clear about the structure of reasoning, including any implicit elements, is crucial to the further step of evaluation.

CASTING

A graphic system for representing argument structure should do what an organizational flow chart does for understanding any complex system. Ideally, the graphic system should be capable of representing an indefinitely large number of elements (or claims, in the case of arguments) and an indefinitely large number of relevant relationships between them. Notice in the two diagrams above how the complexity of the graphic system of representation grows with the complexity of the analysis. A great deal can be done with colours, shapes, typefaces, symbols, arrows, and two spatial dimensions, but we also want a system that is simple enough to learn and re-member and that applies to the types of material—such as newspaper stories and magazine articles—we are likely to encounter in our everyday lives. To this end we now present a simplified variation on the above mapping system—a system we will call "casting." The casting system follows essentially the same steps as used earlier in mapping the argument (see the accompanying figure). The claims that constitute the argument are isolated and marked for identification and then arranged in two-dimensional space to reflect the relationships of support among them.

Tip: Try using 7.6 cm × 12.7 cm (3" × 5") cue cards to puzzle out your casting diagrams. They offer great flexibility.

Here is a basic illustration:

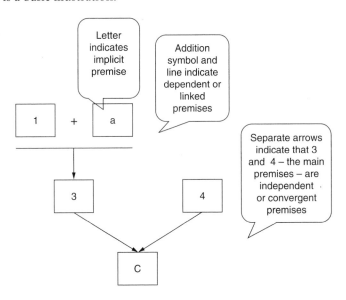

Using the above example, the casting system works as follows (see the accompanying figure and compare the earlier figure on page 98):

[(1) Canadians wait too long for access to many public health care services], (because) [(2) such services tend to be overly bureaucratized]. [(3) Some degree of medical privatization would help the problem], (because) [(4) privatization gives vendors a heightened moti-vation to increase efficiency]. (Therefore,) [(C) Canada should take immediate steps to in-troduce two-tiered health care.]

TABLE 4.1   Casting Checklist

❏ **Identify the elements of the reasoning**

- Count as claims only material that belongs to the logical substance of the passage. You should disregard extraneous material.

- Put brackets at the beginning and end of each claim.

- Number the claims consecutively in their order of appearance in the passage. You should, however, label the overall conclusion as C to distinguish clearly the thesis or upshot of the reasoning from the contributing elements. A conclusion can be implied, in which case you should use the convention C*.

❏ **Create a diagram that shows the structural relations among the elements**

- The *conclusion,* or overall point, should appear alone at the very bottom of the diagram on its own level.

- *Main premises* appear on the level that is closest to the conclusion (that is, on the second lowest level).

- *Supporting premises* appear on various levels (as appropriate) above the main premises.

- Main premises that are supported by other premises are *internal conclusions* within the larger inference. (Not all main premises have supporting premises.)

- Each claim may appear only once.

❏ **Distinguish explicit and implicit premises**

- Use numbers to indicate *explicit premises:* those stated openly by the writer or speaker.

- You should use letters to indicate *implicit premises* (hidden or unstated elements, in other words) that you include because you believe the writer's or speaker's reasoning relies on such ideas. When you point out an assumption you should do so with an eye to some type of textual "anchor" or indication; otherwise, you run the risk of making an uncharitable attribution.

❏ **Distinguish dependent and independent premises**

- *Dependent* or *linked* premises are propositions that must be taken together to generate the intended conclusion of the inferential movement. Their relation is indicated by an addition symbol (+), as well as a line underneath the dependent premises.

- *Independent* or *convergent* premises are propositions that do not need to be taken together in this respect. Note that a practical reality holds sway here: A dependent or linked premise that is problematic affects the evaluation of all associated premises, while independent or convergent premises do not generate this type of effect.

❏ **Follow good technical protocols**

- Use arrows that point downward to indicate inferential movement. You should always read such arrows as having this form: "x is the case; therefore, y is the case."

- An arrow may point to one and only one conclusion (whether the overall conclusion or an internal conclusion).

- A premise or premise group does not generate normally more than one (overall or internal) conclusion. If you find yourself drawing more than one conclusion, you are most likely wrong and should rethink this aspect of your casting diagram.

- A proper casting diagram key or legend—a list or itemization of all claims in the diagram—must always accompany a complex diagram.

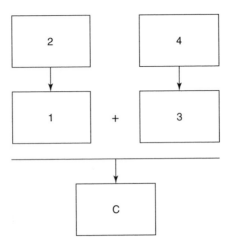

The system can be extended to represent hidden or unstated elements within the argument. To keep this distinction clear (the one between explicit and implicit claims of the argument), we could use letters instead of numbers to represent hidden or unstated elements. Using the same example, the casting would look like this (see the accompanying figure and compare the figure on page 99):

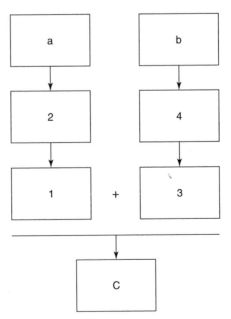

Here the letter "a" represents the claim that public health care services usually involve many organizational channels and restrictions, and the letter "b" represents the claim that people tend to act more effectively when their own money is immediately at stake, as explained above. Implied but unstated conclusions can be handled in a similar way. For example, this argument from *Julius Caesar*

["Yond Cassius has a lean and hungry look . . . (1)] [Such men are dangerous." (2)]

leads obviously to the unstated conclusion: "Cassius is dangerous." We may represent it as a crucial element in the argument by assigning it the convention C*:

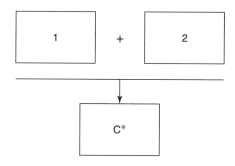

EXERCISE 4.5 | **Basic Casting**

Complete the castings of the following arguments.

(Since) [(1) it is only a matter of time before Canada's submarine fleet becomes obsolete], and (since) [(2) the funds that would be used to develop this technology are sorely needed to reform health care], [(C) now is not the time to invest in a new submarine fleet.]

[(1) The history of technology shows that all technology eventually becomes surpassed and outmoded]. (Therefore,) [(2) it is only a matter of time before Canada's submarine fleet becomes obsolete], and (since) [(3) the funds that would be used to develop this technology are sorely needed to reform health care], [(C) now is not the time to invest in a new submarine fleet.]

[(C) A new submarine fleet is necessary for national defence in this age of possible terrorist infiltration by sea]. (After all,) [(1) any defence system that relies just on surface detection raises the risk of terrorist infiltration by sea], (3) and [(2) this is not a realistic option in today's world]. (3) [A new submarine fleet is the only option yet proposed that does not rely on plain sight detection.]

Although the complexity and variety of arguments you may chance to encounter is practically endless, you can do quite a bit to orient yourself to the argument by using just the few simple tools outlined above (see the accompanying figure). It is important not to confuse the grammatical structure of a passage in a composition with the structure of the argument it conveys. In some cases, with carefully and clearly written passages of argumentation, the grammar and the structure of the argument may coincide. The author may construct the passage so that the grammar can be used as a guide to the argument—but in many cases the author does not. What matters most for argument analysis is not the grammar of the composition but what supports what. Here is a general rule of thumb: Break down a grammatical unit when and only when different parts of the grammatical unit play separate and distinct roles in the argument when it comes to support relationships. By the same token, disregard grammatically distinct repetitions of the same claim.

Finally, remember to stay focused on the argument. In many cases the composition you are analyzing will contain material that is extraneous to the argument: tangential asides, background information, entertaining embellishments, rhetorical flourishes, and so on. Occasionally we may encounter passages in which the author draws and defends a conclusion while at the same time conceding a point to the opposition. Such "concession claims" may be germane to the discussion, and they may make a "diplomatic" contribution to the reception of the author's thesis, though they do not by themselves lend support to it. Here is another general rule of thumb: Be thorough but stay relevant. If you think you understand and can explain the distinct contribution a given claim makes to the argument, include it in your analysis. Otherwise, leave it out. Here is a brief example of a concession claim:

> Lowering the GST will be a good thing for Canadians. It's true that lowering the tax will decrease government revenues, but the increase in spending and business expansion that will flow from such a tax cut will exceed any decrease.

We can account for the concession claim diagrammatically in the following way:

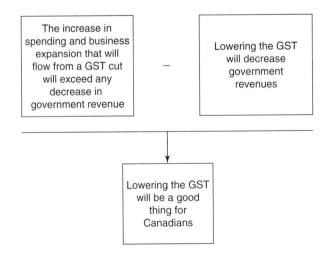

As you can see, the arguer intends the conclusion to follow "on balance" from the two premises. The conclusion is the net result of considering both the positive (supporting) premise and the negative (concession) premise (signalled by a minus sign [−] to the left of the concession premise). You might wonder why anyone would ever make concession claims, as they obviously count against the truth of the conclusion. The answer is simple: Making concession claims can strengthen an argument by showing that the arguer has taken into account major concerns whatever their import, and that the arguer's claim is still reasonable despite some contrary indications. In addition, making concession claims right at the outset of a debate can take the wind out of an opponent's sails by anticipating likely objections, so this can be an especially effective way of gaining dialectical and rhetorical advantage.

EXERCISE 4.6 | Circling and Basic Casting

Practice is the best way to build and hone your skills in this area. Use the circling, highlighting, and casting system outlined above on the following examples.

1. That cell phone we looked at yesterday stores a half-hour's worth of messages, as opposed to this one's 20 minutes. It also has better automated dialing features than this one; and this one's $30 more expensive. I think we should get that other one.

2. A university education makes you aware of interests you didn't know you had. This helps you choose a satisfying job. Job satisfaction is itself your best assurance of personal well-being. Certainly, personal well-being is a goal worth pursuing. Therefore, a university education is a worthy goal.

3. Capital punishment should not be permitted because it in fact involves killing human beings, and killing human beings should never be permitted by society.

4. Because the killing of human beings should never be permitted by society, capital punishment should not be permitted; for it in fact involves killing human beings.

5. Most marriages between people under 20 end in divorce. This should be enough to discourage teenage marriages. But there is also the fact that marrying young reduces one's life options. Married teenagers must forget about adventure and play. They can't afford to spend time "finding themselves." They must concentrate almost exclusively on earning a living. What's more, early marriages can make parents out of young people, who can hardly take care of themselves, let alone an infant.

6. "Suicide no longer repels us. The suicide rate is climbing, ... What's more, suicide has been appearing in an increasingly favorable light in the nation's press. When we surveyed all articles on suicide indexed over the past 50 years in the *Reader's Guide to Periodical Literature,* we found that voluntary deaths . . . generally appear in a neutral light. Some recent articles even present suicide as a good thing to do. . . . They are written in a manner that might encourage the reader to take his own life under certain circumstances. . . ."[1]

7. We must stop treating juveniles differently from adult offenders. Justice demands it. Justice implies that people should be treated equally. Besides, the social effects of pampering juvenile offenders

have sinister social consequences. The record shows that juveniles who have been treated leniently for offences have subsequently committed serious crimes.

8. More and more silent evidence is being turned into loudly damning testimony. Over the past ten years, no area has developed faster than the examination of blood stains. Before we used to be satisfied with identifying a blood sample as type A, B, AB, or O. Now we have three or more different antigen and enzyme systems. The probability that any two people will share the same assessment of their blood variables is 0.1% or less. The size, shape, and distribution of blood spatters tell much about the location and position of a person involved in a crime. The use of bite-mark evidence has skyrocketed. Even anthropology is making a courtroom contribution. Some anthropologists can identify barefoot prints as well as match a shoe to its wearer.[2]

9. Capital punishment does ensure that a killer can never strike again. But it involves killing human beings, and the killing of human beings should never be allowed. Therefore, capital punishment should not be permitted.

10. A university education increases your earning potential. In addition, it makes you aware of interests you didn't know you had. Most important, it teaches one the inherent value of knowledge. It is true, of course, that a university education is expensive. Nevertheless, a university education will be worth every penny it costs.

INTERMEDIATE CHALLENGES

Ever since the beginning of this book we have noticed that we must often account for hidden claims in argument analysis. Critical Thinking Tip 1.1 was to Be Aware of Assumptions, especially "between" and "underneath" claims presented persuasively in arguments. We have used several examples involving hidden claims in illustrating the tools of argument analysis presented earlier. In dealing with such hidden elements, the hard part is not the diagramming. It is not at all difficult to handle hidden claims in the mapping or casting systems presented above (just use letters instead of numbers). The hard part is figuring out *where* and *what* the hidden elements are. Sometimes people give almost open indications as to the assumptions upon which they rely in making their explicit claims; other times, we find that we must tease out assumptions to make sense of the reasoning, with little direction from the writer or speaker. Whenever we make explicit what we take to be implicit ideas, we must be as faithful as possible to what the writer or speaker appears to believe or intend.

This is not *always* hard. Sometimes it is quite obvious. Suppose someone says, "Do you trust your textbooks? I don't. I'm convinced they contain mistakes because they're written by human beings." Now look at the argument in this sentence:[3]

[I'm convinced they (textbooks) contain mistakes Ⓒ] [they're written by human beings. ①]

It should be obvious that a hidden premise exists in here, namely, "Human beings make mistakes," or something similar to that, represented by the letter "a" in the accompanying figure:

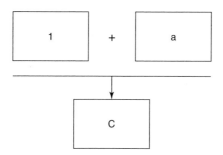

In an obvious case such as this one, the question of *just how* we figure this out does not arise, any more than the questions of where and what the hidden premise is. All this is just "obvious." The problem is that such matters are not *always* obvious. In fact, as one would expect, typically it is not at all obvious where or what the hidden claims in an argument might be, for the simple—and obvious—reason that they are hidden.

Suppose you and a friend are solving a puzzle in which you are supposed to match the names and brief biographies of 20 people from a set of clues, and your friend says, "Pat must be a man because here in the fifth clue it says that Pat is Jason's *father*." You can see right away from the claim—that Pat is Jason's father—that Pat must be a man, but this conclusion does not follow from the claim that Pat is Jason's father *alone*. It also depends on the fact that (by definition) a father is a male parent, and the claim that a parent is presumably an adult, and the fact that (again by definition) a man is an adult human male.

Ordinarily it is not necessary to spell out these three claims explicitly as premises to appreciate fully the reasoning, any more than it is necessary to spell them out in the original presentation of the reasoning. In general, we go to the trouble of spelling out these hidden elements in the reasoning where the hidden or missing elements are both crucial *and controversial* and where they *bear on the evaluation of the argument*. It is important to go to this sort of trouble especially where there seems to be something *wrong* with a particular argument, for example: "You say textbooks don't contain mistakes? Here, I'll prove it to you that they do. My science book says that whales are mammals. But everybody knows that whales live in the sea, which is what a fish is, an animal that lives in the sea."[4] We will reconstruct this argument fragment shortly. For now, noting that the reasoning evidently has *some* weaknesses in it *somewhere* is sufficient. Spelling out all its elements, even the ones that are obvious, becomes useful when we attempt to pinpoint those weaknesses.

In the "real world of public discourse," arguments are often presented as sketches or fragments—what logicians traditionally refer to as *enthymemes*. This means that parts of the reasoning are left for readers or members of the audience to recognize on their own, guided by the context and logic of the argument. This is something that happens with great frequency in the media and in everyday conversation. Why is this? This happens for several reasons, some good, some not so good. Here is a good reason. Sometimes, as in the "human beings make mistakes" example, things are *so* obvious that spelling them out completely and explicitly is unnecessary, needlessly time-consuming, or even insulting to the intelligence of your audience. So we often leave things out of our presentation of the argument as a matter of economy or common courtesy. Sometimes people leave things out because they are not completely aware of all of the assumptions on which their reasoning depends. Sometimes there is even an attempt to gloss over elements in an argument whose maker would just as soon we not notice or consider carefully. In any case, since this is something that happens with great frequency in the real world of public discourse, it is well worth focusing on the question of just how we figure out where and what the hidden claims in an argument may be.

It is worth reminding ourselves what we are up to here. When we reconstruct argument fragments, we are trying to make sense of what people say (and *do not* say). Imagine that you are waiting to be seated at a busy beachfront restaurant immediately behind an attractive couple who happen to be barefoot. The server looks at the barefoot couple, says not one word but points to a sign that reads "No shirt, no shoes, no service." In this context it is reasonable to understand the server's gesture as a justification for refusing to seat the couple. In other words, it functions as an argument in support of his refusal to seat them. So, if we were casting the argument, we might represent his refusal to seat the barefoot couple by assigning it the convention C*. So far, the argument looks like this:

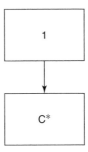

where "1" stands for "If you are not wearing a shirt and shoes, you will be refused service" (what the sign means); and where "C*" stands for "you are being refused service" (addressed to the barefoot couple). An unstated premise exists as well; namely, that the couple are not wearing shoes. You can easily understand why it is not stated: Again, this is because it is obvious—especially, we may presume, to the couple. If we want our casting to reflect this as a part of the justification for the refusal of service (which it obviously is), we assign it the letter "a." So the fully analyzed argument looks like this:

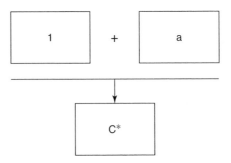

where "a" stands for "you are not wearing shoes" (addressed to the barefoot couple). The server says not one word, but the *context and the inner logic of the argument itself help us to make sense* of his gesture as a meaningful one and to grasp its meaning as an argument. So now let us return to our obvious example. How do we know that the hidden claim is "Human beings make mistakes" and not something different, such as "Elephants make mistakes," or something completely different, such as "Cycling is a great way to meet other single people"? You could say, "We know that 'Human beings make mistakes' is the hidden claim because it's the one that makes the most sense of what the arguer *did* say."

EXERCISE 4.7 | Casting Hidden Claims

Formulate the missing elements and complete the casting for each of the following arguments. Pay close attention to your own reasoning as you work through each of these examples. See if you can feel the "force of logic" at work.

I'm sorry, but [you may stay in the country only if you have a current visa;①] [your visa has expired.②]	**Casting**
Hidden Claim(s)	
[God has all the virtues, ①] (so) [God must have benevolence.②]	**Casting**
Hidden Claim(s)	
[Either the battery in the remote control is dead or the set's unplugged,①] but [the set is plugged in.②]	**Casting**
Hidden Claim(s)	
[All species of mammal suckle their young,①] and [all primates are mammals,②] and [orangutans are primates.③]	**Casting**
Hidden Claim(s)	

So far the examples are all relatively "obvious," but many cases are much more difficult. Frequently, *several different ways* of "making sense" of what someone says exist. Then, too, sometimes what people say just does not make much sense. It is not always possible to know, with certainty, which of several different statements should be cast in the role of missing premises, or whether one should be bothering to look for missing premises at all. The "bad news" is that no simple algorithm exists for making sense of what people say. Instead, making sense of discourse involves the discretionary application of multiple criteria that sometimes conflict with one another. Hence, this process tends to yield multiple solutions, each with advantages and disadvantages. The most one can expect by way of systematic guidance to this sort of process is to have a set of guidelines—rules of thumb, as we will continue to present here. The "good news" is that you already know how to do this sort of interpretive work, at least in obvious cases like those discussed already. As you work with these guidelines, building experience and cultivating sensitivity and judgment—keeping in mind that you may expect to find exceptions to any rule of thumb—you will get even better at it.

Our interest in making sense of what people say by reconstructing their arguments from fragments ultimately concerns assessing the merits of these arguments as reasoning. Ultimately what we want to know is how good or bad the argument is, because we are trying to determine how much sway to give the argument in our own deliberations and decision making. What this means in common-sense terms is that we want as complete and as fair a rendition of the argument as we can determine.

COMPLETENESS

We return once again to our obvious example (see the figure on page 105). The argument as originally stated was, "I'm convinced textbooks contain mistakes because they're written by human beings." Now let us consider how we know that an unstated premise exists in the argument in the first place. In other words, how do we know that the original statement of the argument is not complete? Just focus on the premise for a moment: "Textbooks are written by human beings." True enough, but *from this claim alone* the conclusion "Textbooks contain mistakes" does not follow. If it is clear that the conclusion does not follow from the premise (or more precisely from the totality of the premises) explicitly presented in the argument, then we should be on the lookout for hidden premises. When we say "does not follow," we are using an important and fundamental concept of logic—the concept of deductive validity (which we will discuss more thoroughly in Chapter 6). For the time being, let us understand deductive validity to mean simply that even if the premise is true, the conclusion could still be false.

When we identify an argument as an enthymeme—when we determine, in other words, that its conclusion does not follow from its explicitly stated premises alone—we in effect sense a gap or hole in it. We can be more specific than this. The hole has a more or less definite shape that we can discern, to some extent at least, by paying close attention to what surrounds it—to the argument's conclusion and explicit

---

EXERCISE 4.8 | Does It Follow?

For each pair of claims, suppose that the first claim is true, then determine whether the second one "follows."

Follows	Prisons do not rehabilitate anyone.
Does not follow	Prisons are ineffective as punishment for criminal behaviour.

Follows	Japan must become energy-independent.
Does not follow	Japan should develop solar energy on a widespread basis.

Follows	Abortion involves the taking of a human life.
Does not follow	Abortion should never be encouraged.

Follows	There are 35 students registered in this class.
Does not follow	At least 30 students are registered in this class.

Follows	God is perfect.
Does not follow	Therefore, God is good.

Follows	Everything with any commercial potential eventually gets absorbed into the corporate
Does not follow	world, so the Internet will eventually get absorbed into the corporate world.

Follows	People who were born at exactly the same time often have vastly different life
Does not follow	histories and personalities. Therefore, astrology is not a reliable predictive system.

---

premise(s). Think of this as similar to searching for a missing piece in a jigsaw puzzle. You study closely the shapes and colours of the pieces that surround the one for which you're searching. This helps you find the missing piece. When the puzzle is an incompletely stated argument and what we seek is a missing premise, we can guide ourselves by paying close attention to what the conclusion and explicit premise(s) of the argument are "about." This helps us get a better sense of the "shape" of the hole or gap we are trying to fill, and also of the missing premise that can fill it. This is *heuristics*, generally construed: the process of trying to develop solutions by way of "thought experiments." So, in the example we have been discussing, the conclusion is about textbooks and things that contain mistakes, while the premise is about textbooks and things written by human beings. What we seek is something that will "complete this circle of relationships." What we should seek, then, is a claim that makes some sort of connection between things written by human beings and things that contain mistakes.

EXERCISE 4.9 | **Completing the Argument**

Complete the following arguments, using all and only the words from the following list:
benevolence, depends, develop, effective, fails, homicide, never, unless, virtues, why

1. God has all the virtues. And _____ is one of the _____. So God must have benevolence.

2. Abortion involves the taking of a human life. And that's _____, and you would _____ encourage homicide, would you? So, abortion should not ever be encouraged.

3. Prisons do not rehabilitate anyone. No criminal penalty that _____ to rehabilitate can be _____. That's _____ prisons are ineffective as punishment for criminal behaviour.

4. Japan must become energy-independent. _____ Japan develops solar energy on a widespread basis, its survival _____ on increasingly scarce and expensive petrochemical energy. That's why Japan should _____ solar energy on a widespread basis.

FAIRNESS

We assume that anyone reading this book has a "sense of fairness." If we all have an intuitive sense of fairness, though, we also all know how easy it is to fall into dispute over—and how difficult it can be to resolve—*issues* of fairness. A common-sense rule of thumb in applying the concept of fairness in pursuit of the truth would be "when in doubt, don't be *unfair*."

CRITICAL THINKING TIP 4.1

When in doubt, don't be Unfair.

What does this rule of thumb mean in practice? Remember that argument analysis is a means to the end of determining how good or bad the argument is. In practice, then, the general rule of thumb, "When in doubt, don't be *unfair*," means that in analyzing a given argument, we should *try to avoid discrediting* the argument. When we have two or more otherwise equally reasonable competing interpretations (or two or more interpretations that are not equally reasonable!), we should subscribe to the one that does the argument the most credit. In other words, as indicated above, we should favour the interpretation that *makes the most sense of* what the arguer did say.

As applied to argument analysis, the first consideration regarding fairness would be *accuracy*. Analysis is a form of interpretation. Whenever we "complete" an argument by attributing an unstated claim to it, we are interpreting the "text" of the argument, and in so doing we go beyond what the "text" of the argument actually says. "Text" means the retrievable record of what was said. With written arguments we do not *generally* have the convenient opportunity to question the author if we think hidden elements exist in the argument. We have only—or primarily—the text of the argument to consult. In oral contexts, when we listen to someone present an argument, the opportunity for questioning the person is often available. Even so, as we already pointed out, people are not always fully aware of all the assumptions they make, and they may on occasion even exhibit an unwillingness to learn or to admit that some particular claim is assumed or implied within a given argument or position. So again, we fall back on the text. In assessing the accuracy of the analysis of an argument, remember from Chapter 2 that we are entitled to assume a conventional understanding of the words in the text of an argument. We may also use logic (as we will explain further in Chapter 6) as a guide to our analysis. Of course, all this is governed by the general rule of thumb: "When in doubt, don't be *un*fair."

Here is a short example that offers a pronounced interpretive difference so you can see the point clearly. "Many problems result from lack of self-knowledge. Therefore, know yourself." We could interpret "Know yourself" to mean, "Know yourself fully in every conceivable respect," or "Know yourself better (to some appreciable degree)." In the second interpretation, the claim is sensible enough and the result is achievable in principle (for most people), whereas the first interpretation yields a claim that is awfully demanding and probably impractical. (For example, trying to know oneself fully in every conceivable respect by way of Freudianism might take literally years of psychotherapy and would be fraught with a relentless string of serious challenges—assuming that one could even get to the bottom.) Indeed, the arguer may intend the first interpretation, but this is unlikely, given the strong nature of the formulation. Unless we have a compelling reason to think that the arguer intends the first interpretation, we should follow the second interpretation, which gives the argument more credit. Following the first interpretation would lead us inevitably to criticize the central idea here as substantially problematic, but if we cannot be sure that the arguer intends it, we ought to be charitable and follow the more modest formulation. Note that charity also does not mean making a piece of reasoning better despite its flaws. Being fair as a critical thinker means simply trying to develop an accurate understanding of what the arguer is doing by (in part) avoiding misattributions and distortions, whether negative or positive.

PLAUSIBILITY

For example, when formulating a hidden claim, we should favour the most "plausible" of the available alternative formulations. "Plausibility" is a concept we will develop and apply more deeply and extensively in Chapter 7. The word *plausibility* literally means "deserving of applause," but it has a more precise technical meaning relating to credibility or believability. In technical terms plausibility is an estimate of a claim's power to survive close critical examination. If we were to devise strenuous tests designed to *falsify* a claim, how well would the claim survive such tests? A claim is "plausible" to the extent that we think it likely the claim would survive such tests. A claim is "implausible" to the extent that we think it unlikely the claim would survive such tests. Plausibility, in other words, is a *preliminary estimate* of a claim's truth value. Consider this example:

Since Ng is a police officer, he's probably in favour of gun control legislation.

Here, the conclusion, "Ng is probably in favour of gun control legislation," does not follow from the premise "Ng is a police officer" alone. To complete the inference, we need a claim that makes some sort of connection between being a police officer and favouring gun control legislation. A number of distinct alternatives emerge for the role of missing premise. Take, for example, these two alternatives:

1. All police officers favour gun control legislation.
2. Most police officers favour gun control legislation.

The first formulation is less plausible than the second one because the first formulation makes a stronger claim than the second one. The stronger a claim is, the harder it is to prove (and the more vulnerable it is to refutation). So we should favour the second alternative in reconstructing this argument.

EXERCISE 4.10 | Plausibility

Rank the plausibility of the following sets of claims. Compare your rankings with those of someone else in the class. Wherever your rankings conflict, explain your initial ranking. Compare notes and see whether your ranking is affected.

1. a. Some of the produce sold in the major supermarkets is irradiated.

   b. A lot of the produce sold in the major supermarkets is irradiated.

   c. Most of the produce sold in the major supermarkets is irradiated.

2. a. Tax evasion is a common practice.

   b. Everybody cheats on their taxes.

3. a. Cell phone usage is on the rise.

   b. The cell phone industry is growing at the rate of 65.89% a month.

4. a. It is probable that the al-Qaeda terrorist movement is still actively planning further attacks.

   b. It is possible that the al-Qaeda terrorist movement is still actively planning further attacks.

   c. It is certain that the al-Qaeda terrorist movement is still actively planning further attacks.

5. a. Intelligent life exists in outer space.

   b. Some nonhuman animals have the capacity for language.

6. a. The increasing sophistication of technology increases the risk of unwarranted invasions of privacy.

   b. The perfection of a restrained system of high-tech government surveillance of citizens is feasible.

7. a. Some of the radical anarchists from the 1960s are still alive.

   b. Some of the radical anarchists from the 1960s presently hold high office in Ottawa.

8. a. Adult human beings generally use less than 10% of the capacity of their minds.

   b. The universe is finite.

Now let us put this all together and apply it to the example mentioned earlier:

You say textbooks don't contain mistakes? Here, I'll prove it to you that they do. My science book says that whales are mammals. But everybody knows that whales live in the sea, which is what a fish is, an animal that lives in the sea.

Let us begin by numbering the claims, for our casting:

[You say textbooks don't contain mistakes? Here, I'll prove it to you that they do. (C)] [My science book says that whales are mammals. (1)] But everybody knows that [whales live in the sea, (2)] which is what [a fish is, an animal that lives in the sea. (3)]

Notice that we have bracketed the first two sentences as the conclusion. This is an example of grammatical structure and logical structure diverging from each other. The first two sentences evidently express the conclusion, and we can easily capture it in a single sentence: "Textbooks contain mistakes." You may also have noticed that we ignored the (bad) grammar of the sentence in bracketing claim #3. Claim #3 really needs to be reworded, however, to reflect accurately the argument. What the arguer is evidently trying to say is "Any animal that lives in the sea is a fish." This, at any rate, is how we would paraphrase the conclusion. Claim #1 is offered as direct support for the conclusion. What about claims #2 and #3, though? They both seem intended to contribute support for the conclusion, but the support is not direct. As well, some missing links seem to be involved. Nonetheless, a preliminary casting of these relationships might be helpful at this stage.

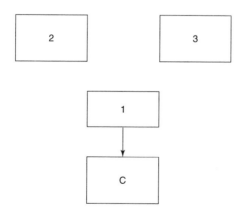

Suppose it is true that the arguer's science book says that whales are mammals (claim #1). The conclusion that textbooks contain mistakes would not follow from that alone. What claim would complete the inference from this premise to the conclusion? One additional implied claim is that the arguer's science book is a textbook. A second additional implied claim is that the statement that whales are mammals is mistaken, or simply "Whales aren't mammals." The first of these claims is pretty obvious and also pretty obviously part of the arguer's position. The second is implausible—indeed false—but it *must be* part of the arguer's position, as we can see quite clearly from claims #2 and #3, which are offered in support of it. So, in spite of the falsity of the claim that whales are not mammals, it is *not* un*fair to attribute it to the argument. So let us assign the letter "a" to the first and the letter "b" to the second of these hidden claims.

"a" = "My science book is a textbook."
"b" = "Whales aren't mammals."

We can now cast the result as follows:

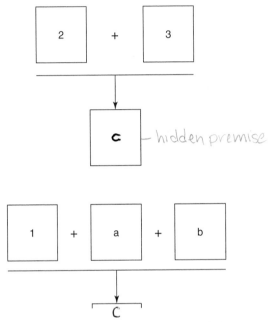

Now let us consider the relationship between claims #2 and #3 and "b." Suppose it is true that whales live in the sea (claim #2) and that any animal that lives in the sea is a fish (claim #3). It would not follow from these two claims alone that whales are not mammals. What would follow from these two claims alone is the claim that whales are fish. From this claim alone, however, the claim that whales are not mammals still would not follow. If, however, we add the claim that no fish are mammals, which is highly plausible—indeed true by definition—and again obviously part of the arguer's position, then the argument is complete. So let us assign the letter "c" to the claim that whales are fish and the letter "d" to the claim that no fish are mammals.

"c" = "Whales are fish."
"d" = "No fish are mammals."

Now we can complete the casting:

In this case, the analysis of the argument enables us to pinpoint precisely the argument's weakness: claim #3. Everything else in the argument is either true, presumably true, or logically derived from what is offered in its support.

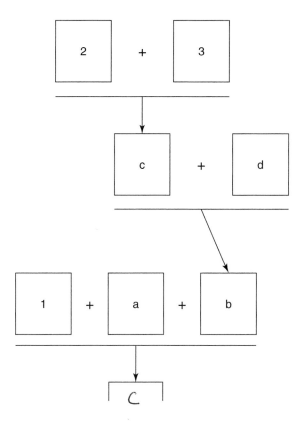

EXERCISE 4.11 | Reconstructing Missing Premises

Select the best reconstruction of the missing premise from the alternatives offered for each of the following enthymemes:

Everything with any commercial potential eventually gets absorbed into the corporate world, so the Internet will eventually get absorbed into the corporate world.	Corporations have the power to absorb any business assets they desire.
	Corporations are inherently profit oriented, and so are naturally drawn to anything with commercial potential.
	The Internet has commercial potential.

Some of these people can't be golfers. They're not carrying clubs.	Some golfers are carrying clubs.
	Everyone carrying clubs is a golfer.
	All golfers carry clubs.

If capital punishment isn't a deterrent to crime, then why has the rate of violent crime increased since capital punishment was outlawed?		Because the rate of violent crime has increased since capital punishment was outlawed, it must be a deterrent.
		An increase in the rate of crime following the abolition of a punishment proves that the punishment is a deterrent.
		An increase in the rate of crime following the abolition of a punishment is evidence that the punishment is a deterrent.

"I feel that since we are doing a science fiction show, morals don't enter into it—because none of it is true." —X-Files director Kim Manners		All science fiction is immoral.
		All science fiction is false.
		Morals do not enter into fictional worlds.

Add naught to MacNaughton—because you don't dilute a great Canadian whisky.		MacNaughton is a great Canadian whisky.
		Adding something to a great Canadian whisky would dilute it.
		MacNaughton is a great Canadian whisky, and adding something would dilute it.

"Murphy's law of [computer] programming states that no nontrivial program is free of bugs. A corollary states that any program with more than 10 lines is by definition nontrivial. The bottom line—your program will have bugs."[5]		Any computer program with 10 lines or less is trivial.
		Your computer program is nontrivial.
		Your computer program has more than 10 lines.

People who were born at exactly the same time often have vastly different life histories and personalities. Therefore, astrology is not a reliable predictive system.		People who believe in astrology are superstitious.
		Astrology predicts that people born at exactly the same time would not have vastly different life histories and personalities.
		No two people are born at exactly the same time.

Since no human system of justice is infallible and capital punishment imposes an irreversible penalty, capital punishment is an unacceptable form of punishment.	If we could perfect our system of justice so that all and only guilty people got convicted, then capital punishment would be acceptable.
	No irreversible penalty is acceptable as a form of punishment in a fallible system of justice.
	You can let a person out of prison if the person turns out to be innocent, but you can't bring a person back to life.

Just as we did with Chapter 3, we close this chapter on basic tools and techniques of argument analysis with a few more examples to practise on. Do your best to analyze the arguments contained in the passages assembled below, using any or all of the techniques of argument analysis presented in Chapters 3 and 4. As you work, especially with the more lengthy and complex passages, do not be surprised or discouraged if you find that the casting becomes as hard to construct and grasp as the passage itself. Keep the goal of argument analysis in mind—a fair and accurate understanding of the argument in detail. Also bear in mind that the best measure of success in achieving this goal is what we will work on in the next chapter—the paraphrase of the argument.

EXERCISE 4.12 | TERM PROJECT: ARGUMENT ANALYSIS

At the end of Chapter 3 (Exercise 3.14) you were instructed to research the issue articulated in your Issue Statement and to identify at least three extended arguments representing at least two distinct positions on the issue. Now in one of these three extended arguments locate and highlight the thesis (or conclusion). Next, locate and highlight the premises that support the thesis directly. Then locate and highlight the premises that support these main premises. Construct a casting of these elements of the argument.

ADDITIONAL EXERCISES

Do your best to analyze the arguments contained in the following passages, using any or all of the techniques of argument analysis presented in Chapters 3 and 4. Take note of any areas of difficulty you encounter. Then go on to Chapter 5.

▪ **Exercise 4.13** "Evolution is a scientific fairy-tale just as the 'flat earth theory' was in the 12th century. Evolution directly contradicts the Second Law of Thermodynamics, which states that unless an intelligent planner is directing a system, it will always go in the direction of disorder and deterioration. Evolution requires a faith that is incomprehensible!"[6]

Exercise 4.14   "Repeated attacks on the rising cost of postsecondary education have spawned a widespread view that high tuition fees constitute a barrier to entry for Canadians in lower-income brackets . . . . [A recent study shows that] [p]eople significantly overestimate the costs of a higher education and underestimate its benefits . . . . This misconception, coupled with cultural and class issues, appears to be much more of a barrier to education than the actual cost of tuition. Student groups have a vested interest in keeping tuition costs as low as possible. But as the results of this study show, their argument that current levels are an insuperable barrier for people in low-income brackets does not hold up to scrutiny. Fees have been rising, but not to unaffordable levels as critics have claimed."[7]

Exercise 4.15   "A scientific colleague of mine, who holds a professorial post in the department of sociology and anthropology at one of our leading universities, recently asked me about my stand on the question of human beings having sex relations without love. Although I have taken something of a position on this issue in my book, . . . I have never quite considered the problem in sufficient detail. So here goes. In general, I feel that affectional, as against non-affectional, sex relations are desirable. It is usually desirable that an association between coitus and affection exist—particularly in marriage, because it is often difficult for two individuals to keep finely tuned to each other over a period of years."[8]

Exercise 4.16   "The whole public discourse of Canada is one of rights—yours against mine, mine against governments, mine against all comers . . . . [What about responsibilities?] After all, rights are linked inherently to responsibilities . . . . Today, the ubiquitous 'rights talk' that so permeates public discourse and fills appeals to the courts reflects an increasingly pluralistic but also narcissistic society, in which self-affirmation, self-absorption and self-enrichment trump collective notions of what we owe each other . . . [We need] a Canadian political leader [who] will develop a narrative of responsibility, tease out its implications, frame it compellingly and say, as a U.S. President once did: Ask not what your country can do for you; ask what you can do for your country."[9]

Exercise 4.17   "To the extent that it is working at all, the press is always a participant in, rather than a pure observer of, the events it reports. Our decisions on where (and where not) to be and what (and what not) to report have enormous impact on the political and governmental life we cover. We are obliged to be selective. We cannot publish the Daily Everything. And so long as this is true—so long as we are making choices that 1) affect what people see concerning their leaders and 2) inevitably cause those leaders to behave in particular ways—we cannot pretend we are not participants."[10]

Exercise 4.18   "Scientists are human beings with their full complement of emotions and prejudices, and their emotions and prejudices often influence the way they do their science. This was first clearly brought out in a study by Professor Nicholas Pastore in 1949. In this study Professor Pastore showed that the scientist's political beliefs were highly correlated with what he believed about the roles played by nature and nurture in the development of the person. Those holding conservative political views strongly tended to believe in the power of genes over environment. Those subscribing to more liberal views tended to believe in the power of environment over genes. One distinguished scientist (who happened to be a teacher of mine) when young was a socialist and environmentalist, but toward middle age he became politically conservative and a firm believer in the supremacy of genes!"[11]

Exercise 4.19   "Many a reader will raise the question whether findings won by the observation of individuals can be applied to the psychological understanding of groups. Our answer to this question is an emphatic affirmation. Any group consists of individuals and nothing but individuals, and psychological mechanisms which we find operating in a group can therefore only be mechanisms that operate in individuals. In studying individual psychology as a basis for the understanding of social psychology, we do something which might be compared with studying an object under the microscope. This enables us to discover the very details of psychological mechanisms which we find operating on a large scale in the social process. If our analysis of socio-psychological phenomena is not based on the detailed study of human behavior, it lacks empirical character and, therefore, validity."[12]

Exercise 4.20   "Flextime (Flexible Working Hours) often makes workers more productive because being treated as responsible adults gives them greater commitment to their jobs. As a result it decreases absenteeism, sick leave, tardiness and overtime, and generally produces significant increases in productivity for the work group as a whole. For example, in trial periods in three different departments, the [government] measured productivity increases averaging about 20%. None has reported a decline."[13]

Exercise 4.21   "Government control of ideas or personal preferences is alien to a democracy. And the yearning to use governmental censorship of any kind is infectious. It may spread insidiously. Commencing with suppression of books as obscene, it is not unlikely to develop into official lust for the power of thought-control in the areas of religion, politics, and elsewhere. Milton observed that 'licensing of books . . . necessarily pulls along with it so many other kinds of licensing.' Mill notes that the 'bounds of what may be called moral police' may easily extend 'until it encroaches on the most unquestionably legitimate liberty of the individual.' We should beware of a recrudescence of the undemocratic doctrine uttered in the seventeenth century by Berkeley, Governor of Virginia: 'Thank God there are no free schools or preaching, for learning has brought disobedience into the world, and printing has divulged them. God keep us from both'."[14]

Exercise 4.22 "What, after all, is the foundation of the nurse's obligation to follow the physician's orders? Presumably, the nurse's obligation is to act in the medical interest of the patient. The point is that the nurse has an obligation to follow physician's orders because, ordinarily, patient welfare (interest) thereby is ensured. Thus when a nurse's obligation to follow a physician's order comes into direct conflict with the nurse's obligation to act in the medical interest of the patient, it would seem to follow that the patient's interests should always take precedence."[15]

Exercise 4.23 "[Our] institutions were fashioned in an era of vast unoccupied spaces and pre-industrial technology. In those days, collisions between public needs and individual rights may have been minimal. But increased density, scarcity of resources, and interlocking technologies have now heightened the concern for 'public goods,' which belong to no one in particular but to all of us jointly. Polluting a lake or river or the air may not directly damage any one person's private property or living space. But it destroys a good that all of us—including future generations—benefit from and have a title to. Our public goods are entitled to a measure of protection."[16]

Exercise 4.24 "These days music is truly global in sweep. The genie's out of the bottle, never to return, with MP3, Napster/Scour, and Freenet and Gnutella rendering all previous lines of demarcation meaningless. There's a revolution in progress, leveling everything in its path. Copyrights, masters, negatives, books, records, and films; it's all the same to a binary number, or a carbon atom and hydrogen qubit. Legislation, global police monitoring by knocking on two million doors—I don't think so. All I know is, you can't afford to make the customer your enemy. They no longer want to purchase a CD with ten or twelve songs on it to get the two they really want. They are also hip enough to know about artists' earnings and no longer want to pay the price for all the people in the middle of the distribution chain. These technological changes have provided an unexpected and highly efficient platform for rebellion for the current generation. We better get together and figure it out—and quickly!"[17]

Exercise 4.25 "In policy debates one party sometimes charges that his or her opponents are embracing a Nazi-like position . . . . Meanwhile, sympathizers nod in agreement with the charge, seeing it as the ultimate blow to their opponents . . . . The problem with using the Nazi analogy in public policy debates is that in the Western world there is a form of anti-Nazi 'bigotry' that sees Nazis as almost mythically evil beings . . . . Firsthand knowledge of our own culture makes it virtually impossible to equate Nazi society with our own. The official racism of Germany, its military mentality, the stresses of war, and the presence of a dictator instead of a democratic system make Nazi Germany in the 1940s obviously different . . . . "[18]

GLOSSARY

casting a graphic system for representing the structural relationships within an argument; or a graphic representation of a particular argument

enthymeme an unstated premise, or an inferential configuration involving an unstated premise

heuristics the process of trying to find solutions by way of "thought experiments"

main premises the premises offered as direct support for a thesis or conclusion

paraphrase a reformulation intended to capture the same meaning as the original statement

plausibility the credibility or believability of an idea that we estimate as likely to survive critical scrutiny

relevant related to the topic under discussion

thesis conclusion, especially of an extended argument

Go to http://www.criticalthinking1ce.nelson.com for additional study resources for this chapter.

ENDNOTES

[1] Elizabeth Hall and Paul Cameron, "Our Failing Reverence for Life," *Psychology Today,* April 1976, p. 108.

[2] Bennett H. Beach, "Mr. Wizard Comes to Court," *Time,* March 1, 1982, 90.

[3] Howard Kahane, *Logic and Contemporary Rhetoric,* 5th ed. (Belmont, CA: Wadsworth, 1997).

[4] Howard Kahane, *Logic and Contemporary Rhetoric,* 5th ed. (Belmont, CA: Wadsworth, 1997).

[5] Daniel Appleman, *How Computer Programming Works* (Emeryville, CA: Ziff-Davis Press, 1994).

[6] Dr. Edward Blic, *21 Scientists Who Believe in Creation* (Harrisonburg, VA: Christian Light Publications, 1977).

[7] Editorial, *Globe and Mail,* July 9, 2005, p. A18. Reprinted with permission from The Globe and Mail.

[8] Albert Ellis, *Sex Without Guilt* (New York: Lyle Stuart, Inc., 1966).

[9] Jeffrey Simpson, "Ask not what your country can do for you . . ." *Globe and Mail,* June 18, 2005, p. A17. Reprinted with permission from The Globe and Mail.

[10] Meg Greenfield, "When the Press Becomes a Participant," *The Washington Post Company, Annual Report,* 1984, 21.

[11] Ashley Montagu, *Sociobiology Examined* (Oxford: Oxford University Press, 1980), 4.

[12] Eric Fromm, *Escape From Freedom* (New York: Avon Books, 1965), 158.

[13] Barry Stein, et al., "Flextime," *Psychology Today,* June 1976, 43.

[14] Jerome Frank, dissenting opinion in *United States v. Roth,* 354 U.S. 476, 1957.

[15] E. Joy Kroeger Mappes, "Ethical Dilemmas for Nurses: Physicians' Orders versus Patients' Rights," in T. A. Mappes and J. S. Zembatty, eds., *Biomedical Ethics* (New York: McGraw-Hill, 1981), 100.

[16] Amitai Etzioni, "When Rights Collide," *Psychology Today,* October 1977.

[17] Quincy Jones, *Q: The Autobiography of Quincy Jones* (New York: Doubleday, 2000), 299.

[18] Gary E. Crum, "Disputed Territory," *Hastings Center Report,* August/September 1988, 31.

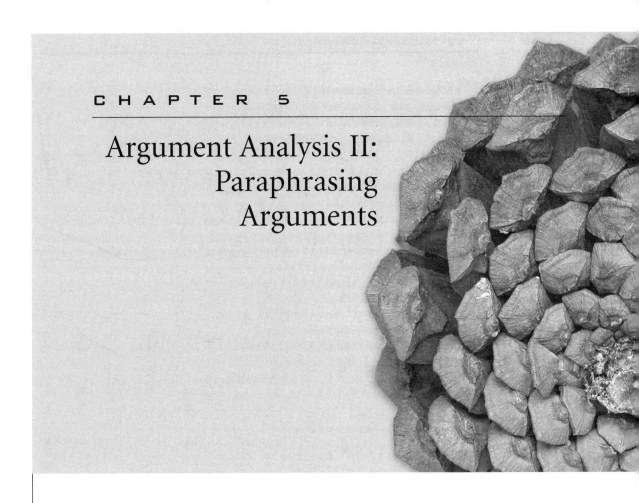

CHAPTER 5

Argument Analysis II: Paraphrasing Arguments

If you want to complain about Marilyn Manson, start from the beginning. Start with Shakespeare. What was *Romeo and Juliet* about? Suicide! OZZY OSBOURNE

In Chapter 4 we introduced the concept of *paraphrasing* as the best test of one's understanding of an argument. Paraphrasing means taking apart and then reassembling a text in your own words. This is both easier and harder than it sounds. We hope and expect that the simple tools, procedures, and guidance presented in Chapter 4 will prove to be useful in paraphrasing arguments, but you will soon see that paraphrasing arguments takes us beyond the simple and mechanical application of Chapter 4's tools and procedures. Let us begin by looking at paraphrasing in general and trying to explain the mysterious remark we just made about paraphrasing being both easier and harder than it sounds. Try the following exercise.

© The New Yorker Collection 1999 Richard Cline from cartoonbank.com. All Rights Reserved.

"Here it is—the plain, unvarnished truth. Varnish it."

Look at the text below. Imagine that it's a newspaper headline—the "joke" kind that we often see in comedy. Write out in a grammatically correct sentence what you think the "actual" (imaginary) news story might be.

NORTH KOREAN HEAD SEEKS ARMS

Complete this sentence: The "real story" is that . . .

_____

_____

_____

_____

_____

We imagine that most of you have easily come up with something like this: The "real story" is that the leader of North Korea is trying to get weapons. This is paraphrasing. The hard part is explaining how you did it.

Jokes of this type depend on ambiguity. Two meanings hold sway here: the one about the leader of North Korea and one about body parts. "Getting" the joke depends on recognizing both meanings. In effect, understanding a joke of this type depends on paraphrasing the same text twice. Again, this is both easy (to do) and hard (to explain). We know this is easy to do because people "get" jokes like this pretty routinely. Whole batches of these "Believe It or Not . . . Real Headlines from Actual Newspapers" jokes circulate widely on the Internet. In fact, here is a short list of them.

| **Topic for Class Discussion**

Pay close attention to your own reasoning processes as you read these headlines. See whether you can figure out precisely how you "get" these jokes. Are you following any "rules"?

"Believe It or Not . . . Real Headlines from Actual Newspapers"

Police Campaign to Run Down Jaywalkers

Safety Experts Say School Bus Passengers Should Be Belted

Drunk Gets Nine Months in Violin Case

Survivor of Siamese Twins Joins Parents
Farmer Bill Dies in House
Prostitutes Appeal to Pope
Panda Mating Fails; Veterinarian Takes Over
British Left Waffles on Falkland Islands
Eye Drops off Shelf
Teacher Strikes Idle Kids
Harper Wins on Budget, But More Lies Ahead
K9 Squad Helps Dog Bite Victim
Stolen Painting Found by Tree
Two Russian Ships Collide, One Dies
Red Tape Holds Up New Bridge
Typhoon Rips Through Cemetery; Hundreds Dead
Astronaut Takes Blame for Gas in Spacecraft
Kids Make Nutritious Snacks
Air Head Fired

We think that you followed a lot of rules in processing these items. For example, paraphrasing the "real story" meaning of "Teacher Strikes Idle Kids" seems to depend on figuring out that *idle* is the verb and *strikes* is a noun. Here you are applying a rule of *syntax,* or grammar, but distinguishing the "parts of speech" is not much help when you get to "Stolen Painting Found by Tree." In this case, distinguishing the "real story" meaning from the "joke" meaning depends on making a *semantic* distinction. In the "real story," the preposition "by" means "next to"; in the joke, it means "through the action or agency of." Plenty of rules exist. How do you know when to apply which rule?

Now here is something even more fascinating. We would not be at all surprised if many of our readers were baffled to one degree or another by what we have just said about syntax and semantics—and maybe even by our explanations of the two jokes—but still you get the jokes. The point here is that getting the joke, which involves paraphrasing the text twice, *does not seem to depend on being able to explain—or even being able to* state—*the rules you follow* as a speaker of the language when you paraphrase. Easy to do—hard to explain.

This is an example of a larger phenomenon: the awesome complexity of human intelligence. What we each do routinely as fluent speakers of a language—and getting jokes is a good measure of one's fluency—is *so* complex and subtle that to reduce it to a set of calculations and mechanical procedures is a huge undertaking (called *linguistics*). This process certainly involves rules and calculations that we can identify and articulate, yet in its totality it is vastly sophisticated. We would need a large book indeed to account for this process within a comprehensive system. A huge amount of computer power would be necessary, as well, even to approximate the process mechanically in practice. This complexity, by the way, pretty much captures the challenge of artificial intelligence as applied to conversation.

The moral of this story is that following the steps and procedures presented in Chapter 4, especially in a "mechanical" way, will not *by itself* do the trick of argument analysis if we understand argument analysis as a particular variety or application of paraphrasing. At the start of Chapter 4 we indicated that in the end it is your paraphrase of an argument—*your grasp of the meaning of the text, expressed in your own words*—that counts. Underlining, highlighting, mapping, casting—these are all merely means to this end. As useful as these tools may be in many cases, they are to full-fledged argument analysis as training wheels are to riding a bike.

For example, look again at the quotation from rock musician Ozzy Osbourne that was used as the opening epigram for this chapter:

> If you want to complain about Marilyn Manson, start from the beginning. Start with Shakespeare. What was *Romeo and Juliet* about? Suicide![1]

Osbourne clearly presents an argument here. Unless you can paraphrase it, however, you will not get anywhere trying to cast it. So how do we go about paraphrasing an argument like this?

EXERCISE 5.3 | Paraphrasing an Argument I

Thought experiment/Topic for class discussion: Start with this question: What do we need to *know* to *understand* the argument? Go through the argument and list the things that a person would need to know or be familiar with to understand what Ozzy Osbourne is saying.

What do you need to know or be familiar with to understand what Osbourne is saying? Here is our list: You need to know who Marilyn Manson is. You need to know what the complaints about Marilyn Manson are. You need to know who Shakespeare was. It helps to know the plot of *Romeo and Juliet*. It also helps to know who Ozzy Osbourne is. Just for fun (and this is good exercise, too), *before* you read any further, continue this exercise as a research assignment. Find out this stuff. Look it up.

EXERCISE 5.4 | Paraphrasing an Argument II

Research assignment: Who is Marilyn Manson? What are the complaints about him? Who was Shakespeare? What is the plot of *Romeo and Juliet*? Who is Ozzy Osbourne? When you have all this information, see whether you can paraphrase the argument.

_____

Marilyn Manson is the stage name of a 1990s gothic rock act whose lead singer took on the persona "Anti-Christ Superstar." Once you know who Marilyn Manson is, you can easily figure out the nature of the complaints. His work was controversial, of course. Concerts were banned, boycotts were organized against the sale of his merchandise, and so on, because of concern that Marilyn Manson's music, music videos, and stage show might exert a satanic influence on teenagers and lead them into depravity. Shakespeare, of course, is the great Elizabethan playwright, whose most famous tragedy, *Romeo and Juliet,* tells the story of the double suicide of two young lovers kept apart by their feuding families.

Ozzy Osbourne rose to prominence in the 1970s as lead singer of the British heavy metal band Black Sabbath. He, too, was the subject of much controversy like that provoked by Marilyn Manson, including a landmark legal battle over the 1981 song "Suicide Solution," allegedly the cause of a teenage gunshot suicide. Now, with this information, go back to paraphrasing Osbourne's argument, starting with the conclusion.

EXERCISE 5.5 | Paraphrasing an Argument III

What is Osbourne's main point?

_____

_____

What is Osbourne's basis of support for this main point?

_____

_____

With the above information, we can see easily that Osbourne's point is to defend Manson (as well as Osbourne's own work) against censorship, based on a comparison with Shakespeare. There you have it: a paraphrase of Osbourne's argument. We accomplished this by *situating the text we are trying to paraphrase in a meaningful context.* This is important enough to qualify as a rule of thumb:

TABLE 5.1 Guidelines for Paraphrasing

- **The Goal:** To establish a fair, accurate, and detailed understanding of the argument—as a preliminary step to rendering a judgment of its quality.
- **The Measure:** The paraphrase of the argument—your grasp of the meaning of the text, expressed in your own words—is what counts most.
- **Rule of Thumb:** Orient yourself to the argument's context.
- **Rule of Thumb:** Find the conclusion first.
- **Rule of Thumb:** When in doubt, don't be unfair—make the argument out to be as reasonable as possible.

Whenever we undertake to paraphrase an argument, we should pause to orient ourselves to the context in which the argument appears. We should begin with the question: What does a person need to know to understand this argument? Of course, we should make sure that we *do* know whatever a person needs to know to understand the argument.

CRITICAL THINKING TIP 5.1

When paraphrasing, orient yourself to the context.

It is time to apply what we have learned to some examples that are more advanced. Let us briefly review. Here are the important guidelines for argument analysis.

ADVANCED APPLICATIONS

So far, the arguments we have used for purposes of illustration have all been quite short. Many of the arguments you encounter will be much longer. Arguments are often presented in the form of letters, speeches, essays, and even whole books. As you already know, analyzing short arguments is challenging in several ways. The results of the analysis of short arguments, or more precisely, short presentations of arguments, can easily be longer and more complex than the texts analyzed. This was the case, for example, with the argument analyzed at the end of Chapter 4 about textbooks, mistakes, whales, mammals, and fish.

Longer arguments present an additional and "opposite" challenge: the challenge of compressing or distilling a lengthy presentation into something that can be grasped more quickly than the original. Fortunately, however, this challenge can be met by approaching it with the guidelines discussed above. The goal and the measure of success remain the same, and the rules of thumb still apply. We shall now illustrate all this with an example. We suggest that you try your hand at paraphrasing the example *before* you read what we have to say about it. Try the following exercise *before reading the rest of this chapter.*

EXERCISE 5.6 | Paraphrasing an Argument

After reading the following passage, apply the above guidelines and *paraphrase the argument in 50 words or less*.

Child Porn: Definition Curbs Expression

When the Canadian Senate approved a new child protection bill last week, it did so with plenty of reservations. One provision that came in for hearty and well-deserved criticism from the Upper Chamber was a "vague and subjective" new definition for child pornography.

The Senate was right to red flag it. The new, broader definition of child pornography could dangerously curb the free expression of writers, artists and, most likely, private citizens with dirty minds and pencils, but no plans to hurt real children.

. . . The new bill keeps [the original] definition, but adds a second written category which labels as child porn any written material "whose dominant characteristic is the description, for a sexual purpose, of a sexual act with a person under the age of 18 years that would be an offence under this Act." The key difference in the second category is that the "advocates or counsels" bit has been erased. Why does this matter? It's the difference between drafting a pamphlet encouraging your neighbours to abuse children and, say, a 17-year-old's love affair with a 14-year-old.

To make matters worse, the new law waters down the defence that artists and authors used to be able to offer if accused of making or possessing child porn. Whereas before they simply had to prove the material had artistic, scientific, educational or medical merit, now they have to show the items have a "legitimate purpose."

. . . In truth, the new law probably won't prompt police to seize copies of *Lolita* from library shelves, although the possibility can't be ruled out.

As repugnant as [infamous convicted child pornographer John Robin Sharpe's unpublished] writings may have been, they were still the products of his imagination [not representations of actual persons or events]. The High Court was right to protect them. Criminalizing private stories, diaries and drawings borders on thought control. Someone like Sharpe will have a tough time proving the "legitimate purpose" of his pornographic scrawlings. That is, after all, precisely why Parliament tweaked the law's language.

The House of Commons should heed the Senate's advice and revisit this legislation before its mandatory review is due. When it does, it should remove language that risks criminalizing Canadians' thoughts and private expressions, no matter how vile.

Editorial, *The Windsor Star*, July 28, 2005, A8. Reprinted by permission.

Paraphrase _____

_____

_____

_____

_____

Now that you have paraphrased the editorialist's argument, compare both your process and your results to our own. We will take you through it step by step. We begin with an orientation to the context of the argument. One of the most important contextual dimensions where arguments are concerned is the *issue* to which the argument is addressed. In fact, the issue is probably the single most important contextual landmark you will be able to find in most cases. Having a clear and solid grasp of the issue will make identifying and formulating the thesis of the argument much easier than it would otherwise be. So, the very first thing we would do is formulate a brief issue statement.

EXERCISE 5.7 | **Issue Statement**

We highly recommend reviewing the section of Chapter 1 on Issues, Issue Analysis, and Composing "Issue Statements." When you are finished, answer the following question: What is the issue the editorialist is addressing in her argument? Try to compose your answer in one sentence.

_____

_____

The editorialist's argument addresses the issue of the government's effort to deal with child pornography. Of course, this a complex issue, so we should undertake some analysis of the issue and focus a little more precisely. We could start by making a distinction between child pornography and freedom of expression generally. The editorialist's argument is concerned particularly with the government's response in the area of questionable or borderline cases. In general terms we might express this issue in the form of the question, "Is the Canadian government giving its best response to the problem of child pornography?"

Besides the issue, what else does a person need to know to understand the editorialist's argument? As in the case of the shorter argument discussed above, we can derive this "research agenda" by carefully scanning or reading the argument. Go ahead and try it; then carry out the research. Look up the information (see Exercises 5.3 and 5.4).

In this case, you should appreciate a number of things. You need to know that concern over child pornography is significant due in part to the ready availability of more sophisticated technologies, such as the Internet and personal digital photography. You need to know that the case of John Robin Sharpe was highly contentious because he was acquitted of the charge of possessing privately held writings that sprang solely from his imagination, though he was separately found guilty of possessing child pornography involving actual children. You need to know that, prior to his eventual conviction, Sharpe was originally acquitted of child pornography charges by the highest court in British Columbia, sparking an outcry across the country. The acquittal centred on the contentious exempting principle of "artistic merit" as applied to otherwise illegally pornographic materials.

You need to know that *Lolita* is a novel by Vladimir Nabokov, "a classic tale," the editorialist explains elsewhere, "of an old man violating his pre-teen stepdaughter." You might also find it helpful to know that this account of the novel differs somewhat from the standard account of the stepdaughter as participating voluntarily in the affair—although this qualification hardly diminishes the controversial nature of the book. You need to know that *Lolita*, and other books, such as *Lady Chatterley's Lover* by D. H. Lawrence and *Tropic of Cancer* by Henry Miller, were for years prohibited or restricted by the Canadian government (and other countries) on grounds of obscenity. You need to know that Canada loosened restrictions on *Lolita* and other books only in the 1960s, years after they were originally published. Even the widely known and read Canadian novel *The Diviners* by Margaret Laurence has been subject to significant controversy.

You might also find it helpful to know that Shakespeare's famous *Romeo and Juliet*, to whom Ozzie Osbourne refers at the start of this chapter, are ill-fated 13-year-old lovers who commit suicide rather than be driven apart by their warring families. The editorialist mentions "a 17-year-old's love affair with a 14-year-old," which is similar to *Romeo and Juliet*, and brings to mind the principle of artistic merit in cases where the material might otherwise be questionable or objectionable.

We could go even further, noting that thinkers and policy-makers of all stripes have debated the issue of freedom of expression over the centuries. The 19th-century British philosopher John Stuart Mill, for example, argued in favour of maximal freedom of expression consistent with the basic rights of others, while 20th-century British conservative Lord Devlin, partially in response to Mill's ideas, argued in favour of society's right to significant restriction and prohibition. We already have enough of a context, though, to enable us to take the next step and identify the editorialist's main point, or "thesis." Remember: The editorialist's thesis will be her particularized answer to the question above into which we distilled the following issue:

"Is the Canadian government giving its best response to the problem of child pornography?"

The editorialist's answer to this question is evident. She does not think that the Canadian government is giving its best response to the problem of child pornography, although she supports the intent of the legislative changes.

In particular, the editorialist argues that the revised legislation needs a change of wording. Why?

Asking the question "Why?" at this point directs our attention to the support the editorialist offers for her thesis. Re-reading the text of her argument against the backdrop of the contextual information assembled above, we can now boil down her support to the following. The wording of the new legislation threatens what ought to be allowable literary and artistic expression (such as some now accepted literary classics) as well as purely private creations of the imagination (which, despite their possible distastefulness, are not intended for anyone else's consumption or even knowledge).

So, we have our paraphrase: The editorialist argues that the revised legislation needs a change of wording, because the wording of the new legislation threatens what ought to be allowable literary and artistic expression as well as purely private creations of the imagination. Remember: This paraphrase is only a short version of the argument, created for the purpose of getting a handle on the reasoning as a whole. A full analytical account of the argument would have to include all the contributing elements of the reasoning.

Using Chapter 4 tools, we can now underline, highlight, and cast our paraphrase as follows:

> [The revised legislation needs a change of wording, Ⓒ] because [the wording of the new legislation threatens what ought to be allowable literary and artistic expression as well as purely private creations of the imagination.①]

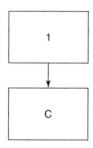

So far, we have arrived at a very short paraphrase of a much longer text. Our paraphrase compresses the editorialist's entire argument into a single sentence of 34 words, consisting of just two claims: her thesis and one supporting premise. In addition, and more importantly, as a result of the process we used to get this far, we are in a good position to explain the argument in greater depth and detail should it be necessary or desirable. The support for the main premise (claim #1) may be found in the paragraphs of contextual information we assembled above. Finally, now that we can see clearly what the editorialist tries to accomplish, we are ready in principle to move into the territory of evaluating the reasoning. We can begin to look for strengths and weaknesses, compelling points, and points against which we might imagine counterarguments forming. While this chapter concerns analysis, not evaluation (we will treat the matter of evaluation in succeeding chapters), keep in mind that proper evaluation rests on proper analysis, as we have done here.

EXERCISE 5.8

Develop and carry out a contextual research agenda for the editorialist's argument. Follow the instructions given in Exercises 5.3 and 5.4.

_____

_____

_____

_____

_____

_____

_____

_____

_____

_____

_____

_____

_____

PRACTICE, PRACTICE, AND MORE PRACTICE   Practice is the only way to get good at paraphrasing. The good news is that the better _you_ get, the easier _it_ gets. We conclude this chapter with a pair of relatively long arguments on which you should practise. These newspaper columns originally appeared together, so you should read them together.

EXERCISE 5.9

The two compositions below present different stances on multiculturalism. Paraphrase each of the two arguments using the procedures illustrated above. The target length for each paraphrase should be 250 words (the rough equivalent of one standard page of double-spaced text).

Our Culture of Accommodation ...

Off to London [United Kingdom] after the terror attacks last week, I swear I might just as well have been in Toronto or Ottawa or Vancouver.

It was all so infuriatingly, weirdly, endearingly familiar—the instant institutional reaction, immediately after the bombs went off, to reach out to British Muslims, from whose very ranks the bombers indisputably sprang; the angst at the BBC about whether the killers should be called terrorists (and the answer in the early days at least was "no") and, more generally, the striving all round for exquisitely careful language, lest anyone's feelings be hurt; the rush to condemn any possible backlash before there was a hint of one; the pronouncements from on high about what a perversion this act was of the wonderful religion of Islam.

I can imagine no other places on Earth but England and Canada where the national preoccupation in the wake of mass murder would be as much about consoling and protecting those who shared the bombers' religion (if in name only) as it was about comforting the families of the murdered and reassuring the wider public. In no other places would the search for a properly sensitive vocabulary be every bit as relentless as that for the perpetrators.

. . . Of course the police should protect Muslims from moronic vigilantism (or any other sort for that matter); of course they should say they will do so; of course they and the rest of us should take racism and hate crime seriously; of course, of course, of course. It's just that it's so damnably British (and Canadian) to be so studiously concerned about all this secondary stuff—and the original sin here is inarguably murder—from the get-go . . . .

My point is that Canucks share with the British a vision of our nations as places where the burden to accommodate social change, some of it sweeping, is not placed on newcomers alone, but as much upon existing and even founding citizens.

I *don't* want a little Muslim child to feel left out [when it comes to public Christmas events], or a Muslim teacher. Neither do I want a little fifth-generation Christian Canadian, or a white Anglo-Saxon teacher, to be deprived of his culture.

Yet it seems to me that in our efforts to make everyone happy, we Canadians are often shamefacedly apologetic about preserving what is good and honourable about our heritage—chiefly, that ours is a graceful, welcoming nation—and sloppily keen to debase ourselves before the new.

Christine Blatchford, "Our culture of accommodation . . . ," Reprinted with permission from *The Globe and Mail,* July 16, 2005.

". . . Is to Some, However, a Culture of Exclusion"

It was Robbie Burns in the 18th century who riffed on the metaphysical differences in the way we see ourselves and others see us. In the aftermath of the [terrorist] attacks on London, we're again looking at this issue of whether we will ever appreciate how these differences can divide the world.

Reading the various commentaries on last week's bombing, I came across this startling observation: "The foreign media are awash with references to 'Londonistan,' describing how this country has become a safe haven for Islamic extremists. . . . They also voice incredulity that the malign impact of multiculturalism and political correctness has for years seen Britain segregated into inward-looking communities that eschew British values while the forces of law and order walk on eggshells."

. . . Blaming everything on multiculturalism is a Pavlovian fashion that still whets the appetites of the gleefully politically incorrect. You rarely hear multiculturalism being maligned in this way when, say, music or food is flavoured with multicultural influences—because for the most part people don't feel threatened by "foreign" food or music. Detonate a bomb, however, and you release the thoughtless police and their attack dogs on the M word.

. . . [W]hen the name [of an attacker] is Hasib Hussain, born and bred in Northern England and identified as one of the London bombers, you just know that someone somewhere is going to blame the whole multicultural tree for failing to adapt its roots to the values of the orchard.

. . . What baffles people from the global South is when host communities in Europe and North America operate housing policy that effectively herds immigrants into ethnic ghettoes which are then branded as "inward-looking societies."

. . . I am not diminishing the London catastrophe, nor the value of those lives that were meaninglessly snatched away. But some of the analysis of why lives were lost does not convince me that we have learned to bridge the gap between how we see ourselves and how others see us.

Ken Wiwa, ". . . is to some, however, a culture of exclusion," Originally published in *The Globe and Mail* July 16, 2005. © 2005 Ken Wiwa. With permission of the author.

ADDITIONAL EXERCISES

At the end of Chapter 4, we supplied examples of argumentation taken from a variety of sources in public discourse for analysis using basic tools and techniques covered in Chapters 3 and 4. Now try these examples again, using the additional tools and techniques of paraphrasing covered in this chapter. See if these tools help you over the rough spots. Keep the goal of argument analysis in mind: a fair and accurate understanding of the argument in detail, expressed in your own words.

EXERCISE 5.10   "Evolution is a scientific fairy-tale just as the 'flat earth theory' was in the 12th century. Evolution directly contradicts the Second Law of Thermodynamics, which states that unless an intelligent planner is directing a system, it will always go in the direction of disorder and deterioration. Evolution requires a faith that is incomprehensible!"[2]

EXERCISE 5.11   "Repeated attacks on the rising cost of postsecondary education have spawned a widespread view that high tuition fees constitute a barrier to entry for Canadians in lower-income brackets . . . [A recent study shows that] [p]eople significantly overestimate the costs of a higher education and underestimate its benefits. . . . This misconception, coupled with cultural and class issues, appears to be much more of a barrier to education than the actual cost of tuition. Student groups have a vested interest in keeping tuition costs as low as possible. But as the results of this study show, their argument that current levels are an insuperable barrier for people in low-income brackets does not hold up to scrutiny. Fees have been rising, but not to unaffordable levels as critics have claimed."[3]

EXERCISE 5.12   "A scientific colleague of mine, who holds a professorial post in the department of sociology and anthropology at one of our leading universities, recently asked me about my stand on the question of human beings having sex relations without love. Although I have taken something of a position on this issue in my book, . . . I have never quite considered the problem in sufficient detail. So here goes. In general, I feel that affectional, as against non-affectional, sex relations are desirable. It is usually desirable that an association between coitus and affection exist—particularly in marriage, because it is often difficult for two individuals to keep finely tuned to each other over a period of years."[4]

■ **EXERCISE 5.13**   "The whole public discourse of Canada is one of rights—yours against mine, mine against governments, mine against all comers. . . . [What about responsibilities?] After all, rights are linked inherently to responsibilities. . . . Today, the ubiquitous 'rights talk' that so permeates public discourse and fills appeals to the courts reflects an increasingly pluralistic but also narcissistic society, in which self-affirmation, self-absorption and self-enrichment trump collective notions of what we owe each other . . . [We need] a Canadian political leader [who] will develop a narrative of responsibility, tease out its implications, frame it compellingly and say, as a U.S. President once did: Ask not what your country can do for you; ask what you can do for your country."[5]

■ **EXERCISE 5.14**   "To the extent that it is working at all, the press is always a participant in, rather than a pure observer of, the events it reports. Our decisions on where (and where not) to be and what (and what not) to report have enormous impact on the political and governmental life we cover. We are obliged to be selective. We cannot publish the Daily Everything. And so long as this is true—so long as we are making choices that 1) affect what people see concerning their leaders and 2) inevitably cause those leaders to behave in particular ways—we cannot pretend we are not participants."[6]

■ **EXERCISE 5.15**   "Scientists are human beings with their full complement of emotions and prejudices, and their emotions and prejudices often influence the way they do their science. This was first clearly brought out in a study by Professor Nicholas Pastore in 1949. In this study Professor Pastore showed that the scientist's political beliefs were highly correlated with what he believed about the roles played by nature and nurture in the development of the person. Those holding conservative political views strongly tended to believe in the power of genes over environment. Those subscribing to more liberal views tended to believe in the power of environment over genes. One distinguished scientist (who happened to be a teacher of mine), when young, was a socialist and environmentalist, but toward middle age he became politically conservative and a firm believer in the supremacy of genes!"[7]

■ **EXERCISE 5.16**   "Many a reader will raise the question whether findings won by the observation of individuals can be applied to the psychological understanding of groups. Our answer to this question is an emphatic affirmation. Any group consists of individuals and nothing but individuals, and psychological mechanisms which we find operating in a group can therefore only be mechanisms that operate in individuals. In studying individual psychology as a basis for the understanding of social psychology, we do something which might be compared with studying an object under the microscope. This enables us to discover the very details of psychological mechanisms which we find operating on a large scale in the social process. If our analysis of socio-psychological phenomena is not based on the detailed study of human behavior, it lacks empirical character and, therefore, validity."[8]

▮ **EXERCISE 5.17**   "Flextime (Flexible Working Hours) often makes workers more productive because being treated as responsible adults gives them greater commitment to their jobs. As a result it decreases absenteeism, sick leave, tardiness and overtime, and generally produces significant increases in productivity for the work group as a whole. For example, in trial periods in three different departments, the [government] measured productivity increases averaging about 20%. None has reported a decline."[9]

▮ **EXERCISE 5.18**   "Government control of ideas or personal preferences is alien to a democracy. And the yearning to use governmental censorship of any kind is infectious. It may spread insidiously. Commencing with suppression of books as obscene, it is not unlikely to develop into official lust for the power of thought-control in the areas of religion, politics, and elsewhere. Milton observed that 'licensing of books . . . necessarily pulls along with it so many other kinds of licensing.' Mill notes that the 'bounds of what may be called moral police' may easily extend 'until it encroaches on the most unquestionably legitimate liberty of the individual.' We should beware of a recrudescence of the undemocratic doctrine uttered in the seventeenth century by Berkeley, Governor of Virginia: 'Thank God there are no free schools or preaching, for learning has brought disobedience into the world, and printing has divulged them. God keep us from both'."[10]

▮ **EXERCISE 5.19**   "What, after all, is the foundation of the nurse's obligation to follow the physician's orders? Presumably, the nurse's obligation is to act in the medical interest of the patient. The point is that the nurse has an obligation to follow physician's orders because, ordinarily, patient welfare (interest) thereby is ensured. Thus when a nurse's obligation to follow a physician's order comes into direct conflict with the nurse's obligation to act in the medical interest of the patient, it would seem to follow that the patient's interests should always take precedence."[11]

▮ **EXERCISE 5.20**   "[Our] institutions were fashioned in an era of vast unoccupied spaces and pre-industrial technology. In those days, collisions between public needs and individual rights may have been minimal. But increased density, scarcity of resources, and interlocking technologies have now heightened the concern for 'public goods,' which belong to no one in particular but to all of us jointly. Polluting a lake or river or the air may not directly damage any one person's private property or living space. But it destroys a good that all of us—including future generations—benefit from and have a title to. Our public goods are entitled to a measure of protection."[12]

▮ **EXERCISE 5.21**   "These days music is truly global in sweep. The genie's out of the bottle, never to return, with MP3, Napster/Scour, and Freenet and Gnutella rendering all previous lines of demarcation meaningless. There's a revolution in progress, leveling everything in its path. Copyrights, masters, negatives, books, records, and films; it's all the same to a binary number, or a carbon atom and hydrogen qubit. Legislation, global police monitoring by knocking on two million doors—I don't think so. All I know is, you can't afford to make the customer your enemy. They no longer want to purchase a CD with ten or twelve songs on it to get the two they really want. They are also hip enough to know about artists' earnings and no longer want to pay the price for all the people in the middle of the distribution chain. These technological changes have provided an unexpected and highly efficient platform for rebellion for the current generation. We better get together and figure it out—and quickly!"[13]

■ **EXERCISE 5.22**   "In policy debates one party sometimes charges that his or her opponents are embracing a Nazi-like position. . . . Meanwhile, sympathizers nod in agreement with the charge, seeing it as the ultimate blow to their opponents. . . . The problem with using the Nazi analogy in public policy debates is that in the Western world there is a form of anti-Nazi 'bigotry' that sees Nazis as almost mythically evil beings. . . . Firsthand knowledge of our own culture makes it virtually impossible to equate Nazi society with our own. The official racism of Germany, its military mentality, the stresses of war, and the presence of a dictator instead of a democratic system make Nazi Germany in the 1940s obviously different."[14]

■ **EXERCISE 5.23**   At the end of Chapter 3 (Exercise 3.14) the instructions were to research the issue articulated in your Issue Statement and to identify at least three extended arguments representing at least two distinct positions on the issue. Now apply all that you have learned about argument analysis to the results of your research. Try to paraphrase each of the arguments you found in your research in 100 words or less.

Go to http://www.criticalthinking1ce.nelson.com for additional study resources for this chapter.

ENDNOTES

[1] Ozzy Osbourne, *Rolling Stone*, #736, 28.

[2] Dr. Edward Blic, *21 Scientists Who Believe in Creation* (Harrisonburg, VA: Christian Light Publications, 1977).

[3] Editorial, *The Globe and Mail*, July 9, 2005, A18.

[4] Albert Ellis, *Sex Without Guilt* (New York: Lyle Stuart, Inc., 1966).

[5] Jeffrey Simpson, "Ask not what your country can do for you . . . ," *The Globe and Mail*, June 18, 2005, A17.

[6] Meg Greenfield, "When the Press Becomes a Participant," *The Washington Post Company, Annual Report*, 1984, 21.

[7] Ashley Montagu, *Sociobiology Examined* (Oxford: Oxford University Press, 1980), 4.

[8] Eric Fromm, *Escape from Freedom* (New York: Avon Books, 1965), 158.

[9] Barry Stein et al., "Flextime," *Psychology Today*, June 1976, 43.

10 Jerome Frank, dissenting opinion in *United States v. Roth*, 354 U.S. 476, 1957.

11 E. Joy Kroeger Mappes, "Ethical Dilemmas for Nurses: Physicians' Orders versus Patients' Rights," in T. A. Mappes and J. S. Zembatty, eds., *Biomedical Ethics* (New York: McGraw-Hill, 1981), 100.

12 Amitai Etzioni, "When Rights Collide," *Psychology Today*, October 1977.

13 Quincy Jones, *Q: The Autobiography of Quincy Jones* (New York: Doubleday, 2000), 299.

14 Gary E. Crum, "Disputed Territory," *Hastings Center Report*, August/September 1988, 31.

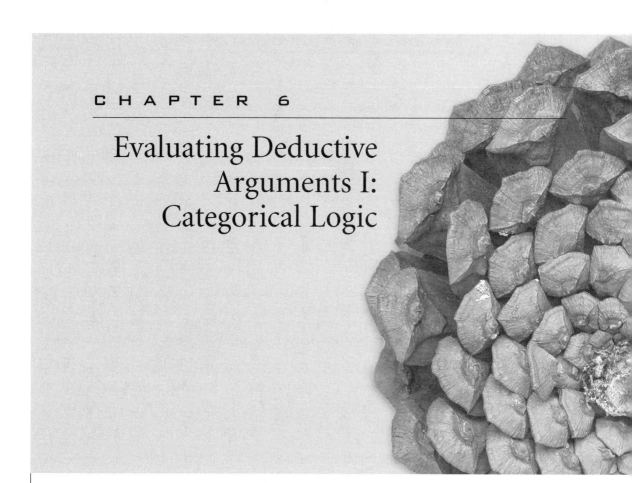

CHAPTER 6

Evaluating Deductive Arguments I: Categorical Logic

Now that we have covered argument identification and analysis, we are ready to address the evaluation of arguments. Most of us intuitively recognize qualitative differences between arguments, especially where the differences are relatively great. We have little difficulty in intuitively recognizing the superiority of an excellent argument to one that is extremely weak.

Our intuitions may fail to guide us, however, where competing arguments are more closely matched. Different people often have conflicting intuitions about which of two closely matched competing arguments is superior, and we may even experience conflicting intuitions as individuals. Furthermore, our intuitions do not help us explain our evaluative judgments. Therefore, we need a bit of theory to support, guide, and explain our evaluative intuitions. For theoretical purposes we will make a basic distinction between the structural features of an argument and the materials used in its construction. One way to understand this distinction

© The New Yorker Collection 1986 Bernard Schoenbaum from cartoonbank.com. All rights reserved.

"I shall now punch a huge hole in your argument."

is to think of an argument as a building. Now suppose, for example, we are evaluating buildings while buying a house. Some houses are obviously and intuitively better built than others. We can tell "intuitively" that 24 Sussex Drive, the prime minister's residence, is a stronger building than an outhouse. Nonetheless, we need a more systematic set of criteria to make reasonable decisions where houses are more closely matched. Buildings are complicated, so we find ourselves faced with many criteria relevant to evaluating buildings. This is why we would want to make the set of criteria "systematic." The system gives us organization.

One way to organize is to divide. When it comes to buildings, a reasonable and powerful first distinction for purposes of evaluation would be to divide between the materials used and how the materials are put together—the design and the execution of the design. So in evaluating arguments we could look at "design factors" and "materials factors." In this comparison (or "analogy") the "materials" are the premises of the argument, and the "design" is the plan according to which the premises are assembled in support of the conclusion. In this chapter we will begin with "design factors," returning to "materials factors" in Chapter 10.

DEDUCTIVE AND INDUCTIVE REASONING

The first consideration in design is always function. In reasoning and its evaluation, an important functional design consideration is "inferential security." In Chapter 3 we introduced the term "inference" as the mental step we take in reasoning from premise(s) to conclusion. In taking this step, we want to know how secure we are against falling into error. Thus, "inferential security" refers to the degree to which an inference is safe. Regarding function, we can sort arguments into two design categories: deductive and inductive. Deductive inferences are designed to achieve "absolute security" in the inference. Inductive inferences are designed to manage risk of error where absolute security is unattainable.

Consider the following two examples:

1. Your neighbour, Al-Timiri, is a member of the Canadian Association of University Teachers. Only members of the faculties of accredited universities are eligible for membership in the Canadian Association of University Teachers. Therefore, your neighbour, Al-Timiri, is a university professor.
2. Your neighbour, Al-Timiri, wears a tweed sports coat with patches on the elbows, carries a battered briefcase stuffed with papers, and rides his bicycle to the university campus every day. Therefore, your neighbour, Al-Timiri, is a university professor.

Notice how much stronger the connection is between the premises and conclusion in the first example as compared with the second example. In the first example we could say that anyone who fully understands what the sentences in the argument mean must recognize that the premises cannot both be true without the conclusion also being true. This is not the case, however, with the second argument. In the second example we could say at most that the premises, if true, make the conclusion reasonable or likely. As we will go on to explain more fully in the next two chapters, deductive reasoning, when it is well designed and constructed ("valid"), completely eliminates all risk of error in the inferential move from the premises to the conclusion. In inductive reasoning, the truth of the premises makes the conclusion reasonable, probable, or likely, but not certain. This difference between deduction and induction will be reflected in different sets of evaluative criteria. Accordingly, an early step in the process of evaluating arguments is deciding which set of criteria should be applied, or in other words, whether the argument should be evaluated as a deduction or as an induction.

Before we address this question, we had better clear up an old and widespread misunderstanding about the essential difference between induction and deduction. It is often said that deduction moves from general premises to particular conclusions, whereas induction moves in the opposite direction from particular premises to general conclusions. *Some* deductive inferences move from general premises to particular conclusions, but this is not an essential distinguishing feature of all deductions. Here is an example:

The major auto manufacturers are Best Buy Motor Company, Capstone Cars, and Ace. Best Buy Motor Company has reported record profits for last year. Capstone Cars has reported record profits for last year. And Ace has reported record profits for last year. Therefore, all the major auto manufacturers made money last year.

This is a deductive argument with particular premises and a general conclusion. Similarly, *some* inductive inferences move from particular premises to general conclusions, but this is not an essential distinguishing feature of all inductive inferences. For example,

> All Nova Scotia premiers have so far been men. Therefore, it is likely that the next Nova Scotia premier will be a man.

is an inductive argument with a general premise and a particular conclusion.

DEDUCTIVE AND INDUCTIVE SIGNALS

Just as the presence of arguments, premises, and conclusions is frequently indicated by means of signal words, so the *modality* of the inference—that is, whether it should be evaluated as a deductive or an inductive one—is often indicated by signal words. Deductive signal words include:

certainly

necessarily

must

See, for example:

> Your neighbour, Al-Timiri, is a member of the Canadian Association of University Teachers. Only members of the faculties of accredited universities are eligible for membership in the Canadian Association of University Teachers. Therefore, your neighbour, Al-Timiri, must be a university professor.

Inductive signals include:

probably

in all likelihood

chances are

it's reasonable to suppose that

it's a good bet that

See, for example:

> Your neighbour, Al-Timiri, wears a tweed sports coat with patches on the elbows, carries a battered briefcase stuffed with papers, and rides his bicycle to the university campus every day. I'd be willing to bet that your neighbour, Al-Timiri, is a university professor.

Just as with argument signal words discussed so far, we need to be aware of ambiguities and other nuances of meaning in context in order to avoid overly mechanical readings of things. In addition, as in all instances of argument analysis, we are guided by the rule of thumb, sometimes called the principle of charity, that we should try to make the argument out to be as reasonable as possible. For example, even if someone said,

> Your neighbour, Al-Timiri, wears a tweed sports coat with patches on the elbows, carries a battered briefcase stuffed with papers, and rides his bicycle to the university campus every day. Therefore, your neighbour, Al-Timiri, (must be) a university professor.

it would still be appropriate to evaluate the argument as an induction. A reasonable and charitable reading would interpret the speaker as having "overstated" the certainty of the conclusion relative to the premises. Similarly, if someone were to say,

> Your neighbour, Al-Timiri, is a member of the Canadian Association of University Teachers. Only members of the faculties of accredited universities are eligible for membership in the Canadian Association of University Teachers. (I'd be willing to bet) that your neighbour, Al-Timiri, is a university professor.

it would be appropriate to evaluate the argument as a deduction. A reasonable and charitable reading would interpret the speaker as having "understated" the certainty of the conclusion relative to the premises.

EXERCISE 6.1 | Deductive/Inductive

For each of the following passages, indicate whether the argument presented should be considered a deductive argument or an inductive argument.

	Deductive	Since the rifle used in the crime could not have been fired more than once every 2.3 seconds, the person arrested for the crime could not have fired three times—hitting Person A twice and Person B once—in 5.6 seconds or less.
	Inductive	

	Deductive	At bottom I did not believe I had touched that man. The law of probabilities decreed me guiltless of his blood. For in all my small experience with guns I had never hit anything I had tried to hit, and I knew I had done my best to hit him.
	Inductive	
		— Mark Twain

	Deductive	All the leading economic indicators point toward further improvement in the economy. You can count on an improved third quarter.
	Inductive	

	Deductive	During an interview with the school paper, Coach Danforth was quoted as saying, "I think it's safe to assume that Jason Israel will be our starting point guard next year. Both of our starting guards are graduating this spring and no one else on the team has Jason's speed and ball-handling skills."
	Inductive	

ARGUMENT FORM

For the rest of this chapter we will concentrate on the first of these two argument design categories, deductive inferences. In Chapter 8 we will focus on inductive inferences. As a first step we must introduce the important notion of argument form. We will focus on syllogisms: a deductive inference from (for the next few pages) two premises. Consider the following argument:

Because [all human beings are mortal ①] [and [all Canadians are human beings, ②]] it follows that [all Canadians are mortal. ③]

Casting the argument shows that premises 1 and 2 together support conclusion 3. Now we want to look more closely at the *way* in which the premises relate to the conclusion. Let us first represent the argument according to a conventional format:

(1)   All human beings are mortal.

(2)   All Canadians are human beings.

∴(3)   All Canadians are mortal.

In this format the premises are listed in order of their appearance above the solid line, and the conclusion is listed below the line. The symbol before #3 (∴) can be read as shorthand for "therefore." Notice that in this particular argument a perfectly strong connection between the conclusion and the premises appears to exist: It is impossible to deny the conclusion without also denying at least one of the premises (or contradicting yourself). Try it. Now consider a second example:

[All corundum has a high refractive index. ①] And [all rubies are corundum. ②] So [all rubies have a high refractive index. ③]

Represented in the same conventional format, the argument looks like this:

(1)   All corundum has a high refractive index.

(2)   All rubies are corundum.

∴(3)   All rubies have a high refractive index.

Notice that here too, the same perfectly strong connection between the conclusion and the premises appears to exist. You might be less acquainted with the optical properties and gemological classification of precious stones, but if you found out that all corundum has a high refractive index and all rubies are corundum, you would then *know* that all rubies have a high refractive index. (So, if a particular stone has a low refractive index, it *cannot* be a ruby.) It would be impossible to deny this conclusion without also denying at least one of the premises (or contradicting yourself). Try it. Now consider the following two claims:

(1)   All mammals suckle their young.

(2)   All primates are mammals.

Suppose these two claims are true. What conclusion could you draw from these two claims as premises?

(1)   All mammals suckle their young.

(2)   All primates are mammals.

∴ (a) ?

If you said, "All primates suckle their young," then notice once again that the same type of perfectly strong connection between your conclusion and the two premises appears to exist. Finally, suppose someone argues as follows:

[All propaganda is dangerous. ⓵] Ⓣhat's why [all network news is dangerous. ⓶]

From what you learned in previous chapters you can see that this argument depends on a missing premise *a*.

   (1) All propaganda is dangerous.

   (a) ?
   _____

∴(2) All network news is dangerous.

What is the missing premise *a*? No doubt you can see that the missing premise is "All network news is propaganda." Notice once again the perfectly strong connection between the conclusion and the two premises. If you suppose that both premises are true, you cannot deny the conclusion without contradicting yourself. Try it. You may have some doubt about the conclusion in this case. If, however, you doubt the truth of the conclusion, you must also doubt the truth of at least one of the premises. Now let us reconsider the four examples we have just examined:

---

   (1) All human beings are mortal.

   (2) All Canadians are human
        beings.
   _____

∴(3) All Canadians are mortal.

   (1) All mammals suckle their
        young.

   (2) All primates are mammals.
   _____

∴(a) ?

   (1) All corundum has a high refractive
        index.

   (2) All rubies are corundum.
   _____

∴(3) All rubies have a high refractive
        index.

   (1) All propaganda is dangerous.

   (a) ?
   _____

∴(2) All network news is dangerous.

These four examples have something important in common. It is a single and simple common feature that explains how we arrive at the conclusion in the third example that "All primates suckle their young" and how we fill in the missing premise in the fourth example that "All network news is propaganda"— and the perfectly strong connection that exists between the conclusion of each of the four arguments and its premises.

All four arguments follow the same pattern or form. Here is what the form looks like schematically:

(1)	All A's are B's		(1)	All _____ are _____ .
(2)	All B's are C's	**or**	(2)	All _____ are _____ .
∴ (3)	All A's are C's		∴ (3)	All _____ are _____ .

DEDUCTIVE VALIDITY

Deductive validity is another name for the kind of connection that holds between the conclusion and premises of arguments that follow this (or any other deductively valid) form. The essential property of a deductively valid argument form is this: *If* the premises of an argument that follows the form are taken to be true, then the conclusion of the argument (no matter what it is) *must* also be true. Because this is a feature of the *form* (or *pattern*) an argument follows, rather than of the argument's specific content, deductive validity is sometimes referred to as "formal validity."

Of course, arguments can follow a great many forms. Some forms are so commonly used and well known that they have been given names. You have just met a variation of "Barbara." Barbara is the name of a specific deductively valid form. For any argument that follows a deductively valid form, accepting the premises forces you to accept the conclusion. Try it. Make some up—even something as absurd as this:

(1)   All fish can fly.

(2)   All snakes are fish.

∴(3)   All snakes can fly.

Even though the premises are in fact false, the conclusion would have to be true *if* the premises were true (in some alternate universe of flying fish and fishy snakes). As you can see, deductive validity is a formal or structural feature that is independent of the actual truth of the premises. Nonetheless, we can distinguish sound and unsound valid inferences. A structurally valid inference that is *sound* has both a deductively valid form and true premises. A structurally valid inference that is *unsound* has a deductively valid form but at least one false premise. In the case above, the argument has a deductively valid form, but its premises are in fact false, so it is a formally valid but ultimately unsound argument.

EXERCISE 6.2 | **Deductive Validity**

	True	A deductively valid argument can have a false conclusion.	Explain your choice and give a supporting example:
	False		

True	A deductively valid argument can have false premises.	Explain your choice and give a supporting example:
False		

True	One cannot tell whether a deductive argument is valid without knowing whether its premises are actually true.	Explain your choice and give a supporting example:
False		

True	A deductively valid argument can have false premises and a true conclusion.	Explain your choice and give a supporting example:
False		

True	A deductively valid argument can have true premises and a false conclusion.	Explain your choice and give a supporting example:
False		

INVALIDITY

Deductively valid argument forms are important because they provide a guarantee that if the premises of the argument are true, the conclusion must be true as well. Not every form or pattern, however, is deductively valid. Consider the following example:

(1) All Canadians are human beings.

(2) All Ontarians are human beings.

∴(3) All Ontarians are Canadians.

Many people initially see nothing deficient in this as a piece of reasoning. This is probably because (1) they can see that the claims are in some way related to each other, and (2) they think that all three claims are true. Notice what happens, however, if you ask whether the truth of the premises *guarantees* the truth of the conclusion. Suppose the premises are true. Could the conclusion still be false? For example, suppose that some Ontarians are not Canadians. This possibility conflicts in no way with either premise 1 or premise 2. So, accepting both premises does not *force* you to accept the conclusion. If this is difficult to grasp, consider this next example:

(1) All men are human beings.

(2) All women are human beings.

∴(3) All women are men.

The falsity of this conclusion is obviously compatible with the truth of these two premises. Nonetheless, this argument follows the same form as the argument about Ontarians. Here is what the form looks like schematically:

(1) All A's are B's		(1) All _____ are _____ .
(2) All C's are B's	**or**	(2) All _____ are _____ .
∴ (3) All C's are A's		∴ (3) All _____ are _____ .

Because it is possible for an argument following this form to move from true premises to a false conclusion, we can easily see that this form is unreliable. The general name for an unreliable inference is *fallacy*. An inference that is unreliable because it follows an unreliable form or pattern is said to be *formally fallacious* or to commit a formal *fallacy*.

TESTING FOR DEDUCTIVE VALIDITY

The two argument forms we have just been studying resemble each other closely, yet one is deductively valid while the other is formally fallacious, and this is a crucial difference for the purposes of argument evaluation. Therefore, it is important to be able to reliably distinguish between deductively valid arguments and formally fallacious ones, though they may look very much alike. One way to do this is to memorize argument forms, but this would be an endless and unmanageable undertaking. Fortunately, a relatively simple and reliably intuitive procedure exists for determining whether a particular argument is deductively valid. It derives from the essential property of deductively valid forms mentioned above. The procedure consists of asking: "Can we assert the premises and deny the conclusion without contradicting ourselves?" If we *cannot* do this—that is, if asserting the premises and denying the conclusion results in a contradiction—then the inference is *deductively valid*. If we *can* assert the premises and deny the conclusion without contradiction, the inference is *not* deductively valid.

CRITICAL THINKING TIP 6.1

To test for deductive validity, ask: "Can I assert the premises and deny the conclusion without contradicting myself?"

EXERCISE 6.3 | **Testing for Deductive Validity**

Which of the following arguments are deductively valid? Which are invalid?

	Valid	God is perfect. Therefore, God is good.	Explain or give example.
	Invalid		

	Valid	Some entertainers are drug users, and all comedians are entertainers, so it stands to reason that some comedians are drug users.	Explain or give example.
	Invalid		

	Valid	Some university professors support the idea of a faculty union, an idea supported by many socialists. So at least some university professors must be socialists.	Explain or give example.
	Invalid		

	Valid	Everyone knows that whales live in the sea, and anything that lives in the sea is a fish. Therefore, whales must be fish.	Explain or give example.
	Invalid		

	Valid	All artists are creative people. Some artists live in poverty. Therefore, some creative people live in poverty.	Explain or give example.
	Invalid		

	Valid	All the justices on the Supreme Court are lawyers, and all members of the prestigious Ottawa Law Society are lawyers, so at least some of the Supreme Court justices are members of the Ottawa Law Society.	Explain or give example.
	Invalid		

Some people find the validity-testing method just described difficult to conceptualize and tricky to keep straight. Here is a variation that may be easier to grasp intuitively. Try to imagine a scenario in which the premises are all true, but the conclusion is false. If you can imagine such a scenario, then the inference is not deductively valid. For example, we can imagine a scenario in which the conclusion of the argument about Canadians, Ontarians, and human beings is false. Simply imagine that there are some Ontarians who are not also Canadians. Imagine, for example, that there are some legal residents of the province of Ontario who are not Canadian citizens, because, let us say, they are foreigners married to Canadians. Notice that both premises would still be true. Thus, this "scenario test" shows that the argument is invalid. Be careful, though. If you cannot imagine such a scenario, the inference is not necessarily deductively valid. It may simply mean that you have not been imaginative enough, so always try to be the best creative thinker you can be. One method you can use is brainstorming: quickly developing the longest possible list of scenarios and considerations, without initially questioning or critiquing.

EXERCISE 6.4   Using Scenarios to Test for Deductive Validity

Create scenarios to test the validity of the six arguments in Exercise 6.3.

Valid	God is perfect. Therefore, God is good.	Scenario:	
Invalid			

Valid	Some entertainers are drug users, and all comedians are entertainers, so it stands to reason that some comedians are drug users.	Scenario:	
Invalid			

Valid	Some university professors support the idea of a faculty union, an idea supported by many socialists. So at least some university professors must be socialists.	Scenario:	
Invalid			

Valid	Everyone knows that whales live in the sea, and anything that lives in the sea is a fish. Therefore, whales must be fish.	Scenario:	
Invalid			

Valid	All artists are creative people. Some artists live in poverty. Therefore, some creative people live in poverty.	Scenario:	
Invalid			

Valid	All the justices on the Supreme Court are lawyers, and all members of the prestigious Ottawa Law Society are lawyers, so at least some of the Supreme Court justices are members of the Ottawa Law Society.	Scenario:	
Invalid			

CONSTRUCTING COUNTEREXAMPLES

One of the best procedures for demonstrating that an inference is unreliable, or fallacious, is to compose an inference that is structured similarly but moves from premises that are obviously true to a conclusion that is obviously false. In the case of the two examples given in the section on "Invalidity," the second argument follows the same pattern as the first (see the figure on page 153) but moves from two premises, each of which is obviously true, to a conclusion that is just as obviously false. By means of such an invented inference we prove that the original argument—indeed any argument following this pattern—is fallacious. Let us try these procedures on a couple of additional examples:

(1) Some entertainers abuse drugs.

(2) All comedians are entertainers.

∴(3) Some comedians are drug abusers.

Is this a deductively valid argument? In other words, if we assert both of the premises and deny the conclusion, does a contradiction result? Now it may well be true that some comedians abuse drugs, but does such a conclusion follow from these two premises? No. It is possible for both of the premises to be true yet the conclusion to be false. Let us try to imagine a scenario in which the premises are both true yet the conclusion is false. Let us suppose it is true that some entertainers abuse drugs and that all comedians are entertainers. What kind of situation would be compatible with these two assumptions, yet incompatible with the conclusion? Suppose that all the drug-abusing entertainers just happen to be accordion players, while the rest of the entertainment industry is totally clean and sober. This may be hard to imagine because it is so at odds with what you may have heard. Nonetheless, it is possible to imagine it. Try it. Now notice that what you are imagining is at odds with the conclusion but perfectly compatible with each of the premises. This shows that the conclusion does not follow from the premises.

Let us now try to demonstrate that this inference is fallacious by producing a structurally or formally similar inference that moves from obviously true premises to an obviously false conclusion. Step one is to reveal the form of the argument. Using the letter "C" (or _____) to represent the category of comedians, the letter "A" (or _____) to represent the category of drug abusers, and the letter "E" (or _____) to represent the category of entertainers, we get from this,

(1) Some entertainers abuse drugs.

(2) All comedians are entertainers.

∴ (3) Some comedians are drug abusers.

to this:

(1) Some E's are A's	(1) Some _____ are _____.
(2) All C's are E's **or**	(2) All _____ are _____.
∴(3) Some C's are A's	∴ (3) Some _____ are _____.

Now, starting with the conclusion, we substitute terms for the abstract placeholders in the formula. We want to pick terms that result in an obviously false conclusion. For example, let "**C**" (or ____) now stand for the category of fathers, and let "**A**" (or ____) now stand for the category of women. This results in the obviously false conclusion that some fathers are women. Now we simply substitute the same terms wherever the abstract placeholders "**C**" (or _____) and "**A**" (or _____) occur in the formula. This gives us:

(1) Some E's are women.   (1) Some _____ are women.

(2) All fathers are E's.   (2) All fathers are _____ .
_____   _____
∴ (3) Some fathers are women.   ∴ (3) Some fathers are women.

Now all we need is a value for "**E**" (or _____) that would make both premises 1 and 2 true. Suppose we let "**E**" stand for the category of parents. This would give us:

(1) Some parents are women.

(2) All fathers are parents.
_____
∴ (3) Some fathers are women.

Here is another example:

(1) Some mysteries are entertaining.

(2) Some books are mysteries.
_____
∴ (3) Some books are entertaining.

Is this a deductively valid argument? In other words, if we assert both of the premises and deny the conclusion, does a contradiction result? No, it is possible for both of the premises to be true yet the conclusion to be false. This may be hard to appreciate, especially if you think just about the conclusion and your actual experience. The conclusion is no doubt true as a matter of fact. Nonetheless, it does not follow from these two premises. It is possible to imagine a scenario in which both premises are true and the conclusion is false. Imagine, for example, that no books are entertaining (in other words, imagine that the conclusion is false). This does not conflict with the first premise. It could easily be the case that some books are mysteries and that no books are entertaining. Nor does it conflict with the second premise. Suppose that all the entertaining mysteries are movies.

Now let us demonstrate that this inference is fallacious by producing a structurally or formally similar inference that moves from obviously true premises to an obviously false conclusion. First we reveal the form of the argument. Using the letter "B" (or _____) to represent the category of books, the letter "M" (or _____) to represent the category of mysteries, and the letter "E" (or_____) to represent the category of things that are entertaining, we get from this:

(1) Some books are mysteries.

(2) Some mysteries are entertaining.
_____
∴ (3) Some books are entertaining.

to this:

(1) Some B's are M's.   (1) Some _____ are _____.

(2) Some M's are E's.   **or**   (2) Some _____ are _____.

∴ (3) Some B's are E's.   ∴ (3) Some _____ are _____.

Again, starting with the conclusion, we substitute terms for the abstract place-holders in the formula. We want to pick terms that result in an obviously false conclusion. For example, let "B" (or _____) now stand for the category of females, and let "E" (or _____) now stand for the category of males. This results in the obviously false conclusion that some females are male. Now simply substitute the same terms wherever the abstract placeholders "B" (or _____) and "E" (or _____) occur in the formula. This gives us:

(1) Some females are M's.   (1) Some females are _____.

(2) All M's are male.   (2) All _____are male.

∴ (3) Some females are male.   ∴ (3) Some females are male.

Now all we need is a value for "M" (or _____) that would make both premises 1 and 2 true. Again, suppose we let the remaining term "M" stand for the category of parents. That would give us:

(1) Some males are parents.

(2) Some parents are females.

∴ (3) Some females are males.

EXERCISE 6.5 | **Constructing Counterexamples**

For each of the invalid arguments in Exercises 6.3 and 6.4 (Testing for Deductive Validity), construct a structurally or formally similar argument that moves from obviously true premises to an obviously false conclusion.

	Invalid Argument	Formally Similar Argument
Premise		
Premise		
Conclusion		

	Invalid Argument	Formally Similar Argument
Premise		
Premise		
Conclusion		

	Invalid Argument	Formally Similar Argument
Premise		
Premise		
Conclusion		

	Invalid Argument	Formally Similar Argument
Premise		
Premise		
Conclusion		

CATEGORICAL LOGIC

The argument forms we have been studying so far in this chapter are called "categorical syllogisms" because they are made up of *categorical statements* (claims about relationships between categories of things). The Greek philosopher Aristotle developed a relatively simple but powerful system of logic based on categorical syllogisms. One of his insights was that anything one might want to say about the relationships between any two categories can be said in one of four ways. In other words, all categorical statements can be reduced to one of the four following standard forms:

Affirmative	Negative
A: Universal Affirmative.	E: Universal Negative.
e.g. All mothers are female.	e.g. No fathers are female.
I: Particular Affirmative.	O: Particular Negative.
e.g. Some women are mothers.	e.g. Some women are not mothers.

These forms are arranged in a matrix that reflects two major distinctions cutting across each other. The categorical statements in the left column *affirm* an *inclusive* relationship between two categories. The categorical statements in the right column each *deny* such a relationship between the two categories; the relationships they indicate are *exclusive*. This is traditionally understood as a "qualitative" distinction and is designated by the terms "affirmative" and "negative." The conventional designations of these statement forms by the letters "A," "E," "I," and "O" derive from this qualitative distinction via the Latin words *AffIrmo* ("I affirm") and n*EgO* ("I deny").

The statements on the top line of the matrix (A and E) assert the *total* inclusion or exclusion of an entire category in or from another. The statements on the bottom line of the matrix (I and O) assert the *partial* inclusion or exclusion of one category in or from another. This is traditionally understood as a "quantitative" distinction and is designated by the terms "universal" and "particular."

One way to measure the "theoretical power" of a system is to divide the number of cases that the system effectively covers by the size of the theoretical apparatus. By this measure, Aristotle's system of categorical logic is extremely powerful. Look at how elemental the theoretical apparatus is: Two major distinctions—Universal (all or none) versus Nonuniversal (some) and Affirmative versus Negative—yield four statement forms, which together cover practically the entire range of claims about category relationships. This is bound to score way up on the scale of theoretical power.

TRANSLATING CATEGORICAL STATEMENTS INTO STANDARD FORM

Nonetheless, a catch exists. Understandably, the power of the system depends heavily on being able to translate the wide variety of things that people actually say about categories in their actual arguments into one or another of the four standard forms. Because, however, language is very flexible and rich in possibilities and people are very imaginative and innovative in their use of language, translation into standard form is a matter of some complexity and uncertainty. We have a few general rules, with exceptions, and an indefinitely large set of interpretive guidelines, of which we shall give you the short "starter kit."

The *General Rules* are:

- Categorical statements begin with a "quantity indicator" ("all," "some," or "no").

- A verb occupies the middle (either "are" or "are not") to indicate the "quality" of the statement (whether it is affirmative or negative).

- Two terms flank the verb, each denoting a category. The term before the verb is called the "subject term," and the term after the verb is called the "predicate term."

- Subject and predicate terms must be nouns or noun phrases. For convenience, we will use angle brackets, < >, to set off the subject and predicate terms from the quantity and quality indicators in standard formulations of categorical statements.

The *Exceptions to the General Rules* are:

- You cannot say "All <A's> are not <B's>" as in "All the <computers on campus> are not <IBM compatible>." This formulation is disallowed because it is ambiguous. It could mean "Not all the <computers on campus> are <IBM compatible>" (which is the same as saying, "*Some* of the <computers on campus> are *not* <IBM compatible>"); or it could mean,

"None of the <computers on campus> are <IBM compatible>." You have to decide whether the statement is supposed to say "Not *all* <A's> are <B's>" or "Not *any* <A's> are <B's>." If the meaning is "Not *all* <A's> are <B's>," use the "O" form: "Some <A's> are not <B's>." If the meaning is "Not *any* <A's> are <B's>," use the "E" form: "No <A's> are <B's>."

- We can make categorical statements about individuals. For example, "Wendy Mesley is a broadcast journalist"; or "Sarah McLachlan is a musician"; or "The Stanley Cup playoff series is an annual event." For all practical purposes (and especially because we are at the beginning of the study of formal logic), we would do well for now to treat any statement similar to the ones above as though it were a Universal Affirmative (or "A") categorical statement, even though there is only one real "category" involved. Categorical logic can handle such statements quite effectively if we pretend that we are, for example, talking about all members of the category <Sarah McLachlan> (a category of which there is only one member) when we say that she is in the category <musicians>.

Some *Interpretive Guidelines* are:

- Turn adjectives into nouns or noun phrases. In some cases this is pretty straightforward and intuitive. For example, "Kenneth Thomson is wealthy" becomes <Kenneth Thomson> is a <wealthy man>.

- Use the context to help determine how to formulate the noun phrase. For example, in the context of the argument "Wealthy individuals enjoy disproportionate access to power. Kenneth Thomson is wealthy. So he must have disproportionate access to power," the premise expressed in the second sentence makes the most sense if we interpret it to mean that Kenneth Thomson is in *precisely* the category indicated by the subject term in the first sentence, <wealthy individuals>. This makes the logic of the inference easier to see. Therefore, "Kenneth Thomson is wealthy" becomes <Kenneth Thomson> is a <wealthy individual>.

- Turn verbs into nouns or noun phrases. Again, in some cases this is pretty straightforward and intuitive. For example, "Deciduous plants shed their leaves" becomes All <deciduous plants> are <things that shed their leaves>.

- Use the context to help determine how to formulate the noun phrase. For example, in this context, "All dancing bears are performing animals. Betty the Bear is dancing the tango. Therefore, Betty the Bear is a performing animal," the logic of the premise expressed in the second sentence makes sense only if we render it thus: <Betty> is a <dancing bear>.

- Use the grammar as a guide, but keep in mind that grammatical structure and logical structure often diverge. For example, in the sentence, "Happy is the man who finds work doing what he loves," the subject term <the man who finds work doing what he loves> is contained in the grammatical predicate. Also, notice that although the subject term is grammatically singular, the meaning for the purposes of categorical logic is plural; "the man who finds work doing what he loves" is meant to stand for the whole category of people who find work doing what they love. So the standard formulation of this statement would be "All <people who find work doing what they love> are <happy people>."

TABLE 6.1a General Rules for Translating into Standard Form

- Categorical statements begin with a "quantity indicator" ("all," "some," or "no").
- A verb occupies the middle (either "are" or "are not") to indicate the "quality" of the statement (whether it is affirmative or negative).
- Two terms flank the verb, each denoting a category. The term before the verb is called the "subject term," and the term after the verb is called the "predicate term."
- Subject and predicate terms must be nouns or noun phrases. For convenience, we use angle brackets < > to set off the subject and predicate terms from the quantity and quality indicators in standard formulations of categorical statements.

TABLE 6.1b Exceptions to the General Rules

- This formulation, "All <A's> are not <B's>," as in "All the <computers on campus> aren't <IBM compatible>," is disallowed because it is ambiguous. If the meaning is "Not all <A's> are <B's>," use the "O" form: "Some <A's> are not <B's>." If the meaning is "Not any <A's> are <B's>," use the "E" form: "No <A's> are <B's>."
- We can make categorical statements about individuals. Treat proper names of individuals as names of categories.

TABLE 6.1c Interpretive Guidelines

- Turn adjectives and verbs into nouns or noun phrases.
- Use the grammar as a guide, but more importantly, use the context to determine how to formulate the noun phrases.

EXERCISE 6.6 | Translating Categorical Statements into Standard Form

Translate each of the following categorical statements into standard form.

All computer hardware have a short shelf life.	C = computer hardware S = things with short shelf life	Standard form:
Some of my beliefs are false.	B = my beliefs F = things that are false	Standard form:
One major corporation is Nortel.	C = major corporations M = Nortel	Standard form:
Some of the members of the Cult of Zarnon are reasonable people.	M = members of the Cult of Zarnon R = reasonable people	Standard form:

Any discipline has rules, or at least regularities of some kind.	D = disciplines R = things with rules or regularities	Standard form:
El Niño is the cause of some of these abnormal weather patterns.	A = these abnormal weather patterns N = things caused by El Niño	Standard form:
I like action movies.	A = action movies L = things I like	Standard form:
Victoria is a city in British Columbia.	S = Victoria C = cities in British Columbia	Standard form:
My favourite actor is a Gemini.	F = my favourite actor G = Geminis	Standard form:
Dogs love trucks.	D = dogs L = lovers of trucks	Standard form:

THE SQUARE OF OPPOSITION

Let us now return to the matrix we used to introduce the four standard forms of categorical statements. This time we will use the same subject and predicate terms in all four examples so as to highlight differences in quality and quantity. Traditionally, in categorical logic, two categorical statements that differ from each other in quality or in quantity, or both, but that are otherwise the same, are said to stand in "opposition" to each other. Several kinds of "opposition" exist, depending on whether the difference is one of quality or quantity, or both. Let us start with what might be described as the "strongest" form of opposition. Look at the "A" statement and the "O" statement together:

	Affirmative		**Negative**
A: e.g.	Universal Affirmative. All <bonds> are <secure investments>.	E: e.g.	Universal Negative. No <bonds> are <secure investments>.
I: e.g.	Particular Affirmative. Some <bonds> are <secure investments>.	O: e.g.	Particular Negative. Some <bonds> are not <secure investments>.

Notice that they cannot both be true, *and* they cannot both be false. This kind of opposition is traditionally called *contradiction*. Now look at the "E" and "I" statements together. Like the "A" and "O" statement pair, if either "E" or the "I" statement is true, the other one must be false; they also *contradict* each other.

Now look at the "A" statement and the "E" statement together:

Affirmative		**Negative**	
A:	Universal Affirmative.	E:	Universal Negative.
e.g.	All <bonds> are <secure investments>.	e.g.	No <bonds> are <secure investments>.
I:	Particular Affirmative.	O:	Particular Negative.
e.g.	Some <bonds> are <secure investments>.	e.g.	Some <bonds> are not <secure investments>.

Notice that they cannot both be true, but they *might* both be false. This is a somewhat weaker form of opposition than contradiction. This kind of opposition is traditionally called *contrariety*. Two categorical statements that stand in this kind of opposition to each other are called *contraries* of each other.

Now look at the "I" statement and the "O" statement together:

Affirmative		**Negative**	
A:	Universal Affirmative.	E:	Universal Negative.
e.g.	All <bonds> are <secure investments>.	e.g.	No <bonds> are <secure investments>.
I:	Particular Affirmative.	O:	Particular Negative.
e.g.	Some <bonds> are <secure investments>.	e.g.	Some <bonds> are not <secure investments>.

Notice that they *could* both be true, but they *cannot* both be false. This kind of opposition is traditionally called *subcontrariety*. Two categorical statements that stand in this kind of opposition to each other are called *subcontraries* of each other.

The technical way in which logicians use the word "opposition" is a little peculiar. So far all of the different kinds of opposition we have discussed seem to involve some sort of "disagreement." Now if you look at the "A" and the "I" statements together you will see that they seem to agree with each other:

Affirmative		**Negative**	
A:	Universal Affirmative.	E:	Universal Negative.
e.g.	All <bonds> are <secure investments>.	e.g.	No <bonds> are <secure investments>.
I:	Particular Affirmative.	O:	Particular Negative.
e.g.	Some <bonds> are <secure investments>.	e.g.	Some <bonds> are not <secure investments>.

In fact, it seems reasonable to say that if the "A" statement is true, then the "I" statement must also be true, "by implication." For example, if it *is* true that all bonds are secure investments, it must surely be true that *some* bonds are secure investments as well. The same relationship also holds between "E" and "O" statements. For example, if it is true that no bonds are secure investments, it must surely be true as well that some bonds are *not* secure investments. This kind of opposition is traditionally called *subalternation*. If two categorical statements with the same subject and predicate terms agree in quality (are both affirmative or both negative) but differ in quantity, the universal statement implies its *subalternate* particular statement. Notice that this is a one-way relationship. The particular statement does not imply the universal statement. Even if it is true that some bonds are secure investments, this does not, all by itself, imply that *all* bonds are secure investments. Similarly, even if it is true that some bonds are *not* secure investments, this does not by itself imply that *no* bonds are secure investments. Let us now summarize the above relationships in what is traditionally called the "square of opposition":

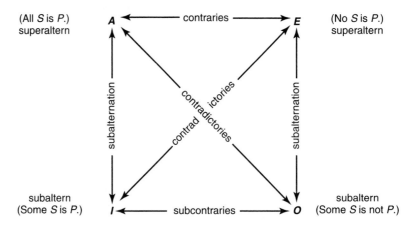

Note: The modern or Boolean square of opposition differs from this traditional or classical (Aristotelian) conception; contrariness, subcontrariness, and subalternation do not obtain. For example, see the section "Mood and Figure" below.

IMMEDIATE INFERENCES AND SYLLOGISMS

Based on the relationships described above and represented in the square of opposition, logic traditionally recognizes certain *immediate inferences* as deductively valid. Inferences such as these are traditionally referred to as "immediate," meaning that they proceed directly from one single categorical statement as a premise to another as the conclusion.

- Assuming that a given "A" statement is true: its contradictory "O" statement is false; its contrary "E" statement is false; its subalternate "I" statement is true.

- Assuming that a given "E" statement is true: its contradictory "I" statement is false; its contrary "A" statement is false; its subalternate "O" statement is true.

- Assuming that a given "I" statement is true: its contradictory "E" statement is false.

- Assuming that a given "O" statement is true: its contradictory "A" statement is false.

Beyond these "immediate inferences" a larger category of inferences exists, called *syllogisms*, which are based on combining two categorical statements as premises. The examples we used above to introduce and illustrate the concept of deductive validity were all syllogisms.

EXERCISE 6.7 | **Immediate Inferences**

In each of the following sets of claims, assume that the first claim (in **bold**) is true, then highlight the claim(s) from the rest of the set that may be validly inferred from it.

All Canada Savings Bonds are safe investments.

No Canada Savings Bonds are safe investments.

Some Canada Savings Bonds are safe investments.

Some Canada Savings Bonds are not safe investments.

No Canada Savings Bonds are safe investments.

Some Canada Savings Bonds are safe investments.

Some Canada Savings Bonds are not safe investments.

All Canada Savings Bonds are safe investments.

Some Canada Savings Bonds are safe investments.

Some Canada Savings Bonds are not safe investments.

All Canada Savings Bonds are safe investments.

No Canada Savings Bonds are safe investments.

Some Canada Savings Bonds are not safe investments.

All Canada Savings Bonds are safe investments.

No Canada Savings Bonds are safe investments.

Some Canada Savings Bonds are safe investments.

An immediate inference involves only two categories. A syllogism always involves three. The three categories, and their corresponding terms, have special names. Let us now introduce this terminology, using one of our earlier examples.

All are <mortals>.

All <Canadians> are

∴ All <Canadians> are <mortals>.

Notice that two of the three terms appear in the conclusion, while the third does not. The term that appears in the predicate position in the conclusion is called the *major term*; the term that appears in the subject position in the conclusion is called the *minor term*. The term that does not appear in the conclusion is called the *middle term*—it is the term that "mediates" the inference. The middle term appears once in each of the premises. The premise in which the major term appears is called the *major premise*; the premise in which the minor term appears is called the *minor premise*. Syllogisms in standard form always follow this order: major premise, minor premise, conclusion.

EXERCISE 6.8 | Standard Form

Put each of the following syllogisms into standard form: major premise first, followed by minor premise, then conclusion.

All Canadians are human beings.

All human beings are mortals.

∴ All Canadians are mortals.

All men are human beings.

All women are human beings.

∴ All women are men.

Some books are mysteries.

Some mysteries are entertaining.

∴ Some books are entertaining.

MOOD AND FIGURE

Remember, only four types of categorical statements exist—A, E, I, and O—as arrayed in the square of opposition, and three claims in any syllogism: major premise, minor premise, and conclusion. Each of these claims may be of any one of the four types. This yields 64 possible combinations (by the formula: 4^3); logicians refer to these combinations as *moods*. The mood of a syllogism is determined by which of the four statement types appears as the major premise, the minor premise, and the conclusion, when the syllogism follows standard form. The mood is indicated by a series of three letters, representing the three statement types in the inference in standard order (e.g., AAA, EAE, EIO, AOO, etc.).

EXERCISE 6.9 | **Mood**

Step 1: Using the square of opposition, identify the statement type of the major premise, minor premise, and conclusion in each of the following syllogisms.

Step 2: Test each syllogism for deductive validity using the procedures outlined above (see Critical Thinking Tip 6.1).

All human beings are mortals.

All Canadians are human beings.

∴ All Canadians are mortals.

All men are human beings.

All women are human beings.

∴ All women are men.

Some mysteries are entertaining.

Some books are mysteries.

∴ Some books are entertaining.

Some mysteries are not entertaining.

Some books are not mysteries.

∴ Some books are not entertaining.

All mysteries are suspenseful.

Some books are not mysteries.

∴ Some books are not suspenseful.

Now look closely at the first two inferences in Exercise 6.8. The mood of each of these syllogisms is AAA. As we have seen since the beginning of this chapter, however, the first inference is valid while the second one is invalid. What is the difference? The difference concerns what logicians call the *figure* of each syllogism, which is determined by the *position of the middle term*. Notice that in the first inference (the valid one), the middle term appears in the subject position in the major premise but in the predicate position in the minor premise. In the second inference (the invalid one), the middle term appears in the predicate position in both premises (see the accompanying figure).

All human beings are mortals.	All men are human beings.
All Canadians are human beings.	All women are human beings.
∴ All Canadians are mortals.	∴ All women are men.

In a standard-form syllogism, the middle term appears once in each premise, but that can be either in the subject or predicate position. Since there are two premises, and each premise has both a subject and a predicate, this gives rise to four possible combinations, or *figures*. Using the letter "S" to indicate the minor term (subject of the conclusion), "P" to indicate the major term (predicate of the conclusion), and "M" to indicate the middle term, we can depict the four figures as follows:

1st Figure	2nd Figure	3rd Figure	4th Figure
M-P	P-M	M-P	P-M
S-M	S-M	M-S	M-S
S-P	S-P	S-P	S-P

Now, with 64 moods and four figures, the total number of possible syllogistic forms comes to 256 (64 × 4). Of these, 15 turn out to be deductively valid. The remaining 241 are invalid. Once a syllogism has been translated into and arranged in standard form, its formal structure (its mood and figure) determines whether or not it is deductively valid in accordance with the following set of rules:

- The syllogism must contain exactly three terms, each used consistently throughout the inference (no ambiguity allowed).
- The middle term of the syllogism must be *distributed* in at least one premise. (A term is distributed when the claim in which it appears says something about *every member of the category* to which the term refers. For example, in the premise "All bonds are safe investments," the term "bonds" is distributed, but the term "safe investments" is not.)

- If either term is distributed in the conclusion, it must be distributed in the premises.
- A valid syllogism may have at most one negative premise.
- If either premise of the syllogism is negative, the conclusion must be negative.
- If the conclusion of the syllogism is negative, one premise must be negative.

Under the modern or Boolean interpretation, an additional rule exists that is suspended for the traditional or classical (Aristotelian) interpretation:

- Existential fallacy: Two universal premises require a universal conclusion.

EXERCISE 6.10 | **Invalid Syllogisms**

In Exercise 6.8, the first syllogism was valid, but all the rest were invalid. Here again are the invalid syllogisms. Which of the above rules is violated in each case?

All men are human beings.

All women are human beings.
_____

∴ All women are men.

Some mysteries are entertaining.

Some books are mysteries.
_____

∴ Some books are entertaining.

Some mysteries are not entertaining.

Some books are not mysteries.
_____

∴ Some books are entertaining.

All mysteries are suspenseful.

Some books are not mysteries.
_____

∴ Some books are not suspenseful.

VENN DIAGRAMS

As you can plainly see, categorical logic can be quite complex. Just as with argument analysis, many people find graphics and visualization helpful in gaining a grasp of this material. For this purpose, British logician John Venn invented a graphic system for representing categorical statements and testing the validity of categorical syllogisms. The system consists of intersecting circles. Each circle represents a category. A shaded area is "vacant"—an area with no examples or members. An X is used to indicate a "populated" area—an area with at least one member. Using two intersecting circles and these simple symbols, we can represent any of the four standard forms of categorical statements (A, E, I, and O). In the accompanying figure the circle on the left represents the category of mothers (the subject), and the circle on the right represents the category of females (the predicate). The shaded area indicates that no members of the category "mothers" occur who are not also members of the category "females." Thus, the figure diagrams the statement that all mothers (subject) are female (predicate).

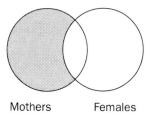

Mothers   Females

In the next figure the circle on the left represents the category of fathers, and the circle on the right represents the category of females. The shaded area indicates that no members of the category "fathers" occur who are also members of the category "females." Thus, the figure diagrams the statement that no fathers are female.

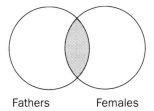

Fathers   Females

In the next two figures the circle on the left represents the category of women, and the circle on the right represents the category of mothers. In the first figure, the X indicates that there are some members of the category women who are also members of the category mothers. Thus, the figure diagrams the statement that some women are mothers. In the second figure, the X indicates that some members of the category women occur who are not also members of the category mothers. Thus, the figure diagrams the statement that some women are not mothers.

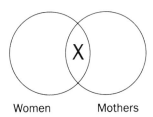

Women   Mothers

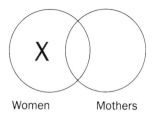

A categorical syllogism contains three terms, corresponding to three categories, two of which appear in the conclusion. In a categorical syllogism each of the premises states a relationship between one of these two categories, which appear in the conclusion and a third (or "middle") category. Thus, to diagram a categorical syllogism we need three intersecting circles, one for each of the categories in the conclusion and a third circle for the middle category:

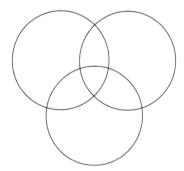

TESTING FOR VALIDITY USING VENN DIAGRAMS

In using the diagram to test for the validity of categorical syllogisms, we should remember the essential characteristic of deductively valid arguments: If the premises of an argument that follows the form are taken to be true, then the conclusion of the argument (no matter what it is) must also be true. In a certain important sense, the conclusion of a deductively valid inference is already "contained in" its premises. Thus, if we represent the information contained in the two premises in the diagram, the conclusion should automatically be represented as well, *if* the argument is a valid one. Let us try this with the first of the examples we considered in this chapter:

(1) All Canadians are human beings.

(2) All human beings are mortal.

∴ (3) All Canadians are mortal.

In the accompanying figure the circle on the left will represent the category of Canadians, the circle on the right will represent the category of mortals, and the lower circle will represent the middle category of human beings.

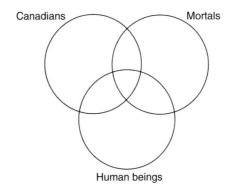

To represent premise 1 in the diagram we must shade all of the human beings circle except where it intersects with the mortal circle:

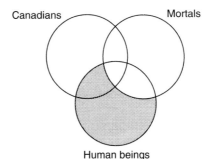

This indicates that no members of the category "human beings" occur who are not also members of the category "mortals." Similarly, we represent premise 2 in the diagram by shading all of the Canadian circle except where it intersects with the human beings circle:

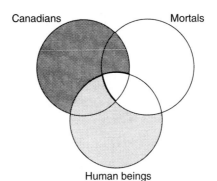

This indicates that no members of the category "Canadians" occur who are not also members of the category "human beings." Lo and behold, this figure already represents the conclusion because the area inside the Canadian circle but outside its intersection with the mortal circle is shaded, indicating that no members of the category "Canadians" occur who are not also members of the category "mortals." Thus, our diagram demonstrates the validity of the inference.

Now let us try the same procedure with the first formally fallacious example we considered above:

(1) All Canadians are human beings.

(2) All Ontarians are human beings.

∴ (3) All Ontarians are Canadians.

In the accompanying figure the circle on the left will represent the category of "Ontarians," the circle on the right will represent the category of "Canadians," and the lower circle will represent the middle category of "human beings."

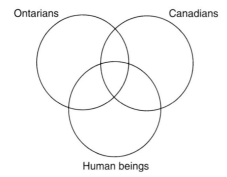

To represent premise 1 we shade the entire Canadian circle except where it intersects with the circle of human beings (see the accompanying figure), indicating that no members of the category "Canadians" occur who are not also members of the category "human beings."

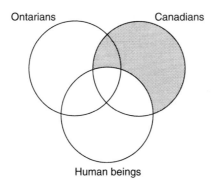

To represent premise 2 we shade in the entire Ontarian circle except where it intersects with the circle of human beings (see the next figure), indicating that no members of the category "Ontarians" occur who are not also members of the category "human beings."

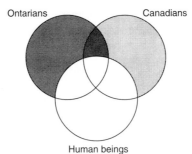

Ontarians   Canadians

Human beings

Does this figure represent the conclusion that all Ontarians are Canadian? It would if the entire area within the Ontario circle were shaded except where it intersects with the Canadian circle. Nonetheless, an unshaded area remains inside the Ontario circle but outside the Canadian circle, indicating that there *may be* some Ontarians who are not Canadian. This shows that even if premises 1 and 2 are both true, the possibility that the conclusion is false is still open. In other words, the inference is not valid.

Some of you may still wonder *why* this is an invalid inference. This may be due to your awareness that Ontario is one of the provinces of Canada. So, you may be thinking, it is not possible to be an Ontarian without also being a Canadian. It *is* possible, however, to be an Ontarian without being a Canadian. One can be a legal, tax-paying, and permanent resident of the province of Ontario without being a Canadian citizen. Suppose a Canadian woman who resides in Ontario marries an Indian man and the couple chooses to reside in Ontario but the husband retains his Indian citizenship. The main point here is that these possibilities do not conflict with either of the premises of the inference. In other words, it is possible for the premises both to be true and the conclusion still to be false, which again, is what the Venn diagram shows.

We have now diagrammed two syllogisms involving universal categorical statements. Let us also try a couple of examples involving particular categorical statements.

(1) All entertainers love attention.
(2) Some drug abusers are entertainers.
──────────────────────────────────
∴ (3) Some drug abusers love attention.

In the figure we will let the circle on the left represent the category of "drug abusers," the circle on the right represent the category of "attention lovers," and the lower circle represent the middle category of "entertainers."

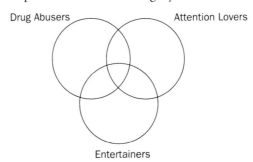

Drug Abusers   Attention Lovers

Entertainers

To represent premise 1 we must shade the entire entertainers circle except where it intersects with the circle of lovers of attention:

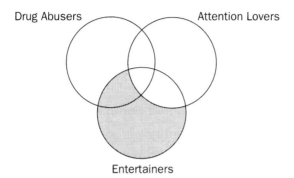

To represent premise 2 we must place an X somewhere in the intersection of the drug abusers and entertainers circles, but only half of the intersection remains open. Thus, the X may appear only in the area where all three circles intersect:

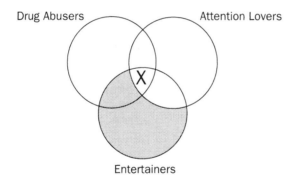

Does this figure represent the conclusion that some drug abusers are attention lovers? Yes, it does. An X already appears in the intersection of the circles representing drug abusers and attention lovers. This shows the inference to be valid.

Compare this last example with the similar one we discussed earlier:

(1) Some entertainers abuse drugs.

(2) All comedians are entertainers.

∴ (3) Some comedians are drug abusers.

In the next figure we will let the circle on the left represent the category of "comedians," the circle on the right represent the category of "drug abusers," and the lower circle represent the middle category of "entertainers."

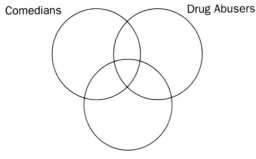

This time we will start with premise 2, following the guideline to diagram a universal premise before a particular one. To represent premise 2 we shade the entire area in the comedians circle except where it intersects with the entertainers circle, indicating that no comedians occur who are not also entertainers:

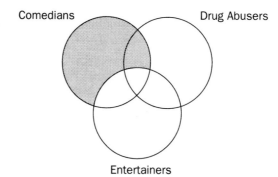

To represent premise 1 we must place an X somewhere in the intersection of the drug abusers and entertainers circles. Do we place it inside or outside the circle of comedians? Nothing in the premises determines the answer to this question. Since we do not know, the X goes on the line:

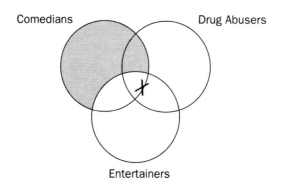

Now, does this figure represent the conclusion that some comedians are drug abusers? It would if the X appeared clearly within the intersection of the comedians and drug abusers circles, but it does not. It appears on the line, indicating that on the basis of our two premises it is not yet clear whether the conclusion is true, and thus that the inference is not valid.

EXERCISE 6.11 | **Invalid Syllogisms**

Here again are the syllogisms from Exercise 6.8. Use Venn diagrams to test for and demonstrate their validity or invalidity.

All human beings are mortals.

All Canadians are human beings.

∴ All Canadians are mortals.

All men are human beings.

All women are human beings.

∴ All women are men.

Some mysteries are entertaining.

Some books are mysteries.

∴ Some books are entertaining.

Some mysteries are not entertaining.

Some books are not mysteries.

∴ Some books are entertaining.

All mysteries are suspenseful.

Some books are not mysteries.

∴ Some books are not suspenseful.

ADDITIONAL EXERCISES

■ **Exercise 6.12**   For each of the following passages, indicate whether it is a deductive argument, an inductive argument, or not an argument.

Deductive	We can't lose. They've got no offence, and they've got no one to stop our leading scorer. They've lost their last four games, and it'll be on our court.	Explain your answer:
Inductive		
Nonargumentative		

Deductive	"In a democracy, the poor have more power than the rich, because there are more of them." —Aristotle	Explain your answer:
Inductive		
Nonargumentative		

Deductive	I've been eating corn on the cob for years, and I always count the number of rows. I have never found an ear of corn with an odd number of rows. I'm convinced that ears of corn always have even numbers of rows.	Explain your answer:
Inductive		
Nonargumentative		

Deductive	Even God makes mistakes. In the Bible, God says, "It repenteth me that I have made man." Now either the Bible is not the word of God, or we must believe that God did say, "It repenteth me that I have made man." But then, if we are to believe the word of God, we must further conclude that He really did repent making man, in which case, either God made a mistake in making man, or He made a mistake in repenting making man.	Explain your answer:
Inductive		
Nonargumentative		

	Deductive	The theory of the unreality of evil now seems to me untenable. Suppose that it can be proved that all that we think evil was in reality good. The fact would still remain that we think it evil. This may be called a delusion or mistake. But a delusion or mistake is as real as anything else. The delusion that evil exists is therefore real. But then it seems certain that a delusion which hid from us the goodness of the universe would itself be evil. And so there would be real evil after all. — J. M. E. McTaggart	Explain your answer:
	Inductive		
	Nonargumentative		

	Deductive	First of all, as the 18th-century Scottish philosopher David Hume pointed out, we never directly observe causal relationships. We have to infer them. Next, we can never infer them with deductive certainty. Since the evidence for a causal relationship is always indirect, some room for doubt will always exist when we infer a cause. In other words, we must reason inductively about them.	Explain your answer:
	Inductive		
	Nonargumentative		

	Deductive	In the entire history of the stock market, every bull market has been followed by a bear market, and vice versa. Therefore, the stock market behaves cyclically.	Explain your answer:
	Inductive		
	Nonargumentative		

		The riding of Grumbleburg has voted for the losing party in every provincial election since 1867. Grumbleburg polls show incumbent MP Press Fleshman running 27 points behind challenger Mary Kay Weedemout. But I'm tired of always voting for losers and lost causes. I'm going to vote for Fleshman, since it looks like he's going to win anyway.	Explain your answer:
	Deductive		
	Inductive		
	Nonargumentative		

■ **Exercise 6.13** Translate each of the following arguments into standard syllogistic form.

All crooks deserve to be punished. But some politicians are not crooks. So some politicians do not deserve to be punished.	C = crooks D = deserve to be punished P = politicians	Standard form:

All artists are creative people. Some artists live in poverty. Therefore, some creative people live in poverty.	A = artists C = creative people P = people who live in poverty	Standard form:

Some reference books are textbooks, for all textbooks are books intended for careful study and some reference books are intended for the same purpose.	R = reference books T = textbooks S = books intended for careful study	Standard form:

Since all birds eat worms, and chickens are birds, chickens must eat worms.	B = birds W = eaters of worms C = chickens	Standard form:

Most poets drink to excess, and some poets are women. So, some women drink to excess.	P = poets D = people who drink to excess W = women	Standard form:

Everyone who smokes marijuana goes on to try heroin. Everyone who tries heroin becomes a junkie. So everyone who smokes marijuana becomes a junkie.	M = marijuana smokers H = people who try heroin J = people who become junkies	Standard form:

This argument must be valid because its premises are true and its conclusion is true and all arguments with true premises and conclusions are valid.	A = anything that is this argument V = things that are valid T = things with true premises and conclusions	Standard form:

This argument must be invalid because its premises are not true and all arguments with untrue premises are invalid.	A = anything that is this argument I = things that are invalid U = arguments with untrue premises	Standard form:

■ **Exercise 6.14**   Using a combination of any two of the procedures discussed in this chapter (the intuitive test, the scenario method, Venn diagrams), determine which of the following are valid deductive arguments. For each invalid argument, compose a formally analogous argument that moves from obviously true premises to an obviously false conclusion.

	Valid	All crooks deserve to be punished. But some politicians are not crooks. So some politicians do not deserve to be punished.	Explain or give an example:
	Invalid		

	Valid	All artists are creative people. Some artists live in poverty. Therefore, some creative people live in poverty.	Explain or give an example:
	Invalid		

	Valid	Some reference books are textbooks, for all textbooks are books intended for careful study and some reference books are intended for the same purpose.	Explain or give an example:
	Invalid		

	Valid	Since all birds eat worms, and chickens are birds, chickens must eat worms.	Explain or give an example:
	Invalid		

	Valid	Most poets drink to excess, and some poets are women. So, some women drink to excess.	Explain or give an example:
	Invalid		

	Valid	Everyone who smokes marijuana goes on to try heroin. Everyone who tries heroin becomes a junkie. So everyone who smokes marijuana becomes a junkie.	Explain or give an example:
	Invalid		

	Valid	This argument must be valid because its premises are true and its conclusion is true and all arguments with true premises and conclusions are valid.	Explain or give an example:
	Invalid		

	Valid	This argument must be invalid because its premises are not true and all arguments with untrue premises are invalid.	Explain or give an example:
	Invalid		

Exercise 6.15   Take any position on the issue you have been working with so far and design an argument in support of the position using any of the deductively valid argument forms discussed in this chapter. Then take an alternative or opposed position and design an argument in support of it using any of the deductively valid argument forms discussed in this chapter.

GLOSSARY

categorical statement   a statement about a relationship between categories

categorical syllogism   a syllogism made up of only categorical statements

contradiction   in categorical logic: a form of opposition between categorical statements; two categorical statements that cannot both be true and also cannot both be false are contradictories

contrariety   a form of opposition between categorical statements; two categorical statements that cannot both be true but that might both be false are contraries

deductive   reasoning designed and intended to secure its conclusion with certainty so that anyone who fully understands what the statements in the argument mean must recognize that the premises cannot both be true without the conclusion also being true

distribution   a term is "distributed" when the claim in which it appears says something about *every member of the category* to which the term refers; for example, in the premise "All bonds are safe investments," the term "bonds" is distributed, but the term "safe investments" is not

fallacy   an unreliable inference

formal fallacy   an inference that is unreliable because it follows an unreliable form or pattern

inductive   reasoning designed and intended to make the conclusion reasonable, probable, or likely, but not certain

invalidity   in a deductive argument, the absence of the essential formal characteristic of a successful deductive argument (see "validity")

soundness   a feature of formally or structurally valid deductive arguments as follows: a structurally valid argument that is sound has both a deductively valid form and true premises; a structurally valid argument that is unsound has a deductively valid form but at least one false premise

square of opposition   in categorical logic, the array of relationships between the four statement forms showing the immediate inferences that may be drawn on the basis of differences of quality and quantity

subalternation   in categorical logic, if a universal statement is true, then the particular version of it (with the same quality) must also be true. As well, if the particular version of it (with the same quality) is false, then the universal statement is false

subcontrariety   a form of opposition between categorical statements; two categorical statements that might both be true but that cannot both be false are subcontraries

syllogism   a deductive inference from two premises

validity   the essential formal characteristic of a successful deductive argument; if the premises are taken to be true, then the conclusion must also be true

Go to http://www.criticalthinking1ce.nelson.com for additional study resources for this chapter.

Evaluating Deductive Arguments II: Truth Functional Logic

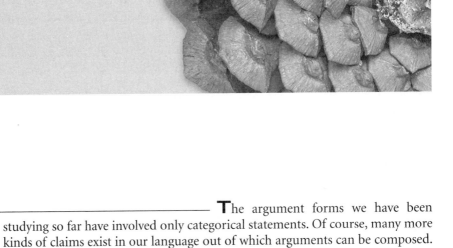

The argument forms we have been studying so far have involved only categorical statements. Of course, many more kinds of claims exist in our language out of which arguments can be composed. Arguments often involve claims similar to these:

- "Either we must make a few sacrifices in the area of privacy, or we will continue to be vulnerable to terrorist attacks."

- "If we allow our civil liberties to be destroyed in the name of greater security, then the terrorists will have won."

As powerful as Aristotle's system of categorical logic is, it is hopelessly awkward to try to translate claims like these into categorical statements. So, because claims like these are so important in reasoning, logicians have developed a system known as truth functional logic (often called "symbolic logic") to deal with them. This is the subject of the present chapter.

TRUTH FUNCTIONAL ANALYSIS
OF LOGICAL OPERATORS

The two examples above have easily recognizable grammatical structures. The first example is a "disjunction," which from the point of view of grammar means an "either . . . or . . ." statement. The second example is called a "conditional," which from the point of view of grammar means an "if . . . then . . ." statement. In studying the role they each play in reasoning and argumentation, however, we need to understand not only their grammatical structure but also their *logical* structure. In order to do this we need to introduce a bit more of the apparatus of modern logic: truth functional analysis of logical operators.

What in the world is a *logical operator*? As a first step, let us distinguish between simple and compound statements. A *simple statement* is one that does not contain another statement as a component part. A *compound statement* is one that does contain at least one other statement as a component part. For example, "The weather is great" and "I wish you were here" are each simple statements, but "The weather is great and I wish you were here" is a compound statement. Think of logical operators as devices for making compound statements out of simple(r) ones. In this example, the word *and* is used to express the logical operator known as conjunction.

NEGATION

Logical operators are defined and distinguished from each other according to how they affect the "truth values" of the compound sentences we make with them. Truth functional analysis is simply a way of keeping track in this regard. The simplest of the logical operators and the easiest to understand truth functionally is *negation*. For example, negating the simple statement "The weather is great" produces the compound statement "The weather is not great." In this example the word *not* is used to express the logical operator negation. How does the logical operator negation affect the truth value of the compound statement "The weather is not great"? If the simple statement "The weather is great" is true, then the compound statement "The weather is not great" is false, and if the simple statement "The weather is great" is false, then the compound statement "The weather is not great" is true. In other words, negation simply reverses the truth value of the component statement to which it is applied.

Here is a simple graphic representation. Let the letter "P" represent any statement. The symbol ~ will be used to represent the logical operator negation. Thus, "~P" represents the negation of P.

P	~P
T	F
F	T

This sort of graphical representation is called a "truth table." We use it here to define the logical operator negation by showing what the truth value of the compound statement produced by negation would be for each of the possible truth values of its component statement. Reading the rows of the truth table, if P is true, then its opposite, ~P, must be false, and if P is false, then its opposite, ~P, must be true.

CONJUNCTIONS

A truth table needs to have as many lines as there are possible combinations of truth value for the number of distinct components involved. Negation operates on a single component statement, P. Since P is either true or false (not true), our truth table for negation required only two lines. However, most logical operators connect two component statements, each of which might be either true or false. So a truth table defining any such operator will require four lines to represent each of the four possible combinations of truth value for the components.

To illustrate, let us use the example of conjunction mentioned above: "The weather is great and I wish you were here." This once again comprises the two simple statements "The weather is great" and "I wish you were here." The components of a conjunction are called "conjuncts." Let "P" stand for the first conjunct and the letter "Q" stand for the second. The symbol "&" will be used to represent the logical operator conjunction. Thus "P & Q" represents the conjunction of P and Q. We can see intuitively that the conjunction "P & Q" is true only if both of its conjuncts are true. "The weather is great and I wish you were here" is true only if the weather really is great and I really do wish you were here. If either conjunct or both were not true, then the conjunction "P & Q" would also not be true, as indicated in the following truth table:

P	Q	P & Q
T	T	T
T	F	F
F	T	F
F	F	F

If P is true and if Q is true (the first row of the truth table), then the conjunction "P & Q" must be true, too. If P and Q differ in value, as they do in the second and third rows of the truth table, then the conjunction "P & Q"—"*both* P and Q are true"—cannot be true (it must be false). If P is false and if Q is false, then the conjunction "P & Q"—"both P and Q are *true*"—cannot be true (it must be false).

DISJUNCTIONS

Like conjunctions, disjunctions assert a truth-functional relationship between the two component statements that comprise them. These component statements are called "disjuncts." Normally the relationship asserted by a disjunction can be expressed as follows: At least one of the disjuncts is true (possibly both). For example, the statement,

> Either the battery is dead or there is a short in the ignition switch.

asserts that at least one of the two statements "The battery is dead" and "There is a short in the ignition switch" is true (and both could be true). This relationship and the logical operator used to make compound statements that assert it we call *disjunction,* and we can represent it by means of the following truth table. Let the letters "P" and "Q" represent the two disjuncts and the symbol "v" represent the operator disjunction. Thus "P v Q" represents the statement "Either P or Q."

P	Q	P v Q
T	T	T
T	F	T
F	T	T
F	F	F

In contrast with the "inclusive" sense of disjunction above in which both disjuncts could be true, another sense of disjunction exists called the "exclusive or," which signifies that either P or Q is the case but not both. For example, "Either I am in Regina at time *t* or I am in Winnipeg at the same time *t*" expresses (in this case) exclusive disjunction (I can be in only one place at a time). "P exclusive or Q" can be symbolized as "(P v Q) & ~(P & Q)."

CONDITIONALS

We are now ready to examine the logical structure of conditionals. First, conditionals are compound statements. They assert that a peculiar kind of relationship (a "truth-dependency" relationship) holds between their component parts. For example, the conditional

> If love is blind, then fools rush in.

comprises the two simple component statements "Love is blind" and "Fools rush in." It does not assert that either of them *is* true, only that the truth of the second one *depends on* the truth of the first one. It asserts that the statement "Love is blind" *implies* the statement "fools rush in." We call both this relationship and the logical operator involved in making conditionals *implication*.

Because this is not a reciprocal relationship—because it only goes in one direction—we need terms to keep track of which statement depends on which. In a conditional statement, the component introduced by the word *if* is called the "antecedent," and the component introduced by the word *then* is called the "consequent." In this example "Love is blind" is the antecedent and "fools rush in" is the consequent.

Sometimes conditionals are used to say more than just that one statement implies another. For example, the statement,

> If abortion is homicide, then by definition it involves the killing of human beings.

expresses also that the consequent *follows (by definition)* from the antecedent. In another example, the statement,

> If the economy doesn't improve, then the prime minister will have a hard time getting re-elected.

expresses also that the antecedent is *causally* connected to the consequent. Finally, the following statement,

> If Parliament overrides the prime minister's proposed policy, then I'll eat my hat.

expresses also that the speaker is *committed* to doing something on a certain condition. In each of these cases, though, the statement expresses at a minimum that the truth of the consequent depends on the truth of the antecedent. This is the logical structure at the core of conditionals, represented in the truth table that follows. Let "P" represent the antecedent and "Q" represent the consequent. The symbol "⊃" will be used to represent the logical operator implication. Thus, "P ⊃ Q" represents the conditional "If P then Q."

P	Q	P ⊃ Q
T	T	T
T	F	F
F	T	T
F	F	T

You may have noticed that according to this truth table, the conditional "If P then Q" comes out false *only* when the antecedent is true and the consequent is false. In all other cases logic treats conditionals as true. It is intuitively reasonable to suppose that a conditional with a true antecedent and a false consequent is false. Generally this is how conditionals are tested for truth. Take the following example:

> If the economy does not improve, then the prime minister will lose her bid for a second term.

We could be certain that this conditional is false only if the economy does not improve (i.e., the antecedent is true) and the prime minister nevertheless is re-elected (i.e., the consequent is false). You might wonder, though, why we would want to call a conditional true whose antecedent and consequent are both false? Suppose you and your friend are scanning the radio dial for something new, and you happen to tune into a station broadcasting the latest in avant-garde electronic music, which sounds to both of you something like a dishwasher full of bone china falling down a flight of stairs. So your friend says:

> If this is music, then I'm the king of Peru.

The *point* of such a statement is to assert the *falsity* of the antecedent, to claim that this is not (*cannot possibly be*) music. Here is how the conditional is being used to make this point: In effect, your friend is saying, "Since the consequent is obviously false (I am not the king of Peru), if the antecedent *were* true the conditional itself would be false. But what I am now saying is true, so the antecedent has to be false too." Alternatively, ponder the fact that "if P then Q" is equivalent to "not both P and not-Q." In other words, it cannot be the case that P is the case but Q is not the case if the conditional statement is true. For example, if we say "If it rains, then it is humid" we are thereby asserting "it can't be the case that it rains but that it isn't humid." Thus, "$P \supset Q$" is equivalent to "$\sim(P\ \&\ \sim Q)$." Since the truth tables for "&" and "$\sim$" are unproblematic, so is the truth table for "$P \supset Q$."

Owing to the complexity and flexibility of language, quite a wide variety of ways of expressing this conditional relationship exist in English. For example, here is a conditional claim: "If I get an A in this class, then my overall average will be A as well." Here are several other ways of expressing the same claim:

- If I get an A in this class, my overall average will be A as well.
- My overall average will be A if I get an A in this class.
- My overall average will be A, provided I get an A in this class.
- My overall average will be A, on the condition that I get an A in this class.

By the same token, not every statement containing the word *if* is a conditional. "You're welcome to wait in the drawing room, if you like" would not ordinarily express a conditional relationship between two component statements. As in so many other situations, recognition of conditionals is an interpretive matter; we need to be aware of nuances of meaning in context.

One subtle but important difference of which we should be aware is the distinction between "if" and "only if." "My overall average will be A, *only if* I get an A in this class" does *not* say the same thing as "My overall average will be A if I get an A in this class." What it really says is "*Unless* I get an A in this class, my overall average *won't* be A." This is the same as saying "If I *don't* get an A in this class, my overall average *won't* be A." In other words, "*In order to* get my overall average up to A, I *must* get an A in this class." This means that if I have an overall average of A, then I will have gotten an A in this class. Thus, "only if" has the effect of reversing the conditional relationship between the antecedent and consequent, as the accompanying figure shows.

P = I get an A in this class   Q = My overall average will be A.

- **If** I get an A in this class, my overall average will be A.   **P ⊃ Q**
- My overall average will be A, **if** I get an A in this class.   **P ⊃ Q**
- My overall average will be A, **provided** I get an A in this class.   **P ⊃ Q**
- My overall average will be A, **on the condition that** I get an A in this class.   **P ⊃ Q**
- My overall average will be A **only if** I get an A in this class.   **Q ⊃ P**
- **Only if** I get an A in this class will my overall average will be A.   **Q ⊃ P**
- **Unless** I get an A in this class, overall average will **not** be A.   **~ P ⊃ ~ Q = Q ⊃ P**
- **If** my overall average will be A, I will have an A in this class.   **Q ⊃ P**

One way to distinguish "P if Q" from "P only if Q" is to note that each of them is one half of "P if and only if Q," symbolized as "P = Q." The so-called biconditional connective means implication in both directions. The truth table for "P = Q" is what we would expect given that "if and only if" is statement identity. In other words, if P and Q have the same values—if they are equivalent—then "P = Q" is true, and if they differ in values then "P = Q" is false:

P	Q	P = Q
T	T	T
T	F	F
F	T	F
F	F	T

EXERCISE 7.1

Translate the following claims into truth functional logical format.

Either the premier will defeat the proposal or she won't be re-elected.	V = The premier will defeat the proposal. R = The premier will get re-elected.	Truth Functional Format:

Judging from that getup, either he's the new Ronald McDonald or he thinks it's Halloween.	R = He's the new Ronald McDonald. H = He thinks it's Halloween.	Truth Functional Format:

We're going to be late and Grandma is not going to be happy.	L = We're going to be late. H = Grandma is going to be happy.	Truth Functional Format:

The weather is great and I wish you were here.	G = The weather is great. W = I wish you were here.	Truth Functional Format:

If you're ever going to become a musician, you're going to have to practice.	M = You're going to become a musician. P = You're going to have to practice.	Truth Functional Format:

Paul will graduate with honours only if he keeps his overall average above B this semester.	H = Paul will graduate with honours. K = Paul keeps his overall average above B this semester.	Truth Functional Format:

Paul will not graduate with honours unless he keeps his overall average above B this semester.	H = Paul will graduate with honours. K = Paul keeps his overall average above B this semester.	Truth Functional Format:

ARGUMENT FORMS

MODUS PONENS

Because of their unique structure, conditionals are extremely powerful reasoning tools, and so they play a crucial role in a great many arguments and argument forms. Let us suppose, for example, that an experimental space probe begins with the following conditional first premise:

(1) If there is life on Mars, then adequate life support exists on Mars.

Now suppose that the space probe establishes that in fact:

(2) Life exists on Mars.

From this as an additional premise together with the first premise, we can conclude that:

(3) Adequate life support exists on Mars.

Notice first that premise 2 is identical with the antecedent of the conditional premise 1, and that the conclusion is identical with its consequent. Notice also that it is impossible to assert 1 and 2 and deny 3 without contradicting yourself. Try it. Thus, this is a deductively valid argument. It follows a form that can be represented schematically as follows:

$$(1)\ P \supset Q$$
$$(2)\ P$$
$$\therefore (3)\ Q$$

Logicians traditionally refer to this argument form by the Latin label *modus ponens,* which means "affirmative mood." Because modus ponens is deductively valid, for any argument whatsoever, as long as the argument follows the form of modus ponens, accepting the premises forces you to accept the conclusion. Try it. Make some up.

FALLACY OF AFFIRMING THE CONSEQUENT

Now let us suppose that our space probe turns up another kind of evidence. Suppose the space probe establishes that:

(2a) Adequate life support exists on Mars.

Suppose we drew the conclusion from this together with premise 1 that:

(3a) Life exists on Mars.

Perhaps conclusion 3a is correct, but do our two premises really guarantee it? No, they do not. It is possible to deny 3a without contradicting the affirmation either of 1 or 2a. Try it (using the scenario method).

If you are having trouble with this, consider the following, formally similar argument:

If a figure is square, then it has four sides.
This rhombus has four sides.

∴ This rhombus is square.

Thus, this argument is not deductively valid. The form it follows, which can be schematically represented as below, is unreliable, or formally fallacious:

> (1) P ⊃ Q
> (2a) Q
> _____
>
> ∴ (3a) P

Logicians traditionally refer to this form as the *fallacy of affirming the consequent* because this is what the second premise does. It affirms the consequent of the conditional first premise. Note: Not all arguments that affirm the consequent are invalid. Some instances of affirming the consequent are valid, and some are invalid, whereas all instances of modus ponens are valid. An example of a valid instance of affirming the consequent is the following:

> (1) If it rains, then it both rains and it is humid.
> (2) It both rains and it is humid.
> _____
>
> ∴ (3) It rains.

MODUS TOLLENS

Now let us suppose that our space probe turns up yet another kind of evidence. Suppose the space probe establishes the following:

> (2b) No adequate life support exists on Mars.

From this together with our first premise, it is possible to conclude the following:

> (3b) No life exists on Mars.

Notice here that premise 2b is the denial of the consequent of premise 1, whereas 3b is the denial of its antecedent. Notice that here again it is impossible to affirm 1 and 2b and deny 3b without contradicting yourself. Try it. Thus, this inference is deductively valid. It follows a pattern that can be represented schematically as follows:

> (1) P ⊃ Q
> (2b) ~Q
> _____
>
> ∴ (3b) ~P

Logicians traditionally refer to this argument form by the Latin label *modus tollens*, which means "denying mood." Because modus tollens, like modus ponens, is deductively valid for any argument whatsoever, as long as the argument follows the form of modus tollens, accepting the premises forces you to accept the conclusion. Try it. Make some up.

FALLACY OF DENYING THE ANTECEDENT

Next, let us suppose our space probe establishes the following:

(2c) No life exists on Mars.

Suppose we drew from this and our first premise the conclusion the following:

(3c) Adequate life support does not exist on Mars.

Again, perhaps 3c is correct, but do premises 1 and 2c guarantee it? No, they do not. It is possible to affirm both 1 and 2c and deny 3c without contradicting yourself. Try it (again using the scenario method).

Recall the earlier example. You can demonstrate the invalidity of this inference by means of a formally similar argument:

If a figure is square then it has four sides.
This figure (a rhombus) is not a square.
_____

∴ This figure (a rhombus) does not have four sides.

Thus, this argument is not deductively valid. The form it follows, which can be schematically represented as follows, is unreliable, or formally fallacious:

$$(1) \quad P \supset Q$$
$$(2c) \ \sim P$$
_____

$$\therefore (3c) \ \sim Q$$

Logicians traditionally refer to this form as the *fallacy of denying the antecedent* because this is what the second premise does. It denies the antecedent of the conditional first premise.

The following table summarizes what we have said about these four conditional forms.

	Valid		Invalid	
Modus Ponens	(1) $P \supset Q$ (2) P		Asserting the Consequent	(1) $P \supset Q$ (2a) Q
	$\therefore$(3) Q			$\therefore$(3a) P
Modus Tollens	(1) $P \supset Q$ (2b) $\sim Q$		Denying the Antecedent	(1) $P \supset Q$ (2c) $\sim P$
	$\therefore$(3b) $\sim P$			$\therefore$(3c) $\sim Q$

EXERCISE 7.2

Demonstrate the fallacious status of affirming the consequent and denying the antecedent by composing arguments of each form that move from intuitively acceptable or obviously true premises to intuitively unacceptable or obviously false conclusions.

_____

_____

_____

EXERCISE 7.3

Analyze and evaluate the following two arguments:

If astrology is correct, then all people born at the same time would have the same sort of personalities, experiences, and opportunities, yet this is not the case.
   i. What is the thesis of this argument?
   ii. The argument is an example of which argument form?
   iii. Is the argument deductively valid or not?

If astrology has been refuted, then we *should* not depend on the predictions in the horoscope. Since, however, astrology has not been refuted, we *should* depend on the predictions.
   i. What is the thesis of this argument?
   ii. The argument is an example of which argument form?
   iii. Is the argument deductively valid or not?

HYPOTHETICAL SYLLOGISM

Another commonly used and important argument form involves two conditional premises. Let us suppose once again, for example, that an experimental space probe begins with the following conditional first premise:

(1) If life exists on Mars, then adequate life support exists on Mars.

This time, however, let us add a second conditional premise:

(2d) If adequate life support exists on Mars, then a mission to Mars by astronauts is feasible.

From this together with our premise 1b, it is possible to conclude the following:

(3d) If life exists on Mars, then a mission to Mars by astronauts is feasible.

Notice here that premise 2d is a conditional whose antecedent is identical with the consequent of premise 1, whereas the conclusion, 3d, is another conditional, whose antecedent is identical with the antecedent of premise 1 and whose consequent is identical with the consequent of premise 2d. Notice that here again it is impossible to affirm 1 and 2d and deny 3d without contradicting yourself. Try it.

Thus, this inference is deductively valid. It follows a pattern that can be represented schematically as follows:

$$(1) \quad P \supset Q$$
$$(2d) \quad Q \supset R$$

$$\therefore (3d) \quad P \supset R$$

Logicians traditionally refer to this argument form as "hypothetical syllogism." Because hypothetical syllogism, like modus ponens and modus tollens, is deductively valid for any argument whatsoever, as long as the argument follows the form of hypothetical syllogism, accepting the premises forces you to accept the conclusion. Try it. Make some up.

Now compare the last example with this one:

(1) If life exists on Mars, then adequate life support exists on Mars.
(2e) A mission to Mars by astronauts is feasible only if adequate life support exists on Mars.

∴ (3d) If life exists on Mars, then a mission to Mars by astronauts is feasible.

This inference is not deductively valid. Remember that "only if" (as in premise 2e) reverses the positions of antecedent and consequent (see the figure on page 192). You can also see the invalidity using the following scenario. Suppose it is true that the existence of life on Mars presupposes adequate life support on Mars (premise 1). Suppose also that a mission to Mars by astronauts is feasible *only if* adequate life support exists on Mars (premise 2e). Now let us also suppose that indeed life on Mars exists, and so also adequate life support on Mars. Intuitively, however, we can see fairly clearly that the feasibility of a mission to Mars by astronauts is still an open question. So the conclusion (3d) does not follow logically from these two premises.

DISJUNCTIVE SYLLOGISM

Like conditional statements, disjunctions are extremely powerful reasoning tools, and so they play a crucial role in a great many arguments and argument forms. Let us suppose, for example, that we have been trying to diagnose the mechanical problem of a car, and we have eliminated all possible problems but two: the battery and the ignition switch. So we now have good reason to believe the following:

(1) Either the battery is dead or the ignition switch has short-circuited.

Now suppose we check the battery and find that it is fully charged and functioning properly. We now know the following:

(2) The battery is not dead.

From this together with our first premise, it is possible to conclude the following:

(3) The ignition switch has short-circuited.

Notice here that premise 2 is the denial of one of the disjuncts of premise 1, whereas 3 is identical with the other disjunct. Notice that here again it is impossible to affirm 1 and 2 and deny 3 without contradicting yourself. Try it. Thus, this inference is deductively valid. It follows a pattern that can be represented schematically as follows:

$$(1) \ P \lor Q$$
$$(2) \ \sim P$$
$$\therefore (3) \ Q$$

Logicians traditionally refer to this argument form as "disjunctive syllogism." Disjunctive syllogism applies if the "or" is either inclusive or exclusive. For example, if either I am in Regina at time t or I am in Winnipeg at the same time t, and I am not in Regina, then it follows that I am in Winnipeg. Nonetheless, the following argument is also valid: "If either I am in Regina or Winnipeg at time t, and I am in Regina at time t, then it follows that I am not in Winnipeg." This illustrates that the following argument form is valid for the *exclusive* sense of "or" only:

$$(1) \ P \lor Q$$
$$(2) \ P$$
$$\therefore (3) \ \sim Q$$

CONSTRUCTIVE DILEMMA AND ENTHYMEMES

One of the oldest and most powerful argumentative strategies combines conditional and disjunctive premises. The strategy aims to prove its point by showing that it is implied by each of two alternatives, at least one of which must be true. The strategy and the argument form that embodies it are called constructive dilemma. For example, suppose that during the CBC "Hockey Night In Canada" pregame commentary you hear Don Cherry say, "If the Leafs beat the Canadiens tonight, then the Oilers are in the playoffs as division champs. But if the Canadiens beat the Leafs, then the Oilers are at least guaranteed a playoff spot."

EXERCISE 7.4

This is an incompletely stated argument. Using the tools presented in Chapter 4, see if you can reconstruct it before you read any further.

- If the Leafs beat the Canadiens tonight, then the Oilers are in the playoffs as division champs. But if the Canadiens beat the Leafs, then the Oilers are at least guaranteed a playoff spot.

The argument as presented consists of two claims, both conditionals, neither of which seems to support the other. The point is apparently that the Oilers are in the playoffs (regardless of the outcome of tonight's game). Thus, the implied conclusion of the argument would be "The Oilers are in the playoffs." Now the argument also depends on a third premise, which is unstated because it is so obvious that it "goes without saying," namely, that either the Leafs will beat the Canadiens or the Canadiens will beat the Leafs. A valid argument with a missing or suppressed premise, or the missing or suppressed premise itself, is called an *enthymeme*. When these elements are filled in, the argument goes like this:

(a) Either the Leafs will beat the Canadiens or the Canadiens will beat the Leafs.
(1) If the Leafs beat the Canadiens, then the Oilers are in the playoffs (as division champs).
(2) If the Canadiens beat the Leafs, then the Oilers are at least guaranteed a playoff spot.

∴ (C*) The Oilers are in the playoffs.

Notice here that antecedent of claim (1) is one of the disjuncts of the implied premise (a), and the antecedent of claim (2) is the other disjunct, while the consequent of each conditional claim is the argument's implied conclusion (C*). Notice that here again it is impossible to affirm the three premises together and deny the conclusion without contradicting yourself. Try it. Thus, this inference is deductively valid. It follows the constructive dilemma pattern, and can be represented schematically as follows:

(1) P v Q
(2) P ⊃ R
(3) Q ⊃ R
_____
∴ (4) R

EXERCISE 7.5

Identify the logical structure of each of the following examples.

Modus Ponens	If Paul keeps his overall average above B this semester, then he will
Affirming Consequent	graduate with honours. And his overall average is A-. So he's going to be
Modus Tollens	graduating with honours.
Denying Antecedent	
Hypothetical Syllogism	
Disjunctive Syllogism	
Dilemma	

	Modus Ponens	
	Asserting Consequence	
	Modus Tollens	
	Denying Antecedent	
	Hypothetical Syllogism	
	Disjunctive Syllogism	
	Dilemma	

Unless [...] overall average above B this semester, he won't gradua[...] [...]age is A-. So he's going to gradua[...]

$\sim P \supset \sim Q$

P

$\therefore Q$

	Modus Ponens	
	Asserting Consequence	
	Modus Tollens	
	Denying Antecedent	
	Hypothetical Syllogism	
	Disjunctive Syllogism	
	Dilemma	

Unless Paul keeps his overall average above B this semester, he won't graduate with honours. And his overall average is C. So he's not going to graduate with honours.

	Modus Ponens	
	Asserting Consequence	
	Modus Tollens	
	Denying Antecedent	
	Hypothetical Syllogism	
	Disjunctive Syllogism	
	Dilemma	

Paul will graduate with honours only if he keeps his overall average above B this semester. He will keep his overall average above B only if he studies an extra 20 hours per week. So Paul will graduate with honours only if he studies an extra 20 hours per week.

	Modus Ponens	
	Asserting Consequence	
	Modus Tollens	
	Denying Antecedent	
	Hypothetical Syllogism	
	Disjunctive Syllogism	
	Dilemma	

We're not going to get to sleep unless the dog stops barking. The dog won't stop barking until the porch light is turned off. So we'll get to sleep only if the porch light is turned off.

	Modus Ponens	
	Asserting Consequence	
	Modus Tollens	
	Denying Antecedent	
	Hypothetical Syllogism	
	Disjunctive Syllogism	
	Dilemma	

Either we turn the porch light off, or that dog will keep on barking. We're not going to get any sleep until the dog stops barking. So we'd better go turn that porch light off.

Modus Ponens	"Every time we talked to higher level managers, they kept saying they didn't know anything about the problems below them. Either the guys at the top didn't know, in which case they should have known, or they did know, in which case they were lying to us."[1]
Asserting Consequence	
Modus Tollens	
Denying Antecedent	
Hypothetical Syllogism	
Disjunctive Syllogism	
Dilemma	

TESTING FOR VALIDITY WITH TRUTH TABLES

In Chapter 6 we found the system of Venn diagrams useful as a graphic means of testing the validity of categorical syllogisms. Venn diagrams do not accommodate particularly well the kind of argument forms we have just been considering, but we can use truth tables for this purpose. We conclude this chapter by demonstrating this feature of truth tables. Thus far we have used truth tables to define and explain logical operators. A truth table lists all possible combinations of truth value for all components of a truth functional compound statement on the left, with the corresponding truth value of the compound statement in the far right column, as, for example, in this truth table for implication:

Components		Compound
P	Q	P ⊃ Q
(premise 2)	(conclusion)	(premise 1)
T	T	T
T	F	F
F	T	T
F	F	T

MODUS PONENS

It so happens that the truth table also represents all the possible truth-value combinations of the premises and conclusion of the argument form modus ponens. The column on the right corresponds to premise 1, the column on the left corresponds to premise 2, and the column in the middle corresponds to the conclusion. So we should also be able to tell from the truth table whether or not it is possible for both of the premises to be true while the conclusion is false. As always, if so, the argument form is not deductively valid, but if not, the argument form is deductively valid. We see only one line (line 1) of the truth table on which both premises are true (see the accompanying figure), and on that line the conclusion is also true. So the argument form is a valid one.

Components		Compound
P	Q	P ⊃ Q
(premise 2)	*(conclusion)*	*(premise 1)*
T	T	T
T	F	F
F	T	T
F	F	T

FALLACY OF AFFIRMING THE CONSEQUENT

It turns out also that the truth table for implication represents all the possible truth-value combinations of the premises and conclusion of the fallacy of affirming the consequent. In this case the column on the right corresponds to premise 1, the column in the middle corresponds to premise 2, and the column on the left corresponds to the conclusion. So again we should also be able to tell from the truth table whether or not it is possible for both of the premises to be true while the conclusion is false. This time, we see two lines (lines 1 and 3) of the truth table on which both premises are true (see the accompanying figure), and on line 3 the conclusion is false. In other words, the truth table shows that it is possible for an argument of this form to have true premises and a false conclusion, and therefore that the argument is not valid.

Components		Compound
P	Q	P ⊃ Q
(conclusion)	*(premise 2)*	*(premise 1)*
T	T	T
T	F	F
Ⓕ	T	T
F	F	T

MODUS TOLLENS

Testing the validity of modus tollens and the fallacy of denying the antecedent is only slightly more complicated. None of the truth tables we have generated so far happens to represent all the possible truth-value combinations for the premises and conclusions of either of these two argument forms. All we need do, however, is merely add a couple of columns to the truth table for implication to accomplish this (see the accompanying figure). These two columns represent the truth values of ~ P and ~ Q, which, according to the truth table for negation, are simply the reverse of the truth values for P and Q respectively.

Components		Compounds		
P	Q	P ⊃ Q	~P	~Q
		(premise 1)	(conclusion)	(premise 2)
T	T	T	F	F
T	F	F	F	T
F	T	T	T	F
F	F	T	T	T

To test the validity of modus tollens we simply need to locate the columns representing the premises and conclusion and check to see whether or not it is possible for both of the premises to be true while the conclusion is false. In our truth table, the third column now represents premise 1, the column on the far right represents premise 2, and the column between them represents the conclusion. We see only one line (line 4) on which both premises are true. Since the conclusion is also true on this line, the argument form is a valid one.

FALLACY OF DENYING THE ANTECEDENT

Similarly, to test the fallacy of denying the antecedent we simply need to locate the columns representing the premises and conclusion and check to see whether or not it is possible for both of the premises to be true while the conclusion is false. In our truth table the third column now represents premise 1, the column immediately to the right of it represents premise 2, and the column on the far right represents the conclusion (see the accompanying figure). This time, however, we see two lines (lines 3 and 4) of the truth table on which both premises are true, and on line 3 the conclusion is false. In other words, the truth table shows that it is possible for an argument of this form to have true premises and a false conclusion, and therefore that the argument is not valid.

Components		Compounds		
P	Q	P ⊃ Q	~P	~Q
		(premise 1)	(premise 2)	(conclusion)
T	T	T	F	F
T	F	F	F	T
F	T	T	T	Ⓕ
F	F	T	T	T

Again we can demonstrate its validity by means of a truth table. This time we are dealing with three distinct components: P, Q, and R. So our truth table (see figure) will need eight lines in order to represent all the possible combinations of truth value for the number of distinct components involved.

Components			Compounds		
P	Q	R	P ⊃ R	Q ⊃ R	P v Q
		(conclusion)	(premise 2)	(premise 3)	(premise 1)
T	T	T	T	T	T
T	T	F	F	F	T
T	F	T	T	T	T
T	F	F	F	F	T
F	T	T	T	T	T
F	T	F	T	T	T
F	F	T	T	T	F
F	F	F	T	T	F

This time, there are three lines (lines 1, 3, and 5) of the truth table on which all the premises are true. Since the conclusion is also true on each of these lines, the argument form is a valid one.

EXERCISE 7.6

Demonstrate the validity of the argument form hypothetical syllogism by means of the truth table below. Highlight the rows in which the truth values of both premises are true. Then determine whether the argument form is valid, as illustrated above.

P	Q	R	P ⊃ R	Q ⊃ R	P ⊃ R
T	T	T	T	T	T
T	T	F	T	F	F
T	F	T	F	T	T
T	F	F	F	T	F
F	T	T	T	T	T
F	T	F	T	F	T
F	F	T	T	T	T
F	F	F	T	T	T

EXERCISE 7.7

Demonstrate the validity of the argument form disjunctive syllogism by means of the truth table below. Highlight the rows in which the truth values of both premises are true. Then determine whether the argument form is valid as illustrated above.

P	Q	P v Q	~P
T	T	T	F
T	F	T	F
F	T	T	T
F	F	F	T

ADDITIONAL EXERCISES

■ **EXERCISE 7.8** Translate the following claims into truth functional logical format.

If a government encourages terrorists, we will hold that government responsible.	G = a government encourages terrorists H = we will hold that government responsible	Truth Functional Format:
If a government encourages terrorists, we will not hesitate to use military force.	G = a government encourages terrorists H = we will hesitate to use military force	Truth Functional Format:
Either the RCMP memo was lost, or CSIS analysts misunderstood the memo's implications.	F = the RCMP memo was lost C = CSIS analysts misunderstood the memo's implications	Truth Functional Format:
Either the RCMP memo was lost, or CSIS analysts did not understand the memo's implications.	F = the RCMP memo was lost C = CSIS analysts understood the memo's implications	Truth Functional Format:
The RCMP memo was lost, and CSIS analysts did not understand its implications.	F = the RCMP memo was lost C = CSIS analysts understood the memo's implications	Truth Functional Format:
Unless interagency communication is improved, national security will continue to be at risk.	I = interagency communication is improved N = national security will continue to be at risk	Truth Functional Format:

■ **EXERCISE 7.9** Translate each of the following arguments into standard form using the scheme of abbreviation provided. Then set up and complete a truth table for each argument and determine each argument's validity status.

If Paul keeps his overall average above B this semester, then he will graduate with honours. And his overall average is A-. So he's going to graduate with honours.	H = "Paul will graduate with honours." K = "Paul keeps his overall average above B this semester." S = "Paul studies an extra 20 hours per week."

H	K	S	Premise 1	Premise 2	Conclusion	Valid	Invalid
t	t	t					
t	t	t					
t	f	f					
f	t	t					
f	t	f					
f	t	f					
f	f	t					
f	f	f					

Unless Paul keeps his overall average above B this semester he won't graduate with honours. But his overall average is A-. So he's going to graduate with honours.	H = "Paul will graduate with honours." K = "Paul keeps his overall average above B this semester." S = "Paul studies an extra 20 hours per week."

H	K	S	Premise 1	Premise 2	Conclusion	Valid	Invalid
t	t	t					
t	t	f					
t	f	t					
t	f	f					
f	t	t					
f	t	f					
f	f	t					
f	f	f					

| Unless Paul keeps his overall average above B this semester he won't graduate with honours. And his overall average is C. So he's not going to graduate with honours. | H = "Paul will graduate with honours."
K = "Paul keeps his overall average above B this semester."
S = "Paul studies an extra 20 hours per week." | |

			Premise 1	Premise 2	Conclusion	Valid	Invalid
H	K	S					
t	t	t					
t	t	f					
t	f	t					
t	f	f					
f	t	t					
f	t	f					
f	f	t					
f	f	f					

| Paul will graduate with honours only if he keeps his overall average above B this semester. He will keep his overall average above B only if he studies an extra 20 hours per week. So Paul will graduate with honours only if he studies an extra 20 hours per week. | H = "Paul will graduate with honours."
K = "Paul keeps his overall average above B this semester."
S = "Paul studies an extra 20 hours per week." | |

			Premise 1	Premise 2	Conclusion	Valid	Invalid
H	K	S					
t	t	t					
t	t	f					
t	f	t					
t	f	f					
f	t	t					
f	t	f					
f	f	t					
f	f	f					

We're not going to get to sleep unless the dog stops barking. The dog won't stop barking until the porch light is turned off. So we'll get to sleep only if the porch light is turned off.	W = we are going to get to sleep D = the dog will stop barking P = the porch light is turned off	

W	D	P	Premise 1	Premise 2	Conclusion	Valid	Invalid
t	t	t					
t	t	f					
t	f	t					
t	f	f					
f	t	t					
f	t	f					
f	f	t					
f	f	f					

Either we turn the porch light off, or that dog will keep on barking. We're not going to get to sleep until the dog stops barking. So we'd better go turn that porch light off.	W = we are going to get to sleep D = the dog will stop barking P = the porch light is turned off	

W	D	P	Premise 1	Premise 2	Conclusion	Valid	Invalid
t	t	t					
t	t	f					
t	f	t					
T	f	f					
f	t	t					
f	t	f					
f	f	t					
f	f	f					

■ **EXERCISE 7.10** Take any position on the issue you have been working with so far, and design an argument in support of that position, using any of the deductively valid argument forms discussed in this chapter. Then take an alternative or opposed position and design an argument in support of it using any of the deductively valid argument forms discussed in this chapter.

GLOSSARY

antecedent in a hypothetical statement, the component introduced by the word *if*

conjunction a compound statement that is true only when both of its components are true; the logical operator *and* used to make such a statement

consequent in a hypothetical statement, the component introduced by the word *then*

contradiction in truth functional logic, a conflict between a statement and its negation

dilemma, constructive an argument form or strategy combining hypothetical and disjunctive premises that seeks to prove its point by showing that it is implied by each of two alternatives, at least one of which must be true

disjunct component of a disjunction

disjunction a compound statement that is true when either one or both of its components are true; the logical operator *or* used to make such a statement

disjunctive syllogism a deductively valid argument form based on a disjunction and the denial of one of its disjuncts

enthymeme an unstated premise, or an inferential configuration involving an unstated premise

fallacy of affirming the consequent a (sometimes) deductively invalid argument form based on a hypothetical statement and the affirmation of its consequent

fallacy of denying the antecedent a (sometimes) deductively invalid argument form based on a hypothetical statement and the denial of its antecedent

hypothetical syllogism a deductively valid argument form based on two hypothetical statements as premises, where the consequent of the first is the antecedent of the second

logical operator in truth functional logic, a device for making a compound statement out of simple(r) ones

modus ponens a deductively valid argument form based on a hypothetical statement and the affirmation of its antecedent

modus tollens a deductively valid argument form based on a hypothetical statement and the denial of its consequent

negation the logical operator that reverses the truth-value of the component statement to which it is applied; a statement formed by applying this logical operator

truth functional analysis system for keeping track of how logical operators affect the truth-values of compound sentences made with them

truth functional logic system of logic based on truth functional analysis

truth table chart used in truth functional logic for listing variable truth values

truth value the truth or falsity of a statement

Go to http://www.criticalthinking1ce.nelson.com for additional study resources for this chapter.

ENDNOTES

[1] Richard Feynman, "Mr. Feynman Goes to Washington: Investigating the Space Shuttle *Challenger* Disaster," *What Do You Care What Other People Think? Further Adventures of a Curious Character* (New York: W.W. Norton, 1988), 212–13.

Inductive Reasoning

CHAPTER 8

Evaluating Inductive Arguments I: Generalization and Analogy

As we have seen in the previous two chapters, deductively valid arguments guarantee their conclusions. If the truth of the premises of a deductively valid argument has been established, no more room exists for doubt about the argument's conclusion. Nonetheless, many arguments that do not provide this "absolute" level of inferential security provide substantial support for their conclusions and are therefore not to be dismissed simply on the grounds that they are not *deductively* valid. Some arguments exist whose premises, though they do not *guarantee* the conclusion, nevertheless make the conclusion more reasonable or probable or likely. Such an argument "stretches" or extends its way toward a conclusion. Here is an example of such an argument:

[Professor Chen has never missed a class. ①] So chances are [she'll be in class today. ②]

If the premise (claim #1) is accepted as true, then it would be reasonable to accept the argument's conclusion (claim #2). Of course, even if the premise is

THE NORM Michael Jantze

WOMEN ARE SO DIFFERENT FROM MEN.

WHAT? LIKE I HAVE TO PROVE IT?

© Michael Jantze King Features Syndicate.

true the conclusion may prove to be false: Professor Chen may not show up for class. Perhaps she is ill or has had an accident or been arrested or has an important conflicting appointment. Nonetheless, the premise does provide reasonable support for the conclusion. Here is another example:

> [It's highly unlikely that any female will play football in the Canadian Football League in the near future, ①] for [none has so far. ②]

Again, if the premise (claim #2) is accepted as true, it provides good—though not deductively valid—grounds for accepting the conclusion (claim #1). These are examples of *inductive* inferences. As we explained in Chapter 6, the essential difference between deductive and inductive reasoning is that deductive inferences are designed to achieve "absolute inferential security," whereas inductive inferences are designed to manage risk of error where absolute inferential security is unattainable.

ASSESSING INDUCTIVE STRENGTH

A deductive argument is either valid or not valid. On the other hand, inductive strength is relative, which means it *admits of degrees*. Some valid inductive arguments are stronger than others. In the absence of *absolute* inferential security— that is to say, when the premises, even if true, leave room for doubt about the conclusion—the essential question becomes "How much room for doubt?" To evaluate inductive reasoning we must estimate the *relative* security of inferences.

EXERCISE 8.1 | **Inductive Strength**

Which is the "stronger" of the following two arguments?

1. The last three cars we have owned have been Ace products, and they've all been trouble free. So we're probably safe to assume that a new Pinnacle will be reliable.

2. In Consumer Safety First nationwide studies of new cars purchased over the last 10 years, Ace had a 30 percent lower frequency-of-repair rate than the other manufacturers. So we're probably safe to assume that a new Pinnacle will be reliable.

In each argument the premise does provide some reason for accepting the conclusion. The first argument, though, leaves more room for doubt than the second one. So the second argument is that much stronger than the first one. If inductive strength is a matter of degree—and the essential question for assessing inductive strength is, "How much room for doubt is left here?"—the answer to this question is, "It depends." Inductive strength depends on a number of variables, according to the *type* of inductive reasoning involved.

INDUCTIVE GENERALIZATIONS

We begin with the simplest and most common of inductive types of reasoning: *inductive generalization,* or simply "generalization." This type of inductive reasoning is involved whenever we draw a general conclusion from a number of particular instances.

Suppose that you work with computers and you have just opened a new shipment of floppy disks. Let us say that the floppy disks are delivered in shipments of 100. The first disk you try is defective. So you try a second one, and it is defective, too. So you try a third disk, which also proves defective. At some point you begin to wonder whether the whole shipment might be defective. So far you have only tried three disks. They have all proven defective, but still you cannot be terribly sure that the entire shipment is defective. In fact, at this point you merely suspect that the entire shipment might be defective, because you have barely sampled the shipment. Suppose you keep going. You try a fourth disk and a fifth disk. Both prove defective. This confirms your suspicion. Obviously, the more disks you try (assuming each one is defective), the more certain you become that the entire shipment is defective. By the time you get to the 35th disk (assuming each one is defective), you will be much more certain—though still not *absolutely* certain—that the entire shipment is defective. This highlights two of the variables that affect the strength of an inductive generalization. From now on, let us refer to the number of disks you have tried as the *sample* and the entire shipment (the general class about which you are concerned) as the *population*. The size of the sample and the size of the population each affect the strength of the inductive inference. *As the size of the sample increases relative to the population, so does the strength of the induction.*

CRITICAL THINKING TIP 8.1

As the size of the sample increases relative to the population, so does the strength of the induction.

Other variables affect inductive strength. If the only variables affecting inductive strength were the size of the sample and the size of the population, then the only way to increase inductive strength—or reduce doubt—would be to keep plodding along, testing the disks one by one until the sample coincides with the population. You do not, however, need to test each and every disk to be reasonably certain about the entire population. A commonsense shortcut would be this: After you have identified the first three or so disks as defective, dig down farther into the shipment and try a disk from the middle and another one from near the bottom. If they, too, turn out to be defective, you can be more certain—although still not *absolutely* certain—that the entire shipment is defective. Notice also that if you followed this procedure and got these results, you would be *more* certain than if you had just tried the *next two* disks. Why? It is much more *unlikely* that by sampling in this more "random" way you would end up picking just those disks that are defective. This highlights another of the variables that affect the strength of an inductive inference: the degree to which the sample is representative of the population as a whole. *The more representative the sample is of the population as a whole, the stronger the induction.*

CRITICAL THINKING TIP 8.2

The more representative the sample is of the population as a whole, the stronger the induction.

How do we determine the degree to which the sample is representative of the population as a whole? This is really a matter of variety. In this example, our "expanded for variety sample" is equal in size to our "keep on plodding along sample" but "covers more variables," as the accompanying figure shows.

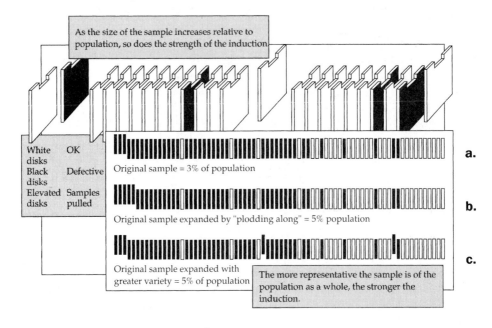

As the size of the sample increases relative to population, so does the strength of the induction

White disks — OK
Black disks — Defective
Elevated disks — Samples pulled

a. Original sample = 3% of population

b. Original sample expanded by "plodding along" = 5% population

c. Original sample expanded with greater variety = 5% of population

The more representative the sample is of the population as a whole, the stronger the induction.

Suppose the disks are packed in the order that they came off the assembly line, and you began by sampling them in (reverse) order. In sampling the middle and both ends of the shipment rather than just the beginning, you are adding to the variety of the sample by including particular examples that represent the entire population, whether packed first, middle, or last. You have added to the variety of the sample in the *dimension* of "numerical order within the shipment." This is significant because numerical order within the shipment— numerical position in the "packing order"—could have something to do with whether a given disk is defective. Maybe a short run of 30 consecutive defective disks occurred. By varying the sample through the dimension of numerical order, you have a way of ruling this out as a possible source of error—a way to reduce the risk of error. Because numerical order within the shipment might have something to do with whether a disk is defective or not, numerical order within the shipment is a *relevant* dimension here. *Generally, you should try to vary the sample as widely and in as many different relevant dimensions as you can conceive.* In science this is called *controlling the variables.* These two factors— sample size relative to population size, and representativeness of the sample— help explain why the first of our two examples of induction was weaker than the second. A *nationwide* comparative study of frequency-of-repair rates involving *not just* Ace products but those of other manufacturers as well constitutes both a larger and more representative sample than the tiny and highly selective "last three cars we have owned."

EXERCISE 8.2 | Inductive Strength II

Rank the following inductive arguments in order of decreasing strength (strongest to weakest). Be prepared to explain your ranking.

- Contrary to current media claims, our schools appear to be doing a superb job of teaching our children to read. A leading news magazine recently tabulated the results of the thousands of responses it received to the survey it published in its May issue. Readers from every province and territory responded. Ninety percent of the respondents believed that their school-aged children's reading skills were good to excellent. Eight percent more believed that their children's reading skills were at least adequate. Less than 1 percent felt that their children were developing less than adequate reading skills. (One percent of the respondents failed to answer this question.)

- In all the studies that have been done over the past 30 years concerning the relationship between standardized test performance and success in school, involving several hundred thousand school-age subjects from a variety of ethnic, regional, and socioeconomic backgrounds, I.Q. (intelligence quotient) tests have been shown to be the single most reliable predictor of success in school. Therefore, if one scores highly on I.Q. tests, one will probably perform well in school.

- An hour in a hot tub will probably impair a man's fertility for up to six weeks. According to one study, three men who sat in a hot tub with water heated to 39°C (most health clubs heat theirs to 40°C) showed reductions in the number and penetrative ability of their sperm cells. In samples taken

36 hours later, the damage was present, but the most dramatic effects did not show up until four weeks later. This indicated that the high heat had harmed even immature sperm cells. (It takes about seven weeks for a newly created sperm cell to mature and pass through a system of storage ducts.) Seven weeks after the men's dip in the hot tub, their sperm returned to normal.

STATISTICAL GENERALIZATIONS

In our example of the defective computer disks, notice that *all* the members of the sample turned out to be one way: defective. Life is rarely so simple. More often, some members of the sample will be one way, and some another. So, a variation on simple inductive generalization involves projecting *trends* or *percentages* observed in the sample onto other instances or onto the population as a whole. This is commonly called *statistical generalization*. For instance, suppose we are interested in how likely university students with different majors are to gain admission to law school. We might survey law school admissions for a certain period. Suppose our survey shows that 20 percent more of those applicants with a major in philosophy were admitted than were admitted from the next most successful major. We might then project inductively that philosophy majors are at least 20 percent more likely to gain admission to law school than other university students.

The same principles used to evaluate the strength of simple inductive generalizations also apply in evaluating the strength of statistical generalizations. In both simple inductive generalization and statistical induction, the strength of the inference increases with the size of the sample relative to the population and with the degree to which the sample is representative of the population as a whole. Suppose our survey of law school admissions was only one year long or was confined to the province of Manitoba. Then we might be overlooking variables that might otherwise show up in a 10-year nationwide survey. Perhaps in a particular year more students with law school aptitude happened to elect philosophy as a major. Perhaps the province of Manitoba has particularly strong instructional programs in philosophy. In any case, the smaller and more selective the sample, the weaker the induction.

MARGIN OF ERROR

Another variable that affects the strength of statistical generalizations is the degree of precision and certainty attached to the conclusion relative to the evidence contained in the premises. A statistical generalization can generally be strengthened by hedging the conclusion with appropriate qualifications: by toning down the language with which the conclusion is presented. This is one reason why statistical arguments often sound so "wishy-washy" in spite of all the numbers in them. Similarly, the degree of precision with which the figures in the conclusion are stated can affect the strength of a statistical generalization. We may lack sufficient evidence to conclude with much certainty that precisely 73.86 percent of the electorate favours the prime minister's new plan for urban development. The same data, however, might well be sufficient to conclude with a much higher degree of certainty that *more than two-thirds* or *most* of the electorate favours it. To handle this variable in a systematic way, statisticians use a conceptual tool known as "margin of error," as in:

> The exit polling predicts that Candidate X will win the election with a 62 percent majority, with a 3 percent margin of error.

Margin of error is an estimate of the likelihood of error in the conclusion of an inductive inference. You may wonder how it would be possible to estimate such a thing so precisely—especially given the size of the sample relative to the population in most public-opinion polling. To give a detailed and systematic answer to this perfectly reasonable question would require a course in statistics, the branch of mathematics concerning the collection and interpretation of numerical data. Nevertheless, here is a way to begin to think about the problem conceptually: Margin of error is an estimate of how well you think the research has controlled the variables. Notice how closely this relates to both the degree of precision and the certainty with which the results of the polling are presented and understood.

EXERCISE 8.3 | Margin of Error

Topic for Class Discussion: Identify two distinct ways in which each of the following inferences might be strengthened. Be prepared to explain your answer in terms of how each of the ways you suggest would lower the margin of error.

1. The last three cars we have owned have been Ace products and they've all been trouble free. So we're probably safe to assume that a new Pinnacle will be reliable.

2. In Consumer Safety First's nationwide studies of new cars purchased over the last 10 years, Ace had a 30 percent lower frequency-of-repair rate than the other manufacturers. So we're probably safe to assume that a new Pinnacle will be reliable.

3. My English teacher has recommended three novels and they've all been wonderful. I think I'm going to enjoy this book of poetry because she just recommended it, too.

REASONING BY ANALOGY

An analogy is a kind of comparison and one of the most useful and powerful reasoning tools we possess. Comparison involves focusing one's attention on similarity. Similarity is an indispensable guide to the environment of any intelligent and sentient being. We must attend to many similarities to get along adequately in the world.

EXERCISE 8.4 | Thought Experiment

Try to think of two things—*any* two things—that are so completely different from each other that they have *nothing* in common. Then see if you can find some similarity between them.

Reasoning with analogies involves the application of three of the most basic intellectual concepts: similarity, difference, and relevance. The connection between analogy and similarity is obvious to the point of being overwhelming. The words *analogous* and *similar* are often regarded as synonymous. What is much less obvious, although no less important, is that comparison always implies its inseparable opposite, its "flip side," contrast—which involves focusing one's attention on difference. Difference, too, is an indispensable guide to the environment of any intelligent and sentient being. We must attend to many differences to get along adequately in the world.

EXERCISE 8.5 | **Thought Experiment**

Try to think of two things—*any* two things—that are so completely identical to each other that they cannot be told apart in any way. Then see if you can find some difference between them.

Analogies are comparisons applied to some specific intellectual purpose. Of course, many such purposes exist. Here, for example, trumpet virtuoso Wynton Marsalis uses an analogy to explain the usefulness of analogies in explaining some of the fascinating features of music:

> As we explore the world of music, we'll be looking for similarities. It's kind of like when you try to begin a conversation with someone you don't know. It's better to talk about what you have in common, rather than be stifled by your obvious differences.[1]

Analogies can be used quite effectively to *explain* new and unfamiliar or abstract and intangible things by comparing them to more familiar and tangible ones. Analogies can be used simply to give a vivid description or to spice up a narrative. Imagine a recent divorcee telling her sister the story of how she fended off unwanted advances at the office: ". . . and I need a date like a fish needs a bicycle." An analogy can be used as the basis for a joke. Lily Tomlin did this when she pointed out that we get olive oil by squeezing olives and corn oil by squeezing kernels of corn and sesame oil by pressing sesame seeds and peanut oil by mashing peanuts, and then wondered how we get baby oil.

EXERCISE 8.6 | **How Many Analogies?**

Topic for Class Discussion: How many analogies can you find in the following passage? What is the author trying to accomplish by means of each of the analogies you notice?

In a *Scientific American* column on innumeracy, the computer scientist Douglas Hofstadter cites the case of the Ideal Toy Company, which stated on the package of the original Rubik cube that there were more than three billion possible states the cube could attain. Calculations show that there are more than 4×10^{19} possible states, 4 with 19 zeroes after it. What the package says isn't wrong; there are more than three billion possible states. The understatement, however, is symptomatic of a pervasive innumeracy which ill suits a technologically based society. It's analogous to a sign at the entrance to the Lincoln Tunnel stating: New York, population more than 6; or McDonald's proudly announces that they have sold more than 120 hamburgers.[2]

Two prominent analogies exist in the above passage: one involving an imagined sign at the entrance to the Lincoln Tunnel in New York City and one involving McDonald's proudly announcing having sold more than 120 hamburgers. The point of each analogy is to make it easier to grasp the magnitude of an understatement that most of us would otherwise find incomprehensible. "Innumeracy" itself is quite possibly an unfamiliar concept, which the author, John Allen Paulos, introduces by means of an analogy with the more familiar concept of illiteracy. This analogy is compressed into his book's title, *Innumeracy: Mathematical Illiteracy and Its Consequences*. Implied in this analogy is also an argument about the importance of overcoming the handicap of innumeracy.

ARGUMENT BY ANALOGY

Analogies can also be used inferentially or argumentatively; that is, to infer conclusions and to support or defend controversial positions. We call this "reasoning by analogy" or "argument by analogy." Like the inductions above, an argument by analogy "stretches" or extends its way to a conclusion. Here is an example in which the 18th-century Scottish philosopher Thomas Reid argued for the probability of extraterrestrial organic life in our solar system:

> We may observe a very great similitude between this earth which we inhabit, and the other planets, Saturn, Jupiter, Mars, Venus and Mercury. They all revolve round the sun, as the earth does, although at different distances and in different periods. They borrow all their light from the sun, as the earth does. Several of them are known to revolve round their axis like the earth, and by that means, must have a like succession of day and night. Some of them have moons, that serve to give them light in the absence of the sun, as our moon does to us. They are all, in their motions, subject to the same law of gravitation, as the earth is. From all this similitude, it is not unreasonable to think that those planets may, like our earth, be the habitation of various orders of living creatures. There is some probability in this conclusion from analogy.[3]

Notice that Reid recognized that the inference is not deductively valid—in other words, that this is a form of inductive inference in which there is room for doubt and error. Nevertheless, he expressed cautious confidence in it as an inference. At some points in history, for instance in the middle of the 20th century, it may have appeared that the conclusion Reid was cautiously drawing was not true, though the question remains an open one to this day. Nonetheless, he was not essentially misguided in placing confidence in the argument. He was following a familiar and generally reliable line of reasoning, which a great many of our everyday inferences follow as well. If you try to enroll in Professor Whitefeather's section of the upper-level poetry course because you have taken three of her introductory courses and found her to be a knowledgeable and stimulating instructor, you are following the same reasoning strategy as Reid was. In effect, you are reasoning as follows:

1. I have observed several items: a, b, and c, each of which has the important characteristic 1 in common with target item d. (*I have taken three courses taught by the instructor of the course I'm contemplating.*)

2. The observed items a, b, and c also have characteristics 2 and 3. (*The three courses I've taken were stimulating and imparted knowledge.*)

3. Therefore, it is likely that target item d will have characteristics 2 and 3 as well. (*The course I'm contemplating is likely to be stimulating and to impart knowledge.*)

The basic inferential strategy of an argument by analogy, as illustrated in these examples, is to infer that if things are similar in some way(s), they are probably similar in other way(s) as well.

In the process of analysis and evaluation of arguments by analogy, we can usefully distinguish the items compared by looking at the roles the items play in the comparison. For this purpose we will call the item(s) used as the basis of the comparison the *analogue(s)*, and we will refer to the item(s) about which conclusions are drawn or explanations are offered as the *target(s)*. So, for example, in Thomas Reid's argument about extraterrestrial life, the planet Earth is the analogue and the other planets in our solar system are the targets. In the example about Professor Whitefeather's poetry class, the three introductory courses you have taken are the analogues and the target is her upper-level class.

EXERCISE 8.7 | **Analyzing Analogies**

Identify the analogues and targets in each of the following analogies. Which analogies are used inferentially or argumentatively, and which are used for explanatory purposes, or something else, such as narrative enhancement or entertainment?

"Suppose that someone tells me that he has had a tooth extracted without an anaesthetic, and I express my sympathy, and suppose that I am then asked, 'How do you know that it hurt him?' I might reasonably reply, 'Well, I know that it would hurt me. I have been to the dentist and know how painful it is to have a tooth stopped [filled] without an anaesthetic, let alone taken out. And he has the same sort of nervous system as I have. I infer, therefore, that in these conditions he felt considerable pain, just as I should have.'"[4] [The context is the question of whether we can know the mental lives of others.]

analogue	target	arg	exp	other

"Cam Neely is like the 'Jim Morrison' of the NHL. A 'live hard die young' approach applied to a career on the ice is what makes him the stuff of legend.

Who is remembered more, a man who is great for a short period of time and then leaves us fans wanting more, or those who linger on years after we have become tired of them?

Neely gave us a brief glimpse of his brilliance and true hockey fans are forever wishing they could have had more memories from him to cherish.

Guys like Messier who linger on long after their expiry date has passed only serve to pad their career stats."[5]

analogue	target	arg	exp	other

"Just like the only way to build your muscles is to go to the gym and actually exercise yourself, the only way to learn how to write good [computer] programs is to actually do programming exercises yourself. In the same way, the only way to really learn how to write proofs is to actually do proving exercises yourself. Just watching someone else solve problems isn't going to help!"[6]

analogue	target	arg	exp	other

"When Dubya wants to sound presidential, he'll try to construct a sentence that suggests some sense of mission, what his father used to call 'the vision thing.' But it's like someone assembling a barbecue—when the sentence is finished there are always a half-dozen parts left over."[7]

analogue	target	arg	exp	other

"What grounds have we for attributing suffering to other animals[?] It is best to begin by asking what grounds any individual human has for supposing that other humans feel pain. Since pain is a state of con-sciousness, a 'mental event,' it can never be directly observed. No observations, whether behavioral signs such as writhing or screaming or physiological or neurological recordings, are observations of pain itself. Pain is something one feels, and one can only infer that others are feeling it from various external indica-tions. The fact that only philosophers are ever skeptical about whether other humans feels pain shows that we regard such inference is justifiable in the case of humans. Is there any reason why the same inference should be unjustifiable for other animals? Nearly all the external signs which lead us to infer pain in other humans can be seen in other species, especially 'higher' animals such as mammals and birds. Behavioral signs—writhing, yelping, or other forms of calling, attempts to avoid the source of pain, and many others—are present. We know, too, that these animals are biologically similar in the relevant respects, having nervous systems like ours which can be observed to function as ours do. So the grounds for inferring that these animals can feel pain are nearly as good as the grounds for inferring other humans do."[8]

analogue	target	arg	exp	other

"If we were to repeat the same note without accents, it would be like our pulse. But what happens if we accent the first of every four **beats**—one, two, three, four, one, two, three, four? Accenting that first note sets up a rhythm we can count. Each note becomes part of a four-beat rhythm, and every four beats is one unit. This could get confusing if we didn't have a way to organize these units. But other things are that way, too. For example, if I ask you how far from home to school, you might say 5 blocks, but you wouldn't say 6,737 steps. Or you might say 10 minutes, not 600 seconds. You divide the distance or organize the time into convenient units."[9]

analogue	target	arg	exp	other

EVALUATING REASONING BY ANALOGY

The variables that affect the strength of inductive inferences generally also pertain in evaluating reasoning by analogy. The number of analogues relative to the number of targets affects the strength of an argument by analogy, just as the size of the sample relative to the size of the population affects the strength of an inductive generalization. An argument based on a large series of analogous cases tends to be stronger than one based on a single analogue, just as an inductive generalization based on many instances is stronger than one based on a tiny sample. Similarly, the number of observed similarities between analogue and target affects the strength of the analogy, just as the representativeness of the sample relative to the population affects the strength of an inductive generalization. This is pretty much intuitively obvious. In general, the more similar that things are *observed to be,* the more likely they will be similar in additional ways as well.

Another variable that affects the strength of both inductive inferences generally and arguments by analogy is the strength of the conclusion relative to the evidence contained in the premises. An argument by analogy can be strengthened by hedging the conclusion with appropriate qualifications, as Thomas Reid did in the example about extraterrestrial life. Had he expressed the conclusion with greater certainty than he did, his argument would have been weaker than it was. These same general considerations apply to differences too, only in reverse. The more differences there are between analogue and target, the weaker the analogy tends to be.

There is another factor to consider in the evaluation of arguments by analogy, one that affects both similarities and differences and is more important than either similarities or differences by themselves. This is the factor of *relevance.* In our earlier example of the defective computer disks, we noted that numerical order within the shipment might have something to do with whether a disk is defective or not. Thus, numerical order within the shipment is a *relevant* variable. Similarly, in evaluating arguments or inferences by analogy, we are most interested in similarities and differences that might reasonably be thought to have something to do with the point of the comparison—the conclusion being inferred about the target. In general, the more relevant the observed similarities between analogue and target are to the conclusion being inferred, the stronger the analogy. By the same token, the more relevant the differences between analogue and target are to the conclusion being inferred, the weaker the analogy. An instance of analogical reasoning can be persuasive rationally only if the things that are compared are similar sufficiently in the respect relevant to establishing the conclusion. Almost any two things may be alike in some respect, but this is often an insufficient basis on which to draw a particular conclusion. On the other hand, the mere fact that two things differ in some respect does not mean they are incomparable; many things that differ also share some similarities. Hence, we must insist on a comparison that focuses on similarities and differences pertinent to getting clear about the exact issue at hand.

Suppose you are shopping for a new car. You decide that the new Ace Pinnacle is likely to be a reliable low-maintenance vehicle because Aces you have owned in the past have been reliable and required minimal maintenance. Your inference is based on a relevant similarity, the identity of the manufacturer. Why? On the other hand, suppose someone drew the same conclusion about a car because it was blue, and the blue cars she had owned in the past had been reliable and required minimal maintenance. This inference would be based on an irrelevant similarity. Why? Answer: Good reasons for thinking that, in general, cars made by the same manufacturer will meet similar standards of reliability do exist, whereas similarly good reasons to suppose that the colour of a car makes a difference as to its reliability do not exist. A plausible explanatory basis exists for linking the identity of the manufacturer to quality control in the production process, but no plausible explanatory link between colour and reliability exists.

Thus, to evaluate an argument or inference by analogy, we must add up the relevant similarities and differences. This can be accomplished in a systematic way by means of a simple form.

	Analogue	Target	Degree of Similarity or Difference	Relevance
Basic points of similarity used as premises				
Conclusion				
Differences				

For purposes of illustration we will use the examples from Exercise 8.7, starting with A. J. Ayer's inference to the conclusion that another person besides himself feels pain. Ayer uses himself as the analogue. The target is some other person. He uses one basic similarity as a premise: similar nervous system. Of course, the conclusion is that the other person would have the same sort of pain that Ayer would.

Ayer's Argument	Analogue Ayer	Target Other Humans	Degree of Similarity or Difference	Relevance
Basic points of similarity used as premises	Central nervous system basic to physiology of sensory experience of pain	Central nervous system basic to physiology of sensory experience of pain		
Conclusion	Ayer experiences pain when undergoing dental work w/o anaesthetic	**Other people experience pain when undergoing dental work w/o anaesthetic**		
Differences				

To evaluate this as an argument by analogy, we would first want to know whether the similarity Ayer asserts in fact holds sway. Is it really the case that people have similar neurophysiology? They do. We should also note that the human central nervous system is a highly complex mechanism with a very high degree of similarity, both physically and functionally, from person to person. Thus, although there is only one similarity claimed here, the similarity is of a very high degree. Next, we want to determine whether this similarity is *relevant* to the conclusion Ayer is trying to draw. It is indeed relevant, because we have good theoretical grounds and empirical evidence to suppose that a body's neurophysiology is the central mechanism involved in the person's sensory experience. So, we might add the following assessments under "Degree of Similarity" and "Relevance":

Ayer's Argument	Analogue Ayer	Target Other Humans	Degree of Similarity or Difference	Relevance
Basic points of similarity used as premises	Central nervous system basic to physiology of sensory experience of pain	Central nervous system basic to physiology of sensory experience of pain	High degree of similarity	Highly relevant to conclusion

Conclusion	Ayer experiences pain when undergoing dental work w/o anaesthetic	**Other people experience pain when undergoing dental work w/o anaesthetic**		
Differences				

At this point we would want to determine whether there are significant relevant differences between the analogue and the target. In the case of this particular argument, since the analogy is between Ayer himself and *any* other human being, the differences would have to relate to characteristics unique to Ayer and that would distinguish him from *any* other human being. Of course, there are many such characteristics, as there are with all human individuals. For example, Ayer was the author of an important work of philosophy published in 1936 entitled *Language, Truth and Logic.* This is true of no other human being. We can't think of any such differences, however, that would be *relevant* to Ayer's conclusion. So, we complete the evaluation as follows:

Ayer's Argument	Analogue Ayer	Target Other Humans	Degree of Similarity or Difference	Relevance
Basic points of similarity used as premises	Central nervous system basic to physiology of sensory experience of pain	Central nervous system basic to physiology of sensory experience of pain	High degree of similarity	Highly relevant to conclusion
Conclusion	Ayer experiences pain when undergoing dental work w/o anaesthetic	**Other people experience pain when undergoing dental work w/o anaesthetic**		
Differences	Ayer was the author of *Language, Truth and Logic,* published in 1936	No other human being was the author of *Language, Truth and Logic,* published in 1936	True	Irrelevant

So Ayer's argument appears to be quite strong, in spite of the fact that it is based on only one similarity.

EXERCISE 8.8 | Analyzing an Argument by Analogy

Now consider Peter Singer's similar argument in Exercise 8.7 about "attributing pain to other animals." Using the above example as a model, set up the form for evaluating Singer's argument by identifying the analogue, the target, the basic points of similarity, and the conclusion in the blank below.

Singer's Argument	Analogue	Target	Degree of Similarity or Difference	Relevance
Basic points of similarity used as premises				
Conclusion				
Differences				

In this case the analogue is human beings and the target is nonhuman animals. The conclusion is that nonhuman animals have experiences of pain similar to those of human beings. This inference rests on two basic points of similarity: similarity of neurophysiology and similarity in behavioural responses to stimuli.

EXERCISE 8.9 | Evaluating an Argument by Analogy

Now complete the evaluation of Singer's argument by assessing the degree and relevance of similarity in the premises, and the degree and relevance of differences you can identify, to Singer's conclusion.

Singer's Argument	Analogue	Target	Degree of Similarity or Difference	Relevance
Basic points of similarity used as premises	Central nervous system basic to physiology of sensory experience of pain	Central nervous system basic to physiology of sensory experience of pain		
	Expressive behavioural responses to sensory stimuli	Expressive behavioural responses to sensory stimuli		

		Nonhuman animals enjoy pleasure and suffer pain		
Conclusion	Humans enjoy pleasure and suffer pain			
Differences				

Here are our findings: To evaluate Singer's argument as an argument by analogy, we would first want to know whether the similarities Singer asserts in fact hold sway. Is it really the case that human and nonhuman animals have similar neurophysiology? It turns out they do. How similar are human and nonhuman animals when it comes to neurophysiology? In some cases—that is, with so-called higher animals—the similarity is extremely high in complex and sophisticated detail, both physically and functionally. Next, do humans and nonhuman animals exhibit similar behavioural responses to stimuli? Again, the answer is "Yes, to a remarkably high and complex degree of similarity in many cases." Next, we want to determine whether these similarities are relevant to the conclusion Singer is trying to draw. It seems that they are relevant, because we have good theoretical grounds and empirical evidence to suppose that a body's neurophysiology is the central mechanism involved in an organism's sensory experience, and similarly good theoretical and evidentiary grounds to connect behavioural manifestations to inner experience. So, we would make the following preliminary assessment:

Singer's Argument	Analogue	Target	Degree of Similarity or Difference	Relevance
Basic points of similarity used as premises	Central nervous system basic to physiology of sensory experience of pain	Central nervous system basic to physiology of sensory experience of pain	High degree of similarity	Highly relevant to conclusion
	Expressive behavioural responses to sensory stimuli	Expressive behavioural responses to sensory stimuli	High degree of similarity	Highly relevant to conclusion
Conclusion	Humans enjoy pleasure and suffer pain	Nonhuman animals enjoy pleasure and suffer pain		
Differences				

At this point we would want to determine whether there are significant relevant differences between the analogue and the target. Of course, many differences between human beings and other species exist, several perhaps that people might think relevant to Singer's conclusion. For example, Singer proceeds in the essay from which the example was taken to consider the issue of language. Now there may be some controversy over the question of whether human beings are the only species of animal with the capability for the development and use of languages. Now for the sake of the argument, let us suppose that this difference genuinely does hold sway. The question at this point is whether this is a relevant difference. Singer argues that it is not, because we do not so much attribute pain to human beings on the basis of their linguistic behaviour as on the basis of the sorts of behaviour exhibited by other animal species. So, on this basis we judge Singer's argument to be, like Ayer's, quite strong:

Singer's Argument	Analogue	Target	Degree of Similarity or Difference	Relevance
Basic points of similarity used as premises	Central nervous system basic to physiology of sensory experience of pain	Central nervous system basic to physiology of sensory experience of pain	High degree of similarity	Highly relevant to conclusion
	Expressive behavioural responses to sensory stimuli	Expressive behavioural responses to sensory stimuli	High degree of similarity	Highly relevant to conclusion
Conclusion	Humans beings enjoy pleasure and suffer pain	**Nonhuman animals enjoy pleasure and suffer pain**		
Differences	Human beings have linguistic capacity	Nonhuman animals do not have linguistic capacity	Plausible, though open to question	Irrelevant to conclusion

ANALOGY AND REFUTATION BY COUNTEREXAMPLE

One use of analogy that deserves special mention is the refutation of arguments by comparison. In this strategy the target is usually an argument (occasionally the thesis of an argument), and the goal is to discredit the target by showing that it is analogous to some other argument (or thesis) that is obviously weak or objectionable. In the following passage from *Alice in Wonderland*, the Mad

Hatter and the March Hare refute Alice. The Mad Hatter has told Alice, who has just said something illogical, that she should "say what she means":

"I do," Alice hastily replied; "at least—at least I mean what I say—that's the same thing, you know."

"Not the same thing a bit!" said the Hatter. "Why, you might just as well say that 'I see what I eat' is the same thing as 'I eat what I see'!"

"You might just as well say," added the March Hare, "that 'I like what I get' is the same thing as 'I get what I like'!"[10]

In Chapter 6 we used an example of refutation by counterexample and explained the concept of a formal fallacy when we compared the two arguments below:

(1) All Canadians are human beings.	(1) All men are human beings.
(2) All Ontarians are human beings.	(2) All women are human beings.
∴ (3) All Ontarians are Canadians.	∴ (3) All women are men.

We also presented a strategy for demonstrating an argument to be fallacious formally by constructing a formally similar argument; that is, one that follows an identical formal pattern but has obviously true premises and an obviously false conclusion.

ADDITIONAL EXERCISES

EXERCISE 8.10   Suppose we were to evaluate the sample in each of the following inductive generalizations. Highlight those among the listed dimensions that, in your opinion, would be relevant to the generalization and would need to be "controlled" to make the sample more "representative." Compare your answers with those of your classmates. Try to resolve any and all points of disagreement rationally, by explaining your answers to each other.

"In Consumer Safety First's nationwide studies of new cars purchased over the last 10 years, Ace had a 30 percent lower frequency-of-repair rate than the other manufacturers. So we're probably safe to assume that a new Pinnacle will be reliable."

- the colour of the car
- the age of the principal driver of the car
- the price paid for the car
- the number of kilometres driven annually
- the size of the car
- the size of the owner's family
- the trim package
- the brand of gasoline used in the car

"Look! The first 10 people to come out of the theatre are all smiling and laughing. I guess this is going to be a good show!"

- the ages of the people
- the gender identities of the people
- the ethnic identities of the people
- the religious affiliations of the people
- the economic status of the people
- the political affiliations of the people
- the social class status of the people

■ **EXERCISE 8.11** Identify and explain as many analogies as you can find in each of the following passages. For each analogy, specify the analogue and the target as well as the purpose (argumentative, explanatory, entertaining, etc.) of the comparison.

- "Well, thish-yer Smiley had rat-tarriers, and chicken cocks, and tom-cats, and all them kind of things, till you couldn't rest, and you couldn't fetch nothing for him to bet on but he'd match you. He ketched a frog one day, and took him home, and said he calculated to educate him; and so he never done nothing for three months but set in his back yard and learn that frog to jump. And you bet he did learn him, too. He'd give him a little punch behind, and the next minute you'd see that frog whirling in the air like a doughnut."[11]

- Therefore, we need a bit of theory to support, guide, and explain our evaluative intuitions. For theoretical purposes we will make a basic distinction between the structural features of an argument and the materials used in its construction. One way to understand this distinction is to think of an argument as a building. Now suppose, for example, we are evaluating buildings while buying a house. Some houses are obviously and intuitively better built than others. We can tell "intuitively" that 24 Sussex Drive, the prime minister's residence, is a stronger building than an outhouse. Nonetheless, we need a more systematic set of criteria to make reasonable decisions where houses are more closely matched. Buildings are complicated, so we find ourselves faced with many criteria relevant to evaluating buildings. This is why we would want to make the set of criteria "systematic." The system gives us organization.

    One way to organize is to divide. When it comes to buildings, a reasonable and powerful first distinction for purposes of evaluation would be to divide between the materials used and how the materials are put together—the design and the execution of the design. So in evaluating arguments we could look at "design factors" and "materials factors." In this comparison (or "analogy") the "materials" are the premises of the argument, and the "design" is the plan according to which the premises are assembled in support of the conclusion.[12]

- "Up to this point we've talked about accents and rests of the same length. But what do musicians like to do most with rhythms? Well, we like to do what everybody likes to do. We like to play. That's right. In basketball, when we first learned how to dribble, it was an achievement just to bounce the ball in a steady motion. You know, you could spend a long time just learning to bounce the ball in one unchanging rhythm. It might take two weeks to learn how to do that comfortably, or a month. But in order to have fun playing, we have to vary the bounces with accents and rests. In a game you would want to fake out an opponent. You wouldn't dribble only at one speed, or in the same predictable rhythm. Sometimes you would go fast, sometimes a little slower, and then maybe real quick between your legs or behind your back. And then sometimes you'd stop dribbling and pass the ball. In a basketball game we dribble the ball to go from one point on the court to another, we hope closer to the basket, and of course we always want to dribble with imagination and style. If you're not going to have imagination and some type of style, it doesn't make sense to play. In music we play with rhythms from tiny fast ones to long slow ones, just like dribbling the ball."[13]

- "When someone writes a piece of music, what he or she puts on the paper is roughly the equivalent of a recipe—in the sense that the recipe is not the food, only instructions for the preparation of the food. Unless you are very weird, you don't eat the recipe. If I write something on a piece of paper, I can't actually 'hear' it. I can conjure up visions of what the symbols on the page mean, and imagine a piece of music as it might sound in performance, but that sensation is nontransferable; it can't be shared or transmitted. It doesn't become a 'musical experience' in normal terms until 'the recipe' has been converted into wiggling air molecules. Music, in performance, is a type of sculpture. The air in the performance space is sculpted into something. This 'molecule-sculpture-over-time' is then 'looked at' by the ears of the listeners—or a microphone."[14]

■ **EXERCISE 8.12** Evaluate each of the following analogy-based arguments using the tools and procedures outlined in this chapter.

Putting up a traffic light after last week's deadly accident is like locking the barn door after the horse has been stolen.

	Analogue	Target	Comment
Basic points of similarity used as premises			
Conclusion			
Differences			

A Good Presentation Is Like a Good Shot of Espresso

After dragging myself out of bed at 6:30 each morning, I shower, shave and head out to order my morning coffee: a single tall mocha, light on the chocolate, extra hot, and double-cup it please. With those relatively simple instructions, you'd think that no matter where I went for my espresso, it would all taste the same. But guess what? It doesn't. Even if I go back to the same coffee shop, my "usual" tastes a little different from one day to the next. All the ingredients remain the same—the coffee beans, the chocolate, the milk—so how can it get screwed up?

The answer, of course, is that the flavor of a single tall mocha depends as much on the person behind the counter as the ingredients in the cup.

When it comes to the quality of the presentations we create, the difference between a good presentation and a great one seldom comes down to software. Instead, it's the person "behind the counter"—crafting the message and using the tools creatively—who ultimately makes the difference.[15]

	Analogue	Target	Comment
Basic points of similarity used as premises			
Conclusion			
Differences			

One of the most well-known instances of argument by analogy is the famous teleological argument for the existence of God. As formulated by the 18th-century theologian William Paley, the argument goes something like this:

Suppose we happened to find a watch lying on the ground in the woods, or on the moon. How could we explain it? Unlike a rock, which we could easily imagine to have just been lying there indefinitely, a watch, we would be forced to conclude, was the product of some intelligent designer, because no other explanation would be adequate to account for the marvelous degree to which the parts and features of the watch seem to be designed, adapted, and coordinated for the purpose of telling time. Now compare the watch to the natural universe or to organic phenomena in the natural universe such as the human eye. The human eye, like the watch, is a complex organ whose parts, like the parts of a watch, seem marvelously well adapted and coordinated for the purpose of enabling visual experience. So, it is reasonable to suppose that the human eye, and other similar phenomena in nature, and indeed the entire natural universe, are the products of an intelligent designer: God.

	Analogue	Target	Comment
Basic points of similarity used as premises			
Conclusion			
Differences			

Return Address at "Giving the Future a Past" Conference, Association for Canadian Studies, Winnipeg, October 20, 2001.

What is [our] public history? I suggest that it is the anatomy and physiology of the evolution of Canada through time. When we discuss that anatomy and physiology most of us would reach a rough agreement on what we have to talk about, just as if we were giving a course on human anatomy and physiology we would largely agree on the organs and processes that we have to cover. We would certainly agree that it would be wrong to give a course on human anatomy and physiology that only included two or three organs, let us say the genitals and the parathyroid glands, or looked at only a couple of processes, such as skin pigmentation and the operations of the sweat glands, ignoring everything else. No doubt our medical friends will tell us that there are many different ways of approaching the study of anatomy and physiology, with differing emphases, but you still have to study the major organs—the brain, the heart, the lungs, and so on— and you have to study the basic physiological processes, respiration, nutrition, the circulation of the blood, and so on.

If we're studying Canadian history honestly, we have not done a very good job if we don't talk about certain key historical episodes or turning points. Have we talked about Canadian history adequately, for example, if we have not talked about the first interactions of Aboriginals with Europeans? Have we talked about Canadian history adequately if we haven't considered the history of New France, if we haven't considered the Conquest, if we haven't considered the effect of the American Revolution, if we haven't considered the evolution of the Canadian economy within the shifting contexts of British trade policy, if we don't talk about the rebellions of 1837, if we don't talk about the coming of responsible government, if we don't talk about Confederation, if we don't talk about Western expansion, if we don't build the CPR, if we don't talk about Canadian contributions to the two Great Wars, if we don't talk about the depression, if we don't talk about Sir John A. Macdonald, Wilfrid Laurier, Mackenzie King, and Pierre Elliott Trudeau, if we don't talk about the crises caused by Quebec nationalism from the 1960s? Have we talked about Canadian history adequately if we don't talk about bilingualism, multiculturalism, constitutional reform and the coming of the Charter of Rights? Have we talked about Canadian history adequately if we haven't talked about the realignment and integration of the Canadian economy with the American economy before and after and including the decision to enter into a free trade agreement?[16]

	Analogue	Target	Comment
Basic points of similarity used as premises			
Conclusion			
Differences			

EXERCISE 8.13   Identify aspects of the issue on which you have been working where generalizations or statistics would be relevant. Identify reliable sources for such information. Pick one such application of inductive reasoning and design the sort of research program or experiment that would be likely to yield reliable results. Next, take any position on the issue on which you have been working and design an argument in support of the position based on an analogy. Then take an alternative or opposed position and design an argument in support of it based on an analogy.

GLOSSARY

analogue   an item used as a basis of comparison in an explanation or argument by analogy

analogy   a comparison

inductive generalization   a variety of inductive reasoning in which general conclusions are projected from a number of particular instances

margin of error   estimate of the likelihood of error in the conclusion of an inductive inference

plausibility   a measure of an idea's likelihood of surviving critical scrutiny

population   the set of instances about which general conclusions are projected in an inductive or statistical generalization

refutation by counterexample   discrediting an argument by showing that it is analogous to another argument that is problematic

relative   as applied to inferential security, means "admits of degrees"

relevance   in inductive reasoning refers to factors that might reasonably be thought to have something to do with the conclusion being inferred

sample   particular observed instances used in inductive or statistical generalizations

sample size   a measure of the number of particular observed instances relative to the population in an inductive or statistical generalization

statistical generalization   a variety of inductive reasoning in which trends or percentages observed in the sample are projected onto other instances or onto the population as a whole

target   an item about which conclusions are drawn or explanations are offered by analogy

Go to http://www.criticalthinking1ce.nelson.com for additional study resources for this chapter.

ENDNOTES

[1] Wynton Marsalis, *Marsalis on Music* (New York: Norton, 1995), 20.

[2] John Allen Paulos, *Innumeracy: Mathematical Illiteracy and Its Consequences* (New York: Hill and Wang, 1988), 9–10.

[3] Thomas Reid, *Essays on the Intellectual Powers of Man,* Essay 1, Chapter 4.

[4] Alfred J. Ayer, "One's Knowledge of Other Minds," *Theoria,* 19 (1953).

[5] Individual contributor, JABO007 at TSN.ca http://www.tsn.ca/nhl/your_call/? messageid=670021&hubname=

[6] François Pitt, "Why learning how to write proofs is like learning how to write programs (is like bodybuilding)!" © Copyright 2000 by François Pitt. Reprinted by permission.

[7] P. J. O'Rourke, "Why I Believe What I Believe," *Rolling Stone,* July 13–27, 1995.

[8] Peter Singer, *New York Review of Books,* April 5, 1973.

[9] Wynton Marsalis, *Marsalis on Music,* 26.

[10] Lewis Carroll, *Alice's Adventures in Wonderland,* Chapter 7.

[11] Mark Twain, "The Celebrated Jumping Frog of Calaveras County."

[12] Joel Rudinow, Vincent Barry, and Mark Letteri, *Invitation to Critical Thinking*, 1st *Canadian ed.* (Toronto: Thomson Nelson, 2007), pp. 145–46,.

[13] Wynton Marsalis, *Marsalis on Music*, 26–27.

[14] Frank Zappa, "All About Music," *The Real Frank Zappa Book* (New York: Poseidon, 1989), 161.

[15] Jim Endicott, "A Good Presentation is Like a Good Shot of Espresso," Reprinted by permission, www.distinction-services.com

[16] "Teaching Canadian National History," Michael Bliss, University of Toronto, Address at "Giving the Future a Past" Conference, Association for Canadian Studies Winnipeg, October 20, 2001, CANADIAN SOCIAL STUDIES VOLUME 36, NUMBER 2, WINTER 2002. Reprinted by permission.

CHAPTER 9

Evaluating Inductive Arguments II: Hypothetical Reasoning and Burden of Proof

When you believe in things that you don't understand, then you suffer....
Superstition ain't the way. STEVIE WONDER

As we explained in Chapter 8, the evaluation of inductive inferences is based on assessing their relative security, which depends on a number of variables, according to the *type* of inductive reasoning involved. In this chapter we will explore two more important and common categories or types of inductive reasoning: hypothetical reasoning and burden-of-proof arguments.

PRESUMPTION AND THE BURDEN OF PROOF

"Burden of proof" reasoning is a kind of inductive reasoning useful in resolving disputes that cannot be compromised or reconciled on a win/win basis—in other words, disputes between two parties or "sides" in which a winner must be declared. Many situations like this often arise in legal contexts. One of the most

241

NEL

© The New Yorker Collection 1985 B. J. Handelsman from cartoonbank.com. All Rights Reserved.

"Let me tell you, folks—I've been around long enough to develop an instinct for these things, and my client is innocent or I'm very much mistaken."

obvious and familiar examples of burden-of-proof reasoning is the "presumption of innocence." In many, though by no means all, of the world's legal systems the accused is presumed innocent unless and until the prosecution meets its "burden of proof." The party (or "side") with the burden of proof is the party (or "side") that has to produce the argument. We can conveniently think of this as a procedural rule in a structured contest according to which one side is assigned the role or position of "offence" while the other side plays "defence." If the side that bears the burden of proof fails to meet its obligation, the issue is decided in favour of the other side. Thus, in Canadian criminal law it is the Crown or prosecution that bears the burden of proof and has to "make its case beyond a reasonable doubt." Meanwhile the defence need not make any argument of its own beyond simply attacking the argument of the Crown and getting "the benefit of the doubt."

In most situations in real life, we will find that the procedural rules are already established, and that we just need to be informed competently as to what they are. Thus, as jurors we are instructed by the judge as to what the rules are and how to weigh the evidence and arguments presented to us in court as we deliberate to a verdict. As plaintiffs and defendants, we will ordinarily be advised by our lawyers as to what our best argumentative strategy may be. Thinking of the burden of proof in this way (as a procedural rule) raises the question of how we decide where—on which side of any given issue—the burden of proof properly belongs. How is the presumption of innocence or any other procedural rule of this kind justified? Why, for example, does the Crown have the burden of proof in Canadian criminal law? Why not the defence? Why should the accused not have to prove his or her innocence? Another similar question concerns the size or "weight" of the burden. For example, the burden of proof is heavier in a criminal trial than in a civil trial. In a criminal trial the prosecution must prove guilt "beyond a reasonable doubt" (a deliberately vague but nevertheless decidedly high standard of proof). In a civil trial, the plaintiff (the one who brings the lawsuit, the one making the complaint) has only the obligation of making a probable case, which obviously places much more stress on the defence. One can imagine many alternatives to such arrangements—many different ways of formulating the procedural rules.

Let us approach these questions at the more general theoretical level. For example, if someone suggested that you invest a small sum of money in a mutual fund, you would want some evidence that the fund is well and profitably managed, but you would want *more* evidence of the security of your investment if it were your entire life savings. In general, the greater the risk of error—and the higher the cost of being wrong—the heavier the burden of proof. In general, then, the burden of proof is placed and the standard of proof is set where they "reasonably belong," which is to say where reasonable explanation and argument will support. Thus, the placement and apportionment of the burden of proof, like many of the concepts we have already encountered in this book, is governed by a number of rules of thumb. One such rule is based on the concept of "plausibility" (as introduced in Chapter 4). In general, the less plausible the arguer's position, the heavier the burden of proof.

Another general rule, derived from the discipline and traditions of rhetoric, has to do with the distinction between the "affirmative" and "negative" positions in a debate. In general, the affirmative side in a debate has the burden of proof because it is in general so much harder to "prove the negative." Thus, the argumentative move known as *ad ignorantiam*, or appeal to ignorance, is a fallacy because it involves trying to prove a claim by arguing that the claim has not been shown to be false. For example, someone who believes in the healing power of the mind, or the therapeutic efficacy of marijuana, or the existence of intelligent extraterrestrial life is expected to produce the evidence. All the affirmative side would need to do to prove conclusively that extraterrestrial intelligent life exists would be to bring forward one specimen. You can see how much harder it would be to prove *conclusively* that extraterrestrial intelligent life does *not* exist. Claiming, "No one has proven that alien life forms do not exist; therefore, they exist," inverts the burden of proof. So, in fairness, the rule is to place the burden of proof on the affirmative position in a dispute.

Fairness is also behind the placement of the burden of proof on the prosecution in Canadian criminal and civil law. In civil law it seems fair to place the burden of proof mainly on the party making the complaint but with a clear need for the defence to respond satisfactorily to the challenge. In criminal law the accused is (usually) an individual, whereas the Crown is the "people" acting collectively through the agency of the government, and the stakes are often some form of punishment. Fairness seems to call for the Crown to produce conclusive proof of guilt, not just a merely probable conclusion. Another rationale exists for placing the burden of proof on the prosecution. Consider the question of how justice could miscarry. Only two kinds of miscarriage of justice seem possible: A guilty party gets off without penalty and an innocent party gets penalized. Which of these two kinds of miscarriage of justice is worse? Some legal traditions— the Canadian system, for example—are based on the idea that punishing an innocent person is worse than letting a guilty person go unpunished.

EXERCISE 9.1 | **Topic for Class Discussion**

Not everyone agrees with this idea. Question: Is it worse to punish an innocent person than to let a guilty person go unpunished? Or is it the other way around? Or are the two equally bad? An interesting exercise would be to consider the arguments that might be made on all sides.

REASONING HYPOTHETICALLY

A subtle and complex, but crucial, variety of inductive reasoning consists in reasoning from facts or observations to explanatory hypotheses. An explanation is an idea or set of ideas that succeeds in reducing or eliminating puzzlement. An "explanatory hypothesis" is an idea or set of ideas put forward for that purpose. The word *hypothesis* means "supposition" or "conjecture." It comes originally from the Greek word *thesis,* which means "idea proposed or laid down for consideration," and the Greek root *hypo,* which means "under." Here, "under" is meant to indicate that the proposed idea is "under investigation."

As the terms suggest, this variety of inductive reasoning, "hypothetical reasoning," is used primarily in trying to understand better the many puzzling things in life—the many things that prompt the question "Why?" Why is the water salty in the Pacific Ocean but not in Lake Athabasca? Why do so many incumbents continue to win re-election in spite of overwhelming anti-incumbent sentiment in the polls? Why does the sound of an approaching train whistle appear to drop in pitch as the train passes? We draw inferences to explanations constantly in all sorts of situations, and when we do, just as when we generalize, we risk error—that is, we reason inductively.

A simple example will illustrate the general structure of inferences to explanatory hypotheses. A professional house sitter, searching for a towel in the linen closet, finds a jar whose lid has become dislodged. Upon examining the contents of the jar, she finds several plastic bags of white powder. What is it? Flour? Sugar? Baking powder? Baking soda? She tests it by tasting it and finds that it is sweet, identifying it as powdered sugar. We might represent her reasoning in the form of the argument or inference:

This tastes sweet.

∴ This is sugar.

In identifying the white powder as sugar, the house sitter has not reasoned deductively. The conclusion does not follow deductively from the premise. Nonetheless, the inference from the taste of the substance to its classification is a reasonable induction. Though room for doubt remains about the truth of the conclusion, the premise does make it *reasonable to suppose* that the conclusion is true. What makes the inference reasonable? How does the premise make it reasonable to suppose that the conclusion is true? What makes the inference reasonable is the idea that *if the conclusion were true, it would explain the truth of the premise*—or—*if the conclusion were not true, it would make the premise much more puzzling.* In other words, the observed fact that the substance tastes sweet *can be best explained* by figuring that it is sugar. This is the general structure of inferences to explanatory hypotheses, or hypothetical reasoning.

The importance of hypothetical reasoning lies in its power to extend or expand our knowledge of the world. Since hypothetical reasoning always takes us beyond what we already know, it always involves the risk of error. Just as with inductive generalizations, the strength of an inference to an explanatory hypothesis is a matter of how well the risk of error is managed or controlled. We have no way of managing the risk of error in hypothetical reasoning on an individual inference-by-inference basis. To manage the risk of error in hypothetical reasoning, we must engage in more and more of it—in effect, using hypothetical reasoning to evaluate hypothetical reasoning. More precisely, the risk of error is measured and managed by way of the relative plausibility of competing explanatory hypotheses, their relative explanatory power, and the degree to which a given hypothesis can be supported by experimental evidence.

PLAUSIBILITY

In Chapter 4 we introduced the idea of plausibility as a measure of how well we think an idea is likely to survive critical scrutiny. How well would the idea hold up were we to devise strenuous tests designed to expose any falsity in the idea? A plausible idea is one that we think would hold up well. An implausible idea is one that we think would not hold up so well. Neither plausibility nor implausibility is "absolute." They both admit of degrees. Some claims are more plausible than others. A good place to look for examples to illustrate this point (implausible though this may sound) is in tabloids, such as the *Weekly World News*. In these publications you will find a steady diet of highly *im*plausible claims, such as "UFO Sighted at Buckingham Palace" or "Elvis Presley Planning Return to United States from Seclusion in Brazil to Expose His Death as Hoax." There are also a good many claims that are somewhat less implausible, such as "Hypnosis Cures Urge to Smoke," alongside a few claims that might be quite a bit more plausible, such as "Avril Lavigne Has New Love Interest." Moreover, our estimates of a claim's plausibility or implausibility are not static. Instead, they are subject to adjustment in accordance with new information. What may appear initially to be a plausible idea may, on further investigation, seem more and more or less and less plausible. Remember: Plausibility is only loosely correlated with truth. A plausible idea may well turn out not to be the case. Furthermore, in a good many cases throughout history initially implausible ideas have nevertheless been confirmed as true. *In general, the more plausible the explanatory hypothesis, the stronger the inference.* Here, we are interested in *relative* plausibility. We need to know how the explanatory hypothesis under investigation compares with others. Does another hypothesis exist that is just as or even more likely to survive critical scrutiny? If not, this strengthens the inference.

CRITICAL THINKING TIP 9.1

The more plausible the explanatory hypothesis, the stronger the inference.

For example, remember the house sitter. As soon as she tastes the white powder, she has occasion to consider the explanatory hypothesis that the powder is sugar. This, of course, is not the only hypothesis that might account for the observed fact that the powder tastes sweet. It could possibly be a new derivative of coca, genetically engineered to have a taste indistinguishable from powdered sugar so as to escape detection as a variety of cocaine. This hypothesis, if true, would account for the observed fact that the powder tastes sweet, and it is certainly within the realm of the "possible," but it is *much* less plausible than the simple powdered sugar hypothesis.

Here is another hypothesis that might account for the observed fact that the powder tastes sweet. Perhaps the powder is cocaine, and the house sitter has suddenly developed a "taste blindness" so that cocaine and powdered sugar taste identical to her. Again, this hypothesis, if true, would account for the observed fact that the powder tastes sweet. This hypothesis, too, is within the realm of the "possible"—but, like the "sweet cocaine hypothesis," also *much* less plausible than the simple powdered sugar hypothesis.

An interesting theoretical problem arises when you compare the taste blindness hypothesis to the sweet cocaine hypothesis. Is one hypothesis more plausible than the other? If so, which one? Or are they equally implausible? How can we tell? In this case it does not matter a whole lot, since a much more plausible option is available in the simple powdered sugar hypothesis. What if we had to choose, however, between competing hypotheses that seemed about equally plausible—or equally implausible? Or what if we could not agree which of several competing hypotheses was the most plausible—or the least plausible? Fortunately, plausibility is not the only standard to which we can appeal.

EXERCISE 9.2 | Plausibility

Topic for Class Discussion: In July 2005, a number of residents of a town in the Yukon reported a sighting of "Bigfoot" or "Sasquatch"—a legendary human-like creature of the western areas of North America. Bigfoot is reputed to be large, covered in hair, quick, and elusive. Rank the following theories about this report in descending order of plausibility. Compare your rankings with those of your classmates. Try to resolve any points of disagreement by explaining your answers to each other.

	The residents saw an actual specimen of the Bigfoot creature.
	Some unexpected animal surprised and confused the residents, but it was not Bigfoot.
	A hoaxer dressed up as Bigfoot fooled the residents.
	The residents are hoaxers.
	The residents experienced a group hallucination due to use of intoxicants.
	The Canadian government arranged the sighting to distract the weary public from fear of terrorism.
	Aliens from outer space arranged the sighting as a test of human reaction to unknown beings.

EXPLANATORY POWER

Remember that an explanatory hypothesis is an idea or set of ideas put forward to reduce or eliminate puzzlement. A good explanation is one that succeeds in reducing or eliminating puzzlement. The "explanatory power" of a given hypothesis is its power to reduce or eliminate puzzlement. *In general, the greater the explanatory power of a given hypothesis, the stronger the inference.* Here, as with plausibility, we are interested in *relative* explanatory power. We need to know how the explanatory hypothesis under investigation compares with others. Does another hypothesis exist that would explain the observed fact(s) in the premise(s) equally well or better? If not, this strengthens the inference. Do other observed facts exist besides the one(s) in the premise(s) that the hypothesis explains better than competing hypotheses? If so, this, too, strengthens the inference.

CRITICAL THINKING TIP 9.2

The greater the explanatory power of a given hypothesis, the stronger the inference.

For example, consider the following case: The neighbours have discovered the body of a well-known but reclusive novelist. The homicide detective arrives at the scene. The body of the deceased is slumped over his prized vintage typewriter, in which there is a sheet of paper with what appears to be an unfinished suicide note. Beside the body is a hypodermic syringe. Traces of white powder are recovered from the table beside the typewriter. The autopsy establishes the cause of death as heroin overdose and fixes the time of death at around 3:00 a.m. A psychiatric history of the deceased reveals several bouts of depression over a 10-year period and two previous suicide attempts. One plausible hypothesis, the obvious one, is that the novelist committed suicide by injecting himself with heroin and lost consciousness while at the typewriter composing the suicide note. Still, the detective is puzzled. She cannot account for the fact that the electric typewriter, an IBM Selectric I, is switched off. Nor can she account for the fact that neither the reading lamp nor the overhead light was on in the room at the time the body was discovered. If the novelist died at 3:00 a.m. while typing, how did he manage to turn off the typewriter and all of the lights?

What the detective needs now is an explanatory hypothesis with greater explanatory power. Perhaps someone murdered the novelist and tried to make the murder look like a suicide. Perhaps the murderer was surprised at the scene of the crime by approaching footsteps, and, to discourage the approaching party from intruding upon the scene and discovering the crime, turned off the lights and the typewriter. This hypothesis, though not nearly as plausible as the suicide hypothesis, nevertheless has greater explanatory power because it accounts for everything that the suicide hypothesis accounts for plus the fact that the typewriter and lights were switched off.

Just as with plausibility, a theoretical problem arises in connection with explanatory power when we have to compare competing hypotheses that seem about equally powerful, or when we cannot agree which of several competing hypotheses is the most powerful. Just as with the earlier problem, we can appeal to the plausibility standard when the explanatory power standard is not decisive. We are still left, however, with the problem of what to do when competing hypotheses seem to measure up roughly equally in both areas. Another theoretical problem exists, too. In our present example, the murder hypothesis is less plausible but more powerful as an explanatory hypothesis. This raises the question: How can we determine the strength of a hypothetical inference when our standards conflict? Does explanatory power outweigh plausibility? Or is it the other way around? Or does it depend? Maybe explanatory power outweighs plausibility when the gap in explanatory power is bigger than the gap in plausibility, and vice versa. It would be nice if we had a good answer to this question that is both simple and straightforward. As far as we know, though, the best approach to resolving any of these problems is just to test hypotheses experimentally.

EXERCISE 9.3 | Explanatory Power

Topic for Class Discussion: Here once again are the theories mentioned in Exercise 9.2. This time, rank the theories in descending order of explanatory power. Compare your rankings with those of your classmates. Try to resolve any points of disagreement by explaining your answers to each other.

	The residents saw an actual specimen of the Bigfoot creature.
	Some unexpected animal surprised and confused the residents, but it was not Bigfoot.
	A hoaxer dressed up as Bigfoot fooled the residents.
	The residents are hoaxers.
	The residents experienced a group hallucination due to use of intoxicants.
	The Canadian government arranged the sighting to distract the weary public from fear of terrorism.
	Aliens from outer space arranged the sighting as a test of human reaction to unknown beings.

TESTING HYPOTHESES

The word *hypothesis* means an idea (or set of ideas) "under investigation." To investigate hypotheses is to search for experimental evidence relevant to their truth or falsity. The "scientific method" for doing so boils down first to using the hypothesis under investigation to predict things, and then seeing whether or not the predictions turn out to be true. *If what the hypothesis predicts turns out to be true, that counts in favour of, or "confirms," the hypothesis. If what the hypothesis predicts turns out not to be true, that counts against, or "disconfirms," the hypothesis.*

For example, let us go back to the house sitter's first hypothesis, that the white powder is sugar. What else do we know about sugar that we could use to test this hypothesis? We know that sugar is soluble in water. So, using the hypothesis, along with this knowledge, we might predict that the powder will dissolve in water. Now if we place the powder in water and it dissolves, this counts as evidence confirming the hypothesis that the powder is indeed sugar. If we place the powder in water and it does not dissolve, this counts as evidence disconfirming the hypothesis that the powder is sugar. Confirming and disconfirming evidence each vary in strength according to the strength of the prediction involved. *The more certain the prediction, the stronger the evidence. In testing hypotheses, we should search for both confirming and disconfirming evidence.*

In quite a few cases we may expect to find evidence of both kinds. For example, in the case of the deceased novelist, some evidence that confirms the suicide hypothesis exists, and some evidence that disconfirms it exists. Naturally, we would be interested in the relative weight of the evidence for and against a given hypothesis. At first there seems to be more evidence in favour of the suicide hypothesis than there is against it. When the disconfirming evidence first emerges, however, the homicide detective quite correctly becomes suspicious. She not only begins to consider other hypotheses but also begins to focus her investigation specifically on the possibility of more evidence disconfirming the suicide hypothesis. Why does she proceed in this way instead of simply concluding that the suicide hypothesis is correct because more confirming evidence than disconfirming evidence exists? The homicide detective is following the general principle that *disconfirming evidence weighs more heavily than confirming evidence.*

CRITICAL THINKING TIP 9.3

Disconfirming evidence weighs more heavily than confirming evidence.

Why does disconfirming evidence outweigh confirming evidence? Again, let us consider the house sitter and the white powder. To test the sugar hypothesis, we derived the prediction that the powder will dissolve in water. So, if it does, we have confirming evidence; if it does not, we have disconfirming evidence. Confirming evidence does not completely verify the hypothesis. Notice, however, that disconfirming evidence completely refutes it. Here is why. Our prediction that the powder will dissolve takes the form of the following hypothetical statement:

If our hypothesis that the powder is sugar is correct, then the powder will dissolve in water.

When our test confirms the hypothesis, what we observe is, in effect, the consequent of this hypothetical statement coming true:

The powder does dissolve in water.

You will remember that from these two statements we cannot validly deduce the conclusion that the powder is sugar. If we simply inferred this as a conclusion, we would be committing the fallacy of affirming the consequent. This makes sense when you consider that other white powdered substances (e.g., artificial sweeteners) that taste sweet and dissolve in water may exist. Nonetheless, the combination of the two statements does, in this sort of situation, provide relevant though not absolutely conclusive evidence in support of the hypothesis under investigation. On the other hand, when our test disconfirms the hypothesis, what we observe is, in effect, the negation of the consequent coming true:

The powder does not dissolve in water.

You will remember that from these two statements we can validly deduce by modus tollens the conclusion that the powder is not sugar. This is why disconfirming evidence is stronger than confirming evidence, and also why this inferential method is often called the "hypothetical deductive" method.

An interesting application of the principle that disconfirming evidence outweighs confirming evidence generates an additional form of confirming evidence. If we search thoroughly for disconfirming evidence and find none, this in itself constitutes a kind of confirming evidence. This is sometimes referred to as "indirect confirmation." Every *unsuccessful* attempt to falsify a hypothesis has the effect of strengthening it. This is why scientists try so hard to *disprove* their hypotheses. Every time they fail, the hypothesis succeeds.

EXERCISE 9.4 | Testing Hypotheses

Essay Assignment: The following is an argument from former University of Toronto business dean and NAFTA (North American Free Trade Agreement) proponent John Crispo. It is titled "Uncle Sam's puzzling decline: Love they neighbour—and I do, which is why I fear for America's future." Write a short essay in which you explain Crispo's argument using the concepts discussed above. What hypotheses does Crispo consider? What evidence does he present? Explain how Crispo uses the evidence to confirm or disconfirm the hypotheses he is considering.

> . . . I believe we are witnessing more than the beginning of the decline and fall of the United States.
>
> . . . The manifestations of the American downfall are becoming more and more apparent. Clearly, the U.S. is overextended militarily, bogged down as it is both in Afghanistan and Iraq. . . .
>
> In terms of its fiscal and trade position, the U.S. is running larger and larger deficits, which cannot be sustained. This is setting the stage for what some have described as "the perfect economic storm." . . .
>
> . . . There are two other critical developments that are at the core of my concerns—one being the deteriorating state of America's education system and the other its declining research and development (R&D) capability.
>
> . . . There is debate in the U.S. about its overstretched military and about its rising fiscal and trade deficits. But there is precious little discussion of its education and R&D shortcomings, which in the end pale in comparison.
>
> The consequence of our neighbour's prospects will be devastating for Canada. But worse still, . . . will be the ramifications for the world at large—economically, militarily, politically and socially. . . .[1]

CAUSAL REASONING

One of the most widespread and important applications of hypothetical inductive reasoning concerns figuring out how things work—determining the *causes* and *effects* of things. Why is the left channel of the stereo intermittently fuzzy and distorted? What is causing that little clicking noise at 90 kilometres per hour? What will be the environmental, psychological, and social consequences of the development of virtual-reality technology? These instances are typical of the kind of causal reasoning problems we encounter so frequently in so many aspects of our lives. Popular accounts of causal reasoning often use cognate words such as *association, connection,* and *linkage* (for instance, a news item might report, "Trans fats linked to heart disease"). Reasoning about causes and effects, however, is tricky. First, as the 18th-century Scottish philosopher David Hume pointed out, we never directly observe causal relationships. We have to infer them. Strictly speaking, according to Hume, we observe directly only event[1] at time[1] and—separately—event[2] at time[2]. Next, we can never infer causal relationships with deductive certainty. Since the evidence for a causal relationship is always indirect, some room for doubt will always exist when we infer a cause. In other words, we must reason inductively about causes. In addition, reasoning about causes by means of simple inductive generalization turns out not to be terribly reliable because inductive generalization by itself provides no basis for distinguishing between a causal relationship and a mere coincidence.

Finally, we must mention the pivotal concept of *correlation*, which is an observed or established statistical regularity (sometimes fallaciously thought to establish a causal connection). An example: We can speculate quite reasonably that a correlation exists between mathematical and scientific ability and success in becoming an engineer. The higher the first is, the more likely the second is. Conversely, the lower the first is, the less likely the second is. Of course, mathematical and scientific ability does not by itself cause people to become engineers, and some people with such ability choose medicine or even the arts instead of engineering. Nonetheless, if we were to investigate the characteristics of (successful) engineers, we would surely find a higher than average level of mathematical and scientific ability. People who exhibit lower levels of such ability are less likely to be represented in the category of engineers. Another example: A correlation exists between alcohol consumption and the grades of university students. Students whose grades are lower tend to drink more than students whose grades are higher. This means that the two variables vary consistently, though inversely: The higher the one is, the lower the other tends to be, and vice versa. We must ask, though: Is alcohol consumption the cause of lower grades for these students—or is greater alcohol consumption a response to (an effect of) disappointingly lower grades? While it is true that a correlation exists here, the existence of a correlation does not by itself answer the question of whether A causes B, or whether B causes A—assuming, as well, that some other variable does not account causally for both. Confirmation is essential in all cases of alleged correlation, as what might appear initially to be a statistical regularity could be mere coincidence, and the establishment of correlation still demands the further step of sorting out causal connections.

MILL'S METHOD OF AGREEMENT

The 19th-century British philosopher John Stuart Mill, best known for his work in moral and political philosophy, also made significant contributions to inductive logic, particularly in its applications to causal reasoning. Mill spelled out a number of guidelines—extensions of the above evaluative principles for inductive generalization—designed to make reasoning about causes and effects more reliable. These guidelines, often referred to as "Mill's Methods," are widely respected and followed as part of what we now call the "scientific method." Mill's method of agreement is a variation of simple inductive generalization. It comprises seeking out some common antecedent condition in all cases of the effect whose cause we are trying to determine. It is based on the (reasonable) assumption that *the cause will be present in every instance in which the effect occurs.* Thus, if we can identify some such common antecedent condition, it is a likely candidate for the cause.

Suppose, for example, that certain people start showing a strange new set of debilitating symptoms in several major cities around the same time. What is the cause of the strange new disease? Right away we would want to know what these people have in common that might account for their symptoms. We know they live in different parts of the world. Let us suppose that no two individuals live within 500 kilometres of each other, that they range in age from 5 to 75 years old, that some are male and some female, that they have no common occupation, and so on. Now if we were to discover that all the people suffering from these symptoms had travelled during the month of June to a particular vacation spot (let us call it Fantasy Island), then we might suppose that the cause of the symptoms is related in some way to vacationing on Fantasy Island in June. The accompanying table illustrates the method of agreement. Let the 10 "instances" represent the 10 individual cases under investigation, the letter *s* represent the "effect" of suffering from the symptoms, and the letters A, B, C, D, E, F, and G represent a range of antecedent conditions, with F representing having vacationed on Fantasy Island in June.

MILL'S METHOD OF AGREEMENT

Instance	Antecedent Conditions							Effect
1	A	B		D	E	F		s
2	A		C		E	F	G	s
3		B		D	E	F	G	s
4			C	D	E	F		s
5	A	B				F		s
6				D		F	G	s
7						F		s
8	A	B	C	D	E	F	G	s
9	A	B				F		s
10			C			F	G	s

Of course, the fact that all the symptom sufferers vacationed on Fantasy Island in June does not *prove* (deductively) a causal connection. It does, though, make it *reasonable to suppose* that such a causal relationship exists, and this is all we can expect from an inductive inference. If having vacationed on Fantasy Island were the *only* common factor we could find among all of the symptom sufferers, we could be even more confident of a causal connection. *In general, the more isolated the common antecedent condition, the more likely it is to be related causally to the effect.*

CRITICAL THINKING TIP 9.4: MILL'S METHOD OF AGREEMENT

In general, the more isolated the common antecedent condition, the more likely it is to be related causally to the effect.

MILL'S METHOD OF DIFFERENCE

The problem, of course, is that any collection of individuals will have not one but many different antecedent conditions in common, most of which will turn out not to have any causal connection with the effect we seek to understand. In this example, having been on Fantasy Island in June together means having not just one but many things in common: exposure to common sources of food and water, exposure to the full range of substances and organisms present in the environment, including the other vacationers, and so on. So we need a way of narrowing the field, of eliminating some of the many candidates we are likely to identify by means of the method of agreement.

Mill formulated the method of difference for this purpose. The method of difference is based on the reasonable assumption that *the cause will be absent from every instance in which the effect does not occur.* To continue with our example, let us suppose that we get a list of all the people who travelled to Fantasy Island in June and it turns out that some of them have not suffered any of the symptoms we are investigating. So next we would want to know what differences exist between these people and the symptom sufferers. Now suppose we discover that the Fantasy Island vacationers who did not get sick also did not go swimming. This would suggest that the cause of the symptoms has something to do with swimming.

The accompanying table illustrates the method of difference. Let the 12 "instances" represent the 12 individuals who vacationed on Fantasy Island in June, the letter *s* represent the "effect" of suffering from the symptoms, and the letters L, M, N, O, P, R, and S represent a range of activities (such as attending the luau, beach volleyball, cycling, drinking rum, and so on), with S representing swimming.

METHOD OF DIFFERENCE

Instance	Antecedent Conditions							Effect
1	L	M	N	O	P	R	S	s
2	L		N	O	P		S	s
3	L	M	N	O	P		S	s
4		M		O	P	R	S	s
5	L	M	N		P	R	S	s
6	L	M	N	O	P	R	S	s
7	L	M		O		R	S	s
8			N	O	P		S	s
9	L		N	O	P	R	S	s
10	L	M		O	P	R	S	s
11	L	M	N	O	P	R	–	–
12	L	M	N	O	P		–	–

Like the method of agreement, the method of difference is a variation of simple inductive generalization. Instead of looking for a correlation between instances of the effect and some common antecedent condition, here we seek a correlation between the *absence* of the effect and the *absence* of an antecedent condition. Also, like the method of agreement, the method of difference is not absolutely conclusive. The discovery of such a correlation—in this example between not having gone swimming and not suffering the symptoms—does not *prove* (deductively) that the symptoms and swimming are causally related, but it does make it reasonable to suppose that they are. If having gone swimming were the *only* difference we could find between the symptom sufferers and the vacationers who did not get sick, we could be even more confident of a causal connection. *In general, the more isolated the difference, the more likely it is to be related causally to the effect.*

CRITICAL THINKING TIP 9.5: MILL'S METHOD OF DIFFERENCE

In general, the more isolated the difference, the more likely it is to be related causally to the effect.

Since the method of agreement and the method of difference each enhance the reliability of inductive inferences about causal relationships when used separately, we can suppose reasonably that using them together in the same investigation (as in our example) would strengthen even further the inductive inference to a causal relationship. In other words, if some antecedent condition is *both* common to all instances of the effect whose cause is under investigation *and* absent from instances where the effect is also absent, a causal connection is even more likely.

METHOD OF CONCOMITANT VARIATION

Now suppose we turn up a Fantasy Island vacationer who went swimming but did not get sick, or a Fantasy Island vacationer who got sick but did not go swimming. We saw earlier how the method of agreement is limited by the fact that any collection of individuals will have not one but many common antecedent conditions, most of which will have no causal connection with the effect we seek to understand. For this reason the method of agreement, by itself, is rarely adequate to identify the cause of any phenomenon. We have now seen how the method of difference helps to identify the cause by a process of elimination. The method of difference has a limitation of its own, however, which in turn limits the joint method of agreement and difference. The method of difference—and therefore also the joint method of agreement and difference—depends upon being able to observe instances from which a suspected cause is *absent*. To apply the method of difference we need to find, or experimentally bring about, an instance in which an antecedent condition that is suspected as a cause is out of the picture.

Let us suppose that by the method of agreement, we have discovered that five antecedent conditions are common to all instances in which the effect we are investigating has been observed. To apply the method of difference thoroughly we would need to be able to observe what happens when each of these five antecedent conditions is missing, yet this is not always easy to do. Sometimes it is practically impossible. Mill's own example of isolating the cause of tides shows this.

When it was suspected that one of the many antecedent conditions that accompanies the ebb and flow of the tides—the position of the moon—was the true cause of tidal motion, it was nevertheless impossible to confirm this suspicion by the method of difference. As Mill said, "We cannot try an experiment in the absence of the moon, so as to observe what terrestrial phenomena her annihilation would put an end to."[2] To overcome this limitation Mill formulated the method of concomitant variation. When it is difficult or impossible to eliminate a suspected cause, it may nevertheless still be possible to *vary* it, or to observe its natural variations, and see whether these variations are accompanied by corresponding variations in the effect under investigation. In the case of the moon and the tides, it turns out that the closer the moon is to a particular coastal region, the higher the tide, and the farther the moon is from a particular coastal region, the lower the tide, which makes it reasonable to suppose that a causal connection exists.

The accompanying table illustrates the joint method of agreement and difference supplemented by the method of concomitant variation for three instances of some effect *s*. The letters L, M, N, O, P, R, and S represent a range of antecedent conditions. By the method of agreement we determine that five of these conditions—L, N, O, P, and S—are present in all cases where *s* is observed. So these are our causal candidates. No cases exist, however, where any of these conditions, or the effect *s*, is absent. So we cannot isolate a cause by the method of difference. Nonetheless, each of the antecedent conditions varies in degree (represented by the plus and minus signs), and only one of them varies in a way that corresponds to variations in the effect. So the condition that we have isolated, O, is most likely to be causally connected to *s*.

MILL'S JOINT METHOD OF AGREEMENT AND DIFFERENCE WITH CONCOMITANT VARIATION

Instance	Antecedent Conditions							Effect
1	L+	M	N−	O	P−	R	S+	s
2	L		N+	O+	P		S−	s+
3	L−	M	N	O−	P+		S	s−

The method of concomitant variation is a widely used experimental strategy in the sciences. For example, pharmacology researchers routinely study the efficacy of experimental drugs by varying the dosage. If the observed effects on the alleviation of symptoms vary with the dosage, going up when the dosage is increased and going down when the dosage is decreased, this counts as confirmation of the causal efficacy of the drug. If the alleviation of symptoms does not vary with the dosage—if, for example, the symptoms are alleviated slightly with small doses, slightly more with slightly larger doses, but not at all with large doses—this would raise doubts about the causal efficacy of the drug.

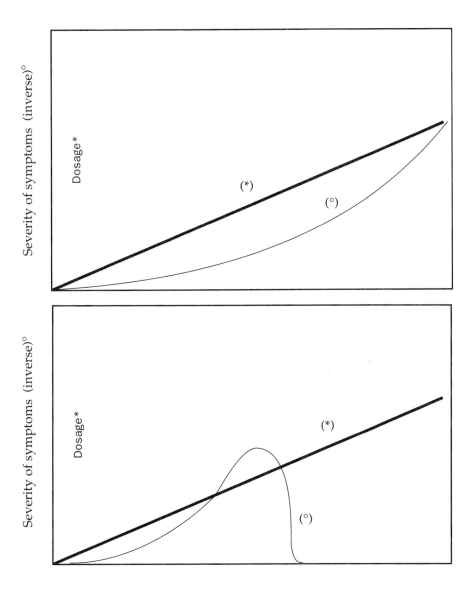

EXERCISE 9.5 | Causal Reasoning

Agenda for Class Discussion:

- Think of all the different areas of routine human interest and concern within which causal reasoning plays a crucial role. Brainstorm a list of such areas.

- Next, as a group, pick some phenomenon of common interest or concern to you whose cause(s) are not yet known.

- Now, develop a list of reasonable causal hypotheses.

- Finally, discuss the design of experiments to test these hypotheses.

ADDITIONAL EXERCISES

EXERCISE 9.6   According to Paul and Nathalie Silver of the Carnegie Institute, California's "Old Faithful" geyser can predict large earthquakes within a radius of 150 miles. They argue for this conclusion on the basis of a 20-year record of geyser eruptions. Ordinarily, the geyser erupts at very regular intervals (which is why it came to be known as "Old Faithful"). On the day before the Oroville earthquake of August 1, 1975, the interval between geyser eruptions suddenly changed from 50 minutes to 120 minutes. In 1984 the geyser was erupting every 40 minutes. But the day before the April 24 Morgan Hill tremor, the pattern became irregular, fluctuating between 25-, 40-, and 50-minute intervals. A change was also noted before the 1989 Loma Prieta quake in the San Francisco area. Two and a half days before the quake, eruption intervals at the geyser suddenly shifted from 90 minutes to 150 minutes. The researchers noted that a number of things, including rainfall, can affect the regularity of eruptions in geysers. However, an analysis of rainfall amounts in the Calistoga area rules this out as an explanation of the abrupt pattern changes preceding each of these earthquakes.

Evaluate the evidence and the reasoning involved here. What strengths can you identify? What weaknesses? What kinds of further evidence would confirm the hypothesis that Old Faithful is an effective earthquake predictor? What kinds of further evidence would disconfirm the hypothesis? What kinds of experiments can you think of to discover such evidence?[3]

EXERCISE 9.7

Research Note: "The Influence of Colour and Incentives on Mail Survey Response Rates," by Chanelle Gallant. Used by permission.

A study examining social democratic values and class, which was conducted during the summer of 1997, has produced unexpected findings concerning response rates. For this study, self-administered questionnaires were distributed to 150 randomly-chosen residents of a Toronto student housing cooperative—56 of whom responded.

One of the methodological aims of this study was to determine the influence of questionnaire colour and incentives on response rates for mail surveys. As it turned out, respondents who received either a questionnaire printed on green paper or a white questionnaire with a lollipop included as an incentive were significantly more likely to respond to the survey than respondents who received a white questionnaire but no incentive. . . .

These findings concerning the influence of questionnaire colour and non-monetary incentives support existing theory and research, yet this study showed an unusually strong effect. . . .

I believe that the increased response rate in this study may be due to the unique characteristics of the group under study: young post-secondary students. This group appears to be strongly enticed by bright colours and candy. These observations suggest that researchers may have underestimated the influence of non-monetary incentives and coloured questionnaires on post-secondary students. . . .[4]

What strengths in the reasoning can you identify? Do you see any weaknesses? How might the researcher's claims be strengthened or weakened by further evidence?

▌ EXERCISE 9.8

"[If, according to Christian creationists, a Biblical flood had suddenly washed over the entire world in the very distant past,] [t]here would be no segregation of fossils. If all organisms lived at the same time, we would expect to see trilobites, brachiopods, ammonites, dinosaurs, and mammals (including humans) all randomly mixed together in the worldwide blanket described in point #1. *This is not what is observed.* The fossil record exhibits an order consistent with the theory of evolution (but inconsistent with creationism), from *simple* forms to more *complex* forms, and from creatures *very unlike* modern species to those *more closely resembling* modern species. There is not one instance of any fossils that have been deposited "out of order."

In addition, there would be no extinction events found in the fossil record. There are at least five major extinction events, a situation where fossils are abundant *below* a certain line within the geological layers, but totally absent above that line. The most notable extinction event is the one that killed off the dinosaurs (and 90% of all other life) 65 million years ago. There is no way to explain these geological features with a global flood."[5]

What strengths in the reasoning can you identify? Do you see any weaknesses? How might the researcher's claims be strengthened or weakened by further evidence?

▌ EXERCISE 9.9 In the first years of our century, so-called reality television became highly popular, noticeably pushing aside more traditional programming. Such shows typically featured documentary-style accounts of personal experiences—for example, romantic dates on *The Bachelor,* or therapy sessions—and tests of skill or endurance—for example, Donald Trump's *The Apprentice* ("You're fired!") and *Fear Factor.* "Documentary-*style*" is truly the appropriate term, since many such shows, though apparently aspiring to present "real-life" experiences, are artificial in character. For example, none of the contestants on the huge hit *Survivor*, who were ostensibly stranded on the proverbial "desert island," were ever in any real danger. Social critics

wondered about the popularity of "reality television" shows and the implications for the general state of culture.

Consider the following list of explanatory hypotheses in terms of plausibility and explanatory power. On this basis narrow the list down to two leading hypotheses. Describe the kinds of experimental evidence that would then be needed in order to choose between the two hypotheses.

- Reality television shows featured "edgier" situations than traditional shows.
- So-called reality television exploited the public's decreasing ability to distinguish fakeness from actual life.
- It was just a fluke.
- It was novelty appeal. Traditional shows were simply getting old. People were looking for something new.
- Reality television was more challenging and rewarding intellectually than traditional shows.

EXERCISE 9.10   Using the concepts and terms of Mill's Methods, explain how, in the following story from the history of medicine, 19th-century medical researcher Ignaz Semmelweis discovered and demonstrated the importance of physician hygiene in patient care.

> Between 1844 and 1846, the death rate from a mysterious disease termed "childbed fever" in the First Maternity Division of the Vienna General Hospital averaged an alarming 10 percent. But the rate in the Second Division, where midwives rather than doctors attended the mothers, was only about 2 percent. For some time no one could explain why. Then one day a colleague accidentally cut himself on the finger with a student's scalpel while performing an autopsy. Although the cut seemed harmless enough, the man died shortly thereafter, exhibiting symptoms identical to those of childbed fever. Semmelweis formed the hypothesis that doctors and medical students, who spent their mornings doing autopsies before making their divisional rounds, were unwittingly transmitting to the women something they picked up from the cadavers. Semmelweis tested this hypothesis by requiring the doctors and students to clean their hands before examining patients. Doctors and students were forbidden to examine patients without first washing their hands in a solution of chlorinated lime. The death rate in the First Division fell to less than 2 percent.

EXERCISE 9.11   Within the context of the issue you have been addressing, identify areas where causal or hypothetical reasoning would be relevant. Formulate causal, interpretive, or other appropriate hypotheses. Evaluate these for plausibility and explanatory power. On this basis, select a "leading hypothesis." Finally, design an experiment to test the leading hypothesis.

EXERCISE 9.12   Research the media stories concerning the Bigfoot example in Exercises 9.2 and 9.3, with special reference to the tests eventually carried out on the alleged physical evidence.

GLOSSARY

burden of proof   obligation to produce the argument in a dispute over an issue; failure to meet the burden of proof settles the issue in favour of the other side

confirming evidence   evidence consistent with what a hypothesis predicts

correlation   an observed or established statistical regularity, sometimes fallaciously thought to establish a causal connection

disconfirming evidence   evidence inconsistent with what a hypothesis predicts

explanatory power   an idea's power to reduce or eliminate puzzlement

hypothesis   an idea or set of ideas under investigation

hypothetical deductive method   a method of scientific investigation involving both hypothetical inductive reasoning and deductive reasoning

inductive generalization   a variety of inductive reasoning in which general conclusions are projected from a number of particular instances

joint method of agreement and difference   a principle of causal reasoning that combines the method of agreement with the method of difference

method of agreement   a principle of causal reasoning that comprises seeking out some common antecedent condition in all cases of the effect whose cause we seek to determine

method of concomitant variation   a principle of causal reasoning that comprises varying a suspected cause and checking for corresponding variations in the effect, useful for situations where it is difficult or impossible to eliminate a suspected cause

method of difference   a principle of causal reasoning that comprises looking for a correlation between the *absence* of the effect and the *absence* of an antecedent condition

Mill's Methods   guidelines for reliable causal reasoning formulated by philosopher John Stuart Mill

plausibility   a measure of an idea's likelihood of surviving critical scrutiny

Go to http://www.criticalthinking1ce.nelson.com for additional study resources for this chapter.

ENDNOTES

[1] John Crispo, "Uncle Sam's Puzzling Decline," *The Globe and Mail,* August 13, 2005, A15. Reprinted by permission.

[2] John Stuart Mill, *A System of Logic,* Book III, Chapter 8, Section 6.

[3] Paul G. Silver, and Nathalie J. Valette-Silver. "Detection of Hydrothermal Precursors to Large Northern California Earthquakes." *Science* 257 (1992): 1363–68.

[4] *Institute for Social Research Newsletter* 13, no. 2, Fall 1988. ISSN: 0834-1729, http://www.isr.yorku.ca/home.html

[5] Ken Harding, "What Would We Find If the World Had Flooded?" http://evolution.mbdojo.com/flood.html Version 2.0 (last updated: November 1, 1999).

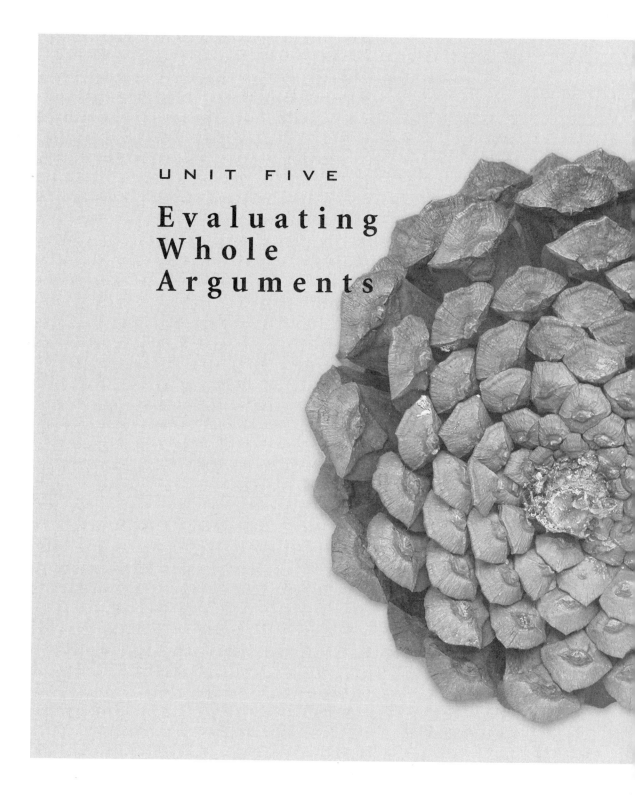

Evaluating
Whole
Arguments

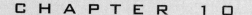

Evaluating Premises: Self-Evidence, Consistency, Indirect Proof

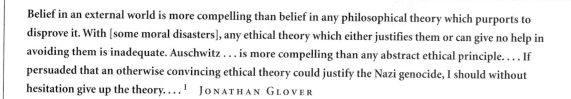

Belief in an external world is more compelling than belief in any philosophical theory which purports to disprove it. With [some moral disasters], any ethical theory which either justifies them or can give no help in avoiding them is inadequate. Auschwitz . . . is more compelling than any abstract ethical principle. . . . If persuaded that an otherwise convincing ethical theory could justify the Nazi genocide, I should without hesitation give up the theory. . . . [1]   JONATHAN GLOVER

In Chapter 6 we distinguished between the structural features of arguments and the materials out of which they are constructed. In Chapters 6 and 7 you learned how to evaluate deductive arguments structurally for validity. In Chapters 8 and 9 you learned how to assess the strength of inductive arguments. Now that you have studied the structural features of arguments in both of these two main argument-design categories, we will look at the standards and practices of evaluating premises. You will be happy (we imagine) to know that there is not much new for you to learn at this stage about evaluating the premises of an argument. Because the premises of any argument are themselves each conclusions of subarguments or internal arguments—or potential conclusions of potential subarguments or internal arguments—evaluating the premises of an argument turns out to be more or less a matter of applying what you have already learned about issues and arguments. If the text of the argument itself offers support for a particular premise, then we have a subargument whose conclusion is

the premise we wish to evaluate, and so we can evaluate the subargument. Eventually, however, you will run into premises that the text of the argument itself does not support. All arguments have to start somewhere, and this means that every argument will have unsupported premises in it.

In designing and constructing an argument, common sense would suggest we establish as firm a foundation as possible. So, experienced arguers generally try to use as their most "basic" premises claims that are as uncontroversial, as easy to accept, and as hard to challenge or refute as possible. For example, the very first article of the United Nations Universal Declaration of Human Rights states that all persons are (should be considered) free and equal. This idea founds the remaining articles. If we were to subtract this starting principle from the list of human rights, the set would become unintelligible. The Universal Declaration of Human Rights in effect says: "Here is a basic idea that does not stand in need of an argument. Any humane person would accept this fundamental stance." We can easily express, but not accept, the contrary: "Not all persons need to be considered free—slavery is allowable—and not all persons need to be considered equal—inequitable treatment is allowable."

EXERCISE 10.1 | **Topic for Class Discussion**

Even if you agree with the United Nations Universal Declaration of Human Rights that a claim as basic as "All persons are free and equal" doesn't (or shouldn't) need to be defended, it's still an interesting question: Why not? Do you think it's true that basic human rights belong equally to each and every human being? Suppose someone challenged this claim. How would you go about supporting a claim as basic as this?

All arguments have to start somewhere. Can an argument, though, move forward without having to back up? The problem critical thinking faces at this point is how to avoid an "infinite regress" of argument evaluation. "Infinite regress" means a kind of "bottomless pit" of premises supported by more premises, supported by more premises, and so on to infinity—so that it becomes logically impossible to complete the evaluation of any argument.

One version of one of Zeno's famous "Paradoxes of Motion" goes like this: Try to go from wherever you are (Point A) to anywhere else (Point B). First you have to go half the distance from Point A to Point B. But before you can go half the distance from Point A to Point B you have to go half that distance. But before you can go half of half the distance from Point A to Point B you have to go half of that distance, and so on to infinity. So not only can you never go from Point A to Point B, you cannot even start! Now, everybody knows from experience that motion is possible, so something has to be wrong with the reasoning in Zeno's Paradox. What can it be?

Philosophers, and theorists generally, tend to run from infinite regresses. In fact, a kind of theoretical rule of thumb exists in many disciplines to the effect that if some hypothesis can be shown to lead to an infinite regress, then the hypothesis is untenable (must be considered incorrect). We can easily understand the urge to apply such a rule of thumb here in critical thinking. If we have no "first premises"— if the demand for deeper support can be made over and over at increasing levels of depth ad infinitum—then no resolution to any issue could ever be achieved, which is simply not reasonable. Consequently, *some* way of avoiding an infinite regress of argument evaluation *must* be found. So we need to inquire as to whether any "self-evident truths" exist beneath which the inquiry cannot or need not go. So, first, do any claims exist that are *completely* beyond question or dispute?

NECESSARY TRUTHS

Do *any claims at all* exist, available for use as premises, that *do not* require their own additional support?

Try to deny the following claim:
    "Either Conrad Black knew about major financial irregularities in his company or he didn't." What do you notice when you attempt to deny this claim?

TAUTOLOGIES

Some people consider certain claims to be "necessarily true," meaning that one cannot deny these claims in a coherent way. For example, when you try to deny the claim in Exercise 10.3, a contradiction results. To deny this claim would in effect say that Conrad Black both knew about major financial irregularities and did not know about major financial irregularities, which is logically impossible.

What "logically impossible" means is that the impossibility can be traced to the logical form of the contradiction. Thus, *any* statement whose formal structure is "either P or not P" must necessarily be true, because the negation of any statement of the form "either P or not P" is self-contradictory (and therefore necessarily false). A claim that you cannot deny without formally contradicting yourself is called a *tautology* and considered to be necessarily true. This can be demonstrated by means of a truth table:

P	~P	P v ~P	~(P v ~P)
T	F	T	F
F	T	T	F

Even though tautologies always carry the value "true," notice that they do not convey much information. The claim "either Conrad Black knew or he didn't" does not by itself tell us much, does it? For this reason, tautologies are often considered "*trivially* true." Nevertheless, they *can* occasionally play a crucial role in an argument. For example:

- Either Conrad Black knew about major financial irregularities in his company or he did not.
- If he did know about such irregularities, then he is guilty of criminal conduct and therefore unworthy of his position.
- If he did not know about major financial irregularities, then he is not in control of his own company and is therefore unworthy of his position.
- Therefore, either way, he is definitely unworthy of his position.

EXERCISE 10.4 | **Topic for Class Discussion**

Do you think the claim in the United Nations Universal Declaration of Human Rights that all persons are free and equal is a "tautology"? Do you think it is "trivially true"? Can you deny it without contradicting yourself?

TRUISMS BY DEFINITION

Do other kinds of statements exist that are "necessarily true"—that "cannot coherently be denied"? Perhaps there are. For example, consider the statement "Murder is a form of homicide," or "All bachelors are unmarried," or "'Phonetic' isn't." It would seem to be impossible to deny any of these statements without contradicting oneself, although this is due not so much to the formal structures of the statements as to the meanings of the terms in them. Murder is, by definition, a subset of the larger category "homicide"; "unmarried" is part of the meaning of "bachelor"; and the word "phonetic" means "spelled the way it sounds." Thus, to deny any of these statements would be a "contradiction *in terms*." So we would expect anyone who understands the meanings of the terms involved to recognize immediately any such statement as true. Such statements might be called "truisms by definition."

EXERCISE 10.5 | **Topic for Class Discussion**

Do you think the claim in the United Nations Universal Declaration of Human Rights that all persons are free and equal is a "truism by definition"? Do you think it would be a "contradiction in terms" to deny it?

EXERCISE 10.6 | **Necessary Truths**

Sort the following statements into these categories: (1) Tautologies; (2) True by Definition; (3) Formal Contradictions; (4) Contradictions in Terms; (5) Statements that Are Neither Necessarily True nor Self-Contradictory. Compare your results with those of your classmates. Be prepared to explain your answers.

	Tautologies	True by Definition	Formal Contradictions	Contradictions in Terms	Neither
A rectangle has four sides.					
This rectangle has only three sides.					
Either she's married or she's not married.					
She is both married and unmarried.					
She is either married or engaged.					
She is neither married nor engaged.					
Abortion is murder.					
Murder is wrong.					
White is a colour.					
White is a shape.					
No statement that contradicts itself is true.					
Rideau Hall is located in Ottawa.					
This sentence has seven words in it.					
This sentence has eight words in it.					
All persons are created equal.					
Wherever you go, there you are.					
All arguments have to start somewhere.					

CONTINGENT CLAIMS

Most claims are neither self-contradictory nor necessarily true. Claims that are neither self-contradictory nor necessarily true are called *contingent,* meaning that their truth or falsity *depends on* something outside themselves, something beyond their formal structures or the meanings of their terms. Let us return now to considering the "self-evident truth" of the United Nations Universal Declaration of Human Rights that all persons are free and equal. Is it a tautology? If someone were to deny it, would a formal contradiction result? We think not. No formal inconsistency appears in the claim that "Not all persons are free and equal," or the logically equivalent claim "Some persons are (inherently) unequal." Nor is the claim that all persons are free and equal "trivially true," as we would expect a tautology to be. It seems actually to say something important. Is it true by definition? Would its denial constitute a contradiction in terms? Again, this apparently is not the case. So, the Declaration's first article evidently means something other than "necessarily true." Let us therefore suppose that the Declaration's "self-evident truth" that all persons are free and equal is a contingent claim. This would mean that its truth value depends on something outside its formal structure and the meanings of its terms. On what does its truth value depend?

Suppose someone were to deny the claim that all persons are created equal. The first question to ask when we come to the evaluation of a contingent claim that has been used as an unsupported premise is: What *kind* of claim is being made here? Does the premise make a factual claim? An evaluative claim? Does it offer an interpretation? This is like asking: If someone were to challenge this claim, what sort of issue would emerge? A factual issue, an evaluative issue, an interpretive issue, or a complex issue involving more than one of these categories? Thinking about these questions helps us to determine what sorts of additional support may be needed to establish a given contingent claim as a premise in an argument.

EXERCISE 10.7 | **Review**

We highly recommend at this point that you review the section in Chapter 1 on issues and issue analysis. It is especially relevant at this point, and it may make even better sense now than it did at the beginning.

FACTUAL CLAIMS

As we pointed out in Chapter 1, most issues are complex and involve elements from all three categories of issues: factual, evaluative, and interpretive. Factual issues often give rise to both evaluative and interpretive issues as well. Thus, establishing a particular premise as a "matter of fact" can turn out to be a tall and complicated order. For example, suppose we are trying to determine as a matter of fact what caused the stock market suddenly to lose 500 points. Right away we are deep into the realm of hypothetical reasoning with all its nuances and complexities, as described in Chapter 9, and a long way from anything that might be considered "self-evident."

Of course, many factual claims are much simpler and more directly linked to our own firsthand experience. Thus, for example, in law, firsthand eyewitness testimony carries great weight in any fact-finding process. "I was there. I saw the crime being committed with my own eyes, . . . " sworn under oath and subject to the penalty for perjury is hard to overcome as evidence at trial. Even here, though, on occasion lawyers find ways to undermine the force of eyewitness testimony. A witness's memory, reliability as an observer, or sanity may be impeached, or contradictory eyewitness testimony may exist. So even eyewitness testimony, as probative (proof-related) and fundamentally unassailable as it may be generally, can still be doubted and overturned, and therefore probably ought not to be considered "self-evident." Still, perhaps *some* factual claims are *so basic* that they might be considered "self-evident." Suppose, for example, you were to say,

> My best friend is over 1.55 metres tall.

The claim made here is a contingent statement of fact. Its truth value depends upon the height of your best friend, something "out there in the world" that can be tested empirically; that is, by reference to sense experience, or to what scientists call "observations." Whenever scientists weigh, measure, or take the temperature of something, they are making observations. Then when they record or report these observations, they are making "observation claims." Suppose someone now challenges your claim that your best friend is over 1.55 metres tall. How do you respond? Well, suppose you say, "I'm 1.58 metres tall and my best friend is taller than I am, so my best friend is over 1.55 metres tall."

Now suppose you are challenged to defend these two claims. How do you know you are 1.58 metres tall? The truth of this sort of observation claim in general depends on the conditions under which the measurements had been made and so on. In this simple instance it is more than sufficient to know that you had been measured, when standing erect, using an accurate standard instrument of measurement, by someone reliable who knew how to use it, in circumstances that did not impair the user's performance. Now, how do you know you were standing erect when your height was measured? How do you know your best friend is taller than you are? At some point, you wind up saying something like this: "Look. There isn't anything *more basic* for me to appeal to here in support of this claim. We stand next to each other, and I look up and he looks down. That's all there is to it! It's a *basic observation!!* It's *self-evident!!!*" Notice that if you say something like this, you are also admitting that *indeed* further claims exist to which you could appeal in support of the observation that your best friend is taller than you are. You have even specified a little empirical experiment (standing next to each other) whose results support the claim. "Self-evident" in this context seems to mean something like this: The supporting claims are no more basic or evident than what they support. This may well be close to what the Declaration means when it offers as an undefended starting point the idea that all persons are free and equal, but it is also pretty clearly evident that the Declaration neither reports a basic observation nor makes any other sort of factual claim.

EVALUATIVE CLAIMS

Probably the best short answer to the question of what sort of claim "all persons are free and equal" *does* express is a "basic moral principle," which would put it in the category of evaluative claims. If the principle were challenged, the issue that would arise would be an evaluative issue. So, on what rational foundation are evaluative issues resolvable? On what rational foundation are evaluative claims to be established as true? One widely held position (which we will call "values relativism") holds that it cannot be done because of the essential difference and an unbridgeable gap between facts and values. Facts are "objective," values are "relative" or even "subjective." The best argument we can conceive in support of values relativism goes something like this:

- Factual claims can be rationally supported empirically.
- This means they are established as true ultimately on the basis of verifiable observations.
- Evaluative claims cannot be rationally supported empirically, nor can they be derived from factual claims alone.
- No other basis besides empirical observations exist on which issues may be rationally resolved or claims rationally established as true.
- Therefore, *no* rational basis exists for the resolution of evaluative issues nor does any rational foundation exist for the establishment of evaluative claims as true.

What we have to say about this view is an extension of what we said about relativism in Chapter 1.

EXERCISE 10.8 | **Review**

We highly recommend at this point that you review the section in Chapter 1 on relativism and limited relativism, under "Obstacles to Critical Thinking."

Values relativism is a specific version of what we identified in Chapter 1 as "limited relativism." As such it is inherently more reasonable and understandable than relativism in general, and even more reasonable still because evaluative issues—which *cannot* be resolved by doing science or looking things up—generally *are* harder to resolve than factual issues. Still, it does not follow from the fact that evaluative claims cannot be established *empirically* that they cannot be established at all. The weakness in the above argument for values relativism lies in the last premise, which claims that no basis other than empirical observation exists on which issues may be rationally resolved or claims rationally established as true. We deny this claim. Another rational basis for resolving issues and establishing claims as true *does* exist: *by considering and evaluating the best available arguments on all sides of the issue (as we are doing here).*

In fact, we will go a step further and argue that certain evaluative claims are already *much more firmly established as true* than certain factual claims are or can hope to be.

EXERCISE 10.9 | **Topic for Class Discussion**

Of the following two claims, which one is evaluative? Which one is factual? Which one do you think is more firmly established as true? Why?

1. Gandhi's political leadership of his people was morally superior to Hitler's political leadership of his people.

2. ~~Intelligent~~ extraterrestrial life exists elsewhere in our galaxy.

We think claim #1 clearly expresses a value judgment. We also think it is much more firmly established as true than (clearly factual) claim #2 either is or will likely be in the foreseeable future. How can this be? Of course, we cannot be *absolutely certain* that Gandhi's leadership of his people was morally superior to Hitler's leadership. Nonetheless, even though this claim expresses a value judgment and even though it may yet be open to challenge and debate, we consider it to be quite firmly established as true. How so?

EXERCISE 10.10 | **Facts and Values**

The following argument—or pair of arguments—adds up in our opinion to a powerful and persuasive case, even though it is chock-full of evaluative claims. How many evaluative claims can you count? Highlight all the evaluative claims you can find. How many factual claims can you count? Highlight all the factual claims you can find. Can you think of any counterarguments? How do the best counterarguments you can find—or imagine—compare? Are they as powerful? Anywhere close?

- Gandhi led his people out of the bondage of colonial rule. He also guided the struggle away from violence. Doing so required great courage and wisdom, saved a great many lives, and provided to the world a model of an effective and humane way to engage in political struggle. Human life is precious. Freedom is better than colonial bondage as a way of life. Therefore, Gandhi was a great leader.

- By contrast, Hitler led his people into World War II. He directed his people to invade and forcibly occupy the territory of neighbouring states. He directed his people to exterminate several million civilian noncombatants. He led the world to develop nuclear and other weapons of mass destruction. Human life is precious. Peace is precious. Therefore, Hitler was a terrible leader.

The example in Exercise 10.10 illustrates how evaluative issues are generally resolved and evaluative claims are established as true—*by considering and evaluating the best available arguments on all sides of the issue (as we are doing here)*.

This brings us back to the problem posed at the beginning of this chapter—how to avoid an infinite regress of argument evaluation. To evaluate an argument you have to evaluate the premises. To do this, of course, you have to evaluate arguments. Can you ever get to the bottom of this? Perhaps you cannot, but once you learn how to swim you stop worrying about "getting (or sinking) to the bottom."

Let us not forget either that the problem of an infinite regress arose also in connection with contingent statements of fact. This does not, however, prevent us from determining matters of fact. At some point, we encounter observation claims so "*basic*" that, even though we *could* go on to support them by appeal to further observations, these would be no more basic or evident than what they support. So, unless there is *good* reason for doubting them, such claims may be taken as "self-evident." Similarly, with value judgments, at some point you get down to an evaluative claim *so basic* that, even if you *could* go on to support it with further arguments based on further claims, these arguments and claims would be no more convincing than the claims they support. So, even if we cannot "get to the *absolute bottom*" of the theoretical heap of premises supported by other premises, supported by other premises, supported by other premises, perhaps we *do* eventually get to a level where the burden of proof shifts decisively in favour of some primal claim.

EXERCISE 10.11 | Topic for Class Discussion

Pick any of the following evaluative claims. Compose (a) the best argument you can in support of it and (b) the best argument you can against it.

- Human life is precious.
- Peace is precious.
- Freedom is better than colonial bondage as a way of life.
- Basic human rights belong equally to each and every human being.

Take a claim like "Human life is precious." If all arguments have to start somewhere, this would be the sort of claim with which one would want to start. It is not the case that one could not possibly argue in support of such a claim—but what would the argument add to the strength of the claim itself? Moreover, what sort of argument could be made against such a claim? The burden of proof does clearly fall on the challenger here. For at least some such claims, the burden of proof seems so substantial that intuitively it is hard to imagine how one might overturn it.

EXERCISE 10.12 | **Topic for Class Discussion**

Here is an argument in support of the claim that basic human rights belong equally to each and every human being. Compare the argument to the claim that it supports. Which do you find more convincing? The argument, or the conclusion itself?

1. Morality presumes consistency.

2. In other words, in the absence of a justification for differential treatment, all moral rules and considerations apply equally to all parties.

3. This includes basic human rights.

4. Apparently no justification exists for differential treatment between individual human beings with respect to basic human rights.

5. Therefore, basic human rights belong equally to each and every human being.

Here is what we would say: The first two premises of the above argument *appear* to reach higher levels of generality and abstraction than the conclusion does, but this does not make them any more convincing than the conclusion itself. Premise #4 makes this a "burden-of-proof" argument, and as such inherently inconclusive. The conclusion itself is much more convincing on its face than *any* "burden-of-proof" argument. This is what we think the Declaration has in mind in offering without defence the idea of basic freedom and equality: not that this idea *cannot* be argued for, but that an argument has to start somewhere, and *this* claim seems as good as *any* candidates for the office of "first premise."

BEYOND "SELF-EVIDENCE"

By far, most claims you will find as premises in the arguments you encounter will be neither necessarily true nor self-evident. For example, we doubt that the question of "self-evidence" really arises in connection with interpretive claims. To recognize a given claim as an "interpretation" is to recognize the possibility of other interpretations and therefore the presence of an interpretive issue. This puts the claim beyond consideration as "self-evident." An interpretation, in other words, is the kind of claim one can always legitimately be challenged to defend argumentatively.

For example, one might claim, "Urbanization leads to fragmented and more superficial social relations." This claim is neither necessarily true nor self-evident in our strict senses of these terms, so the person who makes it must be prepared in principle to defend it. Nor is there a single simple procedure for resolving interpretive issues. So, no single simple procedure exists for establishing interpretive claims as premises in an argument. Instead, as with evaluative claims and indeed with contingent claims generally, it is a matter of considering the best arguments that can be made for and against them and weighing up the arguments and the evidence on all sides. Again, do not worry too much about "getting to the bottom" of this process of rational evaluation of arguments in support of premises in arguments. Just do it.

Here are some additional techniques and strategies, using concepts we have already discussed. Following these procedures can streamline the process and significantly improve results.

CONSISTENCY

One of the most powerful tools for both formal and informal argument evaluation is the concept of consistency. Two statements are "consistent" if they *could* both be true. Two statements are "inconsistent" if we can imagine no possible circumstances in which they could both be true. A group of statements is inconsistent if any two statements in the group are inconsistent. The concept of consistency is crucial to our understanding of deductive validity; more importantly, however, because *inconsistency* is always a sign that something is wrong somewhere, we can also apply it to the evaluation of premises in several highly useful ways. We used it above to explain the concept of a tautology as necessarily true. Similarly, just as a self-contradiction must necessarily be false, and hence its denial or negation necessarily true, a good rule of thumb is to check an argument's entire set of claims *as a group* for consistency. If a given *set* of claims as a group is internally inconsistent, then although you may not know *which* of the premises is false, you know they cannot *all* be true.

CRITICAL THINKING TIP 10.1

Check for consistency. If an argument's premises are not internally consistent as a group, they cannot all be true.

IMPLICATIONS

While the truth value of a claim remains to be determined, one effective strategy is to treat it hypothetically. Assume that the claim is true, and trace out its further implications. What follows logically from the claim? What further claims does it entail or lead us to suppose? The "implications" of a claim are those additional claims that either follow from it by logic or are strongly supported by it inductively. If a claim leads by implication to any further claim that is self-contradictory, or otherwise absurd or known to be false, then good reason exists to doubt the claim. This strategy has traditionally been known by its Latin name *reductio ad absurdum* (which means "to reduce to absurdity"). The strategy can also be inverted to use in defence of a position. This is sometimes called the *method of indirect proof.* In this strategy we assume that the conclusion in favour of which we want to argue is *false*. We then trace the implications of this assumption, hoping to find that it leads to some absurd or contradictory conclusion. This then constitutes good reason to reject the original assumption, which leaves intact our desired conclusion. *Reductio ad absurdum* or indirect proof can be a highly effective technique, and you will find it used frequently in argumentative discourse.

Here is an example drawn from earlier in this chapter: "If we have no 'first premises'—if the demand for deeper support can be made over and over at increasing levels of depth ad infinitum—then no resolution to any issue could ever be achieved, which is simply not reasonable. Consequently, *some* way of avoiding an infinite regress of argument evaluation *must* be found." Here we see concretely the structure of the method of indirect proof: An articulation of the contested idea ("we have no first premises"), a claim that unreasonable results flow from acceptance of the contested idea ("no resolution to any issue could ever be achieved"), and the conclusion that we must reject the contested idea ("some way around this idea must be found"). Here is another example. Consider the radical claim, "Our perceptions are never truthful." Now recall the form of modus tollens from Chapter 7:

P ⊃ Q

~Q

∴ ~P

In natural language, this reads: If P is the case, then Q is the case. [But] Q is not the case. Therefore, P is not the case. We can easily imagine a rebuttal to the claim in the following form:

If our perceptions are never truthful, then no individual perception can ever be truthful.

[But] I perceive myself reading and contemplating these sentences right now (that is, at least one instance of truthful or undeniably real perception obtains).

Therefore, it cannot be the case that our perceptions are never truthful.

If you have a background in philosophy, you may recognize this (paraphrased) argument as part of the philosopher René Descartes's attempt to show that genuine knowledge is possible.

EXERCISE 10.13 | Topic for Class Discussion

The following passage makes a host of interesting claims, each with its own set of implications. Trace the implications to highlight any apparent inconsistencies.

"Most therapies are dualistic. They try to do what seems good and to correct or avoid what seems bad. If they confuse good and bad, as they are sometimes bound to do, their attempt to do good will compound problems and make them harder to resolve. Non-dualistic therapy makes no value judgment about possible alternatives. It looks at the facts, does experiments, and views the results with an open mind. In this way, it is like science, while dualistic therapy is like moralism. Paradoxes should not disturb us. Awareness, if there is enough of it, can always reach the underlying unity of life and merge apparent opposites."[2]

ADDITIONAL EXERCISES

Exercise 10.14   What are the most "basic" premises of each of the following arguments? Include in your analysis any hidden inferential assumptions. If these premises were challenged, how might they be defended?

- "According to modern physics, radio is our only hope of picking up an intelligent signal from space. Sending an interstellar probe would take too long— roughly 50 years even for nearby Alpha Centauri—even if we had the technology and funds to accomplish it. But radio is too slow for much dialogue. The most we can hope from it is to establish the existence (or, more accurately, the former existence) of another civilization."[3]

- How important are professional athletes to society? Not very. They're mere entertainers. They often present bad role models for children—for every Steve Yzerman there's a Bob Probert, or a Don Murdoch, or a Todd Bertuzzi; for every Wayne Gretzky or Mark Messier there's a Dany Heatley. And given the attention they get, they tend to distract us from serious social concerns. At the very least then, the salaries of these prima donnas should be drastically reduced to reflect their social insignificance.

- "If a being suffers, there can be no moral justification for refusing to take that suffering into consideration, and, indeed, to count it equally with the like suffering (if rough comparisons can be made) of another being. So the only question is: Do animals other than man suffer? Most people agree unhesitatingly that animals like cats and dogs can and do suffer, and this seems also to be assumed by those laws that prohibit wanton cruelty to such animals."[4]

- "Are criminal sanctions against cannabis users resulting in greater harm than use of the drug itself? In light of the consistent and well-documented evidence about cannabis's relatively benign effect on users, how is it that public opinion and public policy has been so noticeably misinformed? This may point to the media's choice of what information to share, which in turn shapes whether one views drugs in a positive or negative light. Consider recent advertisements about Zoloft or Viagra. What impact have these commercials had on your opinion about these products? What accurate information do you actually have about these fairly new products and about their short and long-term physiological impact? Now, consider the recent U.S. advertisements that exaggerate the harmfulness of cannabis by depicting how it can contribute to killing people. These television commercials seemed to emerge on the heels of the [2002] Canadian parliamentary reports indicating that evidence supports the decriminalization and potential legalization of cannabis. . . . On the other hand, where are the U.S. or Canadian advertisements about the proven medicinal uses of cannabis?"[5]

- An estimated 2 billion children (persons under age 18) inhabit the world. Since Santa Claus is apparently not responsible for visiting the Muslim,

Hindu, Jewish, and Buddhist children, this reduces his workload to 15 percent of the total, or 378 million children. Assuming an average of 3.5 children per household, this means 91.8 million homes (assuming at least one good child per household). Assuming Santa travels from east to west, and considering the earth's rotation and the different time zones, Santa has 31 hours of Christmas to fulfill his tasks. This works out to 823 visits per second, which means that Santa has a little more than 1/1000th of a second to park, get out of the sleigh, get down the chimney, fill stockings, distribute presents under the tree, eat the snacks left for him, get back up the chimney and into the sleigh, and fly to the next house. Assuming each of the 91.8 million stops to be distributed geographically in an even manner, each stop is 1.25 kilometres apart, which means that Santa's sleigh must travel at 1,046 kilometres per second, thousands of times the speed of sound. Assuming that each child gets nothing more than a medium-sized set of building blocks (approximately 0.9 kilograms), the payload of the sleigh, not counting Santa, must be 291,478 metric tonnes. On land, conventional reindeer can pull about 136 kilograms. Assuming even that "flying reindeer" could pull 10 times this amount, the team required to pull Santa's payload must be 214,200 reindeer, which increases the weight of the loaded sleigh and team to 320,453 metric tonnes (four times the weight of the great yacht *Queen Elizabeth*). An object weighing 320,000 tonnes travelling at 1,046 kilometres per second creates enormous air resistance, with resultant friction and heat, enough to vapourize a reindeer in about 4/1000ths of a second. In conclusion, if Santa ever did deliver presents on Christmas Eve, he's dead now.

Exercise 10.15   *Essay Question:* One of the principles on which our system of criminal law is theoretically based is that punishing innocent people is worse than letting guilty people escape punishment. This principle can be understood as expressing a value judgment. Do you agree with this principle and the value judgment it expresses? If so, formulate three distinct justifications for them. If not, construct three distinct justifications for rejecting them. Write a short essay in which you explain your position.

Exercise 10.16   Here are several justifications for the principle mentioned in Exercise 9.1. For each justification, identify the elements that appeal to consequences and those that appeal to principle. (Do not forget to consider missing premises.) Can you identify any elements that appeal neither to consequences nor to principle? What are the most "basic" premises of each of the three justifying arguments that you created in Exercise 10.15? If these premises were challenged, how might they be defended? Which one of these arguments, a, b, or c, do you find most firmly persuasive? Explain why.

  a. When a society punishes an innocent person, it inevitably increases the unwarranted suffering in the world. It is always wrong to increase the unwarranted suffering in the world.

b. When you punish an innocent person, you turn the person against society, and this leads to an increase in antisocial behaviour.

c. Punishing the innocent is inherently wrong because they've done nothing to deserve punishment. Letting the guilty escape punishment is inherently wrong because they don't get what they deserve. But punishing the innocent is worse because when you punish an innocent person, you are also letting a guilty person escape punishment.

Exercise 10.17 Check for overall consistency in and trace the implications of this excerpt from columnist George Jonas.

A doctor I knew had to flee Canada some 40 years ago to avoid being jailed for performing abortions.

Times have changed. Recently, performing abortions netted Dr. Henry Morgentaler [a well-known Canadian abortion activist] an honorary law degree from the University of Western Ontario.

You've come a long way, baby.

I'd be as reluctant to jail abortionists as to give them medals. . . . If coercing births made for an unfree society 40 years ago, rewarding abortionists denotes a society that's morally tone-deaf.

Being neither pro-choice nor pro-life, I rarely write about abortion. When I do, it's usually to probe the logic of some abstract argument. . . .

[T]he viability test no longer seems adequate. One reason is practical. "Viability" doesn't mean the point at which a fetus can rent its own apartment. It simply means the earliest juncture at which, with some help from medical technology, it can survive outside the womb.

But this juncture changes from year to year.

By now a zygote could survive outside the womb in an up-to-date incubator. Soon, not just a fetus, but an embryo, and eventually even a fertilized cell, will be technically "viable."

. . . A second reason for not liking the viability concept is even more compelling. If viability . . . becomes the test for a right to society's protection, a lot of human beings may lose their right to life.

A suckling infant is no more "viable" than a fetus.

. . . Unconscious, crippled, or elderly people aren't really "viable" either. . . .

Employed as a test, it now seems that viability may prove to be the slipperiest of all slopes. It may provide the most direct route from the social acceptance of abortion to the social acceptance of euthanasia.

The viability test offered at least some check on unbridled abortion on demand. It seemed better than nothing.

But that was before we gave Morgentaler a medal for disposing of our non-viable children.[6]

 Exercise 10.18 All the work you have invested so far in this series of exercises should now be paying off. By carefully stating and researching the issue you have been studying, by finding and analyzing opposed arguments, and by exploring various argument design options, you naturally become much better informed about the issue than when you started. Now it is time to make some decisions. Answer the following question for yourself in 100 words or less: "Where do I stand on this issue?"

GLOSSARY

consistent   two statements are consistent if they could both be true

contingent statement   a claim whose truth value depends on something outside itself

implications   additional claims that either follow logically from or are strongly supported inductively by a given claim

inconsistent   two statements are inconsistent if no possible circumstances exist in which they could both be true; a group of statements is inconsistent if any two statements in the group are inconsistent

indirect proof   argumentative strategy of assuming the negation of some hypothesis and deriving from this idea a clearly false or self-contradictory implication, which then provides a reason to overturn the original idea

necessary truth   a claim that is impossible to deny in a coherent way

reductio ad absurdum   use of the method of indirect proof to refute an opposing position

tautology   a claim that is necessarily true because to deny it would be self-contradictory

Go to http://www.criticalthinking1ce.nelson.com for additional study resources for this chapter.

ENDNOTES

1 Jonathan Glover, *Humanity: A Moral History of the Twentieth Century* (New Haven, CT: Yale University Press, 1999), 406.

2 Ishvara, *Oneness in Living: Kundalini Yoga, the Spiritual Path, and Intentional Community* (Berkeley, CA: North Atlantic Books, 2002).

3 Patrick Moore, "Speaking English in Space: Stars," *Omni*, November 1979, 26.

4 Peter Singer, "Animal Liberation," in James Rachels (ed.), *Moral Problems*, 2nd ed. (New York: Harper & Row, 1975), 166.

5 Jeff Packer, "A Moral Analysis of Canadian Drug Policy," *Perspectives on Canadian Drug Policy, Vol. 2*, The John Howard Society of Canada, http://www.johnhoward.ca/document/drugs/perspect/volume2/volume2.pdf.

6 George Jonas, "The Viability Concept," *Windsor Star*, June 29, 2005, A6. Reprinted by permission.

Informal Fallacies I: Language, Relevance, Authority

In Chapter 6 we introduced the concept of a *fallacy* as an unreliable inference—a crucial concept for argument criticism. Why is it so important? First, because fallacies are *inferences,* they tend to *appear* reasonable. Second, their unreliability tends not to be apparent. In fact, they can be quite persuasive. As a result of their persuasive power they are quite widespread in all sorts of everyday discourse, both public and private. This leads to a lot of confusion and mistakes. So understanding how fallacies work and knowing how to spot them are useful to the critical thinker. We started with formal fallacies because within the framework of formal logic it is possible to demonstrate extremely clearly that a fallacy is unreliable and it is relatively easy to show the formal structure of the fallacy and thus how the fallacy works. Other aspects of reasoning besides the formal structure of inferences, though, can undermine reliability. Thus, an *informal fallacy* is an inference that is unreliable and whose unreliability results from something other than its formal structure.

ROSE IS ROSE. © United Feature Syndicate, Inc.

The informal fallacies constitute a large and mixed bag. The author of one critical thinking textbook estimates that if you were to consult a random selection of informal logic texts, you would likely find several hundred different informal fallacy categories listed. One such text distinguishes over 90 all by itself. This proliferation of categories and terminology makes the study of the informal fallacies bewildering and intimidating for many students. It also leads many students of critical thinking, even quite a few instructors, to approach the informal fallacies as merely a memory challenge—a long list of labels to memorize. This is a terrible way to approach the informal fallacies. Try hard not to fall into this trap. We must be honest here and tell you that one main reason so many categories appear in the literature is that no agreed-upon standard classification system exists for the informal fallacies. This is a good reason *not* to try merely memorizing a list of fallacy labels.

Here is a much better approach. Think of the informal fallacy terminology as part of a tool kit for doing a certain kind of work. Just as a carpenter has carpentry tools, you are assembling a set of tools for critiquing arguments. Your goal should be to attain mastery in their employment, and the best way to pursue this goal is by working with the tools. The tools are mind tools rather than hand tools—concepts rather than hardware. You already have the tools. They are concepts you have studied. In this chapter we will demonstrate a few applications of the tools. From time to time we will also give you a few tips about using the tools, such as:

CRITICAL THINKING TIP 11.1

The work of the carpenter is to construct things out of wood. The mastery of the carpenter shows in the work product. The work of the critical thinker is to produce a form of understanding.

FALLACIES OF LANGUAGE

PROBLEMATIC AMBIGUITY

If a genie came out of a lamp and offered you the gift of everlasting perfect happiness, would you accept? Now suppose the same genie came back a second time and said, "I'll trade you what I gave you last time for this ratty old bowl of leftover party mix," would you accept the offer? In Chapter 2, we presented the concept of ambiguity as a flexible feature of language that enables it to handle multiple meanings at once. Although flexibility in language is essential to effective communication, here we will focus on the downside of ambiguity—the ways it can undermine the reliability of a piece of reasoning. So now suppose the genie offered you the following argument:

> Look, nothing is better than everlasting perfect happiness, but this ratty old bowl of leftover party mix is better than nothing, so you'd really be better off accepting my generous offer.

EXERCISE 11.1 | Problematic Equivocation

What is wrong with the genie's argument? Can you explain the trick?

"Nothing is better than everlasting perfect happiness, but this ratty old bowl of leftover party mix is better than nothing, so the party mix is better than everlasting perfect happiness."

Obviously, *something* is wrong with this argument, but what can it be? It *looks* so logical. Here is a hint. Go back and highlight the terms that appear in both of the premises of the argument. Do these terms each carry the same meaning consistently from premise 1 through premise 2, or do the meanings change? If so, how? The "trick" here is that the word *nothing*, on which the apparently logical comparison hinges, actually changes meaning from the first premise to the second. The first premise can be paraphrased as follows:

> Everlasting perfect happiness is better than *anything else.*

The second premise can be paraphrased as follows:

> *Having* this ratty old bowl of leftover party mix is better than *not having anything at all.*

When the premises have been paraphrased in this way, we are no longer tempted to think that everlasting perfect happiness and this ratty old bowl of leftover party mix are both being compared to *the same thing,* and the apparent logic of the argument falls away. When an argument depends on switching the meanings of an ambiguous crucial term or expression, as in this example, the argument commits the informal fallacy of equivocation, or as we called it in Chapter 2, *problematic equivocation.* The conceptual tool we are using in diagnosing this fallacy is the concept of ambiguity. In critiquing an argument as an instance of this fallacy, one should be able to identify the term(s) or expression(s) being used ambiguously and demonstrate the ambiguity by making clear at least two distinct meanings for each ambiguous item. The best way to do this is to paraphrase the claims in which it is used, as we did here.

EXERCISE 11.2 | Your Turn

- OK, now you try it. Use the cartoon on page 283.

- Then, for comparison, try the following passage from Lewis Carroll's *Through the Looking Glass.* See how well you can explain the tricks in the Queen's reasoning.

  "You couldn't have it if you did want it," the Queen said. "The rule is jam tomorrow and jam yesterday—but never jam today."

  "It must sometimes come to jam today," Alice objected.

  "No it can't," said the Queen. "It's jam every other day: today isn't any other day, you know."

VARIETIES OF AMBIGUITY A good basic understanding of language—for example, the distinction between syntax and semantics—is obviously helpful in diagnosing and explaining informal fallacies of ambiguity. Some ambiguity arises at the verbal level as a result of the power of individual words or idiomatic expressions to support more than one interpretation. Such ambiguity is called "semantic." Thus, the example used above, which we called "equivocation," results from semantic ambiguity—a matter of semantics. Ambiguity can also arise at the grammatical level as a result of grammatical structure or word order. For example:

EXERCISE 11.3 | Amphibole

Can you explain how the ambiguity arises in the following example?

The loot and the car were listed as stolen by the Toronto Police Department.

© The New Yorker Collection 1999 William Haefeli from cartoonbank.com. All Rights Reserved.

"I understood each and every word you said but not the order in which they appeared."

In the example in Exercise 11.3 an ambiguity of reference exists. Which of the two verbs in the sentence does the prepositional phrase modify? The expression is presumably intended to indicate that the police *listed* the loot and car as stolen, not that they *stole* it. This is an example of "syntactical" ambiguity—a matter of syntax. The technical term for an expression whose ambiguity is the result of its grammatical structure or word order is "amphibole." The same sort of thing occurs in the accompanying cartoon.

An argument that exploits or depends on this sort of ambiguity commits the *informal fallacy of amphibole*. Such fallacies are almost always deliberate—for example, in certain sales gimmicks that verge on fraud. For instance, at the end of a direct mail sales offer appears the following guarantee: "We're convinced that you will love your new Acme widget even more than you could begin to imagine. But rest assured. If for any reason you are the least bit dissatisfied, just send it back. We'll give you a prompt and a full refund." Does this mean that you get a full refund promptly? When a dissatisfied customer applies for the refund and receives a nominal reimbursement along with a statement of "service charges," it becomes evident that this is not what the guarantor had in mind—even if it *is* what the guarantor expects *you* to think. Should the customer insist upon a *full* refund, she may expect to wage an indefinitely long and unpleasant battle.

ADVANCED APPLICATIONS The genie's argument we used above to illustrate problematic equivocation is, shall we say, bogus on its face. In other words, it is immediately obvious to nearly any reader that it contains a trick some kind—even if the exact nature of the trick is hard to specify. Fallacies, however, can be much more seductive and difficult to spot.

EXERCISE 11.4 | **False Implication**

Here is an example of a widely used ad strategy known as "false implication." Recently we spotted it on a chocolate bar wrapper with the words "BIGGEST EVER!" imprinted in bright orange 64-point type. Guess the trick if you can.

The widely used advertising strategy known as "false implication" involves *stating* something true while at the same time *implying* something altogether different and false. Of course, the consumer is motivated by the implied falsehood. The implication in this case is that the chocolate bar is bigger now than it was before—that it has been *increased in size*. The literal truth of the matter is that the candy bar is exactly as big as it has ever been—and also as small as it has ever been—because it is the same size as it has always been.

This manoeuvre is standard procedure in writing advertising copy. It explains the conventional advertising industry usage of superlative adjectives, especially in promoting so-called parity products. A "parity product" is one that is practically the same regardless of brand name. Acetylsalicylic acid or ASA—"Aspirin"—is a good example of a parity product. ASA is ASA is ASA. It matters not whether you buy ASA in a bottle with a nationally recognized name on it, or in a bottle with a regional brand name, or in a bottle with a generic label. You get the same number of milligrams of the same chemical formula per tablet. Understandably, producers of parity products work hard in their ads to promote name recognition and brand loyalty, and they frequently use superlatives such as "best," "strongest," "most powerful," and so on to describe their products. "How can this be?" you may ask. "If all the products are identical, they must all be equally good, equally strong, equally powerful, and so on." Assuming no significant differences in other respects, this is indeed the case. If you have this doubt, you probably have it because you recognize that normally a superlative implies a comparison. For example, consider the following sets of adjectives:

Superlative:	Best	Strongest	Sweetest	Biggest	Fastest
Comparative:	Better	Stronger	Sweeter	Bigger	Faster
Descriptive:	Good	Strong	Sweet	Big	Fast

Normally, as you read down the list, each adjective implies the one below. If something is better than something else, this implies that it is good. If something is best, this implies it is better than the rest. As employed in advertising, however, the superlative "best" is taken to mean "none better exists"; the superlative "strongest" is taken to mean "none stronger exists"; and so on. The literal truth of the matter is that the pain reliever is "just as strong as any of the other over-the-counter pain relievers." You are simply getting the maximum dosage legally dispensable without a doctor's prescription, the same as with all the other over-the-counter pain pills.

A special kind of ambiguity is frequently involved in our references to groups of individuals or things. We cannot always be clear whether the members of the group are being referred to individually or collectively. This can result in one or the other of two common informal fallacies. The *informal fallacy of composition* consists in incorrectly inferring characteristics of the group as a collective whole from characteristics of its individual parts or members. For example, someone observes that every member of a local club is wealthy and therefore infers that the club itself must be wealthy, which is not necessarily the case. The confusion results from assuming that what is true of the part must also be true of the whole. In fact, the whole represents something different from simply the sum or combination of its parts. Of course, sometimes a collective whole does have the characteristics of its individual members. It may be the case, for example, that a series of good lectures is a good series of lectures. Nonetheless, no generally reliable equation exists here. For example, a program of short pieces of music (each piece is short) can be a long program indeed (the program might comprise many pieces). A team of highly efficient workers (efficient as individuals) may nonetheless be hopelessly inefficient as a team.

The *informal fallacy of division* works in the opposite direction, incorrectly inferring characteristics of the individual parts or members of a group from characteristics of the group as a collective whole. Observing that a club is wealthy, someone infers that each club member must be wealthy or that a particular member must be wealthy. Just as a property of the part need not imply a property of the whole, so too a property of the whole need not imply a property of the part. The fact that a book is a masterpiece does not mean that each chapter is a masterpiece; the fact that an orchestra is outstanding

"I'm doing a lot better now that I'm back in denial."

© The New Yorker Collection 2005 Pat Byrnes from cartoonbank.com. All Rights Reserved.

does not mean that each member is an outstanding musician. Again, it is sometimes the case that the individual parts or members of a group have some of the characteristics of the group as a whole, but, again, not always. A million-dollar inventory, for example, might be made up of a great many 5- and 10-cent items.

EXERCISE 11.5 | Fallacies of Ambiguity

Cartoonists sometimes provide the most "artful" examples of fallacious reasoning. The above cartoon is an example that hinges on the meaning of a crucial term. Can you explain what is wrong with the woman's reasoning?

PROBLEMATIC VAGUENESS

Chapter 2 presented the concept of vagueness as a feature of language in which questions of definition are left open. Like ambiguity, vagueness is useful. We often need the discretionary flexibility of applying familiar terms and concepts in new and unforeseeable situations. For the same reason, however, vagueness is also prone to certain forms of abuse. Because vague terms and expressions lack exact definition, they lend themselves rather easily and naturally to evasive and manipulative applications. To criticize a piece of reasoning as a case of the abuse of vagueness depends on identifying an instance of vagueness and arguing that it is unreasonably so.

| EXERCISE 11.6 | Topic for Class Discussion |

At the time of this writing, federal Minister of Justice Irwin Cotler proposes revised "lawful access" protocols. Such revisions to investigative regulations, he argues, would enable the Canadian government to fight terrorism more effectively in the post-September 11 world, most notably by broadening the leeway that investigators have regarding electronic and digital communication, such as Internet transactions. Some critics charge that the revised lawful access proposals go too far in the direction of interfering in the private dealings of Canadian citizens, such as allowing police to intercept private communications without the usual judge's order.

Highlight any terms and concepts you find that are used in vague ways in the following passage. Then compare and contrast—where is the vagueness warranted and reasonable; where is it unwarranted or problematic?

> Recently there has been much misunderstanding—and misleading commentary—about the government of Canada's lawful access proposal. Clarification is needed both out of regard for the rule of law and the public's right to know.
>
> . . . It is not about intercepting private communications of all Canadians on a routine basis. It is not about eavesdropping on private communications of Canadians without judicial oversight. . . . And it is not about changing our laws without consulting interested parties, and without due regard for the rule of law.
>
> What lawful access proposals are about is the protection of public safety and ensuring that law enforcement authorities have the ability to keep up with rapid developments in information and communications technology. . . .
>
> There have also been misunderstandings about the government's proposals to clarify how police and CSIS should be able to obtain subscriber information. Basic subscriber information such as a customer's name, address, telephone number and Internet address can be valuable at the initial stages of an investigation. . . .
>
> The underlying principle for me here—as in everything else—remains the same: The enforcement of the law must always comport with the rule of law. Canadians cherish these principles and nothing in the lawful access initiative will undermine this.[1]

No doubt you can see that considerable room exists here for discussion. Some of the terms and ideas here could—or, more to the point, should—be defined more clearly and are therefore arguably vague. Let us consider a few crucial elements that are left open to interpretation, perhaps intentionally.

I. Cotler says that the proposed legislation is not about "intercepting private communications of all Canadians on a *routine* basis [emphasis added]," but this is probably not the claim of his critics. If so, Cotler diverts us from their concern (significant, but not necessarily global, abuse).

II. Cotler repeatedly emphasizes "the rule of law," thus telling us that he views it as foundational and revered. His critics, however, are concerned precisely with the nature and implications of the *revised* rule of law that he suggests (the lawful access proposal). In the eyes of critics, in other words, Cotler could indeed consistently cherish and uphold the rule of law—*right after* changing it in a problematic manner. No necessary logical inconsistency obtains between "following the rule of law" and endorsing a rule of law that is intrinsically excessive (although a moral inconsistency may well exist in such a case). One could conscientiously adhere to a bad law. Cotler, then, leaves his readers with a somewhat fuzzy response to charges of procedural highhandedness in the proposed legislation. (This point also holds true of his claim about consultation. Although consultation is important by anyone's standard, consultation alone does not ensure that the ultimate result is sound or properly reflects the views of those consulted.)

III. Last but definitely not least, Cotler initially states that interceptions would not occur "without judicial oversight" but then states *without qualification*, "[b]asic subscriber information . . . can be valuable at the initial stages of an investigation." While this statement does not at first seem to contradict the initial remark about judicial oversight, a careful reading of this section shows that Cotler does not clearly rule out allowing police to intercept private communications without the usual judge's order. He indeed raises the issue of "*how* police and CSIS should be able to obtain subscriber information [emphasis added]," but does not explicitly reaffirm the necessity for the usual judge's order. Instead, he stresses the need for information about suspects. Is Cotler's earlier statement about judicial oversight perhaps looser than we imagine, leaving room for greater police powers within a weakened regime of judicial supervision? How strictly does he intend the term "judicial oversight"? The expression admits of degrees. If the proposed legislative changes do not remove the traditional necessity for a judge's order, why does he not simply say so? Add to these questions the fact that at the time of writing this book, the public has only summaries of the proposed legislative changes, not the complete text, and you can see why critics will probably not be entirely satisfied with these responses.

EXERCISE 11.7 | **Topic for Class Discussion**

Review Exercise 2.11 (Chapter 2). Then read the "official" Canadian federal government definition of *terrorism* below and consider whether the Canadian government or any of its close allies do or might engage in acts that fall into any of these categories.

[Terrorist action] is taken for political, religious or ideological purposes and intimidates the public concerning its security, or compels a government to do something, by intentionally killing, seriously harming or endangering a person, causing substantial property damage that is likely to seriously harm people or by seriously interfering with or disrupting an essential service, facility or system.[2]

The question posed in Exercise 11.7, whether the Canadian federal government or any of its allies (the United States, for example) do or might engage in activities that would count as terrorism under its own official definition of the term, is a question that the government might find troublesome and would therefore prefer to avoid. Better to leave the concept of terrorism more loosely defined. Understandable reasons also exist as to why the Canadian and allied governments would prefer to keep military options both open and unspecified even if they have been determined. We can be pretty sure, though, that vagueness is being abused when the interpretations of the crucial concepts get so loose and broad as to be internally inconsistent. (Peace is war, war is peace, war is a means to peace, and so on.)

VAGUENESS IN ADVERTISING

Puffery is advertising that praises with vague exaggerations. *Hyperbole,* or "hype" for short, is exaggeration or extravagance as a figure of speech. In advertising, such exaggerations and extravagances exist to create *excitement,* not to convey information. Cultural critic Ivan L. Preston gives a long list of examples, including, "When you say Budweiser, you've said it all"; "You can be sure if it's Westinghouse"; "Toshiba—in touch with tomorrow"; "Waterford—the ultimate gift"; "Diamonds are forever!" The general strategy being pursued here is to raise the level of enthusiasm and excitement without actually making any substantive claims.

EXERCISE 11.8 | **Topic for Class Discussion**

Here is an excerpt from an unsolicited direct mail brochure we received while we were working on this chapter. How many instances of hype and puffery can you find?

This two-day weekend seminar will open you to the wonders of the contemporary experience of modern High-Tech Serendipity Meditation, as your seminar leader and originator of the High-Tech Serendipity Meditation Experience personally conducts this expansive program, demonstrating the power and potential of this contemporary meditative technology. The weekend includes four power-packed sessions of Holodynamic Serendipity material presented in such a way as to enable each participant to personally experience the contemporary ease and the full potential of High-Tech Meditation.

The pitch in the above example sounds intriguing, beneficial, attractive, but what does it all mean? The terminology, though it *sounds* not only positive but also technically precise, is hopelessly vague. This is the important thing to notice here. Because it is so vague, it invites the reader to project onto it whatever meanings are most closely connected with the reader's own fantasies and longings. Of course, if you want to find out in detail what High-Tech Holodynamic Serendipity Meditation is all about, you can sign up for the two-day weekend seminar for a fee of $250. Assuming you can afford it, this might not be such a bad deal for two full days of whatever you want to believe you are hearing.

Already we have seen how an advertiser can exploit ambiguity, by leaving a comparison unfinished, to imply a claim that cannot truthfully be stated in an explicit and straightforward way. In one famous ad we are told, "Ford LTD—700% quieter!" Compared to what? Viewers of this ad are understandably inclined to complete the comparison for themselves in one or another of several ways relevant to choosing a new car. So, for example, many viewers naturally assume that the ad means this year's model is 700 percent quieter than last year's model, or that the Ford LTD is 700 percent quieter than the competitors in its price category. When the Federal Trade Commission (FTC) in the United States challenged the claim, Ford admitted that the real basis of the comparison was exterior noise. The inside of the car was 700 percent quieter than the outside.

Another such device is known as the *weasel word*. The expression is derived from the egg-eating habits of weasels. A weasel will bite into an eggshell and suck out the contents, leaving what appears to the casual observer to be an intact egg. Similarly, a weasel word sucks out the substance of what appears on the surface to be a substantial claim. The weasel word makes the claim in which it is used a *vague* claim, while at the same time at least partially concealing the vagueness.

The word *help* functions in advertising as a weasel. *Help* means literally "aid" or "assist" and nothing more, yet as one author has observed, "'help' is the one single word which, in all the annals of advertising, has done the most to say something that couldn't be said."[3] Once the word *help* is used to qualify a claim, almost anything can be said after it. Accordingly we are exposed to ads for products that "*help* keep us young," "*help* prevent cavities," and "*help* keep our houses germ free." Just think of how many times a day you hear or read pitches that say "*helps* stop," "*helps* prevent," "*helps* fight," "*helps* overcome," "*helps* you feel," and "*helps* you look." *Help* is not the only weasel in an advertiser's arsenal. *Like* (as in "makes your floor look *like* new"), *virtual* or *virtually* (as in "*virtually* no cavities"), *up to* (as in "provides relief *up to* eight hours"), *as much as* (as in "saves *as much as* one gallon of gas"), and other weasels "say" what cannot be said.

Studies indicate that on hearing or reading a claim containing a weasel word, we tend to screen out the weasel word and just hear the claim. Thus, on hearing that a medicine "can provide up to eight hours' relief," we screen out the words *can* and *up to* and infer that the product will give us "eight hours' relief," because this what we want—relief. In fact, according to a strict reading of the wording of the ad, the product may give no relief at all; and if it does give relief, the relief could vary in length from a moment or two to anywhere under eight hours.

DENOTATION

Many issues turn on how things are grouped together in categories. In Chapter 2 we considered several examples, including what we classify as "terrorism" and whether a particular music video is or is not in the category of "pornography." When an argument depends on a claim that either amounts to or presupposes a questionable classification, it is appropriate to challenge the classification. If a premise in an argument has been challenged in this way and the challenge is not met by a defensible essential definition, we may say that some *informal fallacy of classification* has occurred. Of course, all this depends on the essential definition of the category in question. Thus, making such a criticism has the effect of opening the issue of defining the category. In many cases this will be a formidable issue in its own right.

EXERCISE 11.9 | **Topic for Class Discussion**

Review the section on "essential definitions" and Exercises 2.8 to 2.11 in Chapter 2. Then consider the following example:

> Look around the neighbourhood and count the houses and cars. Do you have any trouble deciding which is which? Not likely. But an interesting case in law called even this seemingly obvious classification into question. It seems that police officers had observed a certain vehicle parked for several days during which time individuals and small groups of people were also observed coming and going to and from the vehicle. Suspecting possible drug activity, the police investigated further and indeed found the occupant of the vehicle had drugs in his possession. The occupant was arrested and brought to trial on drug charges. The hitch was that the police had not obtained a search warrant before moving to investigate the vehicle. Why would this be necessary? Police don't need a search warrant to inspect a motor vehicle. But it turned out that the occupant was *living in* the vehicle (a motor home), and it was argued that since the vehicle was the occupant's place of residence, it should be [considered an instance of improper] search and seizure.

Does this argument commit an informal fallacy of classification?

CONNOTATION

In the heat of debate over an issue in which people are passionately engaged, it may be expected that they will use the most powerful language they can muster to make and present their case. So we are well advised to be aware of the connotations of the labels and descriptions used in an argument's text, bearing in mind Critical Thinking Tip 2.1. We may say that some sort of *informal fallacy of loaded language* has occurred when the language distorts the issue under discussion or when the argument leans more heavily on the connotations of the language than it does on the reasoning itself.

As we learned in Chapter 2, a good example of issue-distorting language is the common rhetorical device of *euphemism*. The term *euphemism* derives from the Greek for "good speech" or "good word." It refers to a figure of speech in which things are labelled or described in overly positive terms or terms that understate the negative. The tendency to use and favour euphemisms is natural and understandable as a psychological defence mechanism in many situations. It is nice to be able to express matters in a polite way that is respectful of people's feelings. Unfortunately, euphemisms can also be used to obscure, to mislead, and to confuse—as, for example, when a politician refers to a "tax" as a "revenue enhancement." Nor are euphemisms confined to the political sphere. Euphemism is a strategy of first resort throughout public relations—for instance, when "human resource managers" (otherwise known as the boss) devise ever more artful and evasive ways of saying "you're fired," such as, "your functions have been outsourced" (huh?), or "you've been made redundant." Here is one from the wonderful world of customer service. It seems that Blockbuster Video has stopped charging a "late fee" for videos returned after they are due. Instead they assess "extended viewing fees," which sounds much more agreeable. If we think of euphemism as exaggeration in the positive direction, an obvious and equally powerful strategy consists in exaggerating the negative. This strategy is particularly useful in "demonizing official enemies" of the state—"maniacs"—and thereby motivating public support for aggressive and hostile foreign policy. Following the etymology of euphemism, we might call such negative exaggeration *dysphemism*, from the Greek for "bad speech" or "bad word."

EXERCISE 11.10 | Euphemisms

Here is a collection of 20th-century military euphemisms. See if you can match the euphemism (left column) with the thing described (right column).

This euphemism	means
a "Pacification Centre"	to spy
a "protective reaction strike"	retreat
"incontinent ordnance"	a bombing raid
"friendly fire"	bombs
"force packages"	a concentration camp
"strategic withdrawal"	bombing or shooting someone on your side
to "gather intelligence"	off-target bombs
to "terminate"	to destroy by bombing
to "degrade" the target	civilian casualties caused by your side
"collateral damage"	to kill

LANGUAGE FUNCTIONS

Just as loaded labels can distort an issue, so can inappropriate applications of the rhetorical features and the persuasive power of language. So, we are also well advised to focus our attention on the functions of language, again bearing in mind Critical Thinking Tip 2.1. Be on the lookout for extreme quantifiers (*all, every,* and so on), extreme intensifiers (*absolutely, totally, completely,* and the like), and other universalizing expressions. Heavy reliance on this sort of language often masks weakness in the reasoning. If an argument really is strong, it should not need exaggeration to make its point. Again, we may say that some sort of *informal fallacy of loaded language* has occurred when the argument leans more heavily on the intensity of the language than it does on the reasoning itself.

Sometimes the functions of language are exploited as negotiating tactics or as strategic means of eliciting agreement. For example, a question is a request or invitation to respond, ordinarily at the voluntary discretion of the respondent. We sometimes run across questions—called "rhetorical questions"—that are worded in such a way that only one of the possible answers is invited because all other possible answers are discredited in advance. Rhetorical questions are not illegitimate or problematic in themselves. In "polite" discourse this device can be a perfectly valid and useful way to create an air of "understatement"—surely you agree? On the other hand, rhetorical questions can also unduly amplify and overstate the case. How in the world could you possibly imagine otherwise?! Rhetorical questions are often deployed in lieu of any better argument. When you see this happen, you may say that the *informal fallacy of rhetorical question* has been committed.

EXERCISE 11.11 | Informal Fallacies of Language

In each of the following examples, check all fallacy categories that apply. More importantly, *explain* each fallacious instance you identify.

Airplanes are used for getting high. And airplanes are perfectly legal. Drugs are used for getting high. So they should be legal, too.

		Explain your answer:
	Problematic equivocation	
	Amphibole	
	Problematic vagueness	
	Weasel words	
	Faulty classification	
	Loaded language	
	Euphemism/dysphemism	
	Rhetorical question	

"I passed nobody on the road. Therefore nobody is slower than I am."—Lewis Carroll

		Explain your answer:
	Problematic equivocation	
	Amphibole	
	Problematic vagueness	
	Weasel words	
	Faulty classification	
	Loaded language	
	Euphemism/dysphemism	
	Rhetorical question	

"I don't have a job. I have a *position*."

	Problematic equivocation	Explain your answer:
	Amphibole	
	Problematic vagueness	
	Weasel words	
	Faulty classification	
	Loaded language	
	Euphemism/dysphemism	
	Rhetorical question	

Look! The notice on his office door says "Back Soon." But I've been waiting here for over an hour and a half!

	Problematic equivocation	Explain your answer:
	Amphibole	
	Problematic vagueness	
	Weasel words	
	Faulty classification	
	Loaded language	
	Euphemism/dysphemism	
	Rhetorical question	

God is Love. Love is blind. Therefore, God is blind.

	Problematic equivocation	Explain your answer:
	Amphibole	
	Problematic vagueness	
	Weasel words	
	Faulty classification	
	Loaded language	
	Euphemism/dysphemism	
	Rhetorical question	

News report: "High-level Canadian Security Intelligence Service and Royal Canadian Mounted Police officials will neither confirm nor deny that a would-be terrorist suspect with possible links to al-Qaeda has been apprehended."

	Problematic equivocation	Explain your answer:
	Amphibole	
	Problematic vagueness	
	Weasel words	
	Faulty classification	
	Loaded language	
	Euphemism/dysphemism	
	Rhetorical question	

FALLACIES OF RELEVANCE

Suppose that someone came up to you and said, "Now that I know how to construct a deductively valid argument, I can finally settle the abortion issue once and for all! Here's my argument . . ."

EXERCISE 11.12 | **Brain Teaser**

Clearly something is wrong with the following argument. Can you explain what it is?

If *abortion* is an eight-letter word, then abortion should be against the law. *Abortion is* an eight-letter word. Therefore, abortion should be against the law.

Are you convinced by the argument in Exercise 11.12? No reasonable person would be, but what exactly is wrong with the argument? Since the argument is in the form modus ponens, we cannot fault it formally. So what else might be wrong with it? Are the premises false? The second one is true. Count the letters to verify its truth. This leaves premise 1. Is premise 1 false? Before you answer this question, just suppose for a moment that the conclusion of the argument is true. Now, is premise 1 false? It is hard to tell. You do not know yet whether the conclusion is true, but it might be, and in that case you cannot really be sure that premise 1 is false. (See the section in Chapter 6 on using truth tables to test for deductive validity.)

So what *is* wrong with the argument? The problem here is that both premises are *irrelevant to the issue*. Why? Premise 1 connects superficially with the content of the conclusion (the matter of the legality of abortion appears in both), but in the end it cannot help us to gain clarity about the cogency of the conclusion. The number of letters in the word *abortion*, anyone would agree, is irrelevant to the moral status of the act of abortion and therefore also to the substantive question of abortion law. Here you can see the concept of relevance in bold relief. An important informal consideration in evaluating arguments is whether the premises offered are relevant to the issue at hand. Relevant premises help us to gain clarity about the truth or falsity of the conclusion. If the premises are relevant, so much the better for the argument. If not, some sort of *informal fallacy of relevance*, or *irrelevant appeal*, has been committed. The conceptual tools we use in detecting and diagnosing fallacies of relevance are the concept of relevance and the tools of issue analysis presented in Chapter 1. Generally speaking, the relevance of any premise of any argument to the issue in question may be challenged at any point. Bear in mind, however, that to *challenge* the relevance of a premise is not the same as *establishing* that it is irrelevant. Relevance is not always obvious on the surface. So it remains open to the arguer to meet the challenge by explaining how the premise bears on the conclusion or issue. If a premise *is* relevant, it should be possible to explain the connection. Thus, the most important thing to do is keep the issue(s) clearly in focus as you go.

CRITICAL THINKING TIP 11.2

Keep the issue(s) in focus.

AD HOMINEM

The relevance problem in the argument in Exercise 11.12 is so glaring that the argument is an "obvious" fallacy. Other instances may well be less obvious, though no less fallacious. *Ad hominem,* the Latin phrase for "to the man," refers to the rhetorical strategy of irrelevant personal attack. When people argue ad hominem, they argue that the *person,* not her reasoning or position, is faulty. Ad hominem's frequency and remarkable rhetorical force both probably stem from the general human psychological tendencies to personalize conflict and escalate hostility. As natural as it may be for us to turn attention to the personal weaknesses, flaws, and failures of others, these things—whether real or imagined—are almost always and with only rare exceptions irrelevant to whatever the issue is under discussion.

EXERCISE 11.13 | **Ad Hominem**

Topic for Class Discussion: Here is an excerpt from American right-wing radio personality Rush Limbaugh's book, *The Way Things Ought to Be* (Chapter 10). Identify and explain the ad hominem elements.

> I have spoken extensively in this book about the various fringe movements and the spiritual tie that binds them: radical liberalism. Two groups that are particularly close, to the point of being nearly indistinguishable, are the environmentalists and the animal rights activists. Because I devoted a chapter to the environmentalists. I thought it only fair to include one about animal rights activism. I certainly do not want to be accused of discrimination. Every wacko movement must have its day in my book. . . .
>
> The animal rights movement, like so many others in this country, is being used by leftists as another way to attack the American way of life. They have adopted two constituencies who cannot speak and complain about the political uses to which they are put. One of them is trees and other plant life; the other is the animal kingdom. People for the Ethical Treatment of Animals (PETA) takes in over $10 million every year by preying on people's concern for animals. Most of its contributors think most of the money goes to making sure animals are treated kindly . . . but PETA's real mission is destroying capitalism, not saving animals.
>
> The basic right to life of an animal—which is the source of energy for many animal rights wackos—must be inferred from the anticruelty laws humans have written, not from any divine source. Our laws do not prevent us from killing animals for food or sport, so the right to life of an animal is nonexistent.

The Limbaugh passage in Exercise 11.13 contains a good example of what is often called *abusive ad hominem*—where the personal attack is baseless (for example, "wacko") as well as irrelevant. Think of *abusive ad hominem* as essentially a kind of gratuitous name-calling. The Limbaugh passage also contains a good example of a somewhat more sophisticated strategy, often called *circumstantial ad hominem,* where some piece of actual information about a person that carries unfavourable but irrelevant personal implications (for example, "leftist") is the means of attack.

A special case of *circumstantial ad hominem,* in which the attack is based on the person's relationships with others, is often appropriately called the *informal fallacy of guilt by association.* For example, you might hear someone argue, "Jordan hangs around with Susan, and you know Susan's questionable views, so you shouldn't give too much credence to Jordan's statements." Logically speaking, of course, you ought to assess Jordan's views on their own merits and demerits, not dismiss them out of hand based on a real or perceived association between Jordan and Susan (even if Susan's views are questionable).

A similar strategy—a sort of *circumstantial ad hominem* in advance— attempts to discredit a position before any argument for it has a chance to get a hearing. This strategy is often called *poisoning the well.* The "well" is the reasoning. The "poison" is prejudice, which literally means "prejudgment." A good critical thinker gives due and open-minded consideration to the reasoning *before* arriving at judgment. Anyone who tries to discourage this commits the *informal fallacy of poisoning the well.* For example, 19th-century philosopher/theologian John Henry Cardinal Newman engaged in frequent disputes with clergyman/novelist Charles Kingsley. During the course of one of these disputes, Kingsley suggested that Newman could not possibly value truth above all else because of his Catholicism. Newman rightly objected that this was poisoning the well, since it made it impossible for him (or any Catholic) to state his case. No matter what reasons or arguments Newman might offer to show that he did value the truth and that this value was basic to his faith, Kingsley would have already ruled them out because they had come from a Catholic.

PHILOSOPHICAL DIFFERENCES

Used by permission of Norman Dog.

A similar fallacy, often called *genetic appeal,* consists in evaluating something merely by way of its origin or sources (or "genesis"). For example, certain religious fundamentalists have argued that dancing is evil and should be forbidden because it originated as a form of pagan worship. We have heard conservative arguments against a national daycare program based primarily on the grounds that the idea is "socialist" in origin. Of course, a concern for the source of an idea need not be a distraction in every case. It might turn out to be pertinent. For example, consider the claim, "We have an eyewitness who claims directly to have observed the defendant committing the crime." Assuming the reliability of the testimony, this claim— "We have eyewitness verification" —would be a powerful reason to conclude that the defendant is guilty of the crime. What if, however, the so-called eyewitness has a protracted history of personal animus with the defendant? In this case, the historical circumstances of the testimony would be a relevant consideration in deciding whether to accept it, and indeed we would be remiss if we were to disregard the source of the testimony. (Note: We would not be justified thereby in condemning the testimony out of hand. The eyewitness may have in truth directly observed the defendant committing the crime, notwithstanding the bad blood between them. It is possible in principle.)

EXERCISE 11.14 | Fallacies of Relevance I

In each of the following examples, check all fallacy categories that apply. More importantly, *explain* each fallacious instance you identify.

"No man can know anything about pregnancy and childbirth, because no man can ever go through the experience. So no man is qualified to render an opinion about abortion."

	Explain your answer:
Abusive ad hominem	
Circumstantial ad hominem	
Guilt by association	
Genetic appeal	
Poisoning the well	

"How can you believe anything that this snitch has to say? Can't you see that he has everything to gain by implicating the Prime Minister in this scandal? Look, he's sold his story to *Tabloid Exposé!*"

	Explain your answer:
Abusive ad hominem	
Circumstantial ad hominem	
Guilt by association	
Genetic appeal	
Poisoning the well	

Letter to the Editor: "I was profoundly dismayed by the badgering of witnesses during the hearings by Member of Parliament I. M. Thrasher. Doesn't he realize that such criticism reflects badly on the

Prime Minister? If we can't expect the members of our own party to support the Prime Minister in difficult times, just who can we turn to?"

		Explain your answer:
	Abusive ad hominem	
	Circumstantial ad hominem	
	Guilt by association	
	Genetic appeal	
	Poisoning the well	

"I can't vote for the woman, because I remember some years ago in her law practice she defended that wacko Cat Killer guy."

		Explain your answer:
	Abusive ad hominem	
	Circumstantial ad hominem	
	Guilt by association	
	Genetic appeal	
	Poisoning the welll	

PROVINCIALISM, TRADITION, POPULARITY, NOVELTY, AND POSITIONING

Watch for ad hominem tactics like those described above wherever partisan lines are well known—wherever a well-established divide exists between "us" and "them." In such all-too-frequent contexts, also be on the alert for language that raises considerations of group loyalty, patriotism, nationalism, and so on. Sometimes the group at issue is considerably smaller than a nation—a region, or a city, or perhaps a professional, occupational, or religious group, or a school, or a team. Sometimes the group is even larger than a nation: a gender, for example. The general term for discourse that leans too heavily on irrelevant considerations of loyalty is *provincialism*.

Provincialism is often coupled with an *appeal to tradition*, in which the argument rests heavily on whether something adheres to or departs from tradition. If tradition were the decisive element in science, for example, then science as we know it—ideally as a rigorous but open-minded and continuously unfolding investigation of the physical world—would not exist. Knowing their own inherent fallibility, scientists test and re-test their hypotheses and theories to ensure the best accuracy under the circumstances. Einstein's novel theories, for instance, could never have found purchase if the crucial criterion had been divergence from tradition (considered as a bad thing). *Appeal to popularity* is similar to appeal to tradition: You commit the fallacy of appeal to popularity when you assume or argue that something is true, good, or desirable simply because it is popularly believed or esteemed. Of course, the majority could be wrong, and the minority could be right, so popularity does not by itself tell you whether a position is true or false.

In contrast to the *appeal to tradition,* but just as fallacious, is the *appeal to novelty,* which involves assuming or arguing that something is good or desirable just because it is new or different. Watch for this tactic around election time. Candidates who use slogans like "Leadership for a Change" or "It's Time for New Ideas" *may* have something new and different to offer, something that would advance the public interest, but the *claim* of novelty by itself is irrelevant.

Just as people sometimes attempt to discredit others through *guilt by association,* they can just as effectively promote themselves and others by *positioning*—by appropriating the reputation of a leader in a field to sell a product, candidate, or idea. Here is how it works. In advertising, positioning creates a spot for a company in the prospective buyer's mind by invoking not only the company's image but that of its leading competitor as well. The assumption here is that the consumer's mind has become an advertising battleground. So a successful advertising strategy involves relating to what has already been established in the consumer's mind. Thus, although RCA and General Electric tried in vain to buck IBM directly in the early years of the mainframe computer market, the smaller Honeywell succeeded by using the theme "The *Other* Computer Company." Positioning is hardly confined to advertising. During federal elections, for example, many a local campaign is based almost entirely on party affiliation with the incumbent prime minister or the front-runner. This is called "riding on the coattails." In politics, part of waging a successful campaign often means trading on the reputation of another well-known, popular political figure.

CRITICAL THINKING TIP 11.3

As an antidote to any or all of these corruptions of critical thinking, remember Critical Thinking Tip 11.2: Keep the issue(s) in focus.

EMOTIONAL APPEALS

Emotions can exert a powerful influence over our thinking, but they are not always relevant to the issue at hand. One of the most powerful emotions is anger. Often, anger is powerful enough to overwhelm reason and good common sense, as we recognize, for example, when we speak of crimes of passion and distinguish them from planned crimes. Thus, a powerful persuasive strategy consists in arousing and mobilizing anger in support of a position—a favourite of political campaign strategists, especially when the electorate is relatively poorly informed. When this strategy is pursued in place of reasoning, the *informal fallacy of appeal to anger* is committed. To be sure, we often have good reason to be angry. Anger, when it is reasonably justified, is a strong and appropriate motivator. When little or no specific reason is presented for being angry, however, and instead a vague and rhetorical appeal to general frustration is used to arouse anger, watch out. This is the sort of urging that often leads people to "shoot themselves in the foot." A similar strategy involves attempting to *intimidate* people into accepting a position. The *informal fallacy of appeal to fear* (or *appeal to force*) takes the basic form, "Believe this (or do this), or else!"

A similar strategy consists in attempting to persuade people by making them feel sorrow, sympathy, or anguish where such feelings, however understandable and genuine, are not relevant to the issue at stake. The *informal fallacy of appeal to pity* is frequently used in attempts to get special dispensation or exemption from deadlines and penalties. For example, the student who deserves a C in history might try to persuade his teacher to raise his grade for a variety of lamentable reasons: It is the first grade below a B he has ever received; it spoils an overall A-range average; or he "needs" a higher grade to qualify for law school and has incurred significant student loans to finance his undergraduate education. These considerations are not relevant to the student's actual academic performance in the course, which is the only criterion by which a principled instructor can abide. Note, though, that pity is not *always* irrelevant. For example, when an attorney asks a judge to take into consideration the squalid upbringing of a client in determining a criminal sentence, she is probably not making a fallacious appeal to pity. Although such an appeal would be irrelevant and fallacious in arguing for her client's innocence, it may be perfectly germane to the question of the severity of the sentence. Think of the German youth who in the summer of 1987 flew a small plane into the middle of Red Square in Moscow. That he may have been acting out of simple youthful exuberance rather than some motive more threatening to Soviet national security is irrelevant to whether he acted illegally, but it is not irrelevant to how severely he should be punished.

CRITICAL THINKING TIP 11.4

Pay attention to the *relevance* (or lack thereof) of the emotional appeal. Remember that relevance is not always obvious or apparent on the surface. But it *should* always be explainable.

EXERCISE 11.15 | Emotional Appeals

Identify and explain the fallacious appeal to emotion in each of the following:

Should the government impose even more restrictions and hardships on smokers over the alleged phenomenon of "secondhand" smoke? Let's not forget that smokers are many in number and thus a potent economic and political force. The income and holdings of smokers represent a surprisingly substantial portion of Canada's total wealth, and thus are key to a robust economy. The votes of smokers tally to the millions. Beware a prosperous section of the electorate scorned.

		Explain your answer:
	Appeal to anger	
	Appeal to fear	
	Appeal to pity	

"It may be that some of you, remembering his own case, will be annoyed that whereas he, in standing trial upon a less serious charge than this, made pitiful appeals to the jury with floods of tears, and had his infant children produced in court to excite the maximum of sympathy, I on the contrary intend to do nothing of the sort."— Socrates, in *The Apology,* line 34c.[4]

		Explain your answer:
	Appeal to anger	
	Appeal to fear	
	Appeal to pity	

DIVERSIONARY TACTICS

A common argumentative strategy consists in attempting to divert attention from the issue, especially when one lacks relevant and effective arguments. A general label for diversionary tactics in argument is *red herring.* This colourful term derives from an old ruse used by prison escapees to throw dogs off their trails. (They would smear themselves with herring—which turns red when it spoils—to cover their scent.) Are you stuck for a good argument? Make a joke. Are you stuck for a good defence? Attack! Do you lack a good answer? Evade the question: "Before I answer this question, Ted, let me make a few things clear. . . ." This sort of thing, followed by a tortuous excursion through a number of relatively complicated points, may effectively leave the original topic buried in obscurity. Can you not prove your point? Change the subject.

Sometimes when people have trouble making a cogent argument in favour of a position, they distort the issue or address some alternative issue instead. For example, in opening arguments charging an executive with embezzlement, the Crown may quote harrowing statistics about white-collar crime. Although her statistical evidence may influence the court, it is irrelevant to establishing the objective guilt of this particular defendant. Sometimes when people have trouble making a cogent objection or argument against a position, they distort the position, or in effect set up some alternative position as a target for their objections. This distorted or alternative position is sometimes called a *straw person,* because, like a person made out of straw, it is not real and therefore much easier to knock down than the real position.

When blame is at issue, watch for an attempt to shift the blame. Imagine a police officer stopping a speeding motorist. "Why stop me?" the driver asks. "Didn't you see that Jaguar fly by at 140 kilometres?" (This probably will not get the driver off the hook.) This kind of red herring is often referred to as the *informal fallacy of two wrongs,* which comes from the proverb "Two wrongs don't make a right." A variation of this move is spreading the blame. Caught using company stationery for personal use, an office worker may say, "Everybody else does it." This kind of red herring is often referred to as the *informal fallacy of common practice.*

CRITICAL THINKING TIP 11.5

Remember that issues are complex, so a diversion may on occasion be warranted and reasonable. However, a warranted and reasonable diversion should eventually return to the issue. Keep the issue(s) in mind.

EXERCISE 11.16 | Fallacies of Relevance II

In each of the following examples, check all fallacy categories that apply. More importantly, *explain* each fallacious instance you identify.

And the Lord God commanded man, saying, "You may eat freely of every tree of the garden; but the tree of the knowledge of good and evil you shall not eat, for in the day that you eat of it you shall die." (Genesis 2: 16–17)

		Explain your answer:
	Appeal to anger	
	Appeal to fear	
	Appeal to pity	
	Straw person	
	Two wrongs	
	Common practice	

"Precisely what is Nixon accused of doing that his predecessors didn't do many times over? The break in and wire-tapping at the Watergate? Just how different was that from the bugging of Barry Goldwater's apartment during the 1964 presidential campaign?"[5]

		Explain your answer:
	Appeal to anger	
	Appeal to fear	
	Appeal to pity	
	Straw person	
	Two wrongs	
	Common practice	

"[The fight for the Equal Rights Amendment in Iowa] is about a socialist, anti-family political movement that encourages women to leave their husbands, kill their children, practice witchcraft, destroy capitalism, and become lesbians." (American televangelist and former presidential candidate Pat Robertson.)

		Explain your answer:
	Appeal to anger	
	Appeal to fear	
	Appeal to pity	
	Straw person	
	Two wrongs	
	Common practice	

FEIFFER®

Time DID NOT LIBEL SHARON.

Time MADE UP FACTS ABOUT SHARON.

THE FACTS WERE NOT ACCU- RATE...

BUT EVERYONE KNOWS SHARON'S A BAD GUY.

RONALD REAGAN MAKES UP FACTS ABOUT BAD GUYS ALL THE TIME—

AND HE'S BEEN ELECTED PRES- IDENT **TWICE.**

IF LIES IN THE SERVICE OF A HIGHER TRUTH MAKE FOR GOOD GOVERN- MENT—

WHY NOT GOOD JOURNALISM?

© 1985 Jules Feiffer. Reprinted by permission.

Topic for Class Discussion: In this cartoon the great satirist Jules Feiffer takes a satirical look at journalism. The relevant background information is this: *Time* magazine once published a controversial story about the career of Israeli leader Ariel Sharon. Before Sharon became Israeli prime minister, he served as Israeli defense minister. Before that he was a general in the Israeli army. In this capacity he was commander of Israeli forces during an episode in Lebanon in which Lebanese militia members killed a number of civilian noncombatants in a refugee camp over which he had at least partial control. Sharon brought a libel suit against *Time* over the story. This lawsuit frightened a good many working journalists into some rather extravagant defences of *Time* in particular and journalistic practice and the freedom of speech in general. We count no less than seven distinct fallacious moves in the cartoon. How many fallacies can you find in the columnist's argument?

FALLACIOUS APPEALS TO AUTHORITY

As we discussed in Chapter 1, reliance upon authority is appropriate and understandable in many circumstances. Most of what we learn comes from some authority or other. Since we never arrive at the stage of knowing everything or being expert in *every* field, we continue to rely on authority from time to time throughout our lives. For example, if we want to know about the detailed way of life of a little-known cultural group on the other side of the world a thousand years ago, we will have to rely on the knowledge and discretion of experts, with little or no room for challenges on our part (unless we become experts ourselves). We simply are not in a position to know about such matters on our own, let alone argue with those who do know. Likewise, if you know nothing at all about quantum physics, you would be acting in a perfectly logical way in simply accepting at face value the statements of a known expert in quantum physics. We also noted, however, a risk inherent in reliance upon authority. The risk is that we might rely *too heavily* on authority or rely on authority when we should *not* do so. To the extent that we wind up relying upon unreliable authority, or upon authority whose reliability is open to serious question, we undermine the reliability of our reasoning and may be said to be committing some *informal fallacy of appeal to authority*. How do we know that the authority we are relying upon is in fact reliable? How do we tell when we are relying too heavily on authority or relying on authority when we should not do so? Let us now look more closely at these questions and develop some guidelines.

We must beware of overreliance on authority. When an appeal to authority wipes out all other considerations, it constitutes a fallacious appeal to authority. Such *appeals to invincible authority* have a notorious kind of currency within cults, or groups of any sort whose organizational principles or doctrines depend upon subordinating all personal autonomy. Unquestioning obedience to authority sometimes leads to tragic results. Such appeals, however, are not confined to the restricted world of organizational, political, or religious authoritarianism. Believe it or not, such *appeals to invincible authority* can be found of all places in the history of science. Some of Galileo's colleagues refused to look into his telescope and see the truth of nature for themselves because they were convinced that no evidence whatsoever could possibly contradict Aristotle's accounts of astronomy. This is no isolated aberration, by the way. Galileo himself made a similar argument when he said, "But can you doubt that air has weight when you have the clear testimony of Aristotle affirming that all the elements have weight including air, and excepting only fire?"[6] This suggests that perhaps we should adopt a rule to the effect that any authority worth relying on will remain open to question or challenge.

CRITICAL THINKING TIP 11.6

Any authority that places itself beyond question is unreliable. Any authority worth relying on remains open to question.

Think for a moment about Critical Thinking Tip 11.6. If we regard the reliability of any authority as depending on the authority's remaining open to question, it becomes obvious that any reliable authority must be identifiable. How can we question an authority if we do not know the identity of the authority? In spite of this obvious point, people often merely *allude to* expert opinion, or identify it in such a vague and incomplete way as to make any verification of reliability impossible. This is a favourite device of tabloids, such as the *National Enquirer*, that use phrases such as "experts agree," "university studies show," or "a Russian scientist has discovered" to lend the weight of authority to all sorts of quackery. When an authority is left unspecified, we may say that an *informal fallacy of appeal to unidentified authority* has occurred.

These days real expertise tends to be rather specialized. Although some remarkable individuals excel in more than one area of expertise, probably no one is an expert on *everything*. Accordingly, whenever an appeal to authority is introduced, we would be wise to be aware of the area of expertise of the alleged authority—and to be mindful of the *relevance* of the particular area of expertise to the issue under discussion. When the appeal is made to an authority whose expertise is in some field other than the one at issue, we may say that an *informal fallacy of appeal to irrelevant authority* has occurred. A common variety of appeal to irrelevant authority is the celebrity testimonial used throughout advertising for products ranging from Aspirin to political candidates.

Especially when controversial issues are involved, we may expect to find disagreement even among the experts. What then? We could, of course, simply quote the experts with whom we are in agreement, but the weakness of this as a reasoning strategy is easy to see. Those who disagree with us can quote their own experts, and this leads to a standoff. The simple fact that we find ourselves in agreement with one authority does not by itself make this a more reliable authority than a competing authority with whom we are at odds. Simple appeal to congenial authority, when expert opinion is divided, can be dismissed as the *informal fallacy of division of expert opinion*. Nonetheless, we can sometimes move beyond this sort of standoff. When expert opinion is divided, look into the credentials and affiliations of the experts. See whether you can learn anything about their reputations. How do their peers in their areas of expertise regard them? This may be of some use in sifting through competing appeals to authority.

Sometimes claims are advanced by appeal to experts who do have impressive and genuinely relevant credentials but whose testimony may legitimately be suspect because of a demonstrable *conflict of interest*. The reliability of any authority, even in her own area of specialized expertise, depends also upon her being "impartial." An authority whose impartiality has been compromised is no longer reliable, regardless of the degree or relevance of her expertise. For example, if we find that some scientific study of the effects of secondhand tobacco smoke was underwritten by a research grant from the Tobacco Farmers Marketing Association, we should at least look for other studies with which to compare this one.

EXERCISE 11.17 | Appeals to Authority

In each of the following examples, check all fallacy categories that apply. More importantly, *explain* each fallacy you identify.

The beginning of Chapter 9 contains a cartoon in which a lawyer makes a dubious argument for his client's innocence. Which particular fallacies does the cartoon illustrate?

	Explain your answer:
Invincible authority	
Unidentified authority	
Irrelevant authority	
Division of expert opinion	
Conflict of interest	

Despite occasional annual budget surpluses, Canada is going broke trying to live up to the "quintessentially Canadian" ideal of a welfare state in which the government does everything for everybody. We're indebted over the long term for a frighteningly high sum. We can't afford the liberal dream any longer. The economic analyst U.R. Waysten has said that all the money various governments have spent on social programs over the years represents a vast squandered opportunity to encourage a more robust market economy.

		Explain your answer:
	Invincible authority	
	Unidentified authority	
	Irrelevant authority	
	Division of expert opinion	
	Conflict of interest	

ADDITIONAL EXERCISES

■ **EXERCISE 11.18**   In our experience, the best way to study the material in this and the next chapter is through conversation with other people—in a facilitated discussion section, or in a small autonomous study group, or with a study partner. Take turns critically examining the following examples, using the tools and terms covered in this chapter. Listen to each others' critical assessments and weigh them for their clarity, their explanatory power, and their fairness. As you work your way through the following examples, alternately play the role of finding and explaining the flaw in the argument, and the complementary role of trying to defend the argument against the proposed criticism. Remember: Sometimes the difference between a fallacy and a reasonable argument is a matter of considerable subtlety and delicacy. An argument may look a lot like a fallacy of some kind and yet be deeply defensible. On the other hand, a given argument can have more than one thing wrong with it. The discussion of these examples may well prove to have greater importance than the "answer" to the question of which fallacy, if any, has been committed. If you arrive at a consensus criticism, move on to the next example.

- The end of anything is its perfection. Therefore, since death is the end of life, death must be the perfection of life.

- Pushy father-in-law to new bride: "So, when are you kids planning to make us grandparents?"

- Environment-worshipping tree huggers are misguided and a serious impediment to economic growth and people's happiness. They forget that human beings exist, too, not just plants and animals. And people need jobs to live well, but environmental do-gooding crushes economic health. No one's suggesting that out of control pollution is a good idea, but when enviro-nuts go so far as to shrilly squash development to save some rare species of hummingbird, we're into wacko territory.

- For many years big business has gleefully run roughshod over our natural surroundings, to the detriment of people, animals, and the other life forms.

Government has generally turned a blind eye to corporate enviro-Nazism, corruptly allowing whatever seems politically and economically expedient. We must insist that uncontrolled business predations cease against our natural inheritance.

- Former Prime Minister Pierre Elliot Trudeau's legacy is utterly tainted by his formative dalliances with communist and socialist thought. This aspect of his life is well known; even the U.S. Federal Bureau of Investigation kept tabs on him in the 1950s, well before he became prime minister. We should reject those elements of his policies that still exist in today's legislative and political realms.

- "Should we not assume that just as the eye, the hand, the foot, and in general each part of the body clearly has its own proper function, so man too has some function over and above the function of his parts?"[7]

- From a letter to the editor: "I was most disappointed with your paper for publishing that article about Madonna's book, *Sex,* in your 'Teen Life' section. I feel that the article is encouraging teens to buy and view sordid material on the basis that it is only 'fantasy.' Perhaps we need to remind ourselves that [serial killer] Ted Bundy's career started by viewing soft-core pornography, escalated to hard-core and then, when 'fantasy' was not enough, he decided that only the real thing would do."

- "Many of my colleagues in the press are upset about the growing practice of paying newsmakers for news. The auction principle seems to them to strike somehow at the freedom of the press, or at least the freedom of the poor press to compete with the rich press. But I find their objections pious and, in an economy where everything and everybody has its price, absurd."[8]

- "on june 3 at about 2:45 a.m. elf [Earth Libertation Front] set fire to a luxury home at 145 sterling oaks drive in chico ca. we used a napalm incendiary. it would have burnt to the ground if the pvc pipe containing water didn't put out the flame. the pvc pipe caught on fire and released the water. the damage ended up being minimal to our dissatisfaction. we targeted these luxury homes due to the damage to the bioregion that occurs through development. chico is slowly becoming victim to sprawl and we will not sit back as all that is natural and beautiful is destroyed. civilization as a whole has proved to be detrimental to humans and non human animals. we won't settle for anything less then complete collapse. liberation for all life"[9]

- "We need to recognize the clear importance of economic growth over the fringe concerns of wacky environmentalists. Tree-hugging daintiness is unnecessary and causes big problems for employment- and profit-generating sectors—and let's face it, human beings count more than daisies. We can have a world where every life-form is 'respected,' or we can have a world that works."

- "Can the universe think about itself? We know that at least one part of it can: we ourselves. Is it not reasonable to conclude the whole can?"[10]

- "A term I use to describe the mess that surrounds most issues in the world today and prevents us from getting at what is really so about the world's problems is 'pea soup.' The pea soup is a mass of confusion, controversy, argument, conflict, and opinions. As long as you are asking what more can you do, what better solution have you got, what have you come up with that's different, you cannot see that the confusion, controversy, conflict, doubt, lack of trust, and opinions surrounding the problem of hunger and starvation result inevitably from any position you take. Once you are clear that you cannot take any position that will contribute in any way to the end of hunger and starvation, that any position you take will only contribute to the pea soup that engulfs the problem of hunger and starvation, then hope dies. And when hope dies, hopelessness dies with it: Without hope you can't have hopelessness. You are now close to the source of the problem of hunger and starvation on the planet. If you can see that the problem is without hope, you are no longer hopeless and frustrated. You are just there with whatever is so."[11]

- Beleaguered CEO commenting on allegations of massive accounting fraud: "Sometimes mistakes happen. When mistakes arise, they should be acknowledged. The blame game doesn't help anything."

- Take another look at the example regarding smoking in Exercise 11.15. Consider the following imagined defence of the ad against the possible criticism that it was designed to appeal to fear. "We were just trying to expose people to the issue and get them to think about it, not to frighten them into agreement."

- "How can you deny that abortion is murder? The fetus is certainly alive, isn't it? And it certainly is human, isn't it? And it hasn't done anything wrong, has it? So you're talking about taking an innocent human life. And that's murder! What else is there to say?"

- People object to sexism and racism on the ground that they involve "discrimination." But what is objectionable about discrimination? We discriminate all the time—in the cars we buy, the foods we eat, the books we read, the friends we choose. The fact is there's nothing wrong with discrimination as such.

- "The Dalai Lama says that outer disarmament can only take place through inner disarmament. If the individual doesn't become more peaceful, a society that's the sum total of such individuals can never become more peaceful either."[12]

CALVIN AND HOBBES © 1986 Watterson. Dist. By UNIVERSAL PRESS SYNDICATE. Reprinted with permission. All rights reserved.

Calvin and Hobbes   by Bill Watterson

■ **EXERCISE 11.19** *Essay Assignment:* Is gender relevant? Perhaps an even better question would be, *"When* is gender relevant?" Do you think the young girl commits a fallacy in the Calvin and Hobbes cartoon? Write a short essay in which you explain your answer. Are there any circumstances in which you think gender is relevant?

■ **EXERCISE 11.20** *Essay Assignment:* The following is a portion of the testimony given by former Prime Minister Jean Chrétien at the Gomery Inquiry (February 2005). The Gomery Inquiry investigated alleged large-scale financial fraud and impropriety in the federal government's administration of the sponsorship program, an initiative to win support for national unity in Québec. Is this defence an instance of diversion or not? Explain.

Mr. Commissioner, the question is not whether some action is unusual. The question is whether it is necessary and whether it is right. I am firmly convinced that our national unity strategy was necessary and right. Were some mistakes made in everything we did? I am sure they were. After all, we are all human. Mr. Commissioner, you and I are both trained in the civil law. One of the first things we both learned at law school was the article of the Québec Civil Code that provides a presumption of good faith. I have explained that the sponsorship program was conceived in good faith. Its objectives were noble. When there is a presumption that a program is designed for sinister or corrupt partisan reasons, it is easy to draw all sorts of conclusions about ulterior motives of anyone associated with it particularly when there are hazy recollections of long ago meetings or memos.

A presumption of good faith leads to very different conclusions. For example, there has to be a recognition that people who every day for years dealt with dozens of memos on a whole variety of important issues and who attended sometimes dozens of meetings every day on every conceivable subject may not have total recall about any of them. There is one other important point. As Prime Minister, I received many memos from the Privy Council Office providing advice on every conceivable subject. Most often I accepted the advice. Sometimes I questioned it and my officials convinced me they were right; sometimes I convinced them that my judgment was right. Sometimes, like every prime minister, I did not accept the advice I received. The job of a prime minister, or a minister or a chief executive officer is not to rubberstamp every memo he receives. . . .

Unless staff in ministers' offices or the Prime Minister's Office and public servants can walk in and out of each other's offices, call each other on the phone, seek advice and counsel from each other, the job of government simply does not get done. I urge you not to make recommendations that unwittingly will make it difficult for governments to function and to serve Canadians, difficult for ministers to do their jobs, for members of Parliament to pass representations on behalf of constituents onto public servants, for public servants to work seamlessly with elected officials and their staffs.

I would just conclude in saying that a prime minister has heavy responsibilities and must make decisions that no one else can make, not even auditors general. The single most important priority of every prime minister since 1867 has been to preserve the unity of the country. We all may have been criticized at some time or another for our approach to national unity. But in the case of the unity of Canada every prime minister from Sir John A Macdonald to myself has always put country ahead of anything else.[13]

■ **Exercise 11.21**   At the end of Chapter 10 you were challenged to take a position on your issue in a 100-word "Position Statement" (Exercise 10.18). We bet that what you came up with is an argument. It is a composition designed to be persuasive at a rational level, and it has a thesis or conclusion in it somewhere and some other ideas and claims that support it. It is a draft of an argument—in the "abstract." This means it is short and could be developed more deeply, and it is still open to critique and revision. So, first, analyze your own argument. Then ask yourself, "Is my argument open to any of the kinds of criticisms (does it commit any of the fallacies?) we have just studied?"

GLOSSARY

ad hominem   fallacy consisting of irrelevant personal references or attacks

ad hominem, abusive   fallacy consisting of baseless and irrelevant personal references or attacks

ad hominem, circumstantial   fallacy consisting of irrelevant personal references or attacks based on actual information about a person that carries unfavourable but irrelevant personal implications

amphibole   grammatical ambiguity; a fallacy based on grammatical ambiguity

appeal to anger   fallacious strategy of arousing irrelevant anger in support of a position

appeal to authority   fallacious use of authority in support of a claim

appeal to fear or force   fallacy of attempting to intimidate people into accepting a position

appeal to novelty   fallacy of assuming or arguing that something is good or desirable simply because it is novel or new

appeal to pity   fallacious strategy of arousing irrelevant pity in support of a position

appeal to popularity   fallacy of assuming or arguing that something is true, good, or desirable simply because it is popularly believed or esteemed

appeal to tradition   fallacy of assuming or arguing that something is good or desirable simply because it is old or traditional

common practice   variety of the "two wrongs" fallacy in which one's own wrongdoing is excused by assimilation to widespread practice

composition   fallacy of inferring characteristics of the whole from characteristics of the parts

conflict of interest   any combination of interests that interferes with impartiality; hence, a variety of fallacious appeal to authority where the authority cited has such a combination of interests

division   fallacy of inferring characteristics of a part from characteristics of the whole

division of expert opinion   variety of fallacious appeal to authority where the authorities with relevant expertise are divided over the question at issue

dysphemism   negative exaggeration

equivocation   inconsistent use of an ambiguous expression, or an informal fallacy, problematic equivocation, based on such usage

euphemism   positive exaggeration

false implication   advertising strategy in which important claims are strongly implied but remain literally unstated, often because they are known to be false

genetic appeal   fallacy of assessment merely by way of origin, sources, or genesis

guilt by association   fallacy of supporting negative claims about people or their views or positions solely on the basis of their relationships with others

hyperbole   advertising and public relations strategy in which exaggerated (hyperbolic) terms are used to promote excitement

informal fallacy   an inference that is unreliable and whose unreliability results from something other than its formal structure

invincible authority   variety of fallacious appeal to authority where the authority is taken to outweigh any conflicting consideration

irrelevant expertise   variety of fallacious appeal to authority where the authority cited lacks expertise relevant to the question at issue

poisoning the well   fallacious strategy of attempting to discredit a position, or its advocate, before the argument for the position can be considered

positioning   fallacy of supporting positive claims about people or their views or positions solely on the basis of their relationships with others

provincialism   fallacy of appealing to considerations of group loyalty in support of a claim

puffery   advertising strategy in which vague terms are used to promote enthusiasm

red herring   fallacious argument strategy of diverting attention from the real issue to another one

rhetorical question   question used to mask a claim, or a fallacy based on such usage

straw person   fallacious argument strategy of attacking a weak or distorted representation of an opponent's position

testimonial   advertising and public relations strategy based on testimony of a celebrity, often an instance of the fallacy of irrelevant expertise

two wrongs   fallacy of excusing one's own wrong by pointing to the wrongs of others

unidentified experts   variety of fallacious appeal to authority where the authority is not identified sufficiently to make assessments of expertise, impartiality, or other relevant variables

weasel word   a vague word or expression, often part of advertising and public relations strategies, used to evade responsibility for an implied claim

Go to http://www.criticalthinking1ce.nelson.com for additional study resources for this chapter.

ENDNOTES

[1] Irwin Cotler, "Lawful access proposals protect public safety" (guest column), *Windsor Star*, September 3, 2005.

[2] Department of Justice Canada, "Royal Assent of Bill C-36: The Anti-Terrorism Act," http://canada.justice.gc.ca/en/news/nr/2001/doc_28217.html

[3] Paul Stevens, "Weasel Words: God's Little Helpers," in Paul A. Eschol, Alfred A. Rosa, and Virginia P. Clark (eds.), *Language Awareness* (New York: St. Martin's Press, 1974).

[4] Plato, *The Apology*, trans. by Hugh Tredennick, in *Plato: The Collected Dialogues,* ed. Edith Hamilton and Huntington Cairns, (Princeton: Princeton University Press, Bollingen Series, 1963), 20.

[5] Victor Lasky, "It Didn't Start with Watergate," *Book Digest* (November 1977), 47.

[6] Galileo Galilei, *Dialogues Concerning Two New Sciences,* trans. by Henry Crew and Alfonso de Salvio (Evanston, IL: Northwestern University Press, 1939).

[7] Aristotle, *Nicomachean Ethics,* trans. by Martin Ostwald (Indianapolis: Bobbs-Merrill, 1962), 16.

[8] Shana Alexander, "Loew's Common Denominator," *Newsweek*, April 14, 1975, 96.

[9] (Attributed to) Earth Liberation Front, "ELF Strikes Twice in 48 Hours Against Urban Sprawl in California and Michigan," press release June 4, 2003, http://www.mindfully.org/Heritage/2003/ELF-Urban-Sprawl4jun03.htm

[10] Jose Silva, *The Silva Mind Control Method* (New York: Pocket Books, 1978), 116.

[11] Werner Erhard, *The End of Starvation: Creating an Idea Whose Time Has Come* (San Francisco: The Hunger Project, 1982), 10–11.

[12] Matthieu Ricard, *The Monk and the Philosopher* (New York: Schocken, 1998), 156.

[13] "Gomery Inquiry: Jean Chrétien: a Former PM testifies," CBC News Online February 8, 2005, Reprinted by permission of CBC.

CHAPTER 12

Informal Fallacies II: Assumptions and Induction

Will you forget about logic and give me the benefit of the doubt?!? WOODY ALLEN[1]

In Chapter 1 we discussed the role of assumptions in reasoning and proposed the first of our series of Critical Thinking Tips: Be Aware of Assumptions. Assumptions become more dangerous to reasoning to the extent that they remain hidden. Thus, we should be generally on the alert for hidden assumptions wherever inferences are made from one or more claims to another, and also for hidden assumptions underlying any of the claims explicitly made. In a general sense, this sort of vigilance and awareness constitutes a tool of informal fallacy criticism. Whenever we become aware of the presence of a hidden

© The New Yorker Collection 1988 Roz Chast from cartoonbank.com. All Rights Reserved.

assumption in an argument, and the assumption is questionable or dubious, we may say that the argument commits the *informal fallacy of questionable assumptions.*

FALSE DILEMMA

Of course, the label is not what is important. What is important is the critical activity of carefully pointing out where the assumption is hidden and calling the assumption into question, making clear exactly what is questionable about it. For example, sometimes an argument depends upon the presentation of what is assumed to be an exhaustive range of alternatives. Dilemma is the logical strategy of proving a point by showing that it is implied by each of two alternatives, at least one of which must be true (see Chapter 6). Such an argument depends on the assumption that no *other* alternatives exist. If this assumption is false or doubtful, we may say that the argument commits the *informal fallacy of false dilemma.* Have you ever heard people argue in favour of some course of action by saying something like, "Well, we've gotta do *something*, don't we?" The unstated inferential assumption here is that we must *either* follow the proposed course of action *or* do nothing at all. Why might this be a false dilemma? Doing nothing at all might prove sensible (this is a matter that requires proof, of course), or doing something other than the proposed course of action might prove sensible (this, too, is a matter that requires proof). The strategy best suited to exposing instances of this fallacy is to articulate a specific alternative left out of consideration in the premises. False dilemma is one of the most powerfully persuasive of the common informal fallacies because its structure is deductively valid, conforming to either the disjunctive syllogism or the dilemma argument forms (see Chapter 7). False dilemma is also appealing psychologically due to the natural human tendency to prefer simplicity, to see things by way of pairs of mutually exclusive alternatives, or, as it is sometimes said, in black and white.

LOADED QUESTIONS

Sometimes a question is so worded that you cannot answer it without also granting a particular answer to some *other* question. Such a construction is called a *complex question,* or sometimes simply a *loaded question.* A well-known example is the old vaudeville line, "Have you stopped beating your wife (or husband)?" Such a question boxes you in because, first, it demands either "yes" or "no" as an answer, and second, because either of those answers *presupposes* that you are or were beating your spouse.

INNUENDO

Innuendo is Latin for "by hinting." The *informal fallacy of innuendo* consists of implying a judgment, usually derogatory, by hinting—no argument is offered. Instead, the audience is invited by suggestion, by a nod and a wink, to make the assumption. Someone asks, "Where is Jones? Did he get fired or something?" Someone answers, "Not yet." By innuendo, the response numbers Jones's days. The political candidate who distributes a brochure promising to restore honesty and integrity to an office has suggested, but not thereby *argued,* that the incumbent is crooked.

CIRCULAR REASONING

Three thieves have stolen seven bags of gold. The thief in the middle hands two bags of gold to the thief on the left and two bags of gold to the thief on the right and says, "I'm keeping three for myself." The thief on the left asks, "Why do you get to keep three, when we each only get two?" The thief in the middle says, "Because I'm the leader of this outfit." The thief on the right asks, "What makes you the leader?", to which the thief in the middle responds, "I've got the most gold."[2]

EXERCISE 12.1 | Topic for Class Discussion

Perhaps the moral of this little fable is that thieves have no honour. In any case, it should be readily apparent that the thief in the middle is pulling a logical fast one on his two partners in crime. Can you explain the trick?

The *informal fallacy of begging the question,* or *circular reasoning,* occurs when the conclusion of the argument—or some other claim that presupposes it—is assumed as a premise. Such arguments are objectionable because the premise is just as questionable as the conclusion it is intended to support (hence the name "begging the question"). If you are not already inclined to believe the conclusion, offering a premise that amounts to the same thing clearly will not convince you of its truth. What makes this fallacy particularly tricky to deal with is that arguers are rarely so clumsy as to appeal to a premise that is *obviously* the same as the conclusion. More frequently, the question-begging premise is a subtle rewording of the conclusion or is presupposed by the conclusion in a way that even the arguer may fail to appreciate. The strategy one frequently needs to pursue to effectively diagnose and expose this fallacy therefore involves sensitive use of paraphrase. If the premise and the conclusion can be paraphrased into each other without significant loss of meaning, then we have a plausible case of begging the question.

EXERCISE 12.2 | Fallacious Assumptions

Each of the following examples contains (or points out) at least one major fallacy involving unwarranted assumptions. In each, check all fallacy categories that apply. More importantly, explain each fallacy you identify.

"By the time you have wisely purchased this tome . . . most critics will have undoubtedly savaged it. In many cases, their reviews will have been written before the book was published. How do I know this? Because I do."[3]

		Explain your answer:
	False dilemma	
	Loaded question	
	Innuendo	
	Begging the question	

"We must believe in the existence of God because it is written in the Holy Scriptures, and conversely we must believe in the Holy Scriptures because they come from God."

(René Descartes, "Letter of Dedication," *Meditations on First Philosophy*)

		Explain your answer:
	False dilemma	
	Loaded question	
	Innuendo	
	Begging the question	

Captain L had a first mate who was at times addicted to the use of strong drink, and occasionally, as the slang has it, "got full." The ship was lying in port in China, and the mate had been on shore and had there indulged rather freely in some of the vile compounds common in Chinese ports. He came on board, "drunk as a lord," and thought he had a mortgage on the whole world. The captain, who rarely ever touched liquor himself, was greatly disturbed by the disgraceful conduct of his officer, particularly as the crew had all observed his condition. One of the duties of the first mate is to write up the log each day, but as that worthy was not able to do it, the captain made the proper entry, but added: "The mate was drunk all day." The ship left port the next day and the mate got "sobered off." He attended to his writing at the proper time, but was appalled when he saw what the captain had done. He went back on deck, and soon after the following colloquy took place:

"Cap'n, why did you write in the log yesterday that I was drunk all day?"

"It was true, wasn't it?"

"Yes, but what will the ship owners say if they see it? It will hurt me with them."

But the mate could get nothing more from the Captain than, "It was true, wasn't it?"

The next day, when the Captain was examining the book, he found at the bottom of the mate's entry of observation, course, winds, and tides: "The captain was sober all day."[4]

		Explain your answer:
	False dilemma	
	Loaded question	
	Innuendo	
	Begging the question	

Topic for Class Discussion: Each passage below commits the same informal fallacy of questionable assumption. Can you explain how the fallacy works?

- "Conservative": We must choose between two courses for this country: Continuing in a rut of stagnation and corruption, or choosing the new over the old. And we cannot continue as we've been doing.

- "Liberal": I agree: We are faced with only two choices as Canadians. We can build on the concrete reforms and successes of the past few years, or we can risk everything by allowing a grab for power by those who serve economic elites.

DILBERT

FALLACIES OF INDUCTION

In Chapters 8 and 9 we explained in a general way how to evaluate inductive reasoning. Inductive strength is essentially a matter of degree—the degree to which the conclusion remains open to doubt, assuming the premises are true. The degree to which the conclusion remains open to doubt depends on the *type* of inductive reasoning involved. Looking at the various types of inductive reasoning we discussed in Chapters 8 and 9, we can now highlight some of the more common *informal fallacies of induction*. These involve overestimating the strength of some particular type of inductive inference.

GENERALIZATIONS

In Chapter 8 we explained that the strength of an inductive generalization depends most heavily on two factors: the size and representativeness of the sample. So this highlights two areas of possible overestimation of inductive strength. The *informal fallacy of small sample* consists in overestimating the statistical significance of evidence drawn from a small number of cases. Sometimes what appears to be a significant pattern in a small number of cases disappears altogether when we investigate a larger number of cases. Suppose we take a poll to determine political preferences and of the first 10 responses, 7 favour the challenger over the incumbent. By the time we have interviewed a hundred people, however, we may find the incumbent ahead 75 to 21 (with 4 undecided). One must be careful in applying this result as a criticism, of course. The size of the sample relative to the target population is not the only factor involved in determining the reliability of the inductive inference. Even a relatively small sample can be used to reliably project trends on a massive scale if the study is carefully controlled and based on a representative sample. For example, merely pointing out that a national political preference poll had been conducted on the basis of "only" 5,000 responses would be insufficient basis for criticism. In fact, a poll of only around 1,000 subjects, adhering to all the criteria of a scientifically respectable sample, can yield accurate information about the nation as a whole with a margin of error of only around ± 3 percent.[5]

Suppose, though, that the aforementioned 5,000 responses were all taken from one geographical region. This regional bias would greatly increase liability to error. Thus, the representativeness of a sample is even more important than sample size, since we are trying to project conclusions affected by many variables. If we can control all the relevant variables in a relatively small sample, so much the better for the economy of the study. The important thing is to control all the variables. This can be difficult to accomplish in an area such as political preference, however, since such a wide range of variables affects it. The problem is made greater by the reality that we may not know all the relevant variables. The *informal fallacy of unrepresentative sample* involves overestimating the statistical significance of evidence drawn from a sample of a particular kind.

To see just how tricky this can be, consider the famous case of the 1936 *Reader's Digest* American presidential preference poll, which incorrectly predicted that Alf Landon would defeat the incumbent Franklin Delano Roosevelt. The poll was based on *2 million* respondents selected *at random* from phone books and motor vehicle registration lists. *Random* means that each member of the target population has a roughly equal chance of appearing in the sample. For example, if pollsters wish to find out what the Catholic laity thinks about the sexual abuse scandal, they must ensure that every lay Catholic is *equally likely* to be among those polled. Notice that this does not mean every lay Catholic needs to *be polled*—only that every lay Catholic has an equal chance of *being asked*. If pollsters were to ask only East Coast Catholics or West Coast Catholics, the result would not be random, and so it would not be representative. Now in its 1936 presidential preference poll, *Reader's Digest* picked the names *at random* from the phone book and the motor vehicle registration lists, which leads us to the following exercise.

EXERCISE 12.3 | Unrepresented Sample?

In its 1936 American presidential preference poll *Reader's Digest* picked the names *at random* from the phone book and the motor vehicle registration lists. What did it miss? Can you guess?

The relevant variable the poll overlooked was that in 1936—during the Great Depression—a large part of the electorate could not afford a car or even a phone (and they tended to be angry about it). So, even though the pollsters *tried* to take a random sample, the sample they got was far from random and failed rather spectacularly to reflect the political mood of the electorate as a whole.

Besides the sample size and the degree to which the sample represents the target, other aspects of method can affect the strength of an inductive generalization. The reliability of inductive generalizations can depend in part upon whether other informal fallacies, such as informal fallacies of language or fallacious assumptions, are involved. For example, if a public opinion poll is conducted using loaded or leading questions, or questions that restrict the range of available responses, or questions that contain questionable presuppositions, the results are not to be trusted.

EXERCISE 12.4 | Fallacious Assumptions in Public Opinion Polling

Topic for Class Discussion: Critique the following hypothetical public opinion poll. Suppose that you live in a community where rapid growth has stretched existing waste-management resources to the breaking point, resulting in a glut of garbage serious enough to have raised public concern. Now suppose the local newspaper conducts a readers' poll asking readers to rank the desirability of the following three policy options:

• An increase in municipal property tax to pay for the improvement and expansion of existing facilities.

• A municipal loan to construct new local landfills.

- A provincial initiative to dump excess garbage in newly created landfills in the North.

Now the newspaper reports that public opinion favours a municipal loan to construct new local landfills 48 percent to 35 percent over the next most popular option.

So far we have focused on how inductive evidence is gathered and generalizations are reached. We should also look critically at the way the results are presented and interpreted. Sometimes relevant evidence is deliberately kept from view because it conflicts with the arguer's intended interpretation of the evidence that is presented. This constitutes the *informal fallacy of suppressed evidence*. A common political foible—and a particular favourite in the field of advertising, particularly when statistical data are used—this is an obviously disreputable argumentative strategy. For example, advertisers are forever referring to "scientific" studies that "demonstrate" the superiority of their products but strategically neglecting to mention that they have commissioned the studies themselves, a crucial piece of information relevant to assessing the objectivity of the studies. Moreover, the fallacy of suppressed evidence occurs anytime significant information or evidence—information or evidence that makes a difference to understanding the issue—is omitted. Consider the following example. Canadian columnist Dan Gardner reported that in the 1990s the World Health Organization (WHO) commissioned "the largest global study on cocaine use ever undertaken." He informed his readers that the study "concluded that most users consume cocaine occasionally, that occasional use usually does not lead to compulsive use, and that occasional use does little or no harm to users." These results, Gardner stated, were "a flat contradiction of the [American] drug-war ideology, so the U.S. threatened to pull its funding if the report was released. The WHO buckled, and the report was buried."[6] Such research claims probably seem counterintuitive to most of us, but we should certainly give due consideration to all credible pieces of information that bear upon the issue—even if, in the end, we decide to stick with our original stance. We must at least gain exposure to this information if we are to make a more informed judgment. On Gardner's account, it would seem, if the WHO had published its report using this study after all, then we would have probably received an appreciably "massaged" version of the study results.

Statistics often invite misinterpretation, particularly in the direction of overestimating the significance of some trend. One way that this can happen is by assuming an inappropriate basis of comparison. For example, suppose that you live in a small town and the local weekly newspaper reports a 33 percent rise in the rate of car theft. This sounds rather alarming. The alarm diminishes, however, when we read past the headline and learn that the number of car thefts rose from three in the previous year to four. Now suppose that over the same period the town's population has doubled. In this case, the incidence of car theft *per capita* (relative to population) has significantly dropped. We may call this technique of distorting the implications of statistical data the *informal fallacy of bad baseline*. Be on the lookout for this sort of misrepresentation in political speeches about trends in crime, unemployment, balance of trade, welfare dependency, and other social phenomena. Bear in mind that changing

© Tom Meyer. Reprinted by permission.

the eligibility requirements for employment insurance benefits can make it *look statistically as though* the number of unemployed people is dropping.

ANALOGIES

In Chapter 8 we gave a detailed explanation of the standards and procedures for the evaluation of arguments based on analogies. The examples we used there to illustrate these standards and procedures are quite strong inductive arguments. Using these same standards, the identification and critique of a weak analogy is a matter of adding up relevant similarities and differences. If we find that the argument is based on similarities that are *irrelevant* to the conclusion or that it glosses over relevant differences, then we may object that the argument is based on a questionable, false, or misleading analogy. Note that this is a two-step process. First, we must establish differences between the items compared in the analogy. Second, and more important, we must establish the relevance of the differences to the point of the analogy. Overlooking this second step will result in a misapplication of this criticism. One often hears the objection, "Your argument is like comparing apples and oranges." Notice that this is also an analogy, the point of which is that the analogy under criticism is misleading. Bear in mind that no two items in the universe are so different from each other that they cannot be compared in *some* useful way relevant to *some* purpose. Is a comparison between apples and oranges necessarily misleading? No, not if you are trying to sort the fruit from the vegetables. So, we must keep the point of the analogy we are critiquing clearly in mind as we look for differences. Moreover, we must show that the differences are relevant to the point. When we have done both of these things, we may say that we have identified an instance of the *informal fallacy of faulty analogy.*

EXERCISE 12.5 | Faulty Analogy?

Topic for Class Discussion: Critique the argument in the cartoon on page 325. Do you think any fallacious elements exist in the pig's argument? Explain any criticisms you would offer in detail. What about the fact that the cartoonist puts the argument into the mouth of a pig?

BURDEN OF PROOF

The *informal fallacy of arguing ad ignorantiam* (from Latin for "arguing from ignorance") consists in treating the absence of evidence for (or against) a claim as proof of its falsity (or truth). The fallacy is a perversion of the concepts of "burden of proof" and legitimate presumption discussed in Chapter 9. It essentially involves misplacing the burden of proof. Understandably, many examples of this fallacy concern the unknown and the "supernatural." For example, an argument for the existence of extraterrestrial intelligent life might go like this: Because the universe is infinitely large, we cannot possibly prove conclusively that the only intelligent life that exists dwells on the planet Earth, so we should assume that extraterrestrial intelligent life exists.

PEANUTS: © United Feature Syndicate, Inc.

A related fallacy, which we will call *arguing from invincible ignorance*, consists in refusing to accept one's own burden of proof. For example, in the *Peanuts* episode Snoopy commits this fallacy twice. In the first instance Snoopy dismisses Lucy's expression of doubt as ignorant; later he dismisses the evidence of her research on the basis of the far-fetched assumption of a massive coverup. In each case no reason for dismissing the information emerges other than the uncomfortable fact that it conflicts with the hypothesis to which he is initially, and as it seems inflexibly, committed. In what we might call a definitive case of "sleeping dogmatism," Snoopy simply closes his mind on this subject.

HYPOTHETICAL AND CAUSAL REASONING

A closely related fallacy, in this case a perversion of the concept of explanatory power as discussed in Chapter 9, consists in concluding that some explanation or solution holds simply because no one can think of a better one. Of course, we do not adequately understand many things. For example, as of this writing, the origin of the AIDS virus remains a mystery. Filmmaker Spike Lee once argued that AIDS originated as part of a genocidal attack on gays and black people by the American government. His argument seems to rest largely on the idea that some peculiarities characterize the course of the AIDS epidemic for which no better explanation exists. "All of sudden, a disease appears out of nowhere that nobody has a cure for, and it's specifically targeted at gays and minorities. . . . So now it's a national priority. Exactly like drugs became when they escaped the urban centers into white suburbia. . . . The mystery disease, yeah, about as mysterious as 'genocide'. . . ." To call this an *interesting* hypothesis and one worth investigating would be fair enough. As it stands, however, it is only an empirical hypothesis. This means some hard evidence should exist out there somewhere to confirm it, if it is indeed true. One thing that does *not* count as confirming evidence, however, is the (current) absence of any better explanation. Philosopher Elliott Sober calls this informal fallacy the *Only Game in Town Fallacy.*[7]

Reasoning about causality is tricky because causal relationships are never directly observable, and the things whose causes we most urgently want to understand—our health, the behaviour of the physical world, the economy, and so on—are *so* complicated. For these reasons, we recommend that when confronted by any argument about causal relationships you remind yourself of Mill's Methods of reasoning about causality. Stretch your imagination. Consider as many possible causal factors as you can conceive. Try to imagine the kind of experiment you would design to test these as causal hypotheses. From the discussion of causal reasoning in Chapter 9, we can derive a number of fallacies that we can understand as failing to meet one or more of the standards and criteria of good inductive reasoning. Superstitions provide the most obvious cases of this kind of fallacious thinking, as, for example, when a basketball coach refuses to change his "lucky" socks in an attempt to influence the outcome of the game. A number of more subtle pitfalls of causal reasoning exist, though, and we need to be aware of them.

CRITICAL THINKING TIP 12.1

- Remember Mill's Methods of reasoning about causality.
- Stretch your imagination.
- Consider as many possible causal factors as you can conceive.
- Try to imagine the kind of experiment you would design to test these as causal hypotheses.

One of the most common kinds of evidence for a causal connection is a statistical correlation between two phenomena. For example, medical scientists knew for some time of a statistical correlation between cigarette smoking and lung cancer. The incidence of lung cancer in the smoking population was higher than in the nonsmoking population. Such a correlation is genuinely relevant inductive evidence for a causal connection between lung cancer and smoking. The problem is that by itself it is inconclusive. It suggests, but does not establish, the causal link. For several decades the tobacco industry was successful in eluding the implications—and liabilities—of the causal connection between smoking and cancer on the basis of this distinction between statistical correlation and causality. This is how real and significant a distinction it is. Some people may find this hard to accept and may even be inclined to wonder why we should not, as a society, have been able to move earlier and more decisively against the tobacco industry to establish antismoking policies. Notice, however, that a strong statistical correlation also exists between the incidence of lung cancer and age. Nonetheless, it would be misleading to suggest that age causes lung cancer, or that lung cancer causes aging. So, isolating the causal factor does indeed require further scientific evidence. The *informal fallacy of jumping from correlation to cause* occurs whenever someone interprets an observed statistical correlation as showing a causal connection without first having made a reasonable attempt to isolate the cause by controlling the relevant variables experimentally as described in Chapter 9.

A similar fallacy consists in inferring a causal connection merely from temporal contiguity. In other words, inferring that one thing is the cause of another simply because it is preceded by it in time is a fallacy. For example, someone observes that crime and misbehaviour among youth have increased in Canada since the arrival of punk rock from the United Kingdom and concludes, therefore, that punk rock is causing an increase in juvenile problems. Another instance: Someone observes that every substantial economic downturn in the last century followed the election of a Liberal federal government, concluding therefore that the Liberals caused those downturns. This kind of reasoning came to be known in Latin as *post hoc ergo propter hoc,* which means literally, "after this, therefore because of this."

Two phenomena may be so closely connected that one of them seems to be the cause of the other, though both are really results of some additional, less obvious factor. Suppose a person suffers from both depression and alcoholism. Does the drinking cause the depression or does the depression cause the drinking? Could it be that the depression and the drinking sustain each other causally? Perhaps this is so. We should not, however, overlook the further possibility that some additional cause underlies both the depression and the drinking—for example, a biochemical imbalance or a profound emotional disturbance. The *informal fallacy of overlooking a common cause,* then, consists of failing to recognize that two seemingly related events may not be causally related at all but rather effects of a common cause.

The *informal fallacy of causal oversimplification* consists in assuming that what merely contributes causally to a phenomenon fully explains it. For example, intense debates erupt regularly over the wisdom of increased taxation as a means of balancing the government budgets. Opponents of such measures frequently point to the predictable negative effects that taxation will have on the vitality of the consumer economy, while proponents of such measures stress the effects on real disposable income of the increasing debt burden on the economy as a whole. Both sides likely have a point, but both sides are also likely oversimplifying the economic equation in a number of ways. Tax policy is clearly not the only causal factor that affects the consumer economy. Neither is public indebtedness the only such causal factor. Both factors, and numerous others, are involved and influence each other in a great many ways.

SLIPPERY SLOPE

One specific kind of causal fallacy consists of objecting to something on the grounds of the unwarranted idea that it will inevitably (or quite probably) lead to some evil consequence that will lead to some even more evil consequence that in turn will lead "on down the slippery slope" to some ultimately disastrous consequence. For example, it is commonly argued that marijuana is a dangerous

CALVIN AND HOBBES © 1992 Watterson Dist. By UNIVERSAL PRESS SYNDICATE. Reprinted with permission. All rights reserved.

drug that inevitably (or quite probably) leads to experimentation with harder drugs and eventually to hard drug abuse and addiction. The alleged slippery slope is frequently supported by further fallacious causal inferences such as pointing out that a high percentage of admitted heroin addicts testify to having tried marijuana early in their drug experience. In fact, no slippery slope of this sort exists here, as can easily be established by pointing out that numerous people, who at one time or another have tried marijuana, have never experimented with harder drugs, much less become addicted to them, and have moderated or given up their use of marijuana. A variation on slippery slope reasoning takes the form of posing the rhetorical question, "Where do you draw the line?" This, of course, has the effect of suggesting that no location can exist for a line to be drawn. For example, some people are moved by the arguments like this one:

EXERCISE 12.6 | Slippery Slope?

Topic for Class Discussion: Evaluate the following argument against a form of euthanasia:

"If you permit the withdrawal of life support from terminally ill patients, where do you draw the line between this form of 'mercy killing' and the convenient disposal of one's sick and burdensome elders, or the 'euthanasia' of the mentally or physically or racially 'defective'?"

We think the argument in Exercise 12.6 is an example of slippery slope reasoning. Here the reasoner merely takes for granted that we cannot clearly distinguish between cases of "passive euthanasia" (withholding extraordinary life-prolonging measures) and "active euthanasia" (taking steps to hasten death or bring about death), or between euthanasia done to alleviate pointless suffering of a terminally ill patient and euthanasia done for selfish reasons or with deliberate disregard for the interests of the patient. Now it is easy to see that such distinctions *are* possible, since they have just been made. It is not much harder to see that they are relevant distinctions. Indeed the argument presumes the relevance of such distinctions; otherwise, why assume or suggest that they cannot be made? Thus, an effective strategy for exposing this sort of slippery slope reasoning is simply to draw the relevant distinctions. It is important to recognize, however, that in some contexts the question "Where do you draw the line?", rhetorical question though it is, *does* make a good point. Contexts exist—including some extremely important ones—in which some fundamental principle is at stake that would be irreparably compromised if a certain exception to it were allowed to pass.

GAMBLER'S FALLACY

The so-called *gambler's fallacy* consists in thinking that past outcomes of chance events have any influence on the probability of future outcomes. For example, suppose we are gambling on coin flips and the last 10 flips have come up heads. Many people are tempted to think that tails are therefore *more* likely to come up than heads on the next flip. The problem here is failure to recognize that the chances of heads or tails coming up are the same for each flip (50-50), because each flip is an independent chance event. The chances of a run of 11 heads in a row are of course much lower than 50-50, but the odds against such a run have no bearing whatsoever on the outcome of the next flip. Nonetheless, people persist in the belief to the contrary. Watch people play the slots at any casino. Again and again you will see people pumping coins into a machine that has not paid off for hours, thinking that this fact alone makes it more likely that the machine will pay off soon. Just as unreliable is the inference to continue playing because one has been winning. The idea of "riding a streak" involves the same mistake as thinking that the odds against you eventually have to "even out." If chance determines the outcome of the next play, past outcomes have no bearing whatsoever. Gamblers also tend to be (sometimes pathologically) attracted to "systems" designed to "beat the odds," most of which are completely fallacious products of wishful thinking and do not work at all. (The occasional exception, such as card counting in blackjack, is quickly uncovered and the player is escorted from the premises of the gaming establishment.) One such system consists in "doubling the bet." Suppose you put $2 on red at even money (the odds are 50-50) and you lose. Following this system, you would put $4 on red on the next play. If you win, you will be up $2. If you lose, you will be down $6, but you will also bet $8 on the next play. If you win, you will be up $10. The idea is that eventually you will win, and when you do, you are ahead of the game. The trouble with this system is that the odds remain uniformly stacked against you throughout the game as you continue to raise your stake, which has the effect of digging you more deeply and quickly into a hole. In other words, if you follow this "system," the only probability you will raise is the probability that you will run out of money before you win.

EXERCISE 12.7 | Fallacies of Induction?

In each of the following examples, check all fallacy categories that apply. More importantly, explain each fallacy you identify.

> In spite of the objections of students and faculty, we are moving ahead to implement the new tuition fees recommended by the special committee. We have to do something and we have to do it immediately to restore our reputation as a leading undergraduate educational institution. No one has come forward with a better alternative.

	Explain your answer:
Ad ignorantiam	
Invincible ignorance	
Only game in town	
Correlation to cause	
Post hoc ergo propter hoc	
Overlooking a common cause	
Causal oversimplification	
Slippery slope	
Gambler's fallacy	

A real miracle is something that demonstrably does occur but cannot be scientifically explained. Now we formed a prayer circle over Sadie and her T-cell count has returned to normal and she no longer tests positive for HIV. The doctors have confirmed what the lab work shows, but they can't seem to agree on an explanation. We believe God has sent the virus from her body.

		Explain your answer:
	Ad ignorantiam	
	Invincible ignorance	
	Only game in town	
	Correlation to cause	
	Post hoc ergo propter hoc	
	Overlooking a common cause	
	Causal oversimplification	
	Slippery slope	
	Gambler's fallacy	

"Everything in this book is right and you must be prepared to confront that reality. You can no longer be an honest liberal after reading this entire masterpiece. Throughout the book you will be challenged, because you will actually be persuaded to the conservative point of view. Whether you can admit this in the end will be a true test of your mettle as a human being."[8]

		Explain your answer:
	Ad ignorantiam	
	Invincible ignorance	
	Only game in town	
	Correlation to cause	
	Post hoc ergo propter hoc	
	Overlooking a common cause	
	Causal oversimplification	
	Slippery slope	
	Gambler's fallacy	

"I've always reckoned that looking at the new moon over your left shoulder is one of the carelessest and foolishest things a body can do. Old Hank Bunker done it once and bragged about it and in less than two years he got drunk and fell off of the shot-tower, and spread himself out so that he was just a kind of layer, as you may say; and they slid him edgeways between two barn doors for a coffin, and buried him so, so they say, but I didn't see it. Pap told me. But anyway it all come of looking at the moon that way like a fool."

(Mark Twain, *The Adventures of HOuckleberry Finn*)

		Explain your answer:
	Ad ignorantiam	
	Invincible ignorance	
	Only game in town	
	Correlation to cause	
	Post hoc ergo propter hoc	
	Overlooking a common cause	
	Causal oversimplification	
	Slippery slope	
	Gambler's fallacy	

A FINAL WORD OF CAUTION

By now it should be pretty clear that evaluating arguments, particularly using our "informal" approach, can be a rather messy business. You can expect to encounter a fair number of arguments that you can quite clearly fault in one way or another, and occasionally you will find an argument that is pretty clearly impeccable. A great many arguments, however, are neither clearly fallacious nor clearly not fallacious. In such cases, you should consider your criticisms to be contestable, and therefore you should also recognize the need to supply arguments in support of them, to deal with arguments against them, and perhaps to change your mind. In other words, assessing arguments, like verifying judgments of value, takes you into areas where knowing how to construct and evaluate arguments becomes ever more important.

Bear in mind Critical Thinking Tip 11.1 (see Chapter 11). The point of all this activity is not to vanquish one's opponent, not to humiliate anyone, not to experience the thrill of victory, and not to score points. The point of this activity is to *improve understanding*—to shed light, not generate heat. Moreover, this is not an idle intellectual exercise—not some arcane variety of Trivial Pursuit. Fallacy labels have no *intrinsic* importance at all. Their value is entirely instrumental. Above all, remember that a *fair and accurate understanding* of the argument is an absolute prerequisite to a well-reasoned judgment of its merits. Make sure your criticisms are based on thorough and careful consideration of the argument.

CRITICAL THINKING HALL OF SHAME

Few things are more embarrassing to a discipline such as critical thinking than the kind of inept instruction that provoked the late Jack Smith to publish the following column.

"Critique of an Ironic Writer's Critical Thought," by Jack Smith. Copyright *Los Angeles Times*. Reprinted by permission.

In writing these pieces, it never occurs to me that I am going to be accused of critical thinking, either good or bad.

However, I have received a letter from Howard Holter, professor of history at California State University Dominguez Hills, enclosing an analysis of my critical thinking by one of his students.

Holter explains, "I assigned my students the task of evaluating a piece of newspaper copy in terms of the formal evaluation of critical thinking. They were to use 'fallacies of critical thinking' listed in the textbook to apply to the piece in question."

A student named Melanie Martinez chose to evaluate one of my columns, and Holter says her paper was one of the best. I do not come off too well.

Her paper criticizes a column I wrote about transcendental meditation as taught at Maharishi International University, Fairfield, Iowa. These folks believe, as you may remember, that if enough people meditate together, achieving a state of pure consciousness and connecting with the Unified Field, the basis of all life, they can actually alter events—lowering crime rates, quelling riots, easing international tension and even causing the Dow Jones average to rise.

The theme of my essay was that I did not believe this. However, my tone was irony, which, as we have often seen, is a risky tone to effect.

Martinez aims right at the heart.

"This article," she begins, "contains many vague and ambiguous words and statements, as well as fallacies of presumption."

I am reeling already.

Pinpointing my first fallacy of presumption, she quotes a paragraph: "The meditators held a mass meditation . . . thereby raising the temperature and saving the Florida orange crop, lowering drunken driving arrests is Des Moines, influencing Fidel Castro to give up cigars, and causing the stock market to rally."

Obviously, I hope, I am being ironic. I do not for a moment believe that the meditation had any effect whatever on the events cited.

But Martinez comments:

"This is the fallacy of False Cause, or thinking that because someone did one thing, something else happened as a result. The meditators may have believed that they were the reason for the temperature rise in Florida, but were probably wrongly justified . . ."

My thought exactly.

Later, Martinez observes, while I question the validity of the meditations, I claim that I was the one who meditated the success of Corazon Aquino in her bid for the presidency of the Philippines.

"Not only is this also a Fallacy of False Cause, but this is also a Fallacy of Special Pleading. After denouncing meditation, he does that exact thing."

Obviously, again, I was being ironic when I took credit for meditating Mrs. Aquino into the presidency. I was merely showing how easy it is for anyone to claim the Maharishi Effect for himself.

Martinez also accuses me of the Fallacy of Bifurcation. Bifurcation does not seem the sort of fallacy I might fall into, but let's see.

She quotes me: "I do believe that if we could get millions of people all around the world to sit down and meditate, instead of shooting and bombing one another, conditions would improve."

She says, "Here the author is saying, 'If we do one thing, this will happen.' Actually the opposite could happen: While the majority of people are meditating, a few of the people who aren't participating in the meditation could take advantage and cause destruction."

Alas, Martinez is all too close to the mark on that point. If we had thousands of people sitting around meditating, the barbarians might well say, "Hey, look at those crackpots meditating! Let's kill 'em!"

Or am I bifurcating?

She writes, "The author also included the phrase 'I am out on a limb,' which according to critical thinking, means either he is standing on someone's arm or leg, or he is standing on a tree branch. This is an ambiguous statement."

Nothing ambiguous about "out on a limb." It is an ancient metaphor, much honored in the use, which means, according to A Dictionary of American Idioms, "with your beliefs and opinions openly stated; in a dangerous position that can't be changed."

I am always out on a limb.

ADDITIONAL EXERCISES

EXERCISE 12.8 In our experience, the best way to study the material in this and the previous chapter is through conversation with other people—in a facilitated discussion section, in a small autonomous study group, or with a study partner. Take turns critically examining the following examples, using the tools and terms covered in this chapter. Listen to each other's critical assessments and weigh them for their clarity, their explanatory power, and their fairness. As you work your way through the following examples, alternate between playing the role of finding and explaining the flaw in the argument and the complementary role of trying to defend the argument against the proposed criticism. Remember: Sometimes the difference between a fallacy and a reasonable argument is a matter of considerable subtlety and delicacy. An argument may look a lot like a fallacy of some kind and yet be deeply defensible. On the other hand, a given argument can have more than one thing wrong with it. The discussion of these examples may well prove to be of greater importance than the "answer" to the question of which fallacy, if any, has been committed. If you arrive at a consensus criticism, move on to the next example.

- The Ayatollah Khomeini, former leader of Iran, speaking in defence of state executions of those convicted of adultery, prostitution, or homosexuality: "If your finger suffers from gangrene, what do you do? Let the whole hand and then the body become filled with gangrene, or cut the finger off? . . . Corruption, corruption. We have to eliminate corruption."[9]

- Suppose a survey shows that more than half of all postsecondary students with below-average grades smoke marijuana, while, by contrast, only 20 percent of nonsmokers have below-average grades. On the basis of this information, one person concludes that marijuana use causes students to get lower grades. Another person concludes that getting lower grades causes students to smoke pot. What do you make of this disagreement?

- Argument against raising cigarette taxes: "Taxing cigarettes encourages traffickers in stolen cigarettes by opening up a new and profitable market for them. Support for this measure is support for increased crime. Don't support the smugglers and traffickers and black marketeers."

- Adding a health tax to tobacco products is unfair to the tobacco industry. We're like any other legitimate business in this country. We sell a legal product to willing buyers in a free market, and we pay a fair share into the public purse through various forms of taxation. If tax revenue is to be raised to support health care, let the burden be shared across the board.

- It's a bit mysterious, because Smith's numbers are less than spectacular. He scores fewer points than any of his teammates. We don't let him handle the ball, because he's sure to turn it over. And he's slow and clumsy on defence. But he's a starter and he plays the first few minutes of each game simply because, when he's in the starting lineup, we win 70 percent of our games. When he's not, we only win 50 percent of the time.

- "Is adultery bad for your health? The chances of having a heart attack while making love are infinitesimal, but if you do have one, the chances are you'll have it with your mistress and not your wife. A study of 34 cardiac patients who died during intercourse revealed that 29 of the 34 were having an extra-marital affair." —*Playboy magazine*

- I knew a guy who was so influenced by statistics that numbers ruled his entire life! One time he found out that over 80 percent of all automobile accidents happen to people within five miles of where they live. So he moved!

- "Whatever you do, DO NOT DESTROY THIS LETTER! Send it out to five of your friends. Mildred Wimplebush of Kelowna destroyed her copy of this letter and a week later she died of a stroke. Henry Hinklefrump of Dawson lost his copy of the letter and was fired within a month. Marlena Beauchamp of Lennoxville broke her ankle in a freak accident while tossing a salad only days after throwing her copy away."

- "My last three blind dates have been bombs. This one's bound to be better!"

- A poll is conducted to find out what students think of their university newspaper. A sample is taken in the cafeteria on a Tuesday between 8:00 a.m. and noon. Every fifth person who enters the cafeteria is asked his or her opinion. The results find that 72 percent of the students are highly critical of the newspaper. The student government decides to use these results to revamp the editorial board.

- Professor Gill, wishing to improve her teaching, decides to poll her physics class. She commissions a questionnaire from one of her colleagues in statistics that satisfies all the criteria of a sound polling instrument. She calls each member of her class individually into her office and asks the student to complete the questionnaire. What is wrong with her polling methods?

- Survey question: "Which side do you think Canada should support in the Middle East: Israel or the Palestinians?"

- In 1997 the small town of Sulphur Springs experienced a 200 percent increase in auto theft, according to the Sulphur Springs *Weekly Standard*. This report was based on the fact that joy-riding teenagers stole three cars, compared to 1996, when only one car was stolen.

- "The tsunami in South Asia, Hurricane Katrina in the Gulf of Mexico and especially New Orleans, Louisiana, and the major earthquake in Pakistan and surrounding areas—three huge natural disasters in less than a year. And right around the time evolutionists started blocking the introduction of the teaching of intelligent design alongside the theory of evolution. Is our arrogant resistance to the proper way of considering the nature of our physical world turning against us in the most ironic manner? Is Nature itself teaching us moral consequences?"

- "No woman has the 'right' to an abortion. We don't have a right to do anything we want with our bodies. We can't use our bodies to hurt others. We can't sell our bodies into slavery, or deviance, such as prostitution. We can't even hurt 'just' our own bodies by way of heroin, cocaine, or other dangerous drugs. So the law is clear: We're not free to use our bodies in just any way. Draw the logical conclusion."

- "For three decades ('60s, 70s, 80s) the environmentalists, Greens, tree huggers—choose any epithet that suits your fancy but mainly descriptions of those who've ranted and railed against growth—have managed to defeat every attempt to modernize . . . transportation to handle the growing load. I would like to point out that sticking your head in the sand and saying you're against growth simply won't cut the mustard. You cannot pass a law (urban growth boundaries) against growth; stupid even to think of it. If you can manage to come up with an elixir that can be delivered in the water system a la Big Brother, which will prevent human sexuality, then you can slow growth."[10]

EXERCISE 12.9 *Essay Assignment:* At the beginning of this chapter is a cartoon in which a bunch of dubious "irrefutable" evidence of a UFO landing is presented. Which particular fallacies does this cartoon illustrate?

EXERCISE 12.10 *Essay Assignment:* In frame 11 of the *Peanuts* episode in this chapter, used to illustrate the fallacy of invincible ignorance, Lucy makes reference to medical history. See if you can explain why her argument is not (repeat: NOT) an instance of the informal fallacy of arguing from ignorance.

EXERCISE 12.11 *Essay Assignment:* Read the following commentary from the magazine *The Nation* in which the author makes several distinct criticisms of the general interpretation and reception of a published sociological/psychological study. Explain and evaluate each of these criticisms, using the concepts and terms offered in this chapter.

"In 1989 [Judith] Wallerstein published a [longitudinal] study [of 131 children whose parents had divorced in 1971] claiming that almost half had experienced serious long-term psychological problems that interfered with their love and work lives. This summer she released an update based on twenty-six of these young adults, all of whom had been 2–6 years old when their parents separated. They had been extremely vulnerable to drug and alcohol abuse as teens, she reported, and were still plagued in their 20s and 30s by unstable relationships with their fathers, low educational achievement and severe anxieties about commitment.

But there is good reason to worry about the massive publicity accorded Wallerstein's work. Her estimates of the risks of divorce are more than twice as high as those of any other reputable researcher in the field. Her insistence that the problems she finds were caused by the divorce itself, rather than by pre-existing problems in the marriage, represents an oversimplified notion of cause and effect repudiated by most social scientists and contradicted by her own evidence. Wallerstein studied 60 . . . couples, mostly white and affluent, who divorced in 1971. Her sample was drawn from families referred to her clinic because they were already experiencing adjustment problems. Indeed, participants were recruited by the offer of counseling in exchange for commitment to a long-term study. This in itself casts serious doubt on the applicability of Wallerstein's findings. The people most likely to be attracted to an offer of long-term counseling and most likely to stick with it over many years are obviously those most likely to feel they need it. And after twenty-five years in a study about the effects of divorce, the children are unlikely to consider any alternative explanations of the difficulties they have had in their lives.

Wallerstein admits that only one-third of the families she worked with were assessed as having 'adequate psychological functioning' prior to divorce. Half the parents had chronic depression, severe neurotic difficulties or 'long-standing problems controlling their rage or sexual impulses.' Nearly a quarter of the couples reported that there had been violence in their marriages. It is thus likely that many of the problems since experienced by their children stemmed from the parents' bad marriages rather than their divorces, and would not have been averted had the couples stayed together. Other researchers studying children who do poorly after divorce have found that behavior problems were often already evident eight to twelve years before the divorce took place, suggesting that both the maladjustment and divorce were symptoms of more deep-rooted family and parenting issues."[11]

▍ **EXERCISE 12.12** *Essay Assignment:* Read the following business case in which the writer *explains* several distinct informal fallacies involved in a particular advertising campaign. Can *you* explain each of these fallacies, using the concepts and terms presented in this chapter?

"Everyone loves a sale. Americans have become so used to discounts houses and the lower prices resulting from competition that many people are reluctant to pay the full price for any item. As a result, sales have become more common. But the notion of a 'sale' implies that the item originally sold at a higher price. For how long must it have been sold at that price, and must a store actually have sold any of the item at that price for the item to be legitimately labeled as being 'on sale'? What are customer expectations in this regard, and what constitutes deception? These are not easy questions to answer. The Federal Trade Commission 1964 Guides Against Deceptive Pricing states that before a store can claim that an item is on sale at a reduced price it must have been for sale at its regular price 'for a reasonably substantial period of time . . . honestly and in good faith and not for the purpose of establishing a fictitious higher price.'

May D&F is owned by May Department Stores, Inc., which operates fourteen department store chains. May D&F is not the only store that has been cited for the practices involved in the case, but whereas most stores settle out of court, May D&F defended its case in court. Before being officially charged, it had discussed its policies and its disagreement with the state law department for about a year. The store was officially charged in June 1989. Three counts involved printing inflated prices on its tags, inflating its prices to make its markdowns look larger than they were, and keeping merchandise on continuous sale. As examples, one set of cutlery had been on sale for two years; luggage was continuously sold at a 'special introductory price'; and bedding was kept on sale for eight months.

May D&F claimed that its policy was to offer an item for sale for at least ten days at the beginning of each six-month period. That would establish the original price. Few items sold at that price, which was usually not competitive. The store would then place the item on sale for the remaining 170 days, sometimes offering special soft-term reductions from that price. At the end of the 180-day cycle, it would raise the price to the original price for ten days, and then repeat the cycle. In August 1989, two months after the court case began, it revised its policy so as to charge the original price for 28 out of every 90 days. It further claimed that in a survey 90 percent of its customers did not care whether the item had actually been sold at the original price.

On June 28, 1990, Judge Larry J. Naves of the Colorado State Court decided the case against May D&F, stating that "The clear expectation of May D&F was to sell all or practically all merchandise at its 'sale' price." He fined the company $8,000."[12]

EXERCISE 12.13   At the end of Chapter 11 you were challenged to critique the argument in your original 100-word "Position Statement" (Exercise 10.18). Has your position changed at all as a result of this process? If so, your argument will need revisions. So, when those have been accomplished, reanalyze your own argument. Then ask yourself, "Is my argument open to any of the kinds of criticisms— does it commit any of the fallacies—we have just studied in Chapter 12?"

GLOSSARY

ad ignorantiam   fallacy of inferring a statement from the absence of evidence or lack of proof of its opposite

bad base line   fallacy of statistical inference based on an inappropriate basis of comparison

begging the question   fallacy of assuming or presupposing one's conclusion as a premise

biased method   any method, such as a loaded question, that distorts a statistical study

causal oversimplification   variety of causal fallacy in which significant causal factors or variables are overlooked

circular reasoning   another name for "begging the question"

common cause   variety of causal fallacy in which one of two effects of some common cause is taken to cause the other

correlation   an observed or established statistical regularity, sometimes fallaciously thought to establish a causal connection

false dilemma   fallacy of underestimating or underrepresenting the number of possible alternatives for a given issue

gambler's fallacy   any of a variety of fallacies of inductive reasoning concerning estimating or beating the odds, often based on the use of past outcomes to predict the future outcome of chance events

innuendo   implying a judgment, usually derogatory, by hinting

invincible ignorance   fallacy of refusing to give due consideration to evidence that conflicts with what one is already committed to believing

post hoc   variety of causal fallacy in which order of events in time is taken to establish a cause and effect relationship

slippery slope   fallacy consisting of objecting to something on the grounds that it will lead, by dubious causal reasoning, to some unacceptable set of consequences

small sample   fallacy of statistical inference consisting of overestimating the statistical significance of evidence drawn from a small number of cases

suppressed evidence   persuasive strategy consisting of covering up available evidence that conflicts with an intended conclusion

unrepresentative sample   fallacy of statistical inference involving overestimating the statistical significance of evidence drawn from a sample of a particular kind

Go to http://www.criticalthinking1ce.nelson.com for additional study resources for this chapter.

ENDNOTES

[1] Woody Allen, *The Curse of the Jade Scorpion*. 2001. Allen's character, C.W. Briggs, protests his innocence after being caught in possession of stolen jewels.

[2] Cf. W. Fearnside and W. Holther, *Fallacy: The Counterfeit of Argument* (Englewood Cliffs, NJ: Prentice Hall, 1959), 167.

[3] Rush Limbaugh, *The Way Things Ought to Be* (New York: Simon and Schuster, 1992).

[4] Charles E. Trow, *The Old Shipmasters of Salem* (New York: Macmillan, 1905), 14–15.

[5] For example, see the following Government of Canada website: http://www11.hrdc-drhc.gc.ca/pls/edd/QEE_78017.htm

[6] Dan Gardner, "You can't trust the drug 'experts'." *The Ottawa Citizen,* Tuesday, April 13, 2004, A17.

[7] Elliott Sober, *Core Questions in Philosophy,* 3rd ed. (Englewood Cliffs, NJ: Prentice Hall, 2000).

[8] Rush Limbaugh, *The Way Things Ought to Be* (New York: Simon and Schuster, 1992).

[9] *Time,* October 22, 1979, 57.

[10] Letter to the Editor, *Sonoma County Independent,* February 12, 1998.

[11] Reprinted with permission from the November 17, 1997 issue of *The Nation*. For subscription information call 1-800-333-8536. Portions of each week's Nation magazine can be accessed at http://www.thenation.com.

[12] DEGEORGE, RICHARD, BUSINESS ETHICS, WITH CD, 6th Edition, © 2006. Adapted by permission of Pearson Education, Inc., Upper Saddle River, NJ.

Making Your Case: Argumentative Composition

I write because I don't know what I think until I read what I say.   FLANNERY O'CONNOR

At the beginning of this book we discussed the importance of critical thinking for both personal autonomy and democratic citizenship. As you will recall, our example in the opening pages of this book concerned Canada's troubled political state of affairs at the federal level. At the culmination of our course of study in critical thinking it is appropriate to reflect again on these crucial and connected ideas. An adequate measure of personal autonomy is, of course, fundamental to the ordinary person's conception of a good life, on the assumption that self-directedness and self-responsibility contribute to personal well-being. In addition, for example, Aristotle emphasized the relation between individual flourishing and the health of the community's life.

Let us now focus on the important connection between personal autonomy—the ability to use one's reasoning capability to govern and regulate oneself, to make up one's own mind rationally—and democratic citizenship. The good functioning—and hence the health and very survival—of a free society depends

© The New Yorker Collection 1996 Charles Barsotti from cartoonbank.com. All rights reserved.

"It's plotted out. I just have to write it."

on an intellectually autonomous citizenry. If individual citizens are unprepared to make up their own minds on a rational basis, the collective decision-making processes of the society will be disabled and misguided as a consequence—and will therefore become vulnerable to corruption. The citizenry of a free society that loses its grounding in the "art of reasoning" may expect one day to find its institutions (such as Parliament) and processes (such as elections) corrupted and no longer reliable or effective in serving the public interest. It is better to regain some command of the art of reasoning than to hope blindly that all will be well. Reasonable judgments and decisions do not create themselves—committed individuals and communities do.

Suppose that you have taken this message to heart and are now ready to engage as a citizen in the political processes of your community. Suppose that you care enough about some local issue to go to a city council meeting and witness the process of public deliberation. Suppose a period for public comment presents an opportunity for you to speak. Now suppose you care enough about the issue that you would like to take a turn at the microphone and address the city council members and your fellow citizens. What are you prepared to say?

EXERCISE 13.1 | **Field Trip**

In fact, let's move this out of the realm of the purely hypothetical. Pick some local organization or civic body that holds open public meetings in your community. It could be a city or town council, a local school board, the board of governors of your university, a provincial legislature. Go to a meeting (or two). Witness the process of deliberation. Pay close attention to how decisions are actually made. How is discussion handled? Is opportunity afforded for direct public response to the discussion? What role is assigned to argumentation in the discussion? Find out what issues are coming up on the agenda. See if you can find an issue somewhere in your community that matters to you and is scheduled to come up for discussion and deliberate resolution.

We try to get our students to think along these lines to help them understand and appreciate the value of what they are learning in critical thinking. In the context of living as a member of a free society with the right to free inquiry, what critical thinking provides can be understood and appreciated as follows. Suppose you are about to take your turn at the microphone at a public meeting where an issue of real concern to you is under discussion. Naturally, you want your contribution to the discussion to be treated with respect. Critical thinking is what makes it possible for you to make the kind of contribution *that commands the respectful attention of others* who are interested in the issue, whether or not they share your views. What kind of contribution will command respectful attention in an open discussion of an issue of common interest and concern? Answer: a good argument. An argument, as we defined it in Chapter 3 and have understood it throughout this book, is a composition intended to persuade one's audience by appeal to reason. A *good* argument, whether it is presented as a written composition, as a prepared speech, or "extemporaneously,"[1] will be one that is well suited to the function of persuasion by appeal to reason. It will be a composition that is well informed, well designed as an argument, and well presented.

As much as we might wish it to be otherwise, no reliable shortcuts exist here. A *good* argument is almost always the result of a sustained investment of effort in which all the general areas and many of the specific concepts and skills covered in our study of critical thinking are usefully applied. For this reason, a standing assignment in some critical thinking classes is a sustained project focused on some significant issue, where the work of the project involves research, argument identification, argument analysis, argument evaluation, argument design, and written composition. The finished "work product" is an argumentative essay—or, to put it more plainly, a good argument presented in writing. In this final chapter, we will discuss the composition of an argumentative essay by way of this sort of project.

THE ISSUE STATEMENT

The project begins, of course, with the selection of an issue. Sometimes instructors select an issue as the common focus for the class; sometimes instructors allow the class to select the issue; or sometimes instructors allow each student to select his or her own issue. In any case, attention should fall on issues that would score high on both media visibility (the likelihood of the issue coming under public discussion in the media) and public importance (how much does—or *should*—the issue matter to the general public).

Similarly, an argumentative essay ordinarily begins with a statement of the issue that it will address. The introduction to an argumentative essay should orient the reader to and attract the reader's interest in the topic. At the end of Chapter 1 (Exercise 1.28) you were encouraged to draft a one-page issue statement. Let us now return to that assignment and process it more deeply.

EXERCISE 13.2 | Issues and Disputes: Review

Review the section in Chapter 1 entitled "Looking Ahead: Issues and Disputes."

We propose to evaluate issue statements according to three criteria: articulation, balance, and clarity (ABC—a handy mnemonic acronym). We will comment on each of these criteria in turn, but in reverse order.

CLARITY

In one sense, clarity is the easiest of the three criteria to explain and understand. Clear writing makes the ideas of the composition easy to grasp for the reader (or as easy as possible given the subject matter). Unclear writing—whether through vagueness, wordiness, poor structure, or some other feature—makes the reader struggle to identify and understand the message(s). Clarity applies as a criterion of evaluation not just to the issue statement but to the entire composition. When we evaluate a piece of writing for clarity, we ask, "Is the language used effectively to get the ideas across without confusion?" To the extent that this is so, the composition is clear. To the extent that this is not so, the clarity should be improved. Grammar, vocabulary, idiom, spelling—all play a role here. To check for clarity, we recommend having someone (preferably someone whose writing you respect or admire) read your draft. We will say a bit more about clarity shortly.

BALANCE

Since you are writing about an issue—a topic about which reasonable people may *disagree*—your initial statement of the issue should be "balanced." This means that your statement should not be prejudiced either in favour of or against any of the positions a reasonable person might be inclined to hold about the topic. You do not want to alienate any of your potential readers before they have a chance to consider your argument in its fullness. One of the best ways to achieve this balance is to make a clear distinction between your *issue* statement, in which you bring the topic into focus for your reader, and your *thesis* statement, in which you tell your reader where you stand on the issue. If you can present the issue in a balanced way, your reader will know you understand that room exists for reasonable disagreement on the matter and that you are capable of respectfully understanding divergent positions on the issue. This will encourage your reader to pay respectful attention to *your* argument.

ARTICULATION

As we explained in Chapter 1, articulation concerns the inherent complexity of issues. For any given issue many different ways exist to frame, focus, and organize the inquiry. What do we mean by "framing," "focusing," and "organizing" the inquiry? "Framing" the issue means situating it within a larger context and determining what will be considered within and what will be considered beyond the scope of the discussion. "Focusing" means determining what will be considered central and what will be considered peripheral within the scope of the discussion. "Organizing" refers to the order in which things will be considered. When you enter into a complex area of controversy, you need to make decisions about all these things to develop what we might call an *orderly agenda of inquiry.* This is what we mean by "articulation." An "articulate" issue statement is one that demonstrates careful consideration of how to frame, focus, and organize the discussion of the issue in its inherent complexity and that arrives at and clearly communicates an orderly agenda of inquiry. This is a challenging aspect of the process, but facing the challenge squarely at this early stage will greatly enhance your ability to maintain your bearings as you work your way through the complexity of the issue. It will also make your argument much easier to follow for your reader.

EXERCISE 13.3 | **Issue Statement: Revision**

Revise the issue statement you drafted in Exercise 1.28, paying special attention to the clarity, balance, and articulation of the statement.

Drafting the issue statement is a good way to begin the kind of project we are discussing here, as well as a good way to begin the argumentative essay that comes out of the project as the final "work product." Before we return to a discussion of other elements in the argumentative essay, let us explore the second of the preliminary stages of the project: research. Remember that in the end, a good argument will be a composition that is well informed. Thus, even from the earliest stages of articulating the issue, one of the most important ingredients of a good argument is the quality of the information that goes into it.

RESEARCH AND THE MEDIA

Once an appropriate issue has been selected, an early stage of the project involves research. *Research* means finding out something that we do not already know or know well enough. In researching an issue, we need to gain access to reliable information that is relevant to our topic, and more importantly, since our topic is the subject of debate and disagreement among reasonable people, we need to gain access to arguments of a reasonably high standard representing the range of opinion on our topic. We live in what has come to be known as the Age of

Information. Among the many meanings this label carries with it is the idea that we have unprecedented access to information. Individually and collectively we can now gather, collect, store, sort, process, transmit, and receive more information more quickly than at any previous time in human history. This is both a blessing and a curse for research. The fact that information is so readily available is obviously useful to research. In an information-rich environment such as ours, however, we can easily get lost, distracted, and overwhelmed by the sheer volume of information available. Perhaps even more importantly, we need practical means of assessing the reliability of the information available to us.

Over the last several decades we have seen profound changes in the way research is conducted. A generation ago (when the authors of this book were in university) research meant going to the card catalogue—a paper device—in the university library. The information and the arguments filled books (or periodicals) that were housed in the library and listed in the card catalogue. You simply went there, looked up the items by subject, found them in the stacks, and took them home and read them. Today the library is still the first and best place to go to do research. Now, though, the information and the arguments are located in all kinds of media—not just print—and all over the place—not necessarily housed in the physical library building. Today you can "go to the library" via the Internet. The Age of Information has made do-it-yourself research an easy undertaking, undoubtedly a good thing in itself. At the same time, however, the Age of Information has raised some "quality-control issues" for the do-it-yourself researcher. With so much information so readily available, how can we be sure that the information we are getting is reliable? How do we determine which of the many and often conflicting factual claims we may encounter in our research are accurate? How do we find among the arguments in wide circulation those that represent the broadest spectrum of opinion with the highest standard of reasoning? The best piece of general research advice we have to offer is this: Consult your university reference librarians. Make sure you have your issue clearly defined. Today, librarians are even more crucial as assistants to research than they were a generation ago. They are the university's experts in using new and increasingly powerful information technologies (such as InfoTrac College Edition) to sift through the mountains of information available on nearly any issue. Beyond this piece of general advice, it may be worth saying just a little bit about media, sources of information, reliability, and skepticism.

TELEVISION

In the picture on page 347 "Selectovision" by David Suter, a video camera operator is recording a man fleeing from an attacker with a knife, but the identities of attacker and victim are reversed in the video image. Thus, the artist makes the point that television is capable and often guilty of completely misrepresenting reality. This sort of scepticism about television is much deeper today and more commonplace than it has been throughout most of the medium's short history. We would do well to consider the reasons for this sort of scepticism not only about television but about other sources of information as well.

Used by permission of David Suter.

"Selectovision"

Although the technology was already emerging in the 1920s, television really came into its own after World War II. During the 1950s, television quickly became a dominant communications medium throughout the industrialized world and was widely accepted as a generally reliable source of information. This may be partly attributable to the technology's ability to record and transmit audiovisual imagery of events taking place in real time. It may also be partly attributable to the "realism" of television programming. ("The camera does not lie.") Viewed as a technology and an information medium, television has always had immense potential for human society. It is a highly flexible medium that is able to accommodate information in a wide range of forms, from spoken word, to music, to moving visual imagery, to graphic text—in all manner of combinations. Once programmed, its messages engage the perceiving subject simultaneously through multiple sense modalities, thus giving television unusually high power to attract and hold attention. With the enhancement of general transmission and reception technology, fibre optics, and cable and satellite methods of delivery, television makes possible the instantaneous transmission and reception of huge quantities of audiovisual information on a global basis. Now an international audience of almost any size can witness a significant event—for example, the intense drama of the second hijacked airplane crashing into the North Tower of the World Trade Center on September 11, 2001—as it is occurring (as well as over and over again after the fact).

Even as television technology has become more elaborate and powerful, though, television audiences have become more sophisticated and are coming to understand television not only as a technology and an information medium, but also as a business, indeed a vast industry. Through this process of growth and maturation, television audiences have come to see through certain naïve illusions and become more sceptical, perhaps even cynical. For example, we have all heard the expression "brought to you through the courtesy of . . ." many times on television. Here we are encouraged to understand television as a free entertainment and information service. In its basic form, entertainment and information are delivered to the public free of charge, and Coca-Cola, or McCain, or any of a plethora of advertisers pays for this service. From the vantage of the audience (the vantage most of us occupy), this is no doubt a comfortable way to understand television's institutional role—but it completely misrepresents the economics of the industry. From within the television industry such a description makes no sense at all. Why in the world would the makers of Coca-Cola want to pour money into providing a free entertainment and information service for millions of people?

What the makers of Coca-Cola are purchasing, of course, is public attention. What is really going on is that *we* (the audience) are being brought to *them* (the sponsors) by, for example, CBC. Viewed in these terms, television's primary function in our culture has been as a tool for harvesting public attention for sale in the public-attention market. The primary function of television programming is to round up an audience and hold that audience in place in a receptive attitude (what the industry calls a "buying mood") for the sponsor's message. This explains why television programming is nearly 100 percent entertainment and why the boundaries and distinctions between entertainment (showbiz) and public-service programming (journalism) have gotten blurrier and blurrier. Television audiences are more acutely aware of this nowadays. When we see major network news anchors and journalists make celebrity guest appearances on late-night talk shows, we start to realize that television news is as much a part of showbiz as *Canadian Idol*.

MASS MEDIA

During the 19th century, industrial expansion created so-called economies of scale in many areas of enterprise, including journalism. This meant that the capital costs of acquiring, maintaining, and operating a large industrialized printing press, and the associated need to reach a more and more massive audience, rose by several orders of magnitude. In such a business climate, large businesses dominate, and small businesses get eaten or die. As these trends progress, ownership and control grow increasingly concentrated and further removed from the community. Fewer and fewer, and larger and larger corporations come to control more and more of the flow of information, while small local independent voices are lost. These trends have been studied and documented by media scholar Ben Bagdikian, a Pulitzer Prize-winning journalist and former journalism dean, who writes:

A handful of mammoth private organizations have begun to dominate the world's mass media. Most of them confidently announce that by the 1990's they—five to ten corporate giants—will control most of the world's important newspapers, magazines, books, broadcast stations, movies, recordings and videocassettes. Moreover, each of these planetary corporations plans to gather under its control every step in the information process, from creation of "the product" to all the various means by which modern technology delivers media messages to the public. "The product" is news, information, ideas, entertainment and popular culture; the public is the whole world.[2]

The public is also increasingly aware that the major media, because they are big businesses, have interests to advance and protect which may interfere and conflict with the public interest in access to relevant and accurate information. This applies not just to television but also to the major media generally. Professional journalists who work in the industry are well aware of this potential for conflict of interest as an issue of professional ethics, and the best of them are indeed capable of "biting the hand that feeds them." The public is, however, still right to be sceptical.

Another factor contributing to growing public scepticism is an accumulating history of political and corporate scandal. Adscam, pedophilia in the priesthood, corporate accounting scandals, and similar events, each one with its own series of cover-ups and evasive press conferences, have had the cumulative effect of undermining public trust and confidence in many important social institutions, including the press. The public is now increasingly aware that political press conferences and briefings are "public-relations events" planned and orchestrated to manage public opinion. In short, we have good reason to be sceptical of information made available through the major media and standard outlets and to wonder what may really be going on behind the scenes. A danger exists that we may become so cynical as to suspect the worst at all times and to trust no one, ever. This is a form of intellectual paralysis and something we ought to avoid. We should remember that the events underlying at least some of these scandals (for instance, the pedophile priests) were brought to light through good old-fashioned hard-nosed investigative journalism. Instead of becoming cynical and refusing to trust or believe anything we hear or read, we should become sceptical consumers of information. This means actively seeking out information (rather than passively receiving it) and questioning and challenging the information as it comes in to us (rather than simply accepting it as reliable).

THE INTERNET

The Internet provides an excellent environment within which to practise and develop good habits of active scepticism in research. One reason for this is the *importance* of active scepticism in researching the World Wide Web. When the first edition of this book was published in the 1980s, the Internet was not much more than an obscure and geeky experiment, and the World Wide Web as we now know it did not even exist until well into the 1990s. The Internet is the world's largest and fastest growing computer and communications network, a development that has already brought huge changes in information access generally, and promises more and perhaps even bigger changes to come, especially concerning research and education.

Once connected to the Net, you can gain access to information stored on computers literally all over the world. With a few additional tools and steps you can also publish information to the whole world via the Internet. It is little wonder that so much excitement surrounds the Internet. This is Very Impressive Technology. It literally opens up a "World of Information" on any imaginable subject from astronomy to Zen. You can get into the world's great libraries; you can get into government files and databases; and you can get detailed, up-to-the-minute weather information, celebrity gossip, sports scores, and stock quotations from any part of the world, and on and on. So vast and dynamic is this information environment that it has spawned a gigantically profitable new industry devoted to maintaining up-to-date Internet databases and constructing computer programs called "search engines" to assist people with Internet research.

Anyone with a computer and an Internet connection can publish on the Internet. Many Internet enthusiasts point to this as an indication of the Internet's democratizing potential. By eliminating barriers to publication and wide dissemination, the Internet seems to enhance freedom of speech and expression and freedom of access to information, yet at the same time it raises some of those "quality-control issues" we mentioned earlier. If you look up information about the human genome project in the *New England Journal of Medicine* or the *Journal of the American Medical Association,* you can be confident in the reliability of the information. Why? These and other reputable scientific or academic journals are unusually careful about what they let into their pages, using rigorous peer review processes designed to maintain high standards of accuracy and integrity. On the other hand, no editorial board screens web pages. Anybody—and this includes crackpots and hustlers—can put up a web page. Those who do put up a web page do not have to know what they are doing. They do not need any credentials. They do not have to check their facts. Not only can they put up web pages—they can make it *look* as "professional" as an official University of Toronto web page. So, Internet surfers need to beware: Although the Internet is an abundant information resource, the "garbage-to-good-stuff" ratio is much higher on the Internet than in the Expanded Academic Index.

So, we have to do the evaluation. Many institutional or organizational websites include statements about the type and source of information provided on their web pages, as well as the purpose of the organization itself. If this information is *not* offered, be especially careful when evaluating the data you find there. Here are a few commonsense questions to ask:[3]

CRITICAL THINKING TIP 13.1

Be an "Active Sceptic" in research. Ask questions such as:

- *What are the sources of the information?* Where did the information originate? Who put it there?

  Where to Look: On a web page, look near the top of the page. Check the title, the section headings, and the opening paragraphs to see if some person or organization is named as the person(s) responsible for the content of the web pages. Also look near the bottom of the page for this information. (Keep in mind that the webmaster, or person who designed the web page, is not necessarily the person responsible for the content of the page.)

You can sometimes learn something about the source of a web page by examining the page's URL (the page's address or location on the Internet). The URL often indicates the type of organization and from what country a web page originates.

If you cannot find any information about the author(s) on the page you are viewing, click on "Home," or erase the last part of the URL for the page in your web browser's address bar. Delete from the very end of the URL backwards to the first slash mark("/"), then press the Return or Enter key on your keyboard. If you still do not see any information about the author(s), back up one more directory or slash mark. Keep going until you come to a page that identifies the author(s) of these pages.

- *How authoritative is the source?* What qualifications does this person or organization have to address this topic? Does the author have a university degree in the discipline? Is she or he an amateur, a hobbyist, or merely someone with an opinion to air? If an organization is responsible for the pages, is the organization widely recognized as a source of scholarly and reliable information? (For example, the Canadian Cancer Society is a reliable source of information on cancer-related topics.) What other information can you find about the author or organization responsible for the content of the web page?

  Where to Look: Look near the top and the bottom of the web page. Do you see a link to more information about the person or organization?

  For organizations, you will often see a link called "About Us" or something similar that leads to a page explaining the organization's mission, when and how it was founded, and so forth. Read it for clues.

  For a single person or author, you might find information about the person's educational background, his or her research, or other qualifications for speaking on this topic. You might see a link to his or her faculty or professional web pages.

  Look for links to articles and publications by the person or organization. Look for an address or a phone number by which you could contact the author(s) if so desired.

  If you cannot find any information about the author(s) on the web page, erase the last part of the URL for the page in your web browser's address bar as described above. Keep going until you come to a page that has more information about the person or organization responsible for the pages. Remember: A URL that has a ~ (called a "tilde") in it is almost always someone's personal home page, as distinct from an organization's official page.

  If you cannot find any information about the author(s) anywhere on the web pages, try searching for the person or organization's name using an Internet search engine to see whether you can find related web pages elsewhere. Check some library catalogues and magazine or newspaper databases to see whether the person or organization has published books or articles in the field.

  If you can find no information at all about the web page's author(s), be wary. If you cannot verify that the information is authoritative, do not use it in a class paper or project.

- *What is the purpose of the document?* Does the author claim this page to be factual? Is she or he trying to persuade you of something? To whom is the author of this page speaking? To scholars and experts? To students? To anyone who will listen? Is the author trying to sell you a product discussed on the page? Does the page include advertising? If so, can you tell clearly which parts are advertisement and which parts are informational content? Does the page remind you of a television "infomercial"; that is, does it look like an informational article while actually serving as an advertisement?

Where to Look: If the author or organization has provided an "About Us" page, you can probably determine something about the web page's purpose by reading about the mission of the organization.

- *How "straightforward" is the source?* Does the author or the organization she or he represents have an identifiable vested interest or an obvious bias concerning the topic? Does the author or the organization represent a particular point of view? (For example, the Roman Catholic Church, the National Action Committee on the Status of Women, R. J. Reynolds Tobacco, the Conservative or Green Party, etc.) If you do not know the answer to this question, be sure to read the "About Us" page. If the author does have a vested interest, or particular point of view, is this made clear or is there an attempt to obscure it?

Where to Look: Does the page use inflammatory language, images, or graphic styles (for example, huge red letters or a lot of boldface type) to try to persuade you of the author's point of view?

Examine the URL to see where the web page originates. Is it a commercial site (.com or .biz)? A nonprofit organization (.org)? An educational institution (.edu)? Think again about the person or organization's mission or charge as you read about it in the "About Us" link.

Try some of the same approaches you used to determine the authority of the information source; for example, look for the name of the author(s) using one of the web search engines to see whether you can find other identifying information. Is the organization an advocacy group; that is, one that advocates for a particular cause or point of view?

- *How current is the information?* Can you tell when the web page was originally created? When it was last updated? Is this a topic for which you must have up-to-date information (science, medicine, news, etc.), or is it one where currentness is not as important (history, literature, etc.)?

Where to Look: Look near the top and the bottom of the page to see whether any publication date, copyright date, or "date last modified" is indicated.

Look for other indications that the page is kept current. Do you see a "What's New" section? If statistical data or charts are included, be especially careful to notice what dates are represented there and when the data was collected or published.

Good habits of active scepticism should be applied also in researching newspapers and other periodical literature. One can ask questions similar to those in Critical Thinking Tip 13.1 about the authors and editors of these more traditional sources of information. Who are the authors and editors? What are their qualifications? Did the information they present originate with them, or are they just passing it along? Are they acting with integrity in their capacity as authors and editors? Do they have an "agenda"? Do they have any general political orientation or bias? Are they open and forthright about any such agenda or orientation or bias, or do they try to hide it? Approaching all sources of information in this way will enable you to gather reliable information much more effectively and to weed out the nonsense.

THE THESIS STATEMENT

Let us now return to the matter of composing an argumentative essay. By the time you get to this stage, you should have a pretty good idea of where you stand on the issue you have been considering. The introduction to your argumentative essay should accomplish two essential goals: (1) orienting and interesting your reader in your topic (your issue statement should accomplish this goal); and (2) letting your reader know where you stand. Your "thesis statement" should accomplish this second goal. The word *thesis* comes from Greek and means "proposed idea." As it is used in the discipline of writing, the thesis is the main idea of an essay or longer composition. If the composition is an argumentative essay, the thesis will be in the position of the conclusion of the argument, supported by other ideas that you will present as premises. The essential difference between the thesis statement and the issue statement is that balance is no longer a relevant criterion of assessment. Your thesis statement should be clear and articulate, but it does not need to be "balanced."

As we just said, by the time you come to write an argumentative essay, you *should* have a reasonably clear idea of where you stand. Ideally, your current convictions about the issue will have resulted from the work you have by now invested in researching the issue, finding the arguments both in favour of and against the various positions along the spectrum of opinion, and analyzing and evaluating those arguments. Even after doing all this work, however, many people find formulating a thesis quite an intimidating challenge. This may be because they recognize the risks inherent in taking a position in an area of controversy. "People will disagree with me. I will be called upon to defend my position with an argument. I have no idea yet how I shall argue for my position. What if I'm wrong?" Do not let any of this paralyze you. Yes, people will disagree with you. Yes, you will be called upon to defend your position with an argument. At this stage, though, even if you have no idea yet how the argument will go, you still have time to figure it out. Remember that you are not required to opt for either one of the two "extreme" or "polar" positions along the spectrum of opinion on your issue (if this is how the public debate on the matter has been structured). Indeed, you are not restricted to choosing among positions that have been formulated and articulated by others. You are free to be original and creative and to propose a new "compromise" position if you can think of one. Finally, if you *are* wrong, nothing prevents you from changing your mind and correcting your position. So go ahead and be honest with yourself about where you stand on the subject, and write that down. This is a draft of your thesis statement.

EXERCISE 13.4 | **Thesis Statement**

At the end of Chapter 10 you were challenged to write a 100-word "position statement" (Exercise 10.18), which we expect will contain an argument. Through Chapters 11 and 12 you were prompted to analyze, critique, and revise that argument. Now, draft a thesis statement in 100 words or less. Just the thesis—just what you will go on to support with your argument.

ARGUMENT DESIGN

In general, good argument design flows from a clear and detailed understanding of both the thesis and the issue to which the thesis responds. Depending upon the precise nature of the issue, the subsidiary issues involved in it, and the claim one is defending as one's thesis, different argument design strategies will be more or less viable and promising. The kind of argument we might need to design to support and defend a value judgment effectively may not work so well to support and defend a causal hypothesis. One general principle for argument design, therefore, is simply to study your issue closely and analytically, letting your insights into its character and complexities guide you to a deeper awareness of the strengths and vulnerabilities of your position. Make your argument as logical as you can. If you can, build an argument that is deductively valid. If you cannot find or devise valid deductive support for your thesis, perhaps one or more of the varieties of inductive reasoning will be applicable. In any case, make full use of what you have learned about argument analysis and evaluation in designing your argument. Of course, be careful not to fall into any fallacious patterns or tendencies.

OUTLINING

As you build your case you will want to ensure that your argument hangs together and that your thesis is convincingly and legitimately supported. An excellent device for testing the web of logical relationships in your essay—as well as for guiding and controlling the work of composition—is an outline of your argument. Many student writers (and nonstudent writers, for that matter) fail to exploit fully the outline as an argument design tool. We have seen quite a few outlines that go no further than this:

    I. Introduction

        A. My issue statement

        B. My thesis statement

    II. Body

        A. Reasons in favour of my position

    III. Conclusion

This is *not* what we mean by an outline of your argument. You can do much better. To get the most out of your outline, you will want to go into much greater depth and detail. Concentrate on the argument you are building. Break down item II (Body) further. What *are* the reasons in favour of your position? Be specific. How are those reasons related to each other? What evidence supports those reasons? What positions do you oppose? What are your objections to those opposing positions? Be specific. What objections can you anticipate arising out of those opposing positions? How will you respond to such objections? Be specific. Make sure to define key terms and concepts. Be conscious of the need to support your claims with facts and to illustrate your points with examples. All this material needs to be placed in some order so that your reader can follow your train of thought through your composition. One the most basic functions of outlining is to allow you to think through these details of your argument and get them organized, without at the same time having to work out all the subtleties of wording and presentation that will eventually go into the finished composition. Outlining is a flexible tool. You can use it before *or* after you have written a draft—better yet, use outlining both before *and* after. Use outlining as a tool in *revising* what you have written.

APPRECIATE YOUR OPPONENT'S POSITION

Because your thesis responds to an issue, and because issues are by definition topics about which reasonable people may disagree, your thesis will be debatable to some extent. A second general principle for argument design flows from this, and from the fact that in arguing for your thesis you are essentially trying to be persuasive, to win over your audience. Try to identify premises that are less controversial, less subject to debate, than your thesis. In other words, try to find "common ground" on which to base your argument for your thesis.

This second general principle of argument design suggests some further ideas about argument design and construction. The medieval philosopher and theologian Thomas Aquinas once remarked that when you want to convert someone to your view, you go over to where he is standing, take him by the hand (mentally speaking), and guide him to where you want him to go. You do not stand across the room and shout at him, or call him nasty names, or order him to come over to where you are. You start where he is and work from that position. To put it another way: When you think that someone is wrong and you disagree with her, you should first try to figure out in what way(s) she is right. This is not as paradoxical as it sounds. Suppose you are firmly convinced of some particular position on a complex and controversial subject, such as the death penalty. Are you absolutely certain that you are 100 percent correct? Can you be absolutely certain that those who disagree with you are entirely wrong in everything they might have to say? Would it not be wiser to consider thoughtfully what your opponent might have to say and concede as much as you honestly can? Then when you go on to offer criticisms of your opponent's position, you can reasonably expect to be given thoughtful consideration as well. After all, think about how you would react as a reader to a criticism of your position. If the criticism starts out by identifying your position as out to lunch, you are not likely to be highly receptive, are you? You would be much more open to a criticism that began by stating your position in a way that you would yourself state it, recognizing its intuitive plausibility, its explanatory power, the weight of evidence in its favour, or whatever strengths it may have. If you are going to criticize someone else's argument or position, make sure you state it so that *they* know you have fairly and accurately understood it.

OBJECTIONS AND REPLIES

Just as you should be aware of the possibility that your opponent's position may embody certain strengths, you also should be aware of the possibility that your own position may have certain weaknesses—weaknesses that likely will be more apparent to your opponent than to you. Thus, an additional strategic advantage for the writer of an argumentative essay flows from making a genuine attempt to appreciate the opponent's position. Your opponent's position affords you a much better perspective from which to troubleshoot your own position and argument—to make yourself aware of where your argument needs additional support or where the thesis itself needs to be qualified or refined.

EXERCISE 13.5 | **Outline Your Argument**

Based on your issue statement as revised in Exercise 13.3 and your thesis statement in Exercise 13.4, outline your argument.

THE PRESENTATION

So much good advice is already available about writing and how to get better at it that for us to offer any such advice of our own here would seem to be either a redundant waste of time, arrogant, or both.[4] Do we have anything new and distinctive to add to what the many courses, tutorials, books, tapes, websites, and consultants on becoming a better writer have to offer? We probably do not, but we are not going to let that stop us. We will, however, try to keep this to the point.

Back in Chapter 1 we made a quick comparison, almost in passing, between thinking and writing. We talked about discipline. Our point there was that even though learning a discipline (such as writing, or critical thinking, or music—our other example) involves the mastery of rules and regularities through extensive practice, you still have room to develop your own distinctive individual style. This is important because writing is a means of self-expression. We would be rightly disappointed if to learn how to express ourselves effectively in words we each had to wind up sounding exactly like everybody else. At the same time, just as you can keep on developing and refining your thinking throughout your life by disciplined study, so, too, can you continue to improve your writing, getting better and better with more and more disciplined practice even as you get more and more distinctive in your individual style as a writer.

In Chapter 2 we began our exploration of language by remarking on its amazing flexibility and power as a tool kit for communication. One can accomplish *so many* different things, and undertake so many different tasks, through the use of language. Accordingly, many different kinds of writing exist. What makes for a good piece of writing of one kind (poetry, or a sermon) may not serve well at all the purposes of some other kind of writing (say, a software user manual). We generally do better as writers when we are guided by an understanding of the specific goals of the kind of writing we are creating. Composing an argumentative essay is a rather specialized application of writing. It requires and also helps us to build language skills of certain kinds in certain ways. Some of these skills should come as no surprise, since they have occupied centre stage throughout this course of study and all derive from the function of an argument: to persuade by appeal to reason.

RELEVANCE

We have a friend who tells endless stream-of-consciousness stories. He might start out by saying, "Do you remember Sally so and so from high school? Well, I ran into her the other day in the parking lot outside the supermarket, and she had just been to the deli. You know they have this new deli in the supermarket and they make the greatest pasta salad. They use pine nuts. That's the secret ingredient. And smoothies! You know, since they started making smoothies, I seem to have to go in there every single day! Smoothies have changed my life! But you know I think they've started using less frozen yogurt and more ice. Don't you just hate when they do that? Take some good thing, and just when people start to catch on, raise the price or something. Like my cell phone company . . ." And on and on he goes. We got to the point of taking bets as to whether the story would ever wander back around to Sally so and so from high school.

Try not to write like this. This kind of improvised discourse is acceptable around the campfire—though even there it can be exasperating—but not when you are composing an argumentative essay. Know where you are headed, and go there. Do not wander or interrupt yourself or go off on tangents. If something suddenly occurs to you as an important point that should not be left out, try to find the place in the argument where it is most relevant and insert it there so that the orderly flow of the reasoning is preserved. This is one of the most important applications of outlining. You do not want to leave out anything important, but you do want to present it all in good order.

CARE AND PRECISION IN CHOOSING AND DEFINING TERMS

This precision applies throughout the entire composition. Suppose your issue is "terrorism." Naturally, you will want to define the term *terrorism*. It is not enough, though, just to define the word if in so doing you do not *choose the terms in the definition with great care and precision.* Many students seem unaware of this—or at least this is how it sometimes seems when one reads their essays and notices the general carelessness with which words and phrases are often thrown around. If you do not know the difference in meaning between the words *credible* and *credulous,* you should not use either one. If you do not know the difference between *affect* and *effect,* or between *principal* and *principle,* do not just fake it by alternating between them. If you are not *absolutely certain* what the word you have in mind means, LOOK IT UP! Otherwise, how can you really know if you have made a good vocabulary choice? How can you really know if the word is going to work the way you need it to work in its context? How will you improve your vocabulary? The same holds true for idiomatic phrases. People often seem to shuffle these together like some kind of refrigerator-door poetry kit, ending up with accidental comedy such as, "We need to grab the bull by the tail and look the facts squarely in the eye." Trust us: This is not the effect you want to have on your reader.

CRITICAL THINKING TIP 13.2

How to use your spell checker: The spell checker we have in our word processor highlights <u>misspelled</u> words in red or underlines them. This is supposed to prompt us to revise the spelling. Instead of just tinkering with the spelling until the highlighting disappears, go to a dictionary and look up the word. Use this as an opportunity to learn more about the word.

ECONOMY OF EXPRESSION

Do not waste words. Do not pad your paper. Do not embellish. Many writing instructors advise their students to avoid repetitive use of the same terms throughout a single composition. You may have received such advice. The idea is to spice up the composition by using a variety of synonymous or roughly synonymous terms instead of consistently using the same ones. This may well be good advice if what you are writing is a short story or a travelogue or a biographical essay for a scholarship competition—but when you are writing an argumentative essay, you are trying to enlighten, not entertain. So, you should be more concerned about confusing than about boring your reader.

Also, avoid affectation. Do not try to sound as you think an academic scholar should sound. Academic scholarship, you might as well know, often presents a model of how *not* to write. Here, for example, is a recent winner of the "Bad Writing Contest" sponsored by the academic journal *Philosophy & Literature*.

> Indeed dialectical critical realism may be seen under the aspect of Foucauldian strategic reversal—of the unholy trinity of Parmenidean/Platonic/Aristotelean provenance; of the Cartesian-Lockean-Humean-Kantian paradigm, of foundationalisms (in practice, fideistic foundationalisms) and irrationalisms (in practice, capricious exercises of the will-to-power or some other ideologically and/or psycho-somatically buried source) new and old alike; of the primordial failing of western philosophy, ontological monovalence, and its close ally, the epistemic fallacy with its ontic dual; of the analytic problematic laid down by Plato, which Hegel served only to replicate in his actualist monovalent analytic reinstatement in transfigurative reconciling dialectical connection, while in his hubristic claims for absolute idealism he inaugurated the Comtean, Kierkegaardian and Nietzschean eclipses of reason, replicating the fundaments of positivism through its transmutation route to the superidealism of a Baudrillard.[5]

Is this how you want to sound? Heaven help us! Keep it simple. Be direct. Get straight to your point.

CRITICAL THINKING TIP 13.3

As you write, and especially as you revise, ask yourself, "What exactly is my point in this sentence (or paragraph)?" Then ask yourself, "Can I make my point clear in half the words?" Cut out anything that is not *absolutely* necessary to making the point clear.

RHETORIC

Rhetoric is the classical discipline devoted to the study of expressive discourse. Indeed, the word *rhetoric* derives ultimately from the Greek for "I say." Classical rhetoric classifies all kinds of writing into four basic categories: narrative (story-telling), descriptive (using words to create mental imagery), expository (the presentation or explication of information), and finally, persuasive (using words to change other people's minds). Arguments and argumentative essays fall into this last category, which as it turns out has gotten the most attention of the four categories. The main traditional concern of rhetoric as an academic discipline has been the development and systematic refinement of skills, techniques, and strategies of persuasion—strategies such as rhythmic repetition, alliteration, presenting ideas and examples in groups of three, and so on.

Rhetoric's traditional emphasis on persuasion arose in ancient Greece. In the developing political context of the city-states, citizens found it increasingly important to learn how to make effective and persuasive presentations in the assemblies and law courts, the principal institutions of self-government, where the laws were made and interpreted. So a deep historical connection exists between rhetoric and argument. Argument design is part of rhetoric understood as the general art of persuasion. Argumentative essays, though they may employ narrative, descriptive, and expository discourse as well, fall into the persuasive category. Nonetheless, rhetoric is broader than argument and encompasses more than argument design because persuasion is a broader category than *rational* persuasion. We have other ways to be persuasive than by appeal to reason. So, the question arises when we come to the presentation of the argument, "Should we (and if so, *how* should we) use persuasive strategies and rhetorical devices other than the argument itself in our composition?" Answer: By all means sweeten the presentation as best you can. *Never* forget, however, that the main persuasive tool in the composition should be the argument itself. Do not let the rhetorical sweeteners be a substitute for a good argument. In the absence of a good argument, all rhetoric is "empty."

EXAMPLES

Well-placed and well-chosen examples will do more to enhance your presentation and strengthen your argument than just about anything else we can conceive. Examples assist the reader to grasp difficult and unfamiliar material. Examples also lend support to points that the reader may be inclined to question. In addition, many of the ingredients of a good argument—for example, precisely defined terms and concepts and rigorous logic—tend to make the argument "abstract." Examples help keep it "real." Examples can also be colourful, juicy, spicy, and entertaining. They provide an excellent opportunity to liven up a composition. So, make good use of examples, but just as with the rhetorical sweeteners, make sure the examples *serve*—rather than distract from—the argument.

REVISIONS

Real writers revise, and revise, and revise again. Real writers constantly review and revise—taking the composition apart and reorganizing it, inserting and deleting, making small improvements here and there—because they *care* how the composition comes out. Some of us cannot even stop revising after we are finished. So, take a cue from the best writers, and revise your work. Start early, so you have time to revise. Writing is at least as much a process of *discovering what one thinks* as it is a matter of composing the results of prior thinking. The essay is not merely a format for the presentation of the results of your delibera-tions, a sort of literary Jell-O mould into which you pour your thoughts when they are finished and ready to go to market. The activity of organizing and com-posing the essay is—or can and should be—an integral part of those very delib-erations, an integral part of the process of rationally making up your mind.[6] Sometimes in the course of outlining (or drafting or revising) you may find your argument taking you in unplanned and unanticipated directions, suggesting maybe a different approach or even a different thesis than the one you originally undertook to defend. If this happens, you need not resist. Perhaps what is hap-pening is that you are discovering things about the argument and the issue that are important. Let your reasoning take you where it wants to go. You should adjust your thesis in accordance with the best reasoning you find yourself able to develop. Use the insights you gain through this process of working out your argument to revise your thesis statement. We recommend working with a partner or in a small study group. Have someone else read your draft and offer criticisms. Have someone else read your draft aloud to you. This may help you to detach from your draft enough to hear areas where there may be room or a need for improvement.

We could go on, we suppose, but what is most essential to your learning now is practice. So, we think it is time to wish you the best of luck and let you get to work.

EXERCISE 13.6 | **Your Argumentative Essay**

Based on your issue statement as revised in Exercise 13.3, your thesis statement in Exercise 13.4, and your outline from Exercise 13.5, draft an argumentative essay. Try to make your case in (say) 1,500 words (5–6 pages).

ADDITIONAL EXERCISES

■ **EXERCISE 13.7**   When you have worked out your position and your argument for it at the length prescribed in Exercise 13.6 or by your instructor, try condensing it. Try to compose it as a letter to the editor. Consult the "opinion pages" of your local newspaper for guidance as to length and format.

■ **EXERCISE 13.8**   When you have worked out your position and your argument for it at the length prescribed in Exercise 13.6 or by your instructor, try condensing it for oral presentation. Reduce it to a set of notes from which to speak publicly. Try your speech in front of a mirror, or better yet, a video camera.

GLOSSARY

articulation   as applied to the analysis of complex issues, refers to framing, focusing, and organizing the inquiry

balance   as applied to an issue statement, not prejudiced either in favour of or against any of the positions that a reasonable person might be inclined to hold about the issue

clarity   as applied to a written composition, the use of language to communicate effectively and without confusion

focusing   as applied to the analysis of complex issues, determining what will be considered central and/or peripheral within the scope of discussion

framing   as applied to the analysis of complex issues, determining what will be considered within and outside the scope of discussion

rhetoric   classical discipline devoted to the study of expressive discourse; currently, the art or science of persuasion by stylistic and expressive means

thesis   from Greek, proposed idea; in the discipline of writing, the main idea of an essay or longer composition; the conclusion of an argument

Go to http://www.criticalthinking1ce.nelson.com for additional study resources for this chapter.

ENDNOTES

[1] It is most impressive to see someone present a good argument without any apparent "script" to follow. We should be clear, though, that in nearly every case, this ability to think critically "on one's feet," so to speak, results from the same sort of sustained investment of effort that goes into a well-developed argumentative essay.

[2] Ben Bagdikian, "Lords of the Global Village," *The Nation*, June 12, 1989.

3 This list is derived from a web page developed by reference librarians at Santa Rosa Junior College.

4 We recommend Michael Harvey's *The Nuts and Bolts of College Writing* (Chicago: Hackett Publishing, 2003), and the associated website: http://www.nutsandboltsguide.com

5 From Roy Bhaskar's *Plato etc: The Problems of Philosophy and Their Resolution* (London: Verso, 1994).

6 See V. A. Howard and J. H. Barton, *Thinking on Paper* (New York: Wm. Morrow, 1986).

INDEX